AF539185

MILITARY PENSIONS

SIMPLIFIED

COMMENTARY, CASE LAW & PROVISIONS

NAVDEEP SINGH

Military Pensions Simplified: Commentary, Case Law & Provisions
by Navdeep Singh

ISBN – 978-93-92210-06-8
Edition – II

Published in India by –
J.G.S. Enterprises Pvt Ltd
Imprint: The Browser

Publisher's Address –
SCO 14-15, Sector 8-C, Chandigarh 160 009
Email – service@thebrowser.org
Website – www.thebrowser.org

Printed in India
Cover design, typesetting & layout by 99beagles.com

www.thebrowser.org
Publishers & Booksellers

www.faujidays.com
Oral History and Military Publishing

Dedicated to the Unsung

Foreword

Justice Virender Singh
Former Chief Justice, High Court of Jharkhand &
Former Chairperson, Armed Forces Tribunal

It is indeed a pleasure for me to write this foreword for Major Navdeep Singh's latest treatise - *Military Pensions Simplified.*

This is a subject on which not much has been written. I am glad that this book contains both commentary with case law as well as the various provisions governing pensions in the defence services.

For the uninitiated, this subject can be quite complex but the commentary in the book makes various types of pensionary modalities understandable even to a layperson who may not have a background of the same.

Besides civil and military service law and constitutional issues, Major Singh has played a positive role in matters related to pension and has been of great assistance to both the beneficiaries as well as the Government on the subject. Apart from being a part of many landmark rulings on pensions and other service matters, he has also rendered his views to the Bench whenever asked for.

I hope this book would help in understanding the subject much more soundly and would serve as a guiding light to all those concerned with the subject. I also hope that the provisions are interpreted with a positive outlook as is expected in a welfare state and a democracy.

Justice Virender Singh

The Author

Major Navdeep Singh is a practicing advocate in the Punjab & Haryana High Court. He is the Founder President of the Armed Forces Tribunal Bar Association at Chandigarh. He is a Member of the *International Society for Military Law and the Law of War* at Brussels and International Fellow of the *National Institute of Military Justice* at Washington DC. He writes extensively on military, legal and public policy issues. He is actively engaged in global efforts towards reforms in Military Justice and is a part of a five-member Advisory Committee on the subject constituted by the *Commomwealth Secretariat.*

Navdeep has been a national service volunteer-reservist with the Territorial Army in the past. The Territorial Army is a unique force of volunteers who, while carrying on with their civil vocations, wear uniform for a few days in a year during their spare time in peace so that they can bear arms for the nation's defence during war and national emergencies. He has voluntarily served in counter-insurgency and operational areas during High Court vacations and has been decorated with a record number of 11 commendations from the Army, Air Force and also a Tri-Services Institution.

Besides constitutional law and civil & military service matters, he has enthusiastically worked in the fields of rights of disabled soldiers, military widows & kin and also for military and civil pensioners. He has also worked for the welfare of World War II veterans and for protection of rights, privileges and status of the military community. He strongly advocates judicial independence, including that of tribunals and quasi-judicial bodies.

Based on the sentiment expressed by the Prime Minister for curbing unnecessary litigation, Navdeep was made a part of a short-term high level Committee of Experts constituted by the then Defence Minister for reducing litigation initiated by the Ministry of Defence in service and pension related matters and to strengthen the system of redressal of grievances. The far-reaching, progressive and reformatory recommendations of the Committee, where he functioned pro bono, were widely hailed in Government and military circles, veteran community and by the civil society.

Military Pensions Simplified is his fifth book, the last being *March to Justice: Global Military Law Landmarks.*

Contents

Part II
Provisions

Introduction

I will be very brief here.

The subject of Military Pensions has remained a labyrinth. Not just for the claimants and beneficiaries, but also for those in the establishment. What has further complicated the matter is the plethora of rules, regulations, letters and instructions which makes this subject quite unwieldy and confusing. And then there are judicial pronouncements, many of which have not been incorporated in policy and are applied only to the litigants who approach Courts and Tribunals. To the credit of the successive Governments, the pensionary provisions in India have been quite liberal with a high degree of benefit of doubt to claimants, though their interpretation at times has been literal and narrow at the hands of those handling entitlements.

Needless to state, there is lack of a common platform wherein important letters are consolidated as a compendium. There is also a dearth of a simple commentary on various pensionary concepts in the military, some of which are unique to the defence services and not applicable on civilian employees and retirees. Though we have come a long way from the Army Pension Regulations, 1940 to the 7th Central Pay Commission and the "One Rank One Pension" scheme applicable today, the distance has not been one which was easy to navigate.

It is with the above in mind that I have attempted to compile in this book all important provisions related to military pensions from the time of the 4th Central Pay Commission till date, with an easy-to-understand commentary in non-technical terms to facilitate the comprehension of various types of military pensions and the law governing the same. Wherever necessary, the judicial pronouncements dealing with the subject have been mentioned. The book is broadly divided into two parts – the first dealing with commentary and case law, and the second, containing various provisions governing military pensions.

Many regulations and provisions stand deemingly altered by way of various letters, decisions of the Government and also decisions of the Union Cabinet after acceptance of recommendations of successive pay commissions. Unless specified or indicated, the term "Pension Regulations" in the book refers to the "Pension Regulations for the Army (Part-I), 1961". The Navy and the Air

Force mostly have parallel regulations, though the reference to the same is not quite necessary since pensionary policies are now governed by various Office Memoranda and letters issued by the Government from time to time. The provisions in the second part of the book may not be reproduced date-wise and are clubbed as per subject or in priority of importance. Certain letters contain humungous pensionary tables as appendices, but the same are not being reproduced in order not to burden the book with such lengthy tables. However, anyone who might want to peruse the tables might do so from the official websites which carry them.

The so-called Pension Regulations for the Army (Part-I), 2008 are not being taken into account because the same are only a compendium of various orders and instructions and not valid stand-alone substantive regulations since the same have been drafted by officers of the Defence Accounts Department and got approved from the then Raksha Mantri by conveying that these do not carry out any changes in the existing dispensation, whereas, in reality, many changes in the language of pre-existing regulations have been carried out surreptitiously without specific approval or information to the senior echelons of the Ministry of Defence or the Raksha Mantri. Moreover, these have only been issued for the Army whereas pensionary provisions of all three services are now governed by universal orders issued by the Government from time to time. Hence, wherever there is a clash or conflict between the actual Pension Regulations and Government letters on one side, and the Regulations floated in 2008 on the other, the former must prevail.

Just to provide a rudimentary bird's eye view to the various types of pensions in the military, a table is reproduced in the succeeding pages for assistance, so as to enable a basic understanding at a glance. A glossary is also appended at the end of the book in order to explain the various abbreviations used in the book. An explainer to certain important letters reproduced in Chapter 33 is also appended after the said Chapter.

I hope the provisions in this book are interpreted liberally and in a beneficial manner, in tune with their compensatory character, and not in a hyper-technical way, which might go against the very thought behind them. It was almost 50 years ago, taking a cue from a Full Bench decision of the Punjab & Haryana High Court rendered in 1966, a Constitution Bench of the Supreme Court in Writ Petition 217/1968 **Deokinandan Prasad Vs State of Bihar** decided on 04-05-1971, observed that pension was not a bounty at the discretion, sweet-will or pleasure of the Government but a valuable right of the employee. Of course, the same sentiment was later endorsed by yet another celebrated Constitution Bench in Writ Petition 5939/1980 **DS Nakara Vs Union of India** decided on17-12-1982. Thereafter, the Supreme Court in Civil Appeal 6770/2013 **State of Jharkhand Vs Jitendra Kumar Srivastava** decided on 14-08-2013 reiterated that pension was 'property' of a person within the meaning of Article 300A of the Constitution of India. Lately, again in Civil

Appeal 2463/2015 **Assistant General Manager, State Bank of India Vs Radhey Shyam Pandey** decided on 02-03-2020, a Three Judge Bench of the Supreme Court, while tracing the concept of pension and the law thereon, has held that even if there are multiple interpretations possible or a lack of clarity in matters related to pension, the benefit must go to the employees.

I thank **Pankaj Thakur**, Advocate, from the bottom of my heart, for helping me in compiling and editing this book.

I am also thankful to **Ananya Sharma, Akanksha Duvedi** and **Kanika Sharma** for assisting me on various facets of this project.

That said, I hereby sign off.....

Jai Hind

Major Navdeep Singh

Advocate, Punjab & Haryana High Court
House No 427, Sector 2
Panchkula, Haryana – 134 109
India

Office Phones: 0172- 4186427, 9988853425

Office Web: www.NSA.legal

Email: Office@NSA.legal

Broad Pensionary Types – At a Glance

TYPE OF PENSION	CONDITIONS	BASIC QUALIFYING SERVICE REQUIREMENT
Service/Retiring Pension	No conditions. See Chapter 1	20 years for Officers 15 years for others
Invalid Pension	Granted to those discharged with disabilities considered 'neither attributable to, nor aggravated by service'. See Chapter 9	10 years (minimum service requirement abrogated with effect from 04-01-2019)
Disability Pension comprising both Service Element & Disability Element	Granted to those released with disabilities considered (or deemed to be) 'attributable to, or aggravated by service'. See Chapter 2	No minimum service requirement
War Injury Pension	Granted to those whose disabilities are declared as Battle Casualties under various rules (including for natural illnesses in specified areas), or occur in an Operational area in any notified operation. See Chapter 5	No minimum service requirement

Ordinary Family Pension (OFP)	Granted to families where the death was considered 'neither attributable to, nor aggravated by service' or to the families of deceased pensioners. See Chapter 7	No minimum service requirement
Special Family Pension (SFP)	Granted to those families wherein the death of the individual was considered (or deemed to be) 'attributable to, or aggravated by service'. See Chapter 8	No minimum service requirement
Liberalised Family Pension (LFP)	Granted to those families where deaths occur under same conditions as mentioned in the category of 'War Injury Pension' *supra*. See Chapter 5	No minimum service requirement
Reservist Pension	Granted to individuals recruited in the past under the Colour-Reserve system of service. See Chapter 11	Combined Colour (Physical) and Reserve Service of 15 years, irrespective of the length of Colour Service
Special Pension	Granted to individuals released on reduction of establishment or disbandment of units, etc. See Chapter 10	10 years

Part I

Commentary & Case Law

Chapter-01

Service Pension & Recovery from Pension

Service Pension and Retiring Pension essentially mean the same, with the former term used for ranks other than Commissioned Officers and the latter employed for Commissioned Officers.

The basic qualifying service provisions for earning a pension have more or less remained the same except that for officers, the minimum qualifying service required to earn a pension was only 15 years as per Regulation 21 of the Pension Regulations, 1940, which was later made more stringent at 20 years by the Pension Regulations, 1961, a requirement which continues till date. The minimum qualifying service for ranks other than Commissioned Officers remains the same, that is, 15 years.

However, this is not to state that pension cannot be granted to individuals with less than 15 or 20 years of service in any eventuality. There are certain pensions such as Invalid Pension, Special Pension, Reservist Pension, etc, which are governed by different regulations and varied qualifying service requirements. Further, there is no minimum service requirement for various kinds of Family Pensions and Disability Pension. All these types of pensions are discussed in separate chapters in this book.

As stated above, the minimum qualifying service required to earn a pension in case of officers is 20 years. However, the same is 15 years for late entrants, that is, officers who join service late and are released on reaching the age of superannuation before completing 20 years of service (Regulation 25 of Pension Regulations, 1961).

Not the whole period spent in service qualifies for service and some of the same may be treated as Non Qualifying Service (NQS). Periods such as the period of unauthorised absence (unless pay and allowances are admitted for the said absence), or leave without pay or any period regularised as extraordinary leave without pay and allowances, time spent under imprisonment after conviction, etc, do not count towards pensionable service. This list is not exhaustive and all modalities are spelt out in Regulations 26 and 122 of Pension Regulations, 1961.

1.1

Concept of Rounding-Off of Pensionary Awards - fraction of a year equal to three months and above to be counted as completed half year

The Ministry of Defence (MoD), vide its letter dated 06-08-1984 (Chapter 33.13) had provided that in calculating the length of qualifying service for the purpose of pension/gratuity, a fraction of a year equal to three months and above shall be treated as a completed one half year and reckoned as qualifying service.

In other words, for example, if a person has 17 years and 10 months of service, he or she shall be granted the pension admissible for 18 years.

Similarly, if a soldier has completed only 14 years and 9 months+ of service but less than 15 years, and not granted pension, his or her service as per the above provisions shall be treated as 15 completed years, thereby authorising him or her to Service Pension. Although the establishment is not agreeable to the above interpretation, the same has already been held by the Supreme Court in Civil Appeal 9389/2014 **Union of India Vs Surender Singh Parmar** decided on 20-01-2015 and also in Civil Appeal 2530/2008 **State of Punjab Vs Sucha Singh Rana** decided on 19-02-2014 while dealing with an analogous pensionary provision of the Punjab Government, and hence is binding upon all concerned (please also see Chapter 12).

1.2

The concept of weightage

The concept of weightage was of special importance for personnel of defence services, both for officers as well as others. This concept was meant to compensate officers and *jawans* for their truncated careers as compared to civilian employees who retire much later than defence personnel. Hence, for example, a Colonel or equivalent was given a weightage of 7 years, meaning thereby that if he/she had 23 years of service to his/her credit, he/she would be paid the pension as applicable to 30 years of service. Similar was the case with all other ranks. In fact, the Government kept progressively increasing the weightage for *Other Ranks* from time to time to ameliorate their pensionary woes. The concept of weightage at a universal rate of 5 years was also applicable to civilian employees but restricted to those opting for voluntary retirement only. The improvement in the system of weightages is explained in detail in Chapter 17.

However, the concept of weightage was abrogated by the 6th Central Pay Commission with effect from 01-01-2006 and it was provided that employees would be granted the pension at the rate of 50% of last drawn emoluments at the time of release, irrespective of the length of service, as opposed to the earlier system, wherein it used to be calculated at 50% for 33 years of service, proportionately reduced to the actual length of service (plus weightage) of the employee concerned.

While the system of weightage and linkage with 33 years of service was abrogated for post-2006 retirement cases, the Government continued to proportionately reduce the pensions of pre-2006 civil and military retirees. However, ultimately, the said discrimination was set aside by way of judicial intervention and consequently the Government issued instructions for grant of similar benefits to pre as well as post-2006 retirees with effect from 01-01-2006 (Chapter 30.7). More on this can be read in Chapters 16 and 17.

1.3

Pension on change of nationality

There is no bar on receiving pension on change of nationality. The bar was totally removed by way of MoD letter dated 06-10-2004 (Chapter 33.10) removing the anomaly between civilian and military pensioners. Military pensioners prior to the issuance of the above letter were subjected to hostile discrimination since they alone were fettered with such a prohibition while their civilian counterparts were not. The Government has further initiated very important progressive reforms for pensioners residing outside India vide DoPPW letter dated 20-01-2020 (Chapter 33.11). DoPPW letter 22-09-2021 (Chapter 33.17) and MoD letter dated 13-10-2021 (Chapter 33.18) are also on the same subject.

1.4

Pension on resignation

While pension is not refused to personnel who voluntarily retire, or seek premature retirement or are discharged at own request, however, due to a strange reason, based upon internal circulars and instructions, the pensionary benefits, including gratuity, are refused on a number of occasions to officers who have resigned from service. This sentiment, however, is incorrect and contrary to rules. In the defence services, unlike on the civil side, resignation does not result in automatic forfeiture of service for the purposes of pension. Regulation 16 of the Pension Regulations, 1961, which is often quoted and misinterpreted in this regard, merely tacitly indicates that pension can be refused to officers who are "called upon" to retire or resign, and even in those cases, they can still be allowed pension at the discretion of the Central Government. The said Regulation does not provide for any kind of forfeiture of pension in case a person himself or herself resigns out of own volition. This aspect has already been adjudicated by the Supreme Court in Civil Appeal 252/1988 **Union of India Vs Lt Col PS Bhargava** decided on 10-01-1997.

1.5

Pension on dismissal

In cases of cashiering, dismissal or removal, the Central Government at its discretion (in the name of the President) can still grant pension to a person upto the rate admissible to him/her had he/she retired on the same date as the cashiering/dismissal/removal. In cases of the following eventualities, the power to grant pension has been delegated by the Central Government to the Services Headquarters (Army/Naval/Air HQ) vide MoD Letter dated 14-08-2001 (Chapter 33.3):

- Pensionary awards to officers dismissed from service otherwise than with disgrace/cashiered.
- Pensionary awards to officers who are discharged, called upon to resign or are retired.
- Grant of pension to ranks other than commissioned officers dismissed from service.

MoD letter dated 09-06-1999 (Chapter 33.8) and 10-08-2000 (Chapter 33.9) dealing with the amendment to Regulation 16 (for Commissioned Officers) and Regulation 113 (for ranks other than Commissioned Officers), are also relevant to the subject of grant of pension to dismissed personnel. Further, the MoD through its letter dated 28-07-2020 (Chapter 33.20) has informed all stakeholders on the need to process "mercy appeals" for pension to such cashiered/dismissed/ removed personnel with due alacrity and sensitivity.

1.6

Recovery from Pension

Recovery from pay, allowances, and more particularly any kind of pension, is an issue that has always resulted in heartburn amongst pensioners and serving employees.

The law laid down by the Courts on recovery has always been a little unclear with many contradictory decisions in the past. All such dicta and aspects were, however, discussed by the Supreme Court finally in Civil Appeal 11527/2014 **State of Punjab Vs Rafiq Masih** decided on 18-12-2014, which somewhat brought clarity and stability to the subject.

The one picture that has resultantly emerged over the years is that usually the Courts have eschewed recovery except in cases of fraud or misrepresentation, etc, by the employee or the pensioner.

Just before the decision in *Rafiq Masih's* case, a three Judge Bench of the Supreme Court by way of a short order in SLP (CC) 14563/2010 **Secretary Department of Irrigation Vs Dharmatma Singh**, decided on 29-07-2013, had observed that since the employee himself was not responsible in any manner for the mistake in fixing his pay leading to overpayment "the recovery sought to be effected from him was wholly arbitrary, unjustified and violative of the rules of natural justice."

In *Rafiq Masih's* case, the Supreme Court had the occasion to discuss the complete law related to recovery in great detail. Summing up the circumstances wherein recovery could not be effectuated, the Supreme Court observed the following:

> "12. It is not possible to postulate all situations of hardship, which would govern employees on the issue of recovery, where payments have mistakenly been made by the employer, in excess of their entitlement. Be that as it may, based on the decisions referred to herein above, we may, as a ready reference, summarise the following few situations, wherein recoveries by the employers would be impermissible in law:
>
> i. Recovery from employees belonging to Class-III and Class-IV service (or Group 'C' and Group 'D' service).
>
> ii. Recovery from retired employees, or employees who are due to retire within one year, of the order of recovery.
>
> iii. Recovery from employees, when the excess payment has been made for a period in excess of five years, before the order of recovery is issued.
>
> iv. Recovery in cases where an employee has wrongfully been required to discharge duties of a higher post, and has been paid accordingly, even though he should have rightfully been required to work against an inferior post.
>
> v. In any other case, where the Court arrives at the conclusion, that recovery if made from the employee, would be iniquitous or harsh or arbitrary to such an extent, as would far outweigh the equitable balance of the employer's right to recover."

It may be noted that the above categories are independent from each other and operate separately and only one of the conditions out of them needs to be satisfied.

After the decision in *Rafiq Masih's* case, the Supreme Court had rendered a decision, that is, Civil Appeal 3500/2006 **High Court of Punjab & Haryana Vs Jagdev Singh** decided on 29-07-2016, in which recovery had been upheld based upon an undertaking given by the employee. But the facts of the case were that the employee, a judicial officer who was compulsorily retired, had opted for a higher pay scale (which was already under judicial examination) by particularly and specifically giving an undertaking to the effect that in case he is not found entitled to the same, he shall refund the excess payment. In such circumstances, the Supreme Court upheld the recovery from the said employee.

It must, however, be noted that in *Jagdev Singh's* case, a specific and particular undertaking had been provided for a specific and particular action. Any general undertaking or any old undertaking hence, would not affect the dicta in *Rafiq Masih*. In any case, the effect of *Jagdev Singh's* case has been explained by various High Courts in a number of cases such as by the Punjab & Haryana High Court in CWP 23915/2015 **SS Guraya Vs Union of India** decided on 17-03-2017 and CWP 4575/2019 **Union of India Vs Lt Cdr Dalip Singh & Others** decided on 18-02-2019, the Bombay High Court in WP 3474/2004 **Ravindra Vs Principal Director of Audit (Central)** decided on 17-04-2018, Himachal Pradesh High Court in CWP 839/2015 **Rajeev Kumar Vs Union of India** decided on 27-08-2019, and the Calcutta High Court in WP 22864/2017 **Gita Rani Chakraborti Vs State of West Bengal** decided on 22-09-2017. In fact, in *Chakraborti's* case, the High Court observed that it is common knowledge that declarations are signed by employees under compelling circumstances with no real choice in the matter. In yet another case, that is, WP 22759(W)/2019 **Sumita Badra Vs State Bank of India** decided on 19-02-2020, the Calcutta High Court further explained the effect of *Jagdev Singh's* case and held that the said principle would only operate when any such undertaking is given before accepting any revision of pay-scale on the condition that any excessive amount received would be refunded and that such an undertaking would only matter if it is entered into by an employee as a condition of acceptance of pension being an integral part of the employment package. It was also held in the same case that no undertaking from a family pensioner could be taken which restricted her legal right to receive pension without any fault on her part.

In any case, a Three Judge Bench of the Supreme Court, albeit by way of a short order, in *Dharmatma Singh's* case, has already put the controversy to rest. Not only that, even after *Jagdev Singh's* case, the Supreme Court has continued to decide cases as per *Rafiq Masih's* judgment since the same is a detailed exposition on the matter. Some other recent orders of the Supreme Court following *Rafiq Masih's* dicta are Civil Appeal 6987/2016 **Vijay Kumar Mishra Vs State of Bihar** decided on 11-07-2017, Civil Appeal 6357/2019 **Sabbir Hasan Vs State of Uttar Pradesh** decided on 16- 08-2019 and SLP

(CC) 31384/2017 **Manoranjan Prasad Srivastava Vs State of Bihar** decided on 09-01-2020. The most important out of the above is *Sabbir Hasan's* case where the Supreme Court has reiterated the principles laid down in *Rafiq Masih* and has held a recovery order issued by the department as illegal despite an undertaking by the employee that excess payment could be recovered.

The Supreme Court, yet again in a detailed recent judgment, Civil Appeal 7115/2010 **Thomas Daniel Vs State of Kerala** decided on 02-05-2022, has reiterated the principles of impermissibility of recovery from retirement benefits.

Notwithstanding the judicial dicta on the matter, the whole controversy related to the subject has been laid to rest in view of the issuance of letter dated 02-03-2016 by the DoPT (Chapter 33.5), in which the Government of India has already directed all ministries and departments to comply with the law laid down by the Supreme Court in *Rafiq Masih's* case. Any stand taken contrary to the law laid down by any instrumentality of the Government is, hence, in contravention of the above Office Memorandum, besides being contrary to judicial pronouncements.

Chapter-02

Disability Pension

Disability Pension remains the most vexed and imprecisely understood subject within military pensions when analysed as a whole.

Disability Pension is granted for disabilities (diseases, injuries or other medical conditions) that are either attributable to, or aggravated by (or deemed to be attributable to, or aggravated by) military service.

Disability Pension consists of two elements – **Service Element**, which is the element of pension pertaining to the length of service rendered by an individual (separately explained in greater detail in Chapter 4) and **Disability Element**, which pertains to the percentage of disability suffered by the individual.

The principal provisions governing Disability Pension are Regulations 48 and 173 of the Pension Regulations for the Army, 1961, for Commissioned Officers and personnel other than Commissioned Officers respectively, and the Entitlement Rules for Casualty Pensionary Awards, 1982 (Chapter 23.1), and of course, the parallel and corresponding regulations of the other two services. The minimum percentage of 20% disability required to be eligible for Disability Pension earlier has been abrogated for post-1996 invalidation cases and such personnel are entitled to claim Disability Pension even if the disability percentage is less than 20% and the same is supposed to be paid by rounding it off to 50% for calculation purposes. Prior to 1996, disabled personnel with less than 20% disability were entitled to Service Element of Disability Pension alone, without the Disability Element. Further, as per judicial dicta, explained in succeeding paragraphs, the said benefit of abrogation of the 20% condition is also to be extended to pre-1996 invalidation cases with financial effect from 01-01-1996. For the purposes of Disability Pension, any person who is in a medical category lower than the one in which he or she was recruited, is treated as "invalided" as per Rule 4 of the *ibid* Entitlement Rules (Chapter 23.1), however, the abrogation of the minimum 20% requirement has been made applicable only to those who are actually prematurely boarded out of service on medical grounds before completion of their terms of engagement, while the 20% disability condition remains valid for all other types of release from service even if they fall under the deemed definition of 'invalidation', although in such cases, if the disability is less than 20%, they still remain entitled to Service Element (without the Disability Element). It must still be noted that the 20% condition also stands abrogated for individuals released on medical grounds while on extended service or those who are unwilling for further service/extended service in a sheltered appointment, as clarified by the Government vide letter dated 11-04-2002 (Chapter 23.18).

There is no minimum qualifying service required for Disability Pension. There is no minimum service prescribed for Service Element also, with effect from 01-01-1973. As mentioned above, the various modalities related to Service Element are discussed separately in Chapter 4.

The relevant Pension Regulations dealing with Disability Pension are reproduced in Chapter 23.2 and the Entitlement Rules, 1982 are reproduced in Chapter 23.1. The new Pension Regulations for the Army, published by the Ministry of Defence in 2008, are not actually stand-alone regulations but only a compendium of existing instructions, as explained in the Introduction to this book and hence it is the actual Pension Regulations of 1961 that are being taken note of in this Chapter.

Contrary to popular perception, the attributability and aggravation of disabilities caused in service is not actually to be determined by the medical board or the authorities, but is governed by the provisions of the Entitlement Rules which form a part of the Pension Regulations as 'Appendix II'. In fact, the following lines below the lynchpin provisions of Regulations 48 and 173 of the Pension Regulations, are also a pointer to the same:

> *"The question whether a disability is attributable to or aggravated by military service shall be determined under the rules in Appendix II."*

2.1

Disability Pension in cases of diseases and medical conditions

The rules in Appendix II (Entitlement Rules, 1982) read along with the Guide to Medical Officers for Military Pensions and the Regulations for Medical Services of the Armed Forces provide that the benefit of attributability/aggravation has to go to the claimant who shall not be asked to prove his/her entitlement and that reasons are to be recorded to rebut claims of attributability/aggravation. The Rules also provide that service in peace or field areas has no linkage with grant of Disability Pension. The following provisions of Entitlement Rules, 1982, are specifically pertinent:

- Rule 4, which provides that any person who is in a medical category lower than the one in which he or she was recruited, shall be treated as 'invalided' from service for the purposes of Disability Pension.

- Rules 5 and 14 (b), which provide that in case of discharge from service on medical grounds, the deterioration in health has to be deemed as due to service and any disease that has not been noted at the time of enrolment is deemed to have arisen in service, unless it is recorded that the disease was such which could not have been detected at the time of joining service. Of course, release in low medical category is also treated as 'invalidation' (discharge on medical grounds) by the deeming fiction of Rule 4.

- Rule 9 provides that a claimant shall not be called upon to prove his/her entitlement and shall receive the benefit of doubt.

- Rule 18 of the Entitlement Rules clearly states that 'inherent constitutional tendency' is not a disease in itself as is many a time declared by Medical Boards. In fact, the rule points out that if there is a precipitating or causative factor in service, then it is to be declared as attributable to service.

- Rule 19 provides that if the worsening of a condition persists till the time of discharge, meaning thereby, that if the medical category of an individual remains at a worsened stage at the time of discharge (i.e., he/she remains 'low medical category' at the time of discharge) then aggravation is to be accepted.

- Rule 20(a) points out that in case nothing is known of the disease and if presumption of entitlement is not rebutted, then attributability should be conceded. It may be pointed out here that to 'rebut' entitlement, reasons have to be provided, which if not provided, must result in the acceptance of attributability.

- Annexure III of the Entitlement Rules provides a list of diseases which are affected by stress and strain of service and still it is seen that many such diseases are declared by medical boards as 'not affected or connected with service' and such instances are also in total contravention of the scheduled list which forms a part of rules.

There is a tendency of the authorities concerned to take medical board opinion on its face value while dealing with the claims of the disabled personnel. However, if the said opinion is prima facie not in conformity with rules, or perverse or factually incorrect or without reasons, then relief can be provided by judicial intervention. Also, while dealing with disabilities of military personnel, the much argued comparison with an ordinary person on the street by medical authorities is totally incongruous. There are times when it is remarked that such a disease may also have arisen had the particular person not been in the Army and that the Army is one of the most stress-free organisations in the country. But then the question arises that here is a person who is 24 hours

× 365 days on call, sometimes under the shadow of the gun, mostly away from his/her family, in a strictly regimented routine, and therefore can he or she be simplistically compared with, say, a civilian employee who goes to office at 9 in the morning and returns at 5, only five days a week, lives with family in his/her hometown, enjoys gazetted holidays and retires at 60? As is now well recognised, common ailments such as hypertension or heart disease or minor psychiatric illnesses or psychosomatic disorders are bound to get aggravated by even seemingly insignificant incidents at the home front such as non-performance of children in school, property disputes, red-tapism in other spheres, family problems, etc, which cannot be at all times attended to by military personnel, and such practical aspects of life in general cannot be ignored by taking a highly technical approach which has no link with practical on-ground realities. Further, the curtailment of rights and general freedoms, barrack-living, frequent movements, inability to cater to domestic commitments and invisible reasons such as non-fulfilment of sexual needs, also give rise to stress resulting in aggravation of medical conditions.

Keeping the rules as above in view, the Supreme Court and also various High Courts have ruled a number of times that in case a person joins the military in a fit medical condition, then any medical condition that arises during service is to be treated as attributable to, or at least aggravated by service, thereby authorising the grant of Disability Pension to the soldier concerned. Hence, merely stating that the disability was incurred in a 'peace area' and not in 'field' area, or that it was 'constitutional', or 'idiopathic', etc, cannot result in the denial of Disability Pension unless it is specifically stated that the disability was such that it could not have been detected at the time of entry into service, or, for example, a reason such as excessive smoking leading to a heart disease or hypertension is recorded. It may always be kept in mind that as per rules, the person concerned would always receive the benefit of doubt.

Besides others, the same has been held by the Supreme Court in Civil Appeal 4949/2013 **Dharamvir Singh Vs Union of India** decided on 02-07-2013, Civil Appeal 2904/2011 **Union of India Vs Rajbir Singh** decided on 13-02-2015, Civil Appeal 4357/2015 **Union of India Vs Manjeet Singh** decided on 12-05-2015, Civil Appeal 2633/2017 **Laxmanram Poonia Vs Union of India** decided on 22-02-2017 and Civil Appeal 11208/2011 **Union of India Vs Angad Singh Titaria** decided on 24-02-2015. The matter was also disposed by a Three Judge Bench of the Supreme Court in Civil Appeal 2337/2009 **Union of India Vs Chander Pal** decided on 18-09-2013.

The Chandigarh Bench of the AFT in OA 1366/2019 **Baljeet Singh Vs Union of India** decided on 23-09-2019, carried out a detailed analysis on military disabilities and the case law on the subject and rendered one of the most detailed and pertinent decisions in the matter, also touching upon the cases in which Disability Pension could be denied to the person. In fact, even medical conditions such as cancer, which were earlier thought to have no relationship with military service, are now established by medical research as being aggravated due to stress and strain of military service, except in cases involving tobacco use, etc (See Delhi High Court in WP(C) 5900/2013 **Sneh Lata Vs Union of India** decided on 11-11-2014 and OA 277/2016 **Kanta Katoch Vs Union of India** decided by the Chandigarh Bench of AFT on 24-08-2018).

The law and the rules governing the same are quite similar in most democracies and most nations recognise a presumption of service-connection of any disability arising during military service except in cases of criminal activities or substance abuse. To take an example, the United States, Code Title 38, Section 105 provides the following:

a. **An injury or disease incurred during active military, naval, or air service will be deemed to have been incurred in line of duty and not the result of the veteran's own misconduct when the person on whose account benefits are claimed was, at the time the injury was suffered or disease contracted, in active military, naval, or air service, whether on active duty or on authorized leave,** ***unless*** **such injury or disease was a result of the person's own wilful misconduct or abuse of alcohol or drugs.** Venereal disease shall not be presumed to be due to wilful misconduct if the person in service complies with the regulations of the appropriate service department requiring the person to report and receive treatment for such disease.

b. The requirement for line of duty will not be met if it appears that at the time the injury was suffered or disease contracted the person on whose account benefits are claimed –

   1. was avoiding duty by deserting the service or by absenting himself or herself without leave materially interfering with the performance of military duties;

   2. was confined under sentence of court-martial involving an unremitted dishonorable discharge; or

   3. was confined under sentence of a civil court for a felony (as determined under the laws of the jurisdiction where the person was convicted by such court).

c. For the purposes of any provision relating to the extension of a delimiting period under any education-benefit or rehabilitation program administered by the Secretary, the disabling effects of chronic alcoholism shall not be considered to be the result of wilful misconduct.

In Case No 2007-7241 **James C Groves Vs James B Peake, Secretary of Veteran Affairs** decided on 01-05-2008, the **United States Court of Appeals for the Federal Circuit**, came to the rescue of an old soldier of the US Army whose claim was rejected by the establishment and even whose appeal was dismissed by the *United States Court of Appeals of Veterans Claims*, on the ground that there was no evidence of a medical nexus or an "etiological link" between the disability of the soldier and his military service. The Court of Appeals, however, held that determinations pertaining to service-connection (attributability/aggravation) were to be effectuated with due consideration to the policy of the Department of Veterans Affairs to administer the law under a broad and liberal interpretation. The Court of Appeals further held that the law establishes a presumption of service-connection for a disease which manifests during service and then again at any later date, howsoever remote.

The interpretation of military disability law in American jurisprudence and even the provisions governing the same are, hence, quite similar to the position in India.

It has also been held that in case a medical board has already returned a positive opinion regarding attributability or aggravation of a disability, then the administrative or financial authorities cannot overrule the said opinion by declaring the disability "Neither Attributable Nor Aggravated by Service". The same has been held by the Supreme Court in Civil Appeal 164/1993 **Ex Sapper Mohinder Singh Vs Union of India** decided on 14-01-1993, Civil Appeal 11485/2018 **Madan Prasad Sinha @ Sanatan Baba Vs Union of India** decided on 08-04-2019 and by the Punjab & Haryana High Court in CWP 16324/2003 **Ramesh Kumar Sharma Vs Union of India** decided on 09-12-2003 wherein it was held that the job of such authorities was only to calculate pension and not to sit over the positive findings rendered by a medical board in favour of a disabled soldier.

2.2

Disability Pension in cases of injuries and accidents

The claims of Disability Pension in cases of injuries and accidents (including those on leave) are governed slightly differently than diseases and other medical conditions. As per rules, the Disability Pension claims in Injury cases are now decided by the Adjutant General (and equivalent) in matters relating to officers of the rank of Brigadier and above, by the Additional Director

General Personnel Services (and equivalent) for officers from the rank of Lieutenant to Colonel and the Officer in Charge Records for all other personnel, as per MoD letter dated 01-09-2005 (Chapter 23.4 read with Chapter 23.5).

The above authorities decide upon the attributability of disabilities based upon documents such as Injury Reports and Courts of Inquiry. The provisions governing attributability of injuries are provided in Rules 12 and 13 of the Entitlement Rules, 1982 (Chapter 23.1). It may, however, be noted that the comment upon "aggravation" of disabilities resulting out of injuries which are otherwise "non-attributable" is still within the charter of the medical boards and not the responsibility of executive or administrative authorities.

The grant of Disability Pension for personnel who sustain injuries while strictly on duty is usually not problematic, however, there have been instances wherein the military or financial authorities have not accepted claims of Disability Pension when the injury is sustained outside office hours (though when the person is on duty and not on leave). However, the Courts have usually held that a person should not be denied the benefit only because of the fact that he or she was not strictly performing an official task when the injury was sustained. In fact, the same deeming fiction is covered by Rule 12(f) of the Entitlement Rules, 1982. In CWP 4757/2013 **Rakesh Kumar Sharma Vs Union of India** decided on 12-11-2013, it was held by the Punjab & Haryana High Court that a person who suffered an accident within the city while he was going to the market when he was not on leave would be treated as attributable to service. In TA 1042/2010 **Tarsem Singh Vs Union of India**, it was held by the Chandigarh Bench of the AFT that a person who suffered burn injuries due to a stove-burst would be entitled to Disability Pension although he was at his quarters when the incident occurred. In OA 442/2016 **Tripta Devi Vs Union of India** decided on 12-02-2018, it was held by the Chandigarh Bench that the death of a member of the armed forces in an accident while returning to his unit after watching a movie would be treated attributable to service.

The law on injury while on leave has been a little hazier though. In Civil Appeal 1926/1999 **Madan Singh Shekhawat Vs Union of India** decided on 17-08-1999 and in Civil Appeal 2903/2011 **Pension Sanction Authority, PCDA (P) Allahabad Vs ML George Ex Sgt** decided on 17-09-2014, it was held that a disability sustained while on casual leave would be treated as attributable since casual leave counts as duty. It was also held that it would not matter if the person was travelling on public expense or on private expense, provided that the journey was authorised. In Civil Appeal 2433/2011 **Union of India Vs Surendra Pandey** decided on 18-09-2014, it was further observed that even if the Railway Warrant was issued for a particular place while the injury was suffered at a different station, still the same would be treated as relatable to military service in case the primary aim of such movement was to proceed on leave. However, the Supreme Court in Civil Appeal 6583/2015 **Union of India Vs Ex Naik Vijay Kumar** decided on 26-08-2015, has taken a view that the concerned soldier is not entitled to Disability Pension for an injury sustained by him during annual leave when he was at his sister's place and was walking up the stairs to the roof to smoke a cigarette. In Civil Appeal 4981/2012 **Secretary, Government of India Vs Dharambir Singh** decided on 20-09-2019, again, recently, the Supreme Court has held a person who was injured in a road accident while on leave to not be entitled to Disability Pension and it has been observed that some remote nexus between the injury and military service would have to be demonstrated to claim Disability Pension. There might, however, be some cases wherein a person after suffering an injury while on leave is subjected to prolonged military service including in field areas or in circumstances which are not in consonance with his/her employability restrictions or advisories by medical authorities. Such cases would be on a separate footing and even though the injury might be "non-attributable to service", the disability may fall under the ambit of "aggravation" in terms of Rule 19 of the Entitlement Rules, thereby entitling the person to Disability Pension. This was so held by the Chandigarh Bench of the AFT in OA 1202/2014 **Beant Singh Vs Union of India** decided on 03-01-2018.

Injuries and deaths during leave period while going towards or coming back from Railway Station for undertaking railway reservation to move back to the military unit have been held to be 'attributable to military service' in a number of decisions, including OA 1703/2019 **Renu Vs Union of India** decided by the Chandigarh Bench of the AFT on 08-10-2021. Disability sustained while on an "Out-Pass" has also been treated as "attributable to military service", as directed by the Supreme Court in Civil Appeal 5625/2008 **Ravindran PM Vs Union of India** decided on 11-09-2008. The same was also recently reiterated by the Chandigarh Bench of the AFT in OA 900/2020 **Shamsher Singh Vs Union of India** decided on 03-01-2023

The denial of Disability Pension and attendant benefits by the establishment to personnel suffering injuries while on leave, however, is a bit unfair and it is the Government itself which should have rationalised the system for grant of disability benefits in such cases. This is so because unlike other employees, there is excessive movement of defence personnel during their leave period since they have to take care of domestic requirements of their families during the short period when they are home on leave. Most of such personnel are also out of driving practice being deployed the major part of the year and it is seen from experience that many such injuries result from road accidents. Further, leave has been identified as a basic human right by the United Nations and leave itself is an incidence of service which is therefore recognised by Rule 12(f)of Entitlement Rules, 1982 (Chapter 23.1).

2.3

Constant Attendant Allowance (CAA)

The CAA is paid for those personnel who are 100% disabled and who require the help of an Attendant due to their disability, if so certified by the medical board. It is currently paid at the uniform rate of Rs 6750 per month, irrespective of rank (Para 12 of MoD letter dated 04-09-2017, Chapter 31.2).

2.4

Rank for assessment of Disability Pension

At times it is seen, especially in old cases of ranks other than Commissioned Officers, that Disability Pension is not paid on the basis of the rank held by the person concerned but is released based upon the rank held at the time of sustaining the disability. This approach is incorrect. Regulation 180 of the Pension Regulations, 1961 (Chapter 23.2) provides that for the purposes of assessment of Disability Pension, the rank held at the time of any of the following can be considered, whichever is more favourable – date of discharge/invalidation, date on which the disability was incurred or he/she was first removed from duty on account of the disability, or if he/she rendered further service then the date of later removal from duty on account of disability. Hence, in case the rank held at the time of discharge is higher than the rank held at the time of sustaining the disability, then Disability Pension (both Service Element as well as Disability Element) needs to be released based upon the rank last held.

2.5

Rounding-Off of disability benefits

Disability benefits (Disability Element as well as War Injury Element) are supposed to be rounded off (also known as the concept of "broad-banding") wherein for the purposes of calculation, disability less than 50% is to be calculated by taking it as 50%, disability between 50% and 75% is to be treated as 75% and disability above 76% is to be taken as 100%. Initially, the concept of broad-banding was only extended to those who were invalided out prior to completion of terms of their engagement, but it was held by the Supreme Court in Civil Appeal 5591/2006 **KJS Buttar Vs Union of India** decided on 31-03-2011 as well as in Civil Appeal 418/2012 **Union of India Vs Ram Avtar** decided on 10-12-2014, that the same would apply to all disability pensioners, irrespective of the manner of exit, including those who are released on own request, on completion of terms of engagement or superannuation. A more detailed explanation is provided in Chapter 16 under the heading of "5th Central Pay Commission". There have been cases in the past where even personnel who were released on medical grounds while on extended terms, or due to lack of availability of alternative employment or who were unwilling to opt for alternative employment, were not being treated as "invalided" as provided by Regulations 173 and 173-A of the Pension Regulations, however, this was set right on intervention of the Raksha Mantri vide MoD letter dated 11-04-2002 (Chapter 23.18). Initially, rounding-off was granted by the MoD to pre-1996 cases with financial effect from 01-07-2009 only, vide letter dated 19-01-2010 (Chapter 23.25) though it was granted to post-1996 cases from 01-01-1996, however, after judicial intervention, the said benefit was later extended to pre-1996 cases also with arrears from 01-01-1996 vide MoD letter dated 15-09-2014 (Chapter 23.26).

2.6

Rounding-Off to pre-1996 "less than 20% disability" invalidation cases

As stated earlier, the minimum requirement of 20% disability was abrogated by the Government in 1996 and disabilities even less than 20% were supposed to be rounded-off to 50% in the cases of invalidation, but the same was applied only to post-1996 cases by the MoD, though the DoPPW had issued orders for pre-1996 cases also for similarly placed civilian employees, which till date has not been done by the MoD for the defence services. The Punjab & Haryana High Court, in CWP 16086/2014 **Jaswant Singh Vs Union of India** decided on 23-02-2015, has held that even pre-1996 invalidation cases would have to be granted the same benefits as provided to post-1996 invalidation cases, with effect from 01-01-1996. The High Court has followed the law laid down by the Supreme Court in *KJS Buttar's* case (supra), wherein the cut-off date of 01-01-1996 was read down by the Apex Court.

2.7

Disability Pension on seeking discharge at own request

Initially, the stand of the official establishment based upon Pension Regulations was that Disability Pension is not to be paid to cases of voluntary retirement, that is, those who seek discharge at own request. It was, however, held by the Delhi High Court in CW 2967/1989 **Mahavir Singh Narwal Vs Union of India** decided on 05-05-2004, that any person who was released at own request in low medical category was deemed to be "invalided" for the purposes of Disability Pension as provided by Rule 1 of Entitlement Rules, 1950 (Now Rule 4 of Entitlement Rules, 1982) (Chapter 23.1) and hence, was entitled to Disability Pension. The decision of the High Court was later affirmed by the Supreme Court in SLP (C) 24171/2004 **Union of India Vs Mahavir Singh Narwal** decided on 04-01-2008. Later, the MoD itself allowed Disability Pension to voluntary retirees with effect from 01-01-2006 vide letter dated 29-09-2009 (Chapter 23.23) but the said benefit was only extended to post-2006 retirees. This cut-off date was read down by the Principal Bench of the Armed Forces Tribunal in TA 523/2010 **Gp Capt JK Kaushik Vs Union of India** decided on 12-08-2010 and later upheld by the Supreme Court in Civil Appeal 9827/2011 **Union of India Vs JK Kaushik** vide order dated 03-07-2013 and it was held that even pre-2006 voluntary retirement cases would have to be released Disability Pension but with monetary benefits from 01-01-2006. In CWP 19417/2007 **Ex Naik Parmod Kumar Vs Union of India** decided on 18-02-2009, it was held by the Punjab & Haryana High Court that the purpose of granting Disability Pension is to compensate an individual who has acquired a disability in service and that denial of the same on the pretext such as discharge on compassionate grounds, etc, would clearly be unreasonable, injudicious, illogical and arbitrary. The MoD finally issued a letter dated 17-05-2017 for pre-2006 cases also (Chapter 23.24) which provides for release of disability and war injury benefits to pre-2006 cases with financial effect from 01-01-2006. In case the disability is not of permanent nature, then the said letter provides for holding a fresh medical board to assess disability w.e.f 01-01-2006.

See Chapter 4 for specific commentary on Service Element of Disability Pension.

2.8

Disability Pension to Recruits

Disability Pension is admissible to recruits under the same rules and at the same rates as soldiers calculated for the rank of Sepoy of the lowest Group. The same is provided in Regulation 181 of the Pension Regulations, 1961 (Chapter 23.2).

Normally, in certain disabilities such as psychiatric ones in recruits, there seems to be a tendency to brush aside such conditions as having no connection with military service or training. This would be true in cases wherein the disability is detected soon after commencement of training and the recruit himself provides some kind of a family history on his medical status which can rule out any service-connection. But in cases where there is no family history and no symptoms of any such disability prior to entering service and the same is triggered during training, then the issue must be looked at very closely since the mere fact of a disability getting triggered by military training may bring it into the realm of service-connection. In a milieu where even minor forms of ragging in colleges are viewed seriously and accepted to be reasons for lifelong mental scars in students, it would be unfair to ignore medical conditions in young persons arising during recruit training or stating that military training cannot lead to or trigger any disability or cannot have an adverse effect on the health of a young soldier. In fact, even aggravation of a pre-existing disability or hastening or precipitation of a disability qualifies a person for Disability Pension as per Rule 6(a)(ii) of Entitlement Rules, 1982. The Supreme Court in Civil Appeal 5605/2010 **Sukhvinder Singh Vs Union of India** decided on 25-06-2014, wherein a young recruit was invalided out without any kind of pension and the medical board had ruled that his disability had existed prior to entering service and had remained undetected at the time of recruitment, had observed, "We, just as every other citizen of India, would be extremely disturbed if the authorities are perceived as being impervious or unsympathetic towards members of the Armed Forces who have suffered disabilities, without receiving any form of recompense or source of sustenance, since these are inextricably germane to their source of livelihood", further holding that such personnel could not be encumbered with loss of service without any recompense and deserved to be granted Disability Pension.

2.9

Disability Pension (Ex-Gratia Awards) to Officer-Trainees (also known as Officer-Cadets)

Due to a major policy gap, Officer-Trainees boarded out of military academies are not granted proper Disability Pension but are only granted an ex-gratia allowance containing two elements – monthly ex-gratia and ex-gratia disability award (parallel to Service Element and Disability Element). The awards to Officer-Trainees, however, place them at a sharp disadvantage not only vis-à-vis civilian trainees but even compared to recruits at *jawan* level of the Army since such Officer-Trainees get an amount that is much lesser than both these categories of disabled personnel. The current rates for these awards as made applicable after the 7th CPC are Rs 9000 per month for monthly ex-gratia amount (plus DR) and Rs 16,200 for the monthly ex-gratia disability award for 100% disability proportionately reduced for lesser disability (Paragraph 11 of MoD letter dated 04-09- 2017, Chapter 31.2). The ex-gratia disability award is not paid for disabilities less than 20% but the monthly ex-gratia amount is still payable. The rules regarding attributability/aggravation, etc, are the same for cadets as applicable to commissioned officers as clarified by the MoD in its letter dated 15-09-2003 (Chapter 33.6). The anomaly of disabled Officer-Trainees being paid an amount sharply lower than other similarly placed trainees or even recruits of the Army is pending for resolution with the Government since long.

2.10

Disability Pension on incurring red-ink entries

The official establishment has been taking a view that personnel who are locally/administratively discharged under Army Rules based upon four or more red-ink entries, even if disabled, are not entitled to Disability Pension. This view, however, is absolutely incorrect. Firstly, as per Regulation 113(a) of the Pension Regulations, only dismissed soldiers are not authorised to pensionary benefits, while as per Regulation 113(c), personnel who are discharged from service under provisions of the Army Act and Rules, remain entitled to pensionary benefits under the Pension Regulations. It may be recalled that personnel are 'discharged' on account of red-ink entries, and not dismissed. Secondly, Rule 4 of the Entitlement Rules (Chapter 23.1) is crystal clear on the fact that any person who is released in a medical category lower than the one in which he was recruited, shall be treated as 'invalided' from service for the purposes of disability pension, as interpreted by Constitutional Courts, including the Supreme Court. Thirdly, the matter has already been adjudicated by a Three Judge Bench of the Supreme Court in Civil Appeal 910/1981 **Ram Pal Singh Vs Union of India** decided on 05-10-1983, wherein it was held that the pretext of discharge due to red-ink entries cannot be pressed into service to deny Disability Pension. The matter was also adjudicated in detail by the Punjab & Haryana High Court in CWP 15227/2007 **Jaggar Singh Vs Union of India** decided on 11-05-2009, in which it was held that disability benefits could not be denied to personnel discharged on the basis of red-ink entries. The same view was followed by the Chandigarh Bench of the AFT in TA 83/2010 **Rounki Singh Vs Union of India** decided on 23-04-2010 as well as in OA 114/2016 **Kuldeep Singh Vs Union of India** decided on 27-11-2017.

2.11

Disability Pension when the person himself/herself is negligent

There are many cases, wherein, though the disability is attributable or aggravated or deemed attributable/aggravated as per rules, the same is denied due to apparent misconduct or negligence of the person. This approach is incorrect. As per Rule 13 of the Entitlement Rules, in cases of misconduct or negligence, the disability benefits cannot be denied but the question of reducing the same can be considered. The same is also provided by Regulation 175 of the Pension Regulations for the Army, 1961. The Punjab & Haryana High Court also endorsed the said proposition in CWP 9566/2008 **Kuldeep Singh Vs Union of India** decided on 22-04-2009.

2.12

Disability Pension for disabilities incurred during the period of re-employment

Commissioned Officers can be re-employed in service even after attaining the age of superannuation. Such officers serve in uniform and are 'Commissioned Officers' under the purview of the Army Act and as such are officers under the meaning of Regulation 14 of the Pension Regulations for the purposes of pension and hence, also for the purposes of Disability Pension under the authority of Regulation 47. However, as per an internal instruction issued by the establishment, that is, Special Army Instruction 1/S/80, such officers are denied disability or war injury benefits in case they are disabled during the period of their re-employment. Though logically this makes no sense, since if a person faces a disability or even the bullet of the enemy while serving in uniform during the period of re-employment, there should be no occasion to refuse the corresponding benefits to him/her, but the same has been the practice followed by the establishment.

This prohibitory provision has, however, been read-down by the Chandigarh Bench of the Armed Forces Tribunal in OA 3660/2013 **Col Inder Singh Thind Vs Union of India** decided on 06-05-2015. Relying upon the decision of the Punjab & Haryana High Court in Parmod Kumar (supra), it was held by the tribunal that the manner of exit from service did not matter in such cases. The following lines from *Parmod Kumar's* decision merit reproduction:

> *"...the purpose of giving disability pension is because during the military service, disability is suffered and the same is attributable to or is aggravated by military service; an individual is entitled to disability pension on that account i.e. acquiring disability. Any differentiation, such as the one suggested by the respondents viz. discharge on compassionate ground, would clearly be unreasonable, injudicious, illogical and arbitrary."*

The aspect of grant of disability pension to re-employed officers was also determined by the Supreme Court in Civil Appeal 7352/2013 **Kuldeep Singh Vs Union of India** decided on 05-11-2019.

2.13

Claims of Disability Pension after retiring in fit medical shape

As per Rule 10 of the Entitlement Rules, 1982 (Chapter 23.1), in case a person retires in a fit shape, that is, not in low medical category, but can show that any disease that he may have incurred was a delayed manifestation of a process set in motion by service conditions prior to discharge, then he/she can file a claim for Disability Pension. Usually, any such claim must be supported by some documentary or medical evidence of the same medical condition during the course of service in order to show its origin during military service. The Director General of Armed Forces Medical Services (DGAFMS) is then supposed to hold a Post Discharge Medical Board as per Paragraph 5 of MoD letter dated 01-09-2005 (Chapter 23.4).

The claim for Disability Pension can then be processed in case the board links the disability with military service and endorses some kind of a service-connection. This might so happen in disabilities such as PIVD or spine related problems or even in heart disease, etc, wherein there is evidence of treatment during service but the medical condition was not such that it necessitated lowering of medical category while in service and the said medical condition presents itself as a full blown case after retirement. The service-connection of such disabilities is, however, not done as a matter of routine, and rightly so, and there must be proper evidence or documents to prove the origin in service. It has also been judicially held that such claims must not be administratively rejected and the claimant must be made to undergo a medical board. One such matter in which the same was decided is the decision of the Chandigarh Bench of the AFT in OA 974/2011 **Lt Gen Tej Kumar Sapru Vs Union of India & Others** decided on 03-11-2011.

2.14

Ex-Gratia lumpsum compensation on invalidation

Vide MoD letter dated 26-12-2011 (Chapter 23.28), the concept of ex-gratia payment on invalidation was introduced for those personnel who are invalided out of service prematurely on medical grounds, on account of attributable/aggravated causes. This amount was initially paid at the rate of Rs 9,00,000 for 100% disability and proportionately decreased for lesser disability. This is not payable to disabilities less than 20% and is not supposed to be rounded-off like Disability Pension. This is also not payable to those who are released on completion of terms of engagement or superannuation, since unlike rounding-off, this is not meant to offset medical subjectivity but is meant to compensate the curtailment of tenure. The amount as on date stands at Rs 20,00,000 (Para 9.1 of MoD letter dated 04-09-2017, Chapter 31.2).

2.15

Disability Pension to Short Service and Non-Regular Officers

Short Service Commissioned and Non-Regular Officers are eligible for Disability Pension, including Service Element, at par with Regular Officers. Further modalities of the same are available in Chapter 22.

2.16

Rates of Disability Pension

Disability Element (which is added to Service Pension or Service Element, as the case may be) is essentially granted @ 30% of emoluments or notional emoluments for 100% disability, subject to proportionate reduction. However, the rates as applicable from time to time with all other details are available in Chapter 16 dealing with successive pay commissions and Chapter 17 dealing with various pension enhancements till date.

Chapter-03

Assessment, Re-Assessment, Re-Survey, Review & Post-Discharge Evaluation of Disabilities

The assessment of percentage of disability is the duty of the medical board. However, it must also be kept in mind that such assessment is not sacrosanct and has to adhere to the rules and provisions dealing with the same. To take a very rudimentary example, in case the Guide to Medical Officers (Military Pensions) provides that the minimum permissible percentage for "Hypertension" is 30%, then the assessment at "less than 20%" by a particular medical board is questionable and therefore also challengeable.

However, assessment and re-assessment of disability are governed by certain basic conditions.

3.1

Assessment of disabilities "for life" and the right of a person to claim re-assessment

If the disability percentage is granted only for a particular period for a person who is in receipt of Disability Pension, the authorities concerned are supposed to call him or her for a fresh assessment to ascertain the disability on the expiry of the said period. However, after the year 2001, in case of permanent disabilities, the medical boards are supposed to declare the disability "for life" without calling a person periodically for Re-Survey or Re-Assessment Medical Boards and the percentage once assessed is to be treated as final unless the person himself requests for a fresh assessment of the percentage as per MoD letter 07-02-2001 (Chapter 23.3) read with letter dated 01-09-2005 (Chapter 23.4). Personnel retiring after the effective date mentioned in the above letter are not supposed to be called for re-assessment of disability and the same was also held by the Supreme Court in Civil Appeal 5970/2019 **Commander Rakesh Pande Vs Union of India** decided on 28-11-2019.

By virtue of the above provisions, disabled personnel also have a right to seek a one-time medical board in case they have an objection to the disability percentage or its duration assessed by an earlier board. In case the percentage awarded by a medical board is not acceptable to a disabled person, he or she can claim a "Review Medical Board" with the only caveat that the percentage, as assessed, would have to be accepted by both parties as per the *ibid* MoD letters.

The Review Medical Board (or the incorrectly nomenclatured 'Appeal Medical Board') cannot, however, overturn the positive declaration of attributability or aggravation by an earlier medical board, and at best, can only go into the assessment of extent of disability (percentage of disability) as held in TA 272/2009 **Mohan Singh Thapa Vs Union of India** decided on 22-01-2010 and OA 1824/2011 **Brig Ram Chander Malik Vs Union of India** decided on 02-05-2012 by the Chandigarh Bench of the AFT and upheld by the Supreme Court in Civil Appeal 659/2014 **Union of India Vs Brig Ram Chander Malik** on 10-12-2014.

An individual who is discharged with a disability but claims that there has been substantial increase in the percentage of his disability, can also request to be brought before a medical board vide the *ibid* MoD letters.

3.2

Disability percentage for intervening period

Earlier, Disability Pension claims were not processed between the period intervening the last board and the fresh board. However, the MoD on 10-11-2010 (Chapter 23.36) issued a letter stating that the medical boards would now clearly state the percentage of disability of the person between the last board and the fresh date of assessment and the claims would be processed for release of benefits as per the percentage assessed by the board. There have been instances when Records Offices have been seeking a copy of an undertaking from disabled soldiers that they would not seek disability benefits for the intervening period but the said practice has been held to be incorrect by the Courts and even seeking certificates such as 'non-employment' or 'non-conviction' certificate to process the claims for Disability Pension has been held to be incorrect in cases of personnel who are already in receipt of service pension since such certificates can only be sought from personnel who are non-pensioners and whose pension is to commence for the first time. The above has been held in OA 1827/2011 **Kulbir Singh Vs Union of India** decided on 18-11-2011, OA 653/2014 **Baljit Singh Vs Union of India** decided on 12-05-2015 and OA 1499/2014 **Avtar Singh Vs Union of India** decided on 09-03-2016; all by the Chandigarh Bench of the AFT.

3.3

Post-Discharge Medical Board to claim Disability Pension for a disability arising after release from service

As discussed in the previous chapter on Disability Pensions in detail (Chapter 2.13), a person who has been released in a fit shape (Medical Category AYE/SHAPE-1) can also claim to be brought before a Post-Discharge Medical Board within 10 years of his/her release from service if he/she develops a disability after retirement which has a basis of incurrence when the person was in service.

Chapter-04

Service Element of Disability Pension

As explained in the Chapter on Disability Pension (Chapter 2), the said pension consists of two elements – Service Element and Disability Element.

While Disability Element is granted as per percentage of disability, Service Element is released proportionate to the length of service. There is no minimum qualifying service requirement for Service Element with effect from 01-01-1973.

Earlier, Service Element used to be granted subject to minimum length of service provided for it, which was 10 years till 1968 and 5 years from 1968 to 1972. With effect from 01-01-1973, the minimum service requirement for Service Element was totally abrogated and a person with even a single day of service was made entitled to Service Element of Disability Pension, even if the disability was assessed at less than 20% at the time of release or fell below 20% subsequently. The same dispensation continues till date.

In the past, in case a person was released with a disability below 20% or the disability fell below 20%, the entire Disability Pension used to be discontinued, including the Service Element, except those who were released with the minimum service as prescribed from time to time as mentioned in the preceding paragraph. However, various High Courts had ruled that such a distinction could not be made based upon any cut-off date and that all disabled retirees, irrespective of date of retirement, must be released the Service Element with effect from 01-01-1973. While some High Courts had granted the benefit from 01-01-1973, others had restricted the arrears of Service Element to a period of three years prior to filing of the respective petitions. The Union of India, however, challenged most of the verdicts in the Supreme Court.

The Supreme Court in the year 2012, while hearing the entire bunch of cases, provided an opportunity to the Ministry of Defence to rectify the anomaly on its own. Finally, on a decision taken by the then Defence Minister, the Government agreed to grant the said benefits to all pre-1973 disability pensioners irrespective of the length of service, after which the matter was closed by the Supreme Court after recording the statement of the Union of India.

Thereafter, a policy letter was issued on 10-02-2014 (Chapter 23.31) releasing the benefit to all similarly-placed pre-1973 disability pensioners with financial effect from 01-01-1973.

A controversy since the 2000s has also emerged as to whether Service Element without any linkage with length of service, is available only in cases of 'invalidation' or even to those released on completion of terms of engagement or prematurely at own request. Although the Government maintains that it is only applicable to those who are 'invalided' (medically boarded out before attaining age of retirement or completion of terms of engagement), the fact remains that the definition of 'invalidation' as per rules encompasses all individuals who are released in a medical category lower than the one in which they were recruited (See Rule 1 of Entitlement Rules, 1950 and Rule 4 of Entitlement Rules, 1982, reproduced in Chapter 23.1). Further, rules make it clear that Disability Pension consists of both elements and even spell out how the said Service Element is to be calculated when a person has, and also when he/she does not have, the qualifying service to earn regular pension. An example of the same for ranks other than Commissioned Officers in the Army would be Regulation 183 of the Pension Regulations, 1961.

It was also clarified in Paragraph 14.2 of MoD letter dated 30-10-1987 (Chapter 28.1) specifically that there is no requirement of any minimum service for earning Service Element and how the same is to be calculated if the service is less than the required length for pension. Short Service and Non-Regular officers are also entitled to Service Element (See Chapter 22).

The controversy of entitlement of Disability Pension, including Service Element, for those released at own request before completion of pensionable terms or on resignation and there being no minimum requirement of qualifying service for the same, has been adjudicated judicially in a number of cases including by the Supreme Court in Civil Appeal 4714/2012 **Union of India Vs VR Nanukuttan Nair** decided on 07-11-2019, by the Delhi High Court in CW 2967/1989 **Mahavir Singh Narwal Vs Union of India** decided on 05-05-2004 and CW 6475/1998 **Jai Singh Vs Union of India** decided on 07-03-2005. The Principal Bench of the AFT in OA 603/2014 **Charanjit Singh Medi Vs Union of India** had also decided a similar issue on 09-02-2016 which was affirmed by the Supreme Court in Special Leave to Appeal (C) Diary No 25998/2017 decided on 11-09-2017. The issue was also adjudicated by the Chandigarh Bench of the AFT in OA 2939/2012 **Sanjay Kumar Vs Union of India** decided on 03-07-2015. The matter also came up before the Supreme Court again in Civil Appeal (Diary Number) 28189/2019 **Union of India Vs Mithun Sasi** decided on 27-09-2019 and Civil Appeal (Diary Number) 7938/2019 **Union of India Vs Jeevan Chandra Pandey** decided on 02-09-2022 which upheld the rights of disabled personnel to receive Disability Pension, including Service Element, irrespective of length of service of premature retirees.

Chapter-05

Liberalised Awards (War Injury Pension & Liberalised Family Pension)

The concept of Liberalised Awards assumes much importance in an operationally oriented military like ours.

The concept formally took birth in a regulatory format in the Army Pension Regulations, 1940. For example, as far as Indian Combatants and Non-Combatants were concerned, Regulation 357 of the said Regulations provided two categories/rates of Disability Pension – "field service rate" and "peace area rate". The two categories were akin to the current distinction between War Injury Pension and regular Disability Pension. It needs to be, however, said that the above mentioned then existing regulation was much simpler and balanced since it contained a very relevant clause which provided that if a person is disabled in a peace area but in circumstances which are similar to those encountered in a field area, then the person could be paid "field service rate" of Disability Pension even if the disability was sustained in a peace area. The said Regulation 357 is reproduced hereunder:

> **Circumstances in which field service rates and peace rates of Disability Pension are admissible –**
>
> i. An individual whose disability is certified to be attributable to military service in a "field service" area may be granted field service rate of Disability Pension,if he is otherwise qualified.
>
> ii. If his disability is certified to be attributable to military service in a peace area he may be granted the peace rate of Disability Pension, if otherwise qualified.
>
> iii. If an individual, though not serving in a field service area, is disabled in circumstances which, in the opinion of the local administrative authorities are similar to those encountered on field service, his case shall, provided that claimant is otherwise qualified and his disablement is not due to his own gross negligence or misconduct, be submitted for the orders of the Governor General as to whether the field service rate of pension shall be granted.

Things, however, changed after independence when the Pension Regulations, 1961 were introduced (effective retrospectively from 01-06-1953). These regulations essentially only catered to "non-battle casualty" cases and provided for normal Disability Pension. The concept of "Battle Casualty" as a result of direct action was introduced through an Army Order published in 1952. Declaration of the status of Battle Casualty did not result in higher pensionary benefits at the time.

In 1972 however, the Government introduced the Liberalised Pensionary Awards through Letter dated 24-02-1972 (Chapter 23.6) which took into its ambit essentially all operations after our independence. The important characteristic of this letter, however, was that only cases of 'live action' and mine blast, etc, were covered. It may be noted that present day War Injury Pension at that time was known as "War Injury Pay" and Liberalised Family Pension was called "Liberalised Special Family Pension". Needless to state, while War Injury Pension is granted on sustaining disability, Liberalised Family Pension is awarded on death.

In the year 1985, the Army comprehensively reviewed its existing instructions on "Battle Casualty" as per changing dynamics of operations and consequently issued Army Order 8/S/1985 (Chapter 23.8). This Army Order now included in its ambit death and disability occurring on account of injuries due to booby traps, barbed wires, obstacles in operational areas and also deaths and injuries during natural calamities, etc. It may be recalled that the term "Battle Casualty" now is a misnomer and should not be taken in literal terms. It includes within its ambit many eventualities that go much beyond injuries in a proper war or battle. As mentioned above, it has been progressively altered keeping in view the changing dynamics of operational duties and deployment.

Though the Army continued to grant Battle Casualty status to its soldiers, the same was not recognised for higher pensionary benefits by the Ministry of Defence. Vide letter dated 26-03-1985 (Chapter 23.7), deaths and disabilities occurring in Siachen Glacier (under Operation Meghdoot) on account of avalanches, climatic and terrain conditions were also held eligible for Liberalised Awards. However, in the year 1987, in a very important move after the 4th Central Pay Commission, the Government of India recognised cases declared as battle casualties by the military for grant of War Injury Pension and Liberalised Family Pension vide Part IV of Letter dated 30-10-1987 (Chapter 28.1). Later, in 1991, just like the Siachen Glacier, natural illnesses incurred by personnel operating on the Line of Control and International Borders were also included in the Battle Casualty list for financial purposes, while being continued to be treated as Physical Casualties for statistical purposes (Chapter 23.8).

On 31-01-2001, after the 5th Central Pay Commission, another letter was issued by the Government (Chapter 23.12), further liberalising such benefits in which "Categories D and E" were introduced for Liberalised Awards. “Category D” included mob violence, death & disabilities in earthquake and flood relief, etc, and “Category E” included death & disabilities in wars, war like situations, mine related injuries, and also death & disabilities in notified operations, thereby covering all disabilities occurring in operations such as Operations Rakshak, Rhino, Parakram, etc, notified by the Government. Further, a Note was added under “Category E” which stated that the examples provided were only illustrative and not exhaustive and all other casualties shall continue to be regulated as per existing rules.

Though the above mentioned MoD letter dated 31-01-2001 was based upon DoPPW master letter dated 03-02-2000 (Chapter 23.11), it contained a cut-off date of 01-01-1996 covering only post-1996 cases, although the master letter dated 03-02-2000 was later extended by the DoPPW to pre-1996 cases also vide letter 11-09-2001 (Chapter 23.17) with financial effect from 01-01-1996. Though till date the MoD has not issued implementation instructions as per DoPPW letter dated 11-09-2001 for extension of the benefits of letter dated 31-01-2001 to pre-1996 cases, the Supreme Court in Civil Appeal 5591/2006 **KJS Buttar Vs Union of India** decided on 31-03-2011, has held that the benefits of letter dated 31-01-2001 cannot be denied to pre-1996 cases and need to be extended to such past cases also with arrears from 01-01-1996. Over the years, certain amendments were made and more categories were added into the letter dated 31-01-2001 on 08-09-2009, 05-03-2010, 03-02-2011, 07-03-2018 and 02-09-2021 (Chapters 23.13, 23.14, 23.15, 23.16 and 23.37).

Another Army Order, that is, Army Order 01/2003 (Chapter 23.9) was then later issued in which even more categories were added to the list of “Battle Casualty”, including deaths and disabilities during aid to civil authorities, while performing operational movements and deaths due to electrocution, poisoning and snake-bite in operational areas. Later on 01-04-2013 (Chapter 23.10), it was clarified that disabilities and deaths while the troops were resting when on patrol or while returning to the barracks or due to slipping or falling while patrolling in operational areas were also to be treated as battle casualties.

In the year 2020, yet another Army Order, that is, Army Order 05/2020 (Chapter 23.38) was issued, wherein certain more clauses were added. Though already included in the clarification issued on 01-04-2013 mentioned above, it was now explicitly ordained that falling and slipping while patrolling during ambush or even on operational duty near any type of border would be included in the concept of “Battle Casualty”. A residual clause for considering instances on a case to case basis with the approval of the Chief of the Army Staff, was also added.

Though recently, in a matter titled Civil Appeal 7459/2010 **Kanchan Dua Vs Union of India** decided on 23-09-2019, the Supreme Court was informed by the establishment that Liberalised Awards are only payable in cases of 'live action' by essentially citing the 1972 letter, the same was not an accurate submission of the actual position since the developments on the ever-changing definition of 'Battle Casualty' and various Government instructions, orders and letters were not brought to the notice of the Court. In that sense, it can always be argued that the decision is *sub silentio*. It was also not pointed out that Liberalised Pensionary Awards today have no link whatsoever with the original letter of 1972 or 'live action', since if that argument is to be accepted, then even the rest of the circumstances in Categories D and E of MoD letter dated 31-01-2001 (Chapter 23.12) mentioned as qualifying for liberalised benefits, such as disabilities/deaths while dealing with anti-social elements, quelling agitations by demonstrators, natural calamities, kidnappings, battle inoculation, etc, would become redundant and otiose. Probably when the correct facts are brought to the notice of judicial fora, the result may perhaps turn out to be different. While this is not to say that the wife of the late officer in the said case was entitled to Liberalised Family Pension or whether her case fell in any of the categories for entitlement of the said pension or not, keeping in view the facts of the death, she may or may not have been eligible, but the actuality remains that the changes in the definitions and entitlements were not brought to the knowledge of the Court. In fact, the Court was not even informed that already there is a distinction within battle casualties, wherein War Wounded Battle Casualties, called BC(WW), are provided higher benefits than other battle casualties in matters other than pension (such as in promotion policies), clearly signifying that regular BCs and BCs(WW) are in any case treated separately for certain aspects within the military. There is also a misconception that a 'severity' certificate for 'injuries' is mandatorily required to declare individuals as 'battle casualties'. This is a misreading and misinterpretation of rules since the same is only required in "injury" cases in the category of BC(WW), since such a requirement cannot be in any way met in non-injury or disease cases or those falling in the categories of battle casualty on account of natural illnesses, calamities, climatic conditions in Siachen Glacier, etc.

5.1

Decisions touching upon important modalities of Liberalised Awards

Some important judgments alongwith a gist, with regard to various aspects of Liberalised Awards, are as follows:

In Civil Appeal 5591/2006 **KJS Buttar Vs Union of India** decided on 31-03-2011, it was held by the Supreme Court that the liberalised benefits of the letter dated 31-01-2001 (which was made applicable by the MoD only to post-1996 cases) could not be denied to pre-1996 cases and any such distinction or denial based upon a cut-off date was discriminatory.

In CWP 2976/2007 **Manjit Kaur Vs Union of India** decided on 19-05-2008, the Punjab & Haryana High Court held that under the rules, a death occurring during a training exercise was to be treated as "Battle Casualty" for statistical purposes, and there was no requirement of "live ammunition" in the applicable rules that the official authorities were professing. The High Court had directed the payment of Liberalised Family Pension to the widow.

In OA 1240/2015 **Mandeep F Merchant Vs Union of India** decided on 25-04-2017 by the Chandigarh Bench of the AFT, it was held that a death due to a vehicular accident during Operation Parakram in an operational area was to be treated as eligible for grant of Liberalised Family Pension.

In OA 78/2016 **Gurmel Kaur Vs Union of India** decided on 11-04-2017, the husband of the Petitioner was killed in the 1984 riots. The establishment had refused the grant of Liberalised Family Pension to her on the pretext that deaths in riots, etc, got covered for Liberalised Awards only with effect from 01-01-1996 and the said cut-off date in MoD letter dated 31-01-2001 prevented the Government from releasing her Liberalised Family Pension. The Chandigarh Bench of the tribunal, following the dicta in *KJS Buttar* (supra), however, held that the benefits would have to be released to pre-1996 cases also, with financial effect from 01-01-1996.

In OA 1276/2013 **Gurbax Singh Dhindsa Vs Union of India** decided on 27-08-2015 by the Chandigarh Bench of the AFT, it was held that death of an individual in an operational area on a fighter jet flight or battle inoculation would entitle the next of kin to Dependent Pension (Liberalised).

In TA 07/2014 **Saudamini Mohapatra Vs Union of India** decided on 09-05-2019, the Kolkata Bench of the AFT held that the benefits admissible to casualties which occur on the International Border and the Line of Control (IB and LOC) cannot be denied to similar deaths and disabilities occurring on the Line of Actual Control (LAC).

In OA 48/2016 **Pinky Devi Vs Union of India** decided on 05-03-2018, the Lucknow Bench of AFT held that the benefit of the new categories added by the Government vide MoD letter dated 03-02-2011 (Chapter 23.15) for the admissibility of Liberalised Awards could not be denied to pre-2011 cases based on a cut-off date.

In CWP 3810/2013 **Sumitra Devi Vs Union of India** decided on 17-02-2014, it was held by the Punjab & Haryana High Court that the death of a soldier on account of a heart attack in a notified operation due to service related factors would entitle the widow to Liberalised Family Pension. The SLP filed by the Union of India before the Supreme Court in the matter, was dismissed.

In OA 305/2014 **Kameshwar Gautam Vs Union of India** decided on 15-12-2015, it was held by the Chandigarh Bench of the AFT that the death of a young officer due to cardiac arrest on the Line of Control in an operational area while leading a Ghatak Platoon would entitle the family to Liberalised Pensionary benefits.

In TA 83/2009 **Inder Singh Vs Union of India** decided on 18-04-2011, the soldier who suffered frostbite on both feet while deployed in *Sela-Bomdila* area during the Indo-China War of 1962 was denied War Injury Pension on the pretext that during those times, the said disability was not considered a 'Battle Casualty'. The Chandigarh Bench of the AFT, however, held that such benefits could not be denied to personnel based on cut-off dates and it was the duty of the system to *suo moto* extend the benefits to past retirees whenever any such new category is added to the concept of Battle Casualty or Liberalised Awards.

In OA 3614/2012 **Amar Singh Vs Union of India** decided on 12-07-2017, the soldier who was injured in World War II was granted regular Disability Pension and was denied War Injury Pension on the ground that 'international wars' came to be recognised for Liberalised Awards only with effect from 01-01-1996. The AFT, however, held that such soldiers who were injured in WWII could not be denied the benefit and should be paid War Injury Pension from 01-01-1996. The tribunal had also directed the Respondents to *suo moto* release the same to all similarly placed disabled soldiers too.

In OA 3199/2019 **Anuradha Saini Vs Union of India** decided on 16-03-2023, the Chandigarh Bench of AFT held that the death of a soldier during active operational deployment on the International Border due to a heart attack would fall within the ambit of being a "battle casualty" as per rules, thereby entitling the widow to Liberalised Family Pension. In the said case, the husband of the Petitioner, already suffering from hypertension, was deployed in a bunker on the Indo-Pak border during 'Operation Rakshak' when he suffered a heart attack in the aftermath of twenty five persons trying to infiltrate the border. Though the death was declared attributable to military service in an operational/field area by the statutory Court of Inquiry, the claim was rejected by administrative authorities by overriding the positive declaration of the Court of Inquiry.

5.2

LFP on Remarriage

The rules for LFP on remarriage are provided in detail in Paragraph 6.6 of MoD letter dated 31-01-2001 (Chapter 23.12). There used to be a bar on continuance of LFP on remarriage earlier. It was abrogated for post-1996 pensioners with effect from 01-01-1996. It was also abrogated for pre-1996 pensioners with effect from 24-06-2005 vide MoD letter of the same date (Chapter 26.4).

5.3

LFP to Parents and Dependent Brother/Sister

In case of officers, in case the officer dies a bachelor or as a widower without children, the LFP is paid to parents. The said pension is then known as Dependent Pension (Liberalised). Such pension is paid @ 75% rate of LFP otherwise due in case of both parents and @ 60% for single parent. In the absence of parents, the said pension shall be paid to dependent brother or sister at the rate of 60%. The modalities are provided in Para 6.4 of MoD letter dated 31-01-2001 (Chapter 23.12).

In case of ranks other than Commissioned Officers, the said pension is called Second Life Award (LFP) and the same is regulated differently than officers and the detailed modalities governing the same are available in Paragraph 6.5 of the *ibid* MoD letter.

5.4

Division of LFP

The modalities of division of LFP and the applicable circumstances where the same is permissible, are provided in Paragraphs 6.5 and 6.6 of MoD letter dated 31-01-2001 (Chapter 23.12). Similar modalities in case of Special Family Pension are described in detail in Chapter 8.4 and the same may be perused for more insight on the subject.

5.5

Rates of LFP and WIP

LFP is essentially granted @ 100% of emoluments or notional emoluments subject to the relationship of the deceased with the recipient as discussed above. WIP comprises Service Element and War Injury Element and the said War Injury Element is calculated at 60% of emoluments or notional emoluments for 100% disability, subject to proportionate reduction for lesser disability in case of retirement/discharge cases and at 100% of emoluments or notional emoluments for invalidation cases leading to curtailment of tenure (See Paragraphs 6.4 and 7.1 of MoD letter dated 05-05-2009, Chapter 23.21). However, the rates as applicable from time to time with all other details and calculation modalities are available in Chapter 16 dealing with successive pay commissions and Chapter 17 dealing with various pension enhancements till date. The cap imposed on War Injury Pension, wherein it was provided that the aggregate of Service Element and War Injury Element should not exceed emoluments last drawn, was also removed by MoD on 19-01-2010 (Chapter 23.25). MoD letter dated 31-01-2001 (Chapter 23.12) also provides for other modalities of calculation of War Injury benefits. For example, the calculation of Service Element in cases where the person has been boarded out on medical grounds, is undertaken on the basis of the notional length of service he/she would have actually rendered in normal circumstances had he/she not been boarded out.

Chapter-06

Family Pension

Broadly speaking, Family Pension is of three kinds.

Ordinary Family Pension, that is granted to the eligible member of the family when a person dies in harness due to a reason that is not connected with military service (neither attributable to, nor aggravated by military service), or on the death of any person after retirement/release/discharge who was in receipt of any kind of pension.

Special Family Pension is granted in cases wherein the death is due to a cause attributable to, or aggravated by military service, or deemed as such as per rules, or also in certain cases of death after retirement/release/discharge.

Liberalised Family Pension is granted in cases where the death falls within the parameter of "Battle Casualty" or is due to operational reasons or in operational areas or circumstances as provided in Categories D & E under Paragraph 4 of MoD letter dated 31-01-2001 (Chapter 23.12).

Family Pension is admissible irrespective of any length of service and no minimum qualifying service is prescribed for the grant of any kind of Family Pension.

The above kinds of pensions are discussed in detail in the following Chapters.

Chapter-07

Ordinary Family Pension

As explained in the preceding chapter, Ordinary Family Pension (also known as OFP) is granted to the eligible member of the family when a person dies in service due to a reason that is not connected to military service (neither attributable to, nor aggravated by military service), or on the death of any person after retirement/release/discharge who was in receipt of any kind of pension. OFP is also paid in the cases of suicide. It is paid at 30% of last drawn emoluments of the deceased or 30% of notionally last drawn emoluments admissible to the last rank held by a pensioner. OFP is however paid at an enhanced rate for a certain period.

In normal circumstances, OFP is granted to the widow/widower of the deceased employee if the employee was married.

7.1

Ordinary Family Pension to Children

However, in case of there not being an eligible or surviving widow/widower, OFP is granted to the son or daughter till the date of marriage or till the date he/she starts earning or the age of 25 years, whichever is earlier. The details are available in Paragraph 11 of MoD letter dated 12-11-2008 (Chapter 30.2).

7.2

Ordinary Family Pension to Parents

OFP is also admissible to parents who were wholly dependent upon the employee when he/she was alive, provided the person had not left behind a widow or a child. The dependency criterion is the minimum admissible Family Pension plus dearness relief (See Paragraph 11 of letter dated 12-11-2008, Chapter 30.2, as again revised after the 7th CPC vide MoD letter dated 04-09-2017, Chapter 31.2). The said criterion currently stands at Rs 9,000 + Dearness Relief. It is, however, to be noted that Family Pension to dependent parents (and also unmarried/widowed/divorced daughters) shall be payable only after the other eligible family members in Category I of Paragraph 11 of letter dated 12-11-2008 mentioned above, have ceased to be eligible to receive Family Pension and there is no disabled child to receive the Family Pension. Grant of Family Pension to children in respective categories shall be payable in order of their date of birth and younger of them will not be eligible for Family Pension unless the next above him/her has become ineligible for grant of Family Pension in that category.

7.3

Ordinary Family Pension to Widowed, Unmarried and Divorced Daughters

OFP is also admissible to widowed, unmarried and divorced daughters irrespective of age (till death). However, such pension is not admissible in case the said daughter is earning more than the dependency criterion. The provisions and conditions dealing with this aspect are also available in Paragraph 11 of letter dated 12-11-2008 (Chapter 30.2). These provisions are also governed by the same limitations as applicable to parents, which is, that it shall be payable only after the other eligible family members in Category I of Paragraph 11 of letter dated 12-11-2008 mentioned above, have ceased to be eligible to receive Family Pension and there is no disabled child to receive the Family Pension.

As explained in the preceding paragraph, grant of Family Pension to children in respective categories shall be payable in order of their date of birth and younger of them will not be eligible for Family Pension unless the next above him/her has become ineligible for grant of Family Pension in that category. It was later clarified by the DoPPW and adopted as such by the MoD that only those children of pensioners and also widowed/unmarried/divorced daughters would be considered eligible who were dependent on the pensioner or his/her spouse (the family pensioner) at the time of his or her death, whichever is later. It was also provided for divorced daughters specifically that they shall be eligible for Family Pension if a decree of divorce had been passed by the court during the lifetime of at least one of the parents, so as to prove dependency on them. However, it was later clarified that in case the divorce proceedings had been instituted during the life of one or both (the employee/pensioner or spouse/family pensioner) but none of them remained alive by the time the decree of divorce was granted, in that eventuality, the divorced daughter shall remain eligible for Family Pension. The said provisions and also the modalities mentioned in the above background, become clear from MoD letter dated 17-11-2017 (Chapter 26.12).

The above clarifications by the DoPPW about divorced daughter being eligible only if the decree of divorce had been passed or proceedings initiated during the lifetime of one of the parents, is, however, legally controversial since no such prohibition is imposed in the original policy letter of the DoPPW dated 25-08-2004 (Chapter 26.19) or even the main policy issued by the MoD (Para 11 of Chapter 30.2), and it is setttled law that a 'clarification' cannot result in alteration of a positive or beneficial provision flowing from the main policy. Even otherwise, the very valid income criterion or 'means limit' is the only objective criterion to assess dependency and not the date of divorce or date of death of parent(s) or the date of initiaition of proceedings for divorce, all of which are fortuitous and chance-based conditions.

7.4

Pension to Dependent Disabled Siblings

Vide DoPPW letter dated 17-08-2009 (Chapter 26.6), the definition of 'family' was extended to dependent disabled siblings of central Government employees and pensioners. This provision was extended since it was found that disabled siblings who were dependent upon the said Government employee or pensioner were left to fend for themselves after the death of the employee/pensioner. The same conditions as applicable to dependent disabled sons and daughter were extended to this category. This pension was also made applicable for life and the provisions are available in the abovementioned DoPPW letter.

7.5

Family Pension to Handicapped Children

The son or daughter of an employee or a pensioner who is suffering from any disorder or disability of body or mind so as to render him or her unable to earn a living even after attaining the age of 25 years was made eligible for lifelong Family Pension subject to dependency criterion. However, an additional prohibition was imposed that such a handicapped child will be disqualified from Family Pension if he or she was or got married. The condition of discontinuance of pension on getting married was however removed with financial effect from 24-09-2012 vide MoD letter dated 17-01-2013 (Chapter 26.11).

The income criterion applicable to handicapped children and siblings was earlier pegged at the minimum amount of pension admissible under the Government, for example, Rs 9000 per month plus dearness allowance with effect from 01-01-2016. However, the Government has now changed this criterion and provided that a child/sibling of a deceased employee or pensioner, who is suffering from a mental or physical disability, shall be deemed to be not earning his/her livelihood if his/her overall income from sources other than family pension is less than the entitled family pension at ordinary rate and the dearness relief admissible thereon, payable on death of the employee or pensioner concerned, as per his/her own grade. The same benefit has also been extended to the military side vide letter DESW letter dated 28-09-2021 (Chapter 26.18).

7.6

Ordinary Family Pension on Remarriage

With effect from 01-01-2006, the childless widow of an employee remains eligible for Ordinary Family Pension on remarriage, provided she meets the dependency criterion of having a total income from all sources less than the minimum Family Pension admissible plus dearness relief (Rs 9,000 + Dearness Relief as on date). The same is provided in Paragraph 11.3 of MoD letter dated 12-11-2008 (Chapter 30.2) and latest dependency criterion is reflected in MoD letter 04-09-2017 after the 7th CPC (Chapter 31.2).

As per earlier existing rules, a widow who married the real brother of the employee, irrespective of being childless or otherwise, remained entitled to Special Family Pension. The Delhi High Court in WP(C)1082/1995 **Kashmiro Devi Vs Union of India** decided on 19-05-2008, held that the same shall also apply to Ordinary Family Pension and there could be no discrimination between OFP and SFP in this regard. Hence, as on date, based upon the dicta in *Kashmiro Devi's* case, even a widow with a child, who marries her late husband's brother, remains entitled for continuance of OFP. *Kashmiro Devi's* case was followed by the Chandigarh Bench of the AFT in OA 553/2010 **Vineeta Sur Vs Union of India** decided on 15-09-2010. Situations emerging out of remarriage in cases of SFP and LFP are discussed in the respective chapters.

7.7

Clarification on dependency criterion

While considering the dependency criterion for the purposes of Family Pension, it has been clarified by the DoPPW vide letter dated 30-11-2011 (Chapter 26.7) that any amount of Family Pension already being received by a claimant will not count towards the dependency criterion. However, any other income or earning of the beneficiary under consideration shall continue to be counted towards income for deciding the eligibility for Family Pension as far as dependency criterion is concerned.

7.8

Family Pension to Children born out of Void Marriages

Earlier, the children born out of void marriages were not entitled to Family Pension since any such marriage was not considered legal in the eyes of law. However, the DoPPW changed this rule and provided pension to such children also. The same was then notified by the Ministry of Defence vide Army Instruction 3 of 1995 (Chapter 26.2) which provides that children born out of void marriage in terms of Section 11 of the Hindu Marriage Act, 1955, shall remain entitled to Family Pension if otherwise eligible.

7.9

Division of Ordinary Family Pension

Ordinary Family Pension is not divisible (unlike Special Family Pension and Liberalised Family Pension, which are divisible subject to certain special conditions). It is also not treated as property for the purposes of succession laws, as held by the Supreme Court in Special Leave to Appeal 7254/1980 **Jodh Singh Vs Union of India** decided on 09-10-1980 and in Civil Appeal 9823/2016 **Nitu Vs Sheela Rani** decided on 28-09-2016. However, there might be extraordinary circumstances wherein division of OFP might be possible, such as emerging from a decree of a civil court resulting from an exceptional circumstance such as a settlement, or in other circumstances such as division of pension between a legally wedded wife and children born out of a void marriage as also reflected in DoPPW letter dated 27-11-2012 (Chapter 26.8).

7.10

Ordinary Family Pension to families of Reservists

Ordinary Family Pension is also admissible to families of personnel in receipt of Reservist Pension. Also, and more importantly, Ordinary Family Pension is admissible to families of those reservists who had died during the period of 'Reserves' (that is, while not on physical/colour service) without earning pension. This lesser known provision was introduced vide Army Instruction 3/Special/1977(Chapter 26.1). In modern nomenclature or terminology, the same would be known as Special Army Instruction (SAI) 03/77.

7.11

Family Pension to families of Officer-Trainees (also known as Officer-Cadets)

Families of Officer-Trainees are unfortunately not eligible for grant of proper Ordinary Family Pension or Special Family Pension but are only entitled to a monthly ex-gratia award of Rs 9,000 per month + Dearness Relief at current rates, as per Paragraph 11 of MoD letter dated 04-09-2017 (Chapter 31.2) in case of death declared attributable to or aggravated by military training. The said monthly ex-gratia is also granted to the spouse if the person dies after invalidation due to the same disability for which he/she was invalided out of the training academy. There is currently no provision that caters to grant or continuance of Family Pension or monthly ex-gratia to the spouse of a trainee who dies due to any cause other than the disability for which he/she was invalided, which of course, is discriminatory when compared with other military employees or civilian trainees. The amount as above is also much lesser than even the authorisation of similarly placed recruits at *jawan* level or trainees on the civil side. This anomaly is also discussed in the Chapter dealing with Disability Pension, that is, Chapter 2.

7.12

Dual Family Pension

For many years, families of defence pensioners who were in receipt of two pensions, that is, one from the defence side and the other from the civil side, were entitled to only one Family Pension on the death of such a pensioner. For example, in case a defence pensioner joined a civil department after earning his pension from the military side, and thereafter earned a pension from the civil department, he was entitled to both pensions but his widow was only entitled to one pension. Similarly, if such a military pensioner who had joined a civil department died in harness in the civil employment, then also the widow was entitled to only one Family Pension.

This was considered unjust since the person had earned two pensions by way of separate spells of service and hence, logically, even his/her widow should have remained entitled to two pensions since Family Pension is directly linked with the person's existing pension or the fact that he died in harness. The same logic was applicable to family members other than widows too, in case entitled to Family Pension. This anomaly was finally rectified and it was provided by way of MoD letter dated 17-01-2013 (Chapter 26.9) that such families would remain entitled to both pensions for separate spells of service. The financial benefits were made applicable from 24-09-2012.

It may, however, be noted that the bar of dual Family Pension was not applicable for those cases wherein one Family Pension was through a 'contributory' pension scheme such as Employees' Family Pension Scheme 1971 or Employees' Pension Scheme 1995. This is so since such schemes comprise of part contribution of the employee himself and hence, are not regular 'defined' pension schemes funded by the Government. A letter issued by Employees' Provident Fund Organisation (EPFO) dated 15-01-2002 (Chapter 26.3) also clarifies the said matter.

It has also similarly been held by Courts that when the source of the pension is not purely governmental, for example, it is based upon a pension trust or some special fund or is otherwise contributory such as the ones being run by many banks and financial organisations, even then there would be no bar on dual pension. This also means that in such cases the widows shall remain entitled to the pension from the civil side from the date of entitlement and not from the future cut-off date of 24-09-2012. The same has been held, amongst others, by the Kerala High Court in WP 22963/2007 **Leela Vs Union of India** decided on 27-06-2008 and the Principal Bench of the AFT in OA 116/2012 **Veena Pant Vs Union of India** decided on 31-10-2012.

Another aspect that had created confusion for the grant of dual Family Pension was whether the removal of this bar on dual Family Pension would apply to cases wherein one of the pensions is not OFP but is SFP or LFP or Extraordinary Family Pension under the EOP Rules. This was also recently clarified vide MoD letter dated 08-07-2019 (Chapter 26.13) stating that the provisions shall equally apply to SFP and LFP too, subject to certain conditions.

7.13

Change of name of Wife/Kin in the Records

In certain rare circumstances, there might be a requirement for changing the names of wife or other kin of serving or retired personnel. Such cases are dealt with in accordance with the procedure prescribed by Army HQ letter dated 15-05-2008 (Chapter 33.4).

7.14

Family Pension in case the eligible member of the family is charged with murder or abetment of murder of the employee

As per existing provisions, family pension is not released to the eligible family pensioner if he/she is charged with the murder or abetment of murder of the Government employee concerned. As per the interpretation of the establishment, during the pendency of such proceedings, the family pension was not even paid to other eligible members of the family. For example, if the wife is facing the charge of murder of the Government servant, then during the pendency of the criminal proceedings, the pension was not even being released to his children if eligible in case the widow was deemed ineligible.

The DoPPW has now clarified vide its letter dated 16-06-2021 (Chapter 26.14) that in such cases, the family pension shall be released to the other eligible members of the family and in case the original family pensioner is acquitted ultimately, the pension shall be restored to him/her from the date of acquittal and the family pension to the other member of the family shall stand discontinued from that date. The same provision has also been applied to military family pensioners vide DESW letter dated 05-01-2022 (Chapter 26.15).

7.15

Inclusion of names of Widowed/Divorced/Unmarried Daughters in PPOs

While the procedure and policy existed for inclusion of names of disabled children & siblings and dependent parents in the PPOs, there was no policy for inclusion of names of the widowed/ divorced/unmarried daughters in the PPO, who were otherwise entitled for family pension under existing provisions. The DESW has now issued a policy dated 04-05-2020 (Chapter 26.16) for inclusion of the same in the PPO to avoid any delay in release of benefits to entitled family pensioners.

7.16

Abrogation of minimum length of service to be eligible for Enhanced Ordinary Family Pension

The minimum length of service of seven years required to be eligible for enhanced family pension now stands abrogated with effect from 01-10- 2019 and a letter to the said effect stands issued by the DESW on 05-10-2020 (Chapter 26.17).

Chapter-08

Special Family Pension

(Note: This Chapter may be read in conjunction with the commentary in Chapter 2 on Disability Pension since the rules on attributability and aggravation are the same)

Special Family Pension (SFP) is admissible in cases wherein the death is due to a reason attributable to, or aggravated by military service, or deemed as such as per rules, or also in certain cases of death after retirement/release/discharge. It is paid @60% of last emoluments (or notional emoluments) of the deceased employee.

SFP is dealt by Regulation 213 of the Pension Regulations, 1961 (Regulation 85 in case of families of Commissioned Officers), and the corresponding regulations for the other two services. It reads as follows:

> 213. A special family pension may be granted to the family of an individual if his death was due to or hastened by-
>
> a. a wound, injury or disease which was attributable to military service,
>
> OR
>
> b. the aggravation by military service of a wound, injury or disease, which existed before or arose during military service.

The rules concerning attributability and aggravation qua SFP are essentially the same as Disability Pension both for "injury" as well as "disease" cases. As stated above, the details of the same are available in Chapter 2. Basically, if a person suffers a disability falling (or deemingly falling) within the parameters of attributability/aggravation, he/she is entitled to Disability Pension, while in case of death within the same parameters, the family is entitled to SFP.

8.1

In-Service and Post-Release deaths

As Regulation 213 indicates, a death due to an attributable/aggravated disability leads to the grant of SFP. The said Regulation makes no distinction between in-service or post-release deaths.

Hence, for example, in case a person is released with a Disability Pension for heart disease declared attributable/aggravated by military service and dies due to a heart attack after his retirement, the death shall still fall under an attributable/aggravated death within the meaning of Regulation 213, thereby entitling the family to SFP. However, in case a person is released from service with a Disability Pension but it cannot be medically established that the death is linked with the same disability for which he/she was granted Disability Pension, then the presumption of attributability/aggravation for the grant of SFP shall be in favour of the claimant in case the death has occurred within 10 years from release and in favour of the Government in case the death occurs after 10 years. The same is provided under Rule 11 of the Entitlement Rules, 1982 (Chapter 23.1). It may be remembered that though the term used in Rule 11 is "invalidment", the definition of invalidation as provided in Rule 4 covers all personnel who are in low medical category at the time of release from service. The Government has also waived the requirement of proving any medical certification related to the cause of death as per Circular No 333 issued by the office of the PCDA(P) on 27-01-2005 based on a decision taken by the Ministry of Defence, which runs as under:

* * *

> "If a person who is in receipt of Disability Pension dies within a period of 10 years from the date of receipt of pension, he should be presumed to have died of the disease for which he was granted Disability Pension and a medical certification as to the cause of death stands dispensed with. Cases of death of account of other reasons such as road accident, etc, should be dealt with in accordance with relevant rules and orders"

* * *

A case dealing with the above proposition is OA 1067/2012 **Sunita Mahajan Vs Union of India & Ors** decided on 25-04-2012, by the Chandigarh Bench of the AFT.

8.2

Special Family Pension to Parents

Special Family Pension can also be granted to parents of the deceased employee in case the death is attributable/aggravated by service or deemed to be attributable/aggravated as per rules. When SFP is granted to parents, it is known as "Dependent Pension" in case of Officers and "Second Life Award" for ranks other than Commissioned Officers. The term "Dependent" is as such a misnomer now, since there is no requirement of the parents being actually dependent on the deceased to be eligible for Special Family Pensionary awards. Such SFP to parents (Dependent Pension) is then paid at a rate that is 50% of the normal SFP. Unlike OFP, the dependency criterion (known as the "means limit") for parents to be eligible for SFP has been dispensed with. The same is reiterated in Note 2 under Para 5.6 of MoD letter dated 31-01-2001 (Chapter 23.12).

Paragraph 5 of the above MoD letter dated 31-01-2001 deals with the said provisions in detail.

8.3

Special Family Pension on Remarriage

There used to be a bar on continuance of SFP on remarriage earlier. It was abrogated for post-1996 pensioners with effect from 01-01-1996. It was also abrogated for pre-1996 pensioners with effect from 20-01-2009 vide an MoD letter of the same date (Chapter 26.5). Though there is no bar on grant of SFP on remarriage, the amount to be paid in such a scenario as per different circumstances is provided in Para 5.8 of MoD letter dated 31-01-2001 (Chapter 23.12). The circumstances for regulation of the same are different for Commissioned Officers vis-a-vis ranks other than Commissioned Officers. The various circumstances resulting in different percentages of payout are dependent upon the fact whether the widow continues to support children after remarriage or not, or whether she has any children or not, etc.

8.4

Division of Special Family Pension

Unlike OFP, the amount of SFP can be divided, and in most of the cases, the claim for division is between the wife and the mother. This is not a regular recourse though. The same can only be done after a due verification initiated by military authorities in case the beneficiary refuses to contribute proportionately towards the support of other eligible heirs in the family who were dependent on the deceased as is the requirement of Paragraph 228(a) of Pension Regulations, 1961. Further, such division is only to prevent "destitution" of the rest of the family as provided by Paragraph 42.1 of the Pension Payment Instructions (PPI) issued by the office of the PCDA(P) in 2005 (revised in 2013). Hence, the claimants who seek division of SFP should have been "dependent" upon the deceased and not having other means of livelihood and should be facing the prospects of destitution and fulfilling the criterion of Paragraph 5.8 of MoD letter dated 31-01-2001 (Chapter 23.12). The Supreme Court has already held in Special Leave to Appeal 7254/1980 **Jodh Singh Vs Union of India** decided on 09-10-1980, that the claim to pension belongs to the widow and such benefits are available to her on account of her status as a widow and not on account of the fact that there was some estate of the deceased which devolved on his death. Further, in Civil Appeal 9823/2016 **Nitu Vs Sheela Rani** decided on 28-09-2016, the Supreme Court reiterated that pension cannot be claimed by the mother-in-law based upon Laws of Succession and pension would only go to the widow. The legal position of pension is, however, different from other benefits such as insurance claims, etc, which devolve as per property laws and succession.

8.5

Special Family Pension in cases of negligence or misconduct

Special Family Pension continues to be available even in cases where the death was caused due to serious negligence or misconduct and the same is provided in Regulations 83 and 207 for Officers and Ranks other than Commissioned Officers respectively.

8.6

Rates of Special Family Pension

SFP is essentially granted @ 60% of emoluments or notional emoluments, subject to the relationship of the deceased with the recipient as discussed above and explained in MoD letter dated 31-01-2001 (Chapter 23.12). However, the rates as applicable from time to time with all other details are available in letters referred in Chapter 16 dealing with successive pay commissions and Chapter 17 dealing with various pension enhancements till date.

8.7

Special Family Pension in case of death on account of COVID

Though the DESW had issued (now withdrawn) a convoluted letter on the grant of Special Family Pension due to any death on account of COVID, the same was not in consonance with the rules or practical realities. The rules governing the subject of any infection while in service are very clear. As per Rule 16 of Entitlement Rules, 1982 (Chapter 23.1), any death or disablement occurring from a communicable or infectious disease during service is to be taken as attributable to military service thereby entitling the family to Special Family Pensionary awards. The only caveat provided in the said rule is any infection contracted prior to enrolment or contracted during leave. There are no *ifs and buts* in the rule and the same is very straightforward. Any other negative interpretation articulated is against the explicit exposition of the said rule.

As far as civilian employees are concerned, the DoPPW has inculded COVID in the scheduled list of diseases under Extraodinary Pension (EOP) Rules as per its latest notification issued in January 2023.

Chapter-09

Invalid Pension

Invalid Pension must not be confused with Disability Pension.

While Disability Pension is granted to individuals for disabilities which are attributable to or aggravated by military service or deemed to be attributable/aggravated (See Chapter 2), Invalid Pension is granted to individuals who are released with disabilities which have no link with military service and are neither attributable to, nor aggravated by military service. This can also include disabilities caused by own negligence and those emerging out of alcohol dependence, etc. While Disability Pension comprises two elements – Service Element and Disability Element without any requirement of any minimum qualifying service, Invalid Pension is standalone and granted at rates equivalent to Service Element of Disability Pension but required a minimum length of service of 10 years till the date when the said minimum qualifying service was abrogated with effect from 04-01-2019 (See Chapter 9.2 below).

Regulation 198 of the Pension Regulations, 1961 deals with the (earlier applicable) length of service for grant of Invalid Pension:

> 198. The minimum period of qualifying service actually rendered and required for grant of Invalid Pension is 10 years. For less than 10 years actual qualifying service, Invalid Gratuity shall be admissible.

9.1

Condonation of shortfall in service for grant of Invalid Pension

There were many instances in the past when personnel were invalided out of service prior to completion of 10 years of service. The power to condone shortfall of pension upto 1 year as provided in MoD letter dated 14-8-2001 (See Chapter 12 and Chapter 33.3) was, however, not invoked by the official authorities on the pretext that the same only applies to regular pension and not Invalid Pension. The Courts have, however, held that the said power can be exercised for other types of pension also, and that personnel with 9 years of service or more can be granted Invalid Pension by condoning the period of shortfall by one year. The same was held in TA 184/2009 **Kulwant Singh Rathee Vs Union of India** decided on 11-01-2010 by the Principal Bench of the AFT. As far as disabled personnel with 9 years and 9 months or more but less than 10 years service are concerned, their qualifying service is anyway to be counted as 10 completed years in terms of MoD letter dated 06-08-1984 (Chapter 33.13), which provides that each fraction of a year equal to three months and above shall be treated as a completed one half year and reckoned as qualifying service for determining the amount of pension and gratuity. The same is also discussed in detail in Chapter 12.

9.2

Abrogation of minimum qualifying service by DoPPW

The DoPPW, on prodding by the Supreme Court, however, has abrogated the minimum length of service required for Invalid Pension also, vide a gazette notification reflected through its letter dated 12-02-2019 (Chapter 33.15), with effect from 04-01-2019.

The abrogation of the minimum length of service has been implemented in all departments of the Central Government. However, when the executive instructions were finally issued for defence personnel by the DESW, certain additional words, which did not exist in the gazette notification, were illegally inserted in the policy letter issued on 16-07-2020 (Chapter 33.16) which was essentially drafted for the DESW by the Defence Accounts Department. This has made the entire beneficial letter and abrogation of the minimum qualifying service infructuous for defence personnel.

The following is a comparison:

DoPPW Gazette Notification/Letter dated 12-02-2019 (Chapter 33.15):

> "...a Government servant who retires from service bodily or mental infirmity which **permanently incapacitates him for service** before completing qualifying service of ten years may also be granted invalid pension..."

DESW Letter dated 16-07-2020 (Chapter 33.16) issued on basis of the DoPPW Gazette notification:

> "...Armed Forces personnel with less than 10 years of qualifying service in cases where personnel are invalided out of service on account of any bodily or mental infirmity which is Neither Attributable to Nor Aggravated by military service and which **permanently incapacitates them from military service as well as civil reemployment**."

A close scrutiny reveals that a few additional words i.e. "as well as civil reemployment" were mischievously added in the main text of the letter in vacuum by going beyond what was ordained by the Gazette Notification or the Supreme Court.

As is well known, Military Medical Boards render a certificate of "fitness for civil employment" to all invalided-out and disabled soldiers in order to facilitate their rehabilitation. Now that very benign certificate is being employed by the PCDA(P) to deny Invalid Pension to such soldiers, making the entire concept redundant since the illegally added extra words are being interpreted to the detriment of invalided out soldiers based on the certificate that is rather issued for their benefit and rehabilitation in the civil life than to deny them any pension.

Moreover, it is not that any kind of civil re-employment by the Government is guaranteed or offered on a platter to invalided-out soldiers, and hence, to link the grant of Invalid Pension with some mythical or hypothetical employment in the future, which they may or may not achieve in their lives, is absolutely illogical and also in contravention of the Gazette Notification issued by the Government on orders of the Supreme Court, containing no such condition. Also, Invalid Pension is granted for invalidation from a particular service for the reason that a person has been discharged on account of a disability not out of his/her own choice from a particular Government employment, and such pension has no connection whatsoever with any hypothetical civil re-employment in the future, which, in any case, remains elusive for most of such employees.

All other employees, including those of the Central Armed Police Forces (CAPFs) have already received this benefit which is being surprisingly held back from invalided soldiers. A simple letter on the step of abrogating minimum length of service for Invalid Pension has been totally complicated unnecessarily at the drafting stage by the office of CGDA.

While the DESW has accorded in-principle approval for removal of the illegally inserted additional words, the matter is shuttling from one department to another and the final resolution of the irregularity, by way of issuance of an anomaly-free letter, is still awaited.

Chapter-10

Special Pension

The concept of Special Pension is not widely known. In fact, even certain Records Offices are not aware of the same and many claims of affected personnel have been rejected in the past even when they were fully entitled to Special Pension.

Special Pension is granted under the provisions of Regulation 164 of the Pension Regulations for the Army, 1961, and corresponding regulations of the other two services.

It is granted when personnel are discharged in large numbers and not transferred to the reserves due to the reason of reduction of the strength of the establishment or disbandment.

The qualifying service required for Special Pension is 10 years as per Regulation 167 of the Pension Regulations.

The substantive regulation, that is, Regulation 164, is reproduced hereunder:

> 164. Special Pension or gratuity may be granted at the discretion of the President to individuals who are not transferred to the reserve and are discharged in large numbers in pursuance of Government Policy –
>
> i. of reducing the strength of establishment of the Armed Forces;
>
> OR
>
> ii. of reorganisation, which results in disbandment of any unit/formation.

It may, however, be noted that "the discretion of the President" as it existed in the original regulation has now been deleted and a person is authorised to Special Pension on fulfilment of the criterion without there being any "discretion". The same is provided in Para 11 of MoD letter dated 31-10-1987 (Chapter 28.1).

If a person fulfils the above criterion or can show somehow that he/she was discharged after completion of 10 years service but not transferred to reserve by the Government on the ground of non-availability of vacancies due to reduction of strength of the establishment, then he/she can claim Special Pension. Such reasons are at times recorded in the discharge book which can prove to be a good source of information as to the reasons of discharge or non-completion of full service.

By its very nature, Special Pension is not admissible to voluntary retirees.

The Delhi High Court in Review Petition (RP) 291/2009 in WP(C) 7716/2009 **Ganga Devi Vs Union of India** decided on 23-07-2010, had held that a person with more than 10 years of service discharged on the ground of being surplus would be entitled for Special Pension under Regulation 164. Since the person was no more and the wife had filed the petition, the Court also consequently held the widow of the deceased entitled to Family Pension.

In Civil Appeal 2147/2011 **TS Das Vs Union of India** decided on 27-10-2016, which was a case concerning reservists of the Navy, the litigants had sought the grant of Reservist Pension. The matter ultimately reached the Supreme Court on account of conflicting decisions. The Supreme Court, however, after going into the nuts and bolts of the issue, ultimately held them entitled to Special Pension instead of Reservist Pension since all such individuals were released with 10 or more years of service on (deemed) reduction of establishment.

Chapter-11

Reservist Pension

During the days of yore, defence services used to recruit soldiers under the Colour-Reserve Scheme, wherein the person used to serve for a few years in Colours (physical military service) and then in the Reserves when he could be called out for military service in case of an emergency. The Colour-Reserve system was usually regulated on the 8+7, 9+6 or 10+5 years model.

On completion of 15 years of combined Colour and Reserve Service, the individual used to be granted what is known as 'Reservist Pension'. Earlier, the said pension used to be refused to persons who had sought release from the Reserves at own request, but the Punjab & Haryana High Court had held this to be incorrect in CWP 13784/2006 **Harjinder Singh Vs Union of India** decided on 11-03-2008.

Regulation 155 of the Pension Regulations, 1961, is the provision dealing with the subject and the same is reproduced hereunder as it stands now:

> 155. An OR reservist who is not in receipt of a service pension may be granted, on completion of the prescribed combined colour and reserve qualifying service, of not less than 15 years, a reservist pension equal to 2/3rd of the lowest pension admissible to a Sepoy, but in no case less than Rs 375/- p.m. on his transfer to pension establishment either on completion of his term of engagement or prematurely, irrespective of the period of colour service.
>
> (Note: The above rate of Rs 375 is as per 4th CPC rates, it was amended to Rs 1,275, Rs 3,500 and Rs 9,000 + Dearness Relief after the 5th, 6th and 7th CPCs respectively)

The Naval and the Air Force reservists are also governed by parallel regulations.

There were also cases (mostly in the Air Force), wherein, individuals were recruited on the Colour-Reserve system of engagement but released much earlier by the organisation before they could complete their terms of pensionable engagement of combined Colour and Reserve service. The matters came to be adjudicated by the High Courts and followed by various Benches of the Armed

Forces Tribunal and it was held that if a person was recruited under the Colour-Reserve scheme, then it was incorrect to discharge him prior to completion of pensionable terms. The matter had also reached the Supreme Court in one case, that is, Civil Appeal 4787/2012 **Balbir Singh Vs Union of India** decided on 06-01-2015, wherein the airman was granted relief by the Apex Court when it had been refused by the Chandigarh Bench of the Armed Forces Tribunal.

It may be noted that Ordinary Family Pension is also admissible to families of personnel in receipt of Reservist Pension at par with other retirees. Also, and more importantly, Ordinary Family Pension is also admissible to families of those reservists who had died during the period of 'Reserves' (that is, while not on physical/colour service) without earning pension. This lesser-known provision was introduced vide Army Instruction 3/Special/1977 (Chapter 26.1). In modern nomenclature or terminology, the same would be known as Special Army Instruction (SAI) 03/77 as also noted in Chapter 7 concerning OFP.

Although, the procedural instructions issued after the introduction of the scheme of One Rank One Pension (OROP) with effect from 01-07-2014 (See Chapters 17 and 32) do not take Reservist Pension into their ambit, legally speaking the Reservist Pension of such pensioners cannot be less than 2/3rd of pension granted to Sepoys under OROP as per the spirit of Regulation 155 *supra.*

Chapter-12

Condonation of Shortfall in Service

The Pension Regulations of the three services contain provisions for condonation of shortfall of service for grant of pension upto 6 months by the concerned Regimental Records Offices.

The said power was delegated by the Government to the Army/Naval/Air Headquarters with an enhanced period of 1 year as per Paragraph 1(a)(v) of MoD letter dated 14-08-2001 (Chapter 33.3). Hence, as things stand today, a period of 1 year can be condoned for grant of pension, for example, an individual can be granted service pension in case he/she has 14 years of service.

The said power has given rise to certain controversies, and the major ones are discussed in succeeding paragraphs.

12.1

Condonation of shortfall for personnel of the Defence Security Corps (DSC)

Though the general pensionary provisions as applicable to the regular Army are also applicable to personnel of the DSC, a controversy has repeatedly crept up whether DSC personnel are also authorised to condonation of shortfall in their second stint in the DSC. Though there was no such prohibition in the original rules and the Courts have time and again held that such condonation is available to DSC personnel also, the Government has repeatedly issued letters prohibiting such condonation to DSC personnel, but all such letters and actions of the official establishment have been struck down or read down by Courts. The Courts have also held that such condonation must be granted liberally especially to DSC personnel since many a time, they retire at the cusp of completing pensionable service due to the fact that they join DSC service at a higher age profile than the regular Army, whereas those ex-servicemen who opt to join any civil government organisation become entitled for pension or contributory pension after merely 10 years of service. The larger bench decision by the Armed Forces Tribunal in OA 1238/2016 **Shama Kaur Vs Union of India** decided on 01-10-2019, contains a detailed exposition on the subject. Even earlier, the same was held by the Principal Bench of AFT in OA 60/2013 **Bhani Devi Vs Union of India** decided on 07-11-2013 and more importantly by the Delhi High Court and the Punjab & Haryana High

Court in WP (C) 9593/2003 **Madan Singh Vs Union of India** decided on 31-08-2006 and LPA 755/2010 **Union of India Vs LNK DSC Mani Ram** decided on 05-07-2010, respectively.

12.2

Admissibility of condonation of shortfall to Voluntary Retirees

As per the stand of the official establishment, there is a bar under the rules for grant of condonation to voluntary retirees. However, such a prohibition already stands declared unconstitutional and *ultra vires* by the Bombay High Court in WP (OS) 430/2005 **Gurmukh Singh Vs Union of India** decided on 22-11-2006, in a case involving a Naval retiree. The matter was again discussed in detail by the Supreme Court in Civil Appeal 9389/2014 **Union of India Vs Surender Singh Parmar** decided on 20-01-2015. A similar bar imposed on Army retirees specifically was set aside by the Kochi Bench of the AFT in TA 18/2009 **Vinod Roy John Vs Union of India** decided on 18-03-2010. Condonation of shortfall in service, as on date, hence, is applicable to voluntary retirees/premature retirement cases also, as per judicial dicta.

12.3

Counting of three months or above service as completed half year qualifying service

As per provisions of MoD letter dated 06-08-1984 (Chapter 33.13), each fraction of a year equal to three months and above shall be treated as a completed one half year and reckoned as qualifying service for determining the amount of pension and gratuity. This has been interpreted to mean, for example, that service of 14 years and 9 months shall be treated as 15 completed years for the purposes of pension. Hence, personnel with more than 14 years and 9 months of service are anyway to be treated as having completed 15 years of service without any requirement of condonation. Similarly, individuals with 9 years and 9 months of service can be granted Invalid Pension or Special Pension without any requirement of condonation since the said period is to be treated as 10 completed years. Moreover, individuals with more than 13 years and 9 months of service are to be treated as having 14 years of service and then further condonation upto 1 year can be granted to them in order to make them eligible for pension. This has been so held in *Surender Singh Parmar's* decision of the Supreme Court discussed in the above paragraph. The same interpretation of *pari materia* provisions on the civil side has also been declared by the Supreme Court in Civil Appeal 2530/2008 **State of Punjab Vs Sucha Singh Rana** decided on 19-02-2014 and Civil Appeal 3989/2007 **Indian Bank and Anr Vs N Venkatramani** decided on

30-08-2007. The above concept has also been explained and endorsed by the DoPPW vide letter dated 26-10-2022 (Chapter 33.19)

12.4

Condonation in cases of Pension other than Service Pension

Though the MoD letter dated 14-08-2001 (Chapter 33.3) does not distinguish between various kinds of pensions for grant of condonation of shortfall, the stand of the officialdom has remained that it is applicable only to service pension. The Courts have, however, held that the same must be applied to other types of pension also. More details in this regard are available in the chapter on Invalid Pension (Chapter 9).

Chapter-13

Abrogation of Condition of 10 Months Service in Last Rank

As per the interpretation of the establishment, pre-2006 retirees, other than officers, are not entitled to the pension of the rank last held at the time of retirement unless the said rank was held by the particular pensioner at least for a period of ten months, since in accordance to the pensionary provisions in vogue at that point of time, a minimum service of ten months in the rank was a pre-requisite. However, what has not been realised is that the requirement even prior to the 10 months' stipulation was pegged at 02/03 years' service and was reduced to 10 months after the Constitution Bench decision of the Hon'ble Supreme Court in WP 5939/1980 **DS Nakara Vs Union of India** decided on 17-12-1982. Further, this ten months' condition was altogether abrogated with effect from 01-01-2006, on the recommendations of the 6th Central Pay Commission.

Prior to 1979, pension was calculated on the basis of the emoluments drawn 36 months (3 years) prior to the retirement (2 years in certain cases on the defence side) but the said condition was changed to 10 months with effect from 01-04-1979 for both civilian and defence employees. However, this condition of reduction from 36 months to 10 months was made applicable only to employees retiring after the cut-off date of 01-04-1979, but this cut-off date was struck down by a Constitution Bench of the Supreme Court in *DS Nakara's* case (supra), which held that all employees, irrespective of the date of retirement, would be granted the benefit of the 10 months' formula but with financial effect from the said cut-off date of 01-04-1979. The Supreme Court, hence, had held that the reduction from the 36 months system to 10 months system was applicable to all pensioners irrespective of the date of retirement.

The 6th Central Pay Commission came into effect from 01-01-2006. Accordingly, as mentioned above, after the 6th CPC abrogated the requirement of the 10 months average emoluments system for post-01-01-2006 employees and pension was now to be calculated on the basis of emoluments last drawn. The requirement of 10 months emoluments, hence, was effectively removed. The said 10 months requirement was also abrogated for pre-01-01-2006 employees and it was inter-alia provided in the said notification that the pension of such pre-2006 retirees would either be calculated with respect of the fitment formula (old basic pension X 2.26 = new basic pension) or according to principles of modified parity, it would not be less than 50% of the revised emoluments corresponding to the pre-revised scale of the rank from which the person had retired, that is, the last rank/scale held without any reference to the length of service in the pre-revised scale/rank. The minimum pension for each rank without any reference to the 10 months' period was also reflected in the Annexure appended with the letter issued by the Government for pre-2006 retirees.

Hence, the 10 months system was abrogated, or it can be said that it was brought down to emoluments of the rank/scale last held, both for post-2006 as well as pre-2006 retirees and there was no requirement of the 10 months' criterion in both pre and post-2006 pensionary implementation letters. The same formula was also implemented in the case of civilian employees. This was also in line and consonance with the decision in *DS Nakara's* case which provided that whenever a pensionary calculation formula was revised, it had to be revised for all pensioners irrespective of date of retirement.

Prior to the 6th Pay Commission, the pensions of ranks other than Commissioned Officers were granted on the basis of the *maximum* of the 5th CPC scales which was different than the system followed for all civilian employees and Commissioned Officers of the defence services for whom the pension was calculated on the basis of the *minimum* of pay scale. Accordingly, again to provide an edge to ranks other than Commissioned Officers, as was the case till 6th CPC, the Government constituted a committee under the Cabinet Secretary who opined that the pension of pre-2006 retirees should be calculated based on the notional maximum within the new 6th CPC scales corresponding to the maximum of pre-6th CPC (5th CPC) scales as per the 6th CPC switch-over fitment tables, thereby extending the edge granted to such personnel, which was applicable to them earlier. This new stipulation was applicable with financial effect from 01-07-2009.

The said report was accepted by the Cabinet. **However, when the Ministry of Defence implemented the said report, they, on their own, again added a line re-introducing the 10 months stipulation back into the pensionary provisions for pre-2006 retirees, which by now stood abrogated for pre-2006 as well as post-2006 civilian retirees with effect from 01-01-2006.** The following was the offending part of the re-introduced 10 months' stipulation:

> "The notional pay in the revised pay structure corresponding to the maximum of pay scale applicable from 10.10.1997 for the rank and group, shall be determined as per the fitment tables attached to SAI 1/S/2008 and corresponding instructions for Navy & Air Force, for each rank and group and shall consist of pay in the pay band plus Grade pay plus 'X' Group pay (where applicable) plus Military Service pay plus 50% of the highest classification allowance (revised rates effective from 1.9.2008), if any, **of the rank and group held continuously for 10 months preceding discharge**"

The stipulation was also inserted again when the pensions were again revised in the year 2013 w.e.f 24-09-2012 and also in the OROP tables. Hence, the MoD chose now to re-introduce the 10 months' stipulation which neither existed for post-2006 pensioners of the ranks other than Commissioned Officers category nor for modified parity provisions of pre-2006/post-2006 Commissioned Officer pensioners, nor for similar provisions for pre-2006/post-2006 civil pensioners.

The matter was not to end there. When the new pensionary calculation formula was introduced for pre-2006 personnel, there emerged certain anomalous situations wherein the pension of post-2006 pensioners happened to be lower than pre-2006 pensioners at certain ranks. To address this anomaly, the Government extended exactly the same formula as introduced for pre-2006 pensioners based on notional maximum of 5th CPC scales for post-2006 pensioners also but it was specifically provided in the said Government letter that the 10 months' stipulation would not apply on post-2006 pensioners as becomes clear from the following extract of the letter:

> "The service pension under these orders shall be determined on the basis of the rank/group last held by the individual and the pre-revised/revised pay scales connected thereto, **even if the rank/group was held for less than 10 months before discharge/Invalidment."**

Hence, while the MoD had now extended the formula applicable to pre-2006 pensioners to post-2006 pensioners also, it specifically regressively ensured (based on a Draft Government Letter provided by the Defence Accounts Department) that while all other conditions remained constant, the 10 months' criterion was to apply to pre-2006 pensioners but not to post-2006 pensioners. The same 10 months' stipulation has also been carried on by the Government in various pensionary policies issued thereafter.

These stipulations, by way of a flip-flop and constant somersault in policy, not only resulted in direct infringement of the ratio laid by the Apex Court in *DS Nakara's* case, but also resulted in micro-classification resulting in serious violence to the spirit of Article 14 of the Constitution of India discriminating between various categories of pensioners and also within the category of ranks other than Commissioned Officers, based on a cut-off date. On one hand, while the MoD has made attempts to address incongruities in pensionary provisions, with clever drafting by the other hand, they have re-introduced other anomalies which stood addressed earlier. In direct applicability of the *DS Nakara's* case, the following lines from the landmark judgment are very pertinent:

> *"...How does a fortuitous circumstance of retiring a day earlier or a day later will permit totally unequal treatment in the matter of pension? One retiring a day earlier will have to be subject to ceiling of Rs 8,100 p.a. and average emolument to be worked out on 36 months salary while the other will have a ceiling of Rs 12,000 p.a. and average emolument will be computed on the basis of last 10 months average. The artificial divisions stares into face and is unrelated to any principle and whatever principle, if there be any, has absolutely no nexus to the objects sought to be achieved by liberalising the pension scheme. In fact this arbitrary divisions has not only no nexus to the liberalised pension scheme but it is counter-productive and runs counter to the whole gamut of pensions scheme. The equal treatment guaranteed in Art. 14 is wholly violated inasmuch as the pension rules being statutory in character, since the specified date, the rules accord differential and discriminatory treatment to equals in the matter of commutation of pensions. A 48 hours difference in matter of retirement would have a traumatic effect. Division is thus both arbitrary and unprincipled. Therefore, the classification does not stand the test of Article 14..."*

The above detailed explanation was required only to elaborate the historical basis of the issue.

The matter now stands judicially settled and it has been held that the pensions of all pensioners shall be calculated based upon the rank last held without any linkage with the length of time spent in that rank. The problem, however, is that till date the benefits are only being released to those pensioners who approach the Court for relief and not across the board.

The lead cases wherein the above has been resolved and laid down are OA 404/2015 **Hardev Singh Vs Union Of India** decided on 29-04-2015 and OA 882/2016 **Ex JWO Ashok Kumar Tanwar Vs Union of India** decided on 17-04-2017, by the Chandigarh Bench and the Principal Bench of the Armed Forces Tribunal respectively.

Chapter-14

Cut-Off Dates in Pensionary Policies

Pensionary polices in India, both civil and military, have been subject of massive litigation with regard to cut-off dates. Many a time, at the moment of revision of pension or when a new stipulation is introduced for existing pensioners, the Government introduces a cut-off date, thereby creating a class within a class, wherein it is provided that pensioners retiring prior to the said cut-off date would not be released the benefit of the new provision/revision while those retiring after the cut-off date would be provided the said benefit. However, Constitutional Courts, that is, the Supreme Court and our High Courts, have time and again held that any revision in pension or liberalisation of pensionary benefits or change of a stipulation for existing pensioners, would have to be passed on to past pensioners also, from the same cut-off date.

There are certain exceptions to the above general rule though. Firstly, the said proposition does not apply to one-time payments such as gratuity, and secondly, the same would not apply to situations wherein a completely new dispensation is introduced. For example, this proposition would not apply to a situation wherein, say, the Government introduces a proper/defined pensionary scheme from a particular cut-off date replacing an earlier applicable contributory pension scheme, and in such circumstances, the retirees who were released from service earlier and were existing beneficiaries of the old contributory system, cannot claim to be brought over to the newly introduced defined pension system. However, if the retiree was already in receipt of pension and a revision is introduced, or a new stipulation for pensioners is introduced, or a new formula of pension calculation is brought into force, then the same shall apply to past retirees also, though from the fresh date introduced for new pensioners.

The law on cut-off dates in pension was first authoritatively adjudicated by a Constitution Bench of the Supreme Court in WP 5939/1980 **DS Nakara Vs Union of India** decided on 17-12-1982. Although by then, the Supreme Court had already ruled that pension was not a bounty at the sweet-will or discretion of the Government but was a rightful deferred wage for past services, as held in WP 217/1968 **Deokinandan Prasad Vs State of Bihar** decided on 04-05-1971.

The issue before the Supreme Court in *DS Nakara's* case was that prior to 1979, pension was calculated on the basis of the emoluments drawn 36 months (3 years) prior to retirement but the said condition was changed to 10 months with effect from 01-04-1979 for both civilian and defence employees. However, this condition of reduction from 36 months to 10 months was made applicable only to those employees retiring after the cut-off date of 01-04-1979. This cut-off date was struck down by the Constitution Bench of the Supreme Court in *DS Nakara's* case which held that all employees, irrespective of the date of retirement, would be granted the same benefit of the new formula, but with financial effect from the cut-off date of 01-04-1979. The following observations of the Supreme Court assume importance:

> *"...How does a fortuitous circumstance of retiring a day earlier or a day later will permit totally unequal treatment in the matter of pension? One retiring a day earlier will have to be subject to ceiling of Rs 8,100 p. a. and average emolument to be worked out on 36 months salary while the other will have a ceiling of Rs 12,000 p. a. and average emolument will be computed on the basis of last 10 months average. The artificial divisions stares into face and is unrelated to any principle and whatever principle, if there be any, has absolutely no nexus to the objects sought to be achieved by liberalising the pension scheme. In fact this arbitrary divisions has not only no nexus to the liberalised pension scheme but it is counterproductive and runs counter to the whole gamut of pensions scheme. The equal treatment guaranteed in Art. 14 is wholly violated inasmuch as the pension rules being statutory in character, since the specified date, the rules accord differential and discriminatory treatment to equals in the matter of commutation of pensions. A 48 hours difference in matter of retirement would have a traumatic effect. Division is thus both arbitrary and unprincipled. Therefore, the classification does not stand the test of Article 14..."*

There are many other landmark decisions dealing with the same proposition.

In Civil Appeal 5566/2008 **Union of India Vs SPS Vains** decided on 09-09-2008, again it was held that it was unconstitutional to have a disparity in pension between officers of the same rank retiring on two sides of a cut-off date. The Court was dealing with the pensions of officers of the defence services in the rank of Major General in the said case.

In Civil Appeal 5591/2006 **KJS Buttar Vs Union of India** decided on 31-03-2011, the Court, while dealing with the proposition of liberalised pensionary awards (War Injury and Liberalised Family Pension) introduced only for retirees released after the cut-off date of 01-01-1996, held that all concepts and categories of War Injury and Liberalised Family Pension introduced for pensioners from 01-01-1996 on implementation of the 5th Central Pay Commission, would also apply to similarly placed retirees who were discharged prior to 01-01-1996 and with financial benefits from 01-01-1996.

In Civil Appeal 8848/2012 **Kallakkurichi Taluk Retired Official Association, Tamil Nadu Vs State of Tamil Nadu** decided on 17-01-2013, the Supreme Court discussed the varied rates of pensions made admissible to the officers of the same rank retiring on different dates and ultimately held the discrimination to be bad in law, thereby striking down a notification issued in the year 1989 which discriminated between officers retiring prior to and after 01-06-1988. The Court also held that while dealing with such discriminatory practices, the amounts involved would not be of any consequence.

In Civil Appeal 3349/1996 **MC Dhingra Vs Union of India** decided on 05-02-1996, the question being examined was the counting of past service rendered prior to and after a cut-off date in respect of retirees who had retired on different dates. The Supreme Court observed the following:

> *"... We find no force in the contention. All the persons who rendered temporary service prior to their joining the Government of India Service have been given the benefit of fixation of the pension payable by tagging the temporary service. The cut off date is arbitrary violating Article 14 of the Constitution of India. Having grouped all the similar circumstanced employees, fixing the cut off date and giving benefit to those who retired thereafter is obviously arbitrary..."*

In Civil Appeal 626/2008 **AN Sachdeva Vs Maharshi Dayanand University, Rohtak** decided on 10-08-2015, the Supreme Court again examined the entire case law on cut-off dates with regard to pensionary policies and observed the following:

> *"...it is a case of upward revision of benefit and the classification which is sought to be created by the aforesaid method of not extending benefit to persons appointed directly and by fixing cut-off date cannot be said to be intelligible one; same is discriminatory and thus, the appellants would be entitled for the benefit from the date decision has been taken on 24.12.2001 to compute the previous service rendered in Punjab University/ Kurukshetra University as qualifying service. In other words, they would be entitled for the benefit prospectively from the date of issuance of memorandum dated 24.12.2001..."*

Very recently, in Civil Appeal 10857/2016 **All Manipur Pensioners Association Vs State of Manipur** decided on 11-07-2019, the Supreme Court firmly reiterated the principles on the subject. The Court was examining the non-applicability of certain provisions introduced with effect from 01-01-1996 to those who had retired prior to 01-01-1996 based upon the plank of financial constraints raised by the State. The Court held the distinction discriminatory. The following were the observations of the Apex Court on the subject:

"...we are of the firm opinion that there is no valid justification to create two classes, viz., one who retired pre1996 and another who retired post-1996, for the purpose of grant of revised pension, In our view, such a classification has no nexus with the object and purpose of grant of benefit of revised pension. All the pensioners form a one class who are entitled to pension as per the pension rules. Article 14 of the Constitution of India ensures to all equality before law and equal protection of laws. At this juncture it is also necessary to examine the concept of valid classification. A valid classification is truly a valid discrimination. It is true that Article 16 of the Constitution of India permits a valid classification. However, a very classification must be based on a just objective. The result to be achieved by the just objective presupposes the choice of some for differential consideration/treatment over others. A classification to be valid must necessarily satisfy two tests. Firstly, the distinguishing rationale has to be based on a just objective and secondly, the choice of differentiating one set of persons from another, must have a reasonable nexus to the objective sought to be achieved. The test for a valid classification may be summarised as a distinction based on a classification founded on an intelligible differentia, which has a rational relationship with the object sought to be achieved. Therefore, whenever a cut-off date (as in the present controversy) is fixed to categorise one set of pensioners for favourable consideration over others, the twin test for valid classification or valid discrimination therefore must necessarily be satisfied. In the present case, the classification in question has no reasonable nexus to the objective sought to be achieved while revising the pension. As observed hereinabove, the object and purpose for revising the pension is due to the increase in the cost of living. All the pensioners form a single class and therefore such a classification for the purpose of grant of revised pension is unreasonable, arbitrary, discriminatory and violative of Article 14 of the Constitution of India. The State cannot arbitrarily pick and choose from amongst similarly situated persons, a cut-off date for extension of benefits especially pensionary benefits..."

Cases such as the ones discussed at the beginning of the chapter wherein a new kind of benefit is introduced (such as a switch over from a Provident Fund or Contributory Fund based scheme to a regular Pensionary Scheme) or when the revision involves a one-time payment, would not be amenable to the law of non-applicability of cut-off dates. Such a proposition is aptly dealt by the Supreme Court in Civil Appeal 506/1992 **State of Punjab Vs Justice SS Dewan (Retired Chief Justice)** decided on 25-04-1997 as well as in WP(C) 372/1999 **Subrata Sen Vs Union of India** decided on 18-09-2001.

There is copious amount of case law dealing with cut-off dates with regard to benefits such as War Injury Pension and Liberalised Family Pension specifically related to the military. The same is separately discussed in Chapter 5.

Chapter-15

Ex-Gratia Lumpsum Compensation

Ex-gratia compensation in the current form was introduced vide MoD letter dated 22-09-1998 (Chapter 24.1). The said letter provided for graded ex-gratia lumpsum compensation for deaths in harness in situations such as accidents in the course of performance of duties, in acts attributable to terrorism, enemy action, war, etc. This is not to be confused with the ex-gratia compensation introduced in the year 2011 for invalided disabled personnel that is discussed in the part of the book dealing with Disability Pension (Chapter 2).

The conditions and guidelines to be followed for payment of ex-gratia compensation were appended with the letter dated 22-09-1998 and essentially provided broad rules to be observed for release of such compensation. The guidelines state that there should be some causal connection between the death and Government service and benefit of doubt must be given to the claimant and that contributory negligence of the employee, if any, shall be of no consequence.

The rates of ex-gratia compensation have been increased by the Government from time to time and essentially doubled after every pay commission. In fact, certain new categories have also been inserted even before promulgation and implementation of fresh pay commission recommendations. Chapters 24.1, 24.3, 24.4 and 24.6 can be perused for rates applicable from time to time.

The ceiling imposed for receipt of relief from different sources was removed vide MoD letter dated 17-08-2010 (Chapter 24.5).

Although the guidelines appended with the master letter dated 22-09- 1998 mentioned above only require a causal connection between death and service, essentially just the same as the Entitlement Rules, 1982 (Chapter 23.1), many a time, the office of PCDA (P) had been refusing ex-gratia compensation in varied types of deaths, such as any death occurring while a soldier was returning from or proceeding for authorised leave. In order to address such confusion, the Department of Military Affairs of the MoD has issued a clarification dated 14-07-2021 (Chapter 24.7) wherein admissibility of ex-gratia compensation in various situations, basically covered by the Entitlement Rules, has been reiterated, including while proceeding to or returning from authorised leave or outpass. Vide another letter dated 23-09-2021 (Chapter 24.8), it has again been stressed upon that various situations already covered under the policy should be taken care of by the establishment itself, so as to avoid litigation on these points.

The rates and categories as applicable on date vide MoD letter dated 02-11-2016 (the *ibid* Chapter 24.6) are as follows:

a. Death occurring due to accidents in course of duties – Rs 25 Lakhs
b. Death in the course of duties attributable to acts of violence by terrorists, anti-social elements etc – Rs 25 Lakhs
c. Death occurring in border skirmishes and action against militants, terrorists, extremists, sea pirates – Rs 35 Lakhs
d. Death occurring while on duty in the specified high altitude, inaccessible border posts, on account of natural disasters, extreme weather conditions – Rs 35 Lakhs
e. Death occurring during enemy action in war or such war like engagements, which are specifically notified by MoD and death occurring during evacuation of Indian Nationals from a war-torn zone in foreign countries – Rs 45 Lakhs

15.1

Courts on Ex-Gratia Compensation

Some issues have arisen in matters related to ex-gratia compensation but most such controversies have come about due to a hyper-technical or literal interpretation by the concerned authorities. Some matters that have reached courts and other judicial fora are enumerated below.

In OA 1954/2013 **Paramjit Kaur Vs Union of India** decided on 12-02-2014, the soldier concerned was proceeding from an operational area to a transit camp, from where he further had to proceed on leave. The bus in which he was travelling in the convoy, however, met with an accident leading to his death. Ex-gratia was refused to his widow on the pretext that his death had not taken place during "actual" performance of duties. The Chandigarh Bench of the AFT, however, held that the main letter and master circular simply provided that the death should have occurred in the course of performance of duties and that there should be a causal connection between the two, which already was fully established, and hence the term "actual" even if existing in the appended guidelines could not alter the main provisions in the main body of the letter promulgated by the Government.

In OA 3105/2012 **Daxina Kumari Vs Union of India** decided on 24-07-2013, the soldier, while deployed in a high altitude post on the China border died by slipping in a treacherous terrain while he was going to answer the nature's call. While his wife was released the requisite Special Family Pension, the grant of ex-gratia was refused on the pretext that at the exact point of his death, the soldier was not performing his duty but was answering the nature's call. The Chandigarh Bench of the AFT, however, directed the establishment to release the ex-gratia payment setting aside the hyper-technical interpretation of the authorities.

In CWP 16430/2002 **Daljeet Kaur Vs Union of India** decided on 22-04-2003, the Punjab & Haryana High Court held that an accidental discharge of weapon leading to the death of a soldier would be treated in the course of performance of duty, thereby necessitating release of ex-gratia.

Taking strong objection to the interpretation of the Army authorities in denying the said ex-gratia to the mother of a deceased soldier, the High Court observed:

> *"...Alas even these provisions will, at best, go only a little way towards assuaging the feeling of utter devastation of the mother who loses a son, whilst performing his patriotic duties for the protection of the Nation...Can the benefits sought to be given to the unfortunate legal heir of a deceased military personnel whose case falls clearly within these instructions, be permitted to be negated by a bureaucratic army officer sitting in his Ivory Tower by sheer mis-interpretation of the instructions, is the significant question of law which arises in this petition. We are constrained to give a preface to this judgment with the aforesaid remarks, due to the peculiar facts and circumstances of this case..."*

In CWP 6301/2008 **Smt Santosh Vs Union of India** decided on 20-11-2009, the Punjab & Haryana High Court held that even a heart attack while performing duties, must be taken as an 'accident' for the grant of ex-gratia since it is a sudden event leading to death. The same was also held by the High Court in LPA 575/2011 **Kamlesh Vs Union of India**, decided on 07-07-2011.

Chapter-16

Bird's Eye View of Implementation of Recommendations of Successive Pay Commissions with Regard to Pension

Though a lot can be written on the subject, it would make this chapter unwieldy. Hence, it would only be prudent to touch upon the main recommendations and subsequent changes after their acceptance by the Government in pension regimes in somewhat recent times. The period from January 1986, that is, after the implementation of the 4th Central Pay Commission (4th CPC), would be a nominal starting point.

16.1

4th Central Pay Commission

The 4th CPC was made applicable from 01-01-1986. The minimum pension admissible was Rs 375 and the maximum pension possible was Rs 4,500. Of course, Dearness Relief was meant to be added to the above figures. The minimum Family Pension was also Rs 375 but the maximum family pension was capped at Rs 1,250. The amount of gratuity was also capped at Rs 1,00,000 and the percentage of pension available for commutation was 1/3rd (45% for defence personnel other than officers and 43% for Commissioned Officers). The Rank Pay introduced for officers of the defence services was a part of reckonable emoluments and so was Non Practicing Allowance (NPA), and pension was based upon average emoluments of the last 10 months. Different weightages were also made applicable for various ranks to compensate for lesser length of service due to early retirement. Ranks other than Commissioned Officers were granted a uniform weightage of 5 years. Full Pension was calculated on completion of 33 years' service (after including weightage), proportionately reduced for lesser length of service. The provisions are available in MoD letter dated 30-10-1987 (Chapter 28.1).

Disability Pension continued to comprise of Service Element and Disability Element (without applicability of any minimum service requirement) and was calculated at Rs 750, Rs 550 and Rs 450 for Officers & Honorary Officers, JCOs and Other Ranks & Non Combatants (Enrolled), respectively, for 100% disability with proportionate reduction for lesser percentage of disability.

No Disability Pension was allowed for disability less than 20% (also see Chapter 2). War Injury Pension was calculated differently and was granted to cases declared "Battle Casualty" as per Part IV of letter dated 30-10-1987 (Chapter 28.1). It was now provided that War Injury Pension for 100% disability would be equal to reckonable emoluments last drawn and in case it was less than 100% then the amount was to be reduced proportionately but not below a figure less than 60% of reckonable emoluments for Officers and 80% for ranks other than Commissioned Officers. It was also provided that War Injury Pension shall also be granted if the disability was less than 20% or assessed less than 20% at any later stage.

Liberalised Family Pension was admissible under the same circumstances as War Injury Pension in case the person died and was eligible to be declared a "Battle Casualty". The said pension was to be calculated at a rate equal to the reckonable emoluments last drawn. (Also see Chapter 5)

16.2

5th Central Pay Commission

The 5th CPC gave rise to a host of anomalies and was made applicable from 01-01-1996. The earliest major problem occurred when after rationalisation of scales and trades, certain anomalies were removed with effect from 10-10-1997 rather than 01-01-1996, which was the date of implementation of the 5th CPC. As a result, those who retired prior to 10-10-1997 were not given the benefit of the anomaly-free scales and even retirees were granted pension based upon the anomalous scales of 01-01-1996 and not the anomaly-free replacement scales introduced from 10-10-1997. The Punjab & Haryana High Court, however, held in CWP 15400/2006 **Jai Narain Jakhar Vs Union of India** decided on 14-01-2008, as affirmed later by the Supreme Court in Special Leave Petition 15128/2008 **Union of India and others Vs Jai Narain Jakhar** decided on 21-11-2008, that the removal of the anomaly shall operate from 01-01-1996, that is, the inception of the anomaly, and not any future artificial cut-off date. Of course, the benefit was only granted to litigants and not to others by the Government.

The minimum pension introduced by the 5th CPC was Rs 1,275 and the maximum was Rs 15,000. The minimum family pension was pegged at Rs 1,275 and the maximum at Rs 9,000. The gratuity was enhanced from the earlier rate of Rs 1,00,000 to Rs 3,50,000. The commutation limit was enhanced to 40% for civilian retirees while it remained the same for defence retirees. Ex-gratia lumpsum compensation ranging from Rs 5,00,000 to Rs 10,00,000 was also introduced for deaths during the course of performance of duties in various circumstances ranging from death in course of duty simpliciter to death in a war, etc (See Chapter 15).

Even during the 5th CPC, the pension continued to be calculated on the basis of the 33 years formula for full pension as becomes clear from MoD letter dated 03-02-1998 (Chapter 29.1).

The 5th CPC had introduced certain new concepts for Disability and War Injury Pension too. The concept of "broad-banding" or "rounding-off" of disability percentage for calculation of Disability or War Injury Element was brought into force to overcome medical subjectivity of different boards assessing varied percentage of disability. By this, disability less than 50% was to be calculated as 50% for the purposes of calculating Disability or War Injury Element, between 50% and 75% was to be calculated as 75% and above 75% was to be taken as 100%. This was introduced by DoPPW letter dated 03-02-2000 (Chapter 23.11), which was implemented for defence pensioners by MoD vide its letter dated 31-01-2001 (Chapter 23.12). Different categories for disability awards (A to E) were also introduced with varying rates of disability benefits with Categories D & E being eligible for Liberalised Awards (See Chapter 23.12 alongwith amendments in Chapters 23.13 to 23.16). Disability element was now upgraded to an amount of Rs 2,600, Rs 1,900 and Rs 1,550 for Officers & Honorary Officers, JCOs and Other Ranks & NCs(E) respectively while the rates of War Injury Element were notified at Rs 5,200, Rs 3,800 and Rs 3,100 respectively for the same categories.

While "broad-banding" initially was only granted to those who were medically boarded out prior to completion of terms of engagement, it was held by the Courts that in view of the pensionary provisions which provided that all personnel released in low medical category are to be treated as "invalided" from service, it needed to be extended to all categories of Disability Pensioners irrespective of the manner of exit from the defence services. Civil Appeal 5591/2006 **KJS Buttar Vs Union of India** decided on 31-03-2011 as well as in Civil Appeal 418/2012 **Union of India Vs Ram Avtar** decided on 10-12-2014, are important decisions of the Supreme Court on the same subject. Modalities on applicability on pre-1996 retirees are discussed in Chapter 2.

Important letters concerning 5th CPC are available in Chapter 29.

16.3

6th Central Pay Commission

The 6th CPC was implemented with effect from 01-01-2006. The pay commission introduced running pay band with additional Grade Pay for each Grade/Rank, which was to be added into the applicable Pay Band, thereby abolishing the system of fixed Pay-Scales that were in place as on 31-12-2005. Now, the minimum pension was raised to Rs 3,500 and the maximum was kept at Rs 45,000. The maximum family pension was pegged at Rs 27,000. The limit of gratuity was also enhanced to Rs 10,00,000. The commutation percentage was changed to 50% for defence pensioners while it was retained at 40% for civilians. The ex-gratia compensation was doubled than the earlier rates and now ranged from Rs 10,00,000 to Rs 20,00,000.

Certain other very important changes were also brought in by the 6th CPC. The first was that the system of weightages was abolished and it was now provided that full pension would be granted on being eligible for pension, thereby abrogating the 33 years requirement for earning full pension. The system of calculating pension based on the last 10 months service was also abrogated. Initially, these concepts were only extended to post-2006 retirees, but were later extended to pre-2006 retirees also, with financial effect from 01-01-2006, on judicial intervention as provided by MoD letter dated 30-09-2016 (Chapter 30.7).

The Disability and War Injury Elements were now also directed to be based upon the percentage of emoluments at par with civilians, rather than a fixed amount or slab system followed till the 5th CPC. Disability awards were now to be calculated @ 30% of emoluments for 100% disability (proportionately reduced for lesser percentage of disability) and 60% or 100% of emoluments for War Injury Element depending upon the manner of exit as per letter dated 05-05-2009 (Chapter 23.21).

Under the 6th CPC, additional pension was also granted for old age as follows:

AGE OF PENSIONER	ADDITIONAL QUANTUM OF PENSION
From 80 years to less than 85 years	20% of basic pension
From 85 years to less than 90 years	30% of basic pension
From 90 years to less than 95 years	40% of basic pension
From 95 years to less than 100 years	50% of basic pension
100 years or more	100% of basic pension

Another controversy that had arisen during the regime of the 6th CPC was the calculation of pensions for pre-2006 retirees. The orders that were issued contained two options of calculation, one was the consolidation method, wherein the old pension was to be multiplied with 2.26, and the other one was 50% of minimum pay method, wherein it was provided that pension shall, in no manner, be less than 50% of minimum of the pay in the pay band (and the Military Service

Pay and X Group Pay wherever applicable) plus the Grade Pay. This was interpreted to mean the minimum of the pay band itself rather than the minimum of pay for each grade/rank within the newly introduced pay bands as per the switch-over fitment formula. The matter was again resolved by judicial intervention and the Government issued revised pensions based on the minimum of pay within the pay band rather than the minimum of the pay of the pay band itself, but the arrears were only provided with effect from 24-09-2012 rather than the date of the inception of the anomaly, that is, 01-01-2006. However, the Delhi High Court in WP (C) 1535/2012 **Union of India Vs Central Govt SAG** decided on 29-04-2013, held that arrears were to be paid from 01-01-2006 and not from a later artificial date. The decision was affirmed by the Supreme Court in an SLP filed by the Government. Even a Review and a Curative Petition filed by the Union of India were dismissed and ultimately orders were issued to release revised pension from 01-01-2006 to all civil and military pensioners vide MoD letter dated 03-09-2015 (Chapter 30.6).

The concept of Modified Assured Career Progression Scheme (MACP) was also introduced on recommendations of the 6th CPC. The said scheme provided for upgradation to higher pay-band/grade to offset stagnation, after 10, 20 and 30 years of service (8, 16 and 24 for defence personnel). The MACP was, however, made applicable only from 01-09-2008, and the benefit was not extended to personnel who retired between 01-01-2006 and 30-08-2008. It was, however, held by the Supreme Court that since the recommendations of the 6th CPC related to "pay" were accepted from 01-01-2006 for defence personnel, MACP must also apply from the same date since the concept was related to upgradation of "pay". This was so held in Civil Appeal Diary No 3744/2016 **Union of India Vs Balbir Singh Turn** decided on 08-12-2017.

Another controversy that had arisen during the same period was regarding the pension of Honorary Naib Subedars. Pensioners of the said rank (Havildars granted the Honorary Rank of Naib Subedar) were being paid an additional amount of Rs 100 initially vide MoD letter dated 21-06-2002 (Chapter 29.4) but the 6th CPC recommended, and the Government accepted, that they be paid the pension as admissible to a regularly promoted Naib Subedar vide MoD letter dated 12-06-2009 (Chapter 30.4). The order was, however, implemented by the Government only for post-2006 retirees leading to sharp discrimination between pre and post-2006 pensioners of the same rank with pre-2006 retirees being paid the pension of a Havildar with the additional Rs 100 (upgraded to Rs 226 from 01-01-2006) and post-2006 retirees being paid the pension as admissible to a regularly promoted Naib Subedar. This was held to be discriminatory by the Chandigarh Bench of the AFT in OA 42/2010 **Virender Singh Vs Union of India** decided on 08-02-2010 and later affirmed by the Supreme Court in Special Leave to Appeal (Civil) CC 18582/2010 **Union of India Vs Virender Singh** decided on 13-12-2010. Another detailed decision on the same lines was rendered by the Chandigarh Bench of the AFT in OA 33/2013 **Subhash Chander Soni Vs Union of India** decided on 27-09-2013, dealing with the admissibility of arrears from 01-01-2006, and the same was also upheld by the Supreme Court in Civil Appeal 4677/2014 **Union of India & Others Vs Subhash Chander Soni** decided on 20-05-2015. The Chandigarh Bench of the AFT further held in OA 2755/2013 **Hoshiar Singh Vs Union of India** decided on 27-10-2017 that even the subsequent pension revisions carried out with effect from 2009 and 2012 would apply to pre-2006 Honorary Naib Subedars. Ostensibly in compliance of the same, the MoD has now issued a fresh letter (Chapter 30.5).

Important letters concerning 6th CPC are available in Chapter 30.

16.4

7th Central Pay Commission

The 7th CPC introduced the system of Pay Levels in a newly introduced pay matrix, a system which was a departure from the running pay bands and more akin to pay scales. A total of 18 Pay Levels (Pay Level-1 to Pay Level-18) were introduced and a parallel defence pay matrix was brought into force with the Chief of the Army Staff being placed at the highest Pay Level-18 with the pay of Rs 2,50,000 (fixed).

The figure of minimum and maximum pension admissible was raised to Rs 9,000 and Rs 1,25,000 respectively, and for family pension the amounts were the same as becomes clear from MoD letter 04-09-2017 (Chapter 31.2). The minimum Disability Pension was also raised to Rs 18,000 vide MoD letter dated 29-01-2019 (Chapter 23.34).

The calculation system for pension, however, was radically altered by the 7th CPC. It was recommended that existing pension (as it existed on 31-12-2015) be multiplied by 2.57 and another regime of notional fixation be introduced for all retirees to bridge the gap between old and new retirees. It was recommended that pre-2006 retirees be first fixed in the new pay matrix based upon the pay band and grade pay at which they retired at the minimum of the corresponding level in the new matrix and then the amount be raised to arrive at the notional pay by adding the number of increments he or she had earned in that level while in service at the rate of 3% (increment rate), and 50% of the total amount arrived at shall become the new revised pension with effect from 01-01-2016.

The above system, though appeared and sounded complicated, was a workable solution for bridging the gap to a large extent. It did throw up some problems though, for example, the lack of information of number of increments drawn in a particular scale by old retirees.

Taking into view all aspects of the recommendations, the DoPPW finally issued a letter implementing the notional pay system after tweaking and modulating the original recommendations of the 7th CPC. This was for civil pensioners. A similar letter for defence pensioners was issued by the MoD on 17-10-2018 (Chapter 31.3). Although, in most cases, the pensions of defence pensioners using the 2.57 multiple formula with the OROP tables was more beneficial (Further details on OROP are available in Chapter 17).

Important letters on the 7th CPC are available in Chapter 31 (Also see Chapter 23.35).

Chapter-17

Pensionary Enhancements, One Rank One Pension (OROP) & the Journey Towards It

When I say "journey", I do not mean the political promises and related happenings, but the route towards OROP as far as the policy is concerned.

Over the years, many developments have taken place for the betterment of military pensions, most stemming from the fact that defence personnel retire earlier than other employees, hence, need to be compensated for their truncated careers.

There have been many moves. For example, the grant of One Time Increment (OTI) and also calculation of pensions of ranks other than Commissioned Officers based upon the top-end (maximum) of pay-scale rather than the minimum, and enhanced weightages to Commissioned Officers. It would, however, be unwieldy to embark upon a journey too much into the past. With that in mind, certain developments finally leading to the issuance of the letter for OROP can be enumerated in the following paragraphs.

17.1

Improvement announced in 2006

In January 2005, a Group of Ministers (GoM) was constituted to look into the demand of OROP. Though OROP was not accepted, it was recommended that pensionary benefits of the three lowest ranks of the defence services (Sepoy to Havildar) must be improved. Ultimately, it was accepted by the Government that the pension of pre-1996 retirees would be revised with reference to maximum of post-1996 anomaly-free scales (initially made applicable only from 10-10-1997, see 5th CPC part in Chapter 16) and with increased weightage for past and future retirees in the ranks of Sepoy (which includes the appointment of Lance Naik), Naik and Havildar.

The weightages now provided were 10, 8 and 6 years respectively. Meaning thereby, that in case a Sepoy had retired with 17 years of service, he was now to be paid pension for 27 years of service (17 years + weightage of 10 years), and that too, at the maximum of the pay scale for Sepoy (and not minimum as applicable to civilians and to Commissioned Officers). The MoD letter dated

01-02-2006 is available at Chapter 32.1. The benefits were made applicable from 01-01-2006. Certain anomalies had crept into the letter dated 01-02-2006, such as grant of higher pension to junior ranks, etc, and the same were rectified through another letter issued on 02-05-2006 (Chapter 32.2).

17.2

Pension Enhancement in 2010

Pensions were again enhanced in the year 2010 with retrospective effect from 01-07-2009. This was necessitated since after the 6th CPC, the pensions were again pegged at the minimum of the scales (now pay bands) rather than maximum, as was the case for ranks other than Commissioned Officers as per the formula in vogue till that point of time. It was now decided that the pensions of all pre-2006 pensioners for ranks other than Commissioned Officers would be reckoned with reference to a notional maximum in the post-2006 revised pay structure (6th CPC pay bands) corresponding to the maximum of pre-6th Pay Commission pay scales as per fitment table of each rank. It was also decided that the enhanced weightages earlier applicable would continue to be enforced. The above was implemented through MoD letter dated 08-03-2010 (Chapter 32.3). Further, the rates of Disability and War Injury Pension had already been enhanced even prior to issuance of the above letter and the 'cap' on War Injury Pension linked with the 'last drawn emoluments' was also removed vide another letter issued by the MoD on 19-01-2010 (Chapter 23.25).

17.3

Pension Enhancement in 2013

Another policy of enhancement of pensions was issued in 2013. This enhancement was effectuated with effect from 24-09-2012. The pensions of ranks other than Commissioned Officers were now enhanced by increasing the weightage yet again by 2 years, thereby taking the admissible weightage for Sepoy, Naik and Havildar to 12, 10 and 8 years respectively. Hence, for example, if a Sepoy had physically served the Army for 17 years, he was now to be paid pension for a service of 29 years. Again, the pension was still to be based upon notional maximum of scales and not the minimum. This was provided in MoD letter dated 17-01-2013 (Chapter 32.4) for post-2006 retirees and a letter of the same date for pre-2006 retirees (Chapter 32.5). The anomaly of minimum of pay band vis-à-vis minimum of pay within the pay band for each rank (discussed in more detail in 6th CPC part of Chapter 16) was also resolved by way of a separate letter dated 17-01-2013 for Commissioned Officers at par with similarly placed civilian employees. Of course, this was later implemented with financial effect from 01-01-2006 rather than 24-09-2012 by way of a separate letter dated 03-09-2015 after judicial intervention (Chapter 30.6). A letter based on the same formula for casualty pensionary awards was also issued on 17-01-2013 for post-2006 cases (Chapter 23.28) and separately for pre-2006 cases (Chapter 23.29). There were also many other related letters issued on the subject which are worth perusing and are discussed in Chapters 2, 5, 7, 8 and 16 of this book. A new anomaly had also arisen after implementation of the above, wherein Honorary Commissioned Officers who had retired after 2006 now started facing reverse discrimination wherein pre-2006 retirees were getting more pension than them. This was also resolved on judicial intervention leading to the issuance of letter dated 06-02-2019 (Chapter 32.8).

17.4

One Rank One Pension

OROP was finally brought into effect by way of a MoD letter dated 07-11-2015 (Chapter 32.6) after approval of the Union Cabinet. This was to retrospectively operate from 01-07-2014. The following was the basic premise of OROP as per the said letter:

> "…OROP implies that uniform pension be paid to the Defence Forces Personnel retiring in the same rank with the same length of service, regardless of their date of retirement, which, implies bridging the gap between the rates of pension of current and past pensioners at periodic intervals…"

As per the formula promulgated by the letter, pension was to be re-fixed for all pensioners on the basis of the average of minimum and maximum pension of personnel retired in 2013 in the same rank and with the same length of service. The pension of anyone drawing above the average so calculated was to be protected and anyone drawing lower was to be upgraded, and the exercise was to be carried out every 5 years. The benefit was to be extended to all types of pensions, including family pensions. It was also provided that voluntary retirees, that is, personnel retiring at own request, would not be covered under the OROP dispensation.

Detailed instructions on OROP were issued through a separate letter dated 03-02-2016 (Chapter 32.7). In this letter, certain additional clauses were added by the MoD, such as, re-fixation of pension under OROP subject to the maximum terms of engagement, as applicable from time to time, as per the date of retirement of the individual. Hence, for example, if a person was made to serve for 30 years though the terms of engagement at the time of his retirement were only 24 years, then he would not be paid OROP for more than 24 years of service. Any such negative stipulation was, however, never approved by the Union Cabinet and the OROP scheme as endorsed was simply uniform pension for same rank and same length of service. There was no further categorisation in the length of service as per terms applicable from time to time in the scheme as per the master office memorandum of the scheme issued after approval of the Union Cabinet. This created an anomaly, wherein again, different pension was now sought to be released based on different dates of retirement as per the terms of engagement applicable on the said date of retirement.

The above matter was also subject of litigation and it was decided by the Chandigarh Bench of the Armed Forces Tribunal in OA 411/2018 **Chander Bhan Vs Union of India** decided on 04-10-2019, that such a stipulation went against the concept of OROP as approved by the Cabinet and pension needed to be released based on the actual service, irrespective of date of retirement, and not based upon the terms of engagement applicable at the time of retirement.

Another anomaly that has crept into the pension dispensation after implementation of OROP is the fact that again reverse discrimination is reflected in certain cases wherein pre-2014 cases, that is, retirees who retired prior to the implementation date of OROP, are now getting higher pension than certain post-2014 retirees. This anomaly is yet to be resolved.

There are other issues related to OROP which were considered by a One Man Judicial Committee (OMJC), but the same are currently pending with the Government and no decision has been taken on the same since the report of the OMJC was further endorsed for examination by an Anomalies Committee. However, while dealing with an appeal filed by the Union of India against a judgment of the Armed Forces Tribunal, that is, Civil Appeal Diary No 31127/2022 **Union of India Vs Lt Cdr Mathew Joseph** decided on 12-12-2022, the Supreme Court has asked for a decision to be taken by the Anomalies Committee within a period of four months.

Another matter on OROP was pending in the Supreme Court in which the Petitioners therein had challenged the manner of calculation of figures for grant of OROP and the periodic revision of five years. In the said case, WP(C) 419/2016 **Indian Ex-Servicemen Movement Vs Union of India** decided on 16-03-2022, though the Supreme Court did not direct any change in the manner of calculation or the period prescribed for revision, it was ordered that the long-pending revision with effect from 01-07-2019 should be carried out by the Government.

In compliance of the directions of the Supreme Court, the Government has now issued the much awaited fresh letter dated 04-01-2023 (Chapter 32.9) regarding revision of OROP rates with effect from 01-07-2019 which has now been followed up by OROP pensionary tables that are appended with the procedural instructions issued by the Government on 20-01-2023 (Chapter 32.10). The tables are available for download from the official website of the Principal Controller of Defence Accounts (Pensions).

The said letter dated 04-01-2023, however, contains an anomaly in Para 2.6 regarding those who had sought premature retirement/discharge at their own request and which is contradictory to Para 4 of the actual OROP letter issued on 07-11-2015 (Chapter 32.6). While Para 4 of the actual OROP letter states that those personnel who had sought premature retirement or discharge at own request after issuance of the letter, that is, 07-11-2015 onwards, would be ineligible for OROP prospectively, the letter for revision (Chapter 32.9) in Para 2.6 mentions the said date of ineligibility incorrectly as 01-07-2014. Due to this retrospective mentioning of an incorrect date, those who had sought premature retirement or had been discharged at their own request between 01-07-2014 and 07-11-2015, who are/were eligible for OROP under the actual letter, have now become ineligible due to this apparent oversight or drafting error. The resolution of this anomaly is currently under examination.

Certain other anomalies observed in the new tables are also under examination.

Chapter-18

Re-Employment and Related Modalities

A large number of military pensioners are reemployed after being released from military service, and naturally so, in view of the short service span as compared to civilian employees, most of whom retire at the age of 60.

There are certain modalities of such reemployment that are followed for regulating concepts such as Dearness Relief during reemployed service and also pay fixation which are explained in brief in the following paragraphs.

Earlier, defence pensioners on getting reemployed were not entitled to Dearness Relief (DR) on their pension and were only allowed basic pension along with the pay and Dearness Allowance (DA) from the department/organisation where they were reemployed.

The above system was considered incongruous because there was no reason to deny such personnel the DR on pension since it was meant to offset the rising cost of living and inflation and more so in light of the fact that pension is a deferred wage that a person had already earned by way of his service with the Government.

The Government, based on the recommendations of the 5th CPC, finally resolved the matter and issued detailed instructions through the Ministry of Personnel, Public Grievances & Pensions letter dated 02-07-1999 (Chapter 27.1), which inter alia, provided that ranks other than Commissioned Officers (and grades other than Group A Officers on the civil side) would continue to remain entitled to both DR on Pension and DA on Pay in case they join the fresh appointment at the minimum of the pay of the post. The system of fixation of Pay of Commissioned and Group A Officers was also tweaked. The said letter also contained many other modalities. The benefit of DR was made available with effect from 18-07-1997.

The MoD also issued parallel instructions vide its letter dated 28-08-2000 (Chapter 27.2).

There still remained some problems even after the issuance of the above letter, wherein, due to the fact that certain departments provided a higher start within the applicable pay-scale to fresh joinees or provided advance increments to them, the said benefit of DR started to be refused by the Defence

Accounts Department. The DoPPW, however, clarified vide its letter dated 03-04-2008 (Chapter 27.3) that DR would not be refused even in such cases, though technically, such employees were not being made to join at the minimum of pay in the new department/organisation.

Many more letters have been issued from time to time on fixation of pay, ignorable portion of pension, etc, with respect to reemployed military pensioners, but the latest on the subject issued by the DoPT dated 01-05-2017 (Chapter 27.4) contains all past and existing modalities on the subject.

It may, however, be kept in mind that there are no such fetters on DA/DR or fixation of pay or adjustment of pension, etc, as above either on Commissioned Officers or on other personnel when they are reemployed on contractual terms or as fresh appointees or from open market, as opposed to reemployment terms.

Personnel disabled during the period of re-employment within the military remain entitled to Disability Pension as per military terms as explained in detail in Chapter 2.12 dealing with Disability Pension.

Chapter-19

Pension to Families of Missing Personnel

One aspect that has repeatedly troubled the families of personnel who go missing without trace, has been the non-grant of Family Pension. Despite several progressive policies of the Government and multiple judicial dicta, many Military Records Offices refuse to process the claims of Family Pension for the kin of missing personnel on the pretext of "desertion", not realising the difference between "desertion" vis-a-vis "missing".

Of course, common sense, as also the rules require that a person can only be declared a "deserter" if there is any hint or any intention of desertion and if a person is keeping himself/herself away from service wilfully and not in cases where a person is missing for reasons that are unknown or beyond anybody's control. Naturally, if a person is unheard of and is not apprehended or his whereabouts remain unknown, then he/she is to be declared as "missing" and not a "deserter". Even otherwise, the following lines of Army Order 01/2003 (Chapter 25.5) provide adequate assistance as to what should be done in such situations:

ARMY ORDER 01 OF 2003

> 58. Army personnel may be found missing when there are no operations/hostilities. **Great care must be exercised in dealing with such cases. They would be reported as deserters only after conclusive evidence is obtained.** A few examples are cited below:
>
> a. A person may have drowned in a river and his dead body may not been recovered or seen by a reliable witness.
>
> b. A person may have been abducted.
>
> c. A person may have been on board an aircraft or a ship which is missing, and consequently no trace has been found of it.
>
> d. A person involved in a skirmish whilst in aid of civil authorities to maintain internal security and fighting against armed hostilities, may have been killed but his dead body may not have been recovered or seen by a reliable witness.

e. A person having gone on Annual Leave or in transit through a disturbed area does not report back from Annual Leave or goes missing while in transit. Such a person may have been killed/rendered incapable of reporting in time and as such should be reported missing till conclusive evidence of desertion is found.

Rules for Reporting Personnel Missing:

59. Following instructions will be observed whilst reporting personnel as missing:

a. **A person will be regarded as missing with effect from the day following on which he was last seen.**

b. A "missing" casualty will not be reported until 72 hours from the date he was missing i.e. 96 hours after he was seen, e.g. a man last seen on 17 Nov. will be reported on 21 Nov as missing with effect from 18 Nov.

The policy of the Government of India on the subject first issued on 03-06-1988 (Chapter 25.1) clearly itself provides the answer on how to release such benefits and states that service and pensionary benefits are to be released to families of personnel whose whereabouts are not known. This was to counter the procedure being followed by certain organisations, wherein missing personnel were being dismissed in an ex parte manner after being declared deserters. Earlier, Government departments used to wait for 7 years for presumption of death and then used to release the arrears after the lapse of 7 years, but in the year 1988, the Government issued a policy that some benefits would be released immediately on declaration of disappearance and some other service benefits would be released after one year of declaration of disappearance after lodging a missing report with the police. The declaration of date of disappearance was later prescribed as the date of lodging the police report vide a policy issued on 23-03-1992 (Chapter 25.2) and then again on 26-08-1993 (Chapter 25.3). The indemnity bonds required for processing the claim are appended as Chapter 25.4. The time schedule of one year also was later amended and now it stands at 6 months by way of the latest MoD policy dated 15-02-2011 (Chapter 25.6). The concerned person granted family pension is, however, supposed to provide an indemnity bond as above promising to return the amount in case the person is found living at a later date. Further policies in this regard on the modalities to be observed have also been issued by the DoPPW and MoD respectively on 02-11-2012 and 05-06-2013 (Chapters 25.7 and 25.8). A latest policy issued by the MoD dated 23-12-2014 is available at Chapter 25.9.

Many Records Offices are also under the misconception that being a "deserter" (albeit wrongly declared as such), the said individual forfeits pension under Regulation 123 of Pension Regulations, 1961, not realising that a bare perusal of Regulation 123 would show that service is only forfeited for pension in case a person is convicted for the offence of desertion by way of a court-martial and not in cases where the person remains missing. The Regulation referred above is reproduced below:

Forfeiture of Service for certain offences and its restoration

123. (a) A person who has been guilty of any of the following offences:

i. Desertion, vide Section 38 of the Army Act.

ii. Fraudulent enrolment, vide Section 34 (a) of the Army Act,

shall forfeit the whole of his prior service towards pension or gratuity upon being convicted by court martial of the offence.

(b) A person who has forfeited service under the provisions of the preceding clause but has not been dismissed shall, on completion of any period of three years further service in the colours and/or service in the reserve with exemplary conduct and without any red ink entry, be eligible to reckon the forfeited service towards pension or gratuity.

It becomes clear from the above regulation that service towards pension is only forfeited in case a person is convicted by a court martial for desertion, not otherwise.

There are many decisions on this proposition. The Courts have deprecated time and again how the families of missing soldiers are being treated and how such soldiers are declared deserters rather than 'missing' and then dismissed ex parte rather than releasing the due benefits to families. In fact, the Courts, including the Supreme Court, have held such families entitled to full benefits from the date of issuance of apprehension roll (the date the Police is informed about the person by the military) and not from the date of lodging of police report since the date of first information to the police is naturally the time when the apprehension roll is issued by military authorities. Some such orders are the directions by the Supreme Court in Writ Petition (Criminal) 125-126/2002 **Uma Devi Vs Union of India** decided on 20-07-2011, the Rajasthan High Court in CWP 6620/1997 **Phoola Devi Vs Union of India** decided on 07-12-2006, the Chandigarh Bench of AFT in OA 978/2011 **Palwinder Kaur Vs Union of India** decided on 21-10-2011 and OA 3707/2013 **Phul Maya Gurung Vs Union of India** decided on 12-03-2018.

Chapter-20

Family Pension for Families of Individuals Dying During the Period of Unauthorised Absence or Desertion

There is certain reluctance and inertia on part of some authorities in processing claims of Ordinary Family Pension for widows of those soldiers who die in harness during unauthorised period of absence while in service but before ex parte dismissal. Many such claims are rejected on the pretext that the death occurred during the period of unauthorised absence or desertion, while the correct legal position is that the death of a person who dies prior to dismissal, even during unauthorised absence or desertion, is a death in harness or in service, thereby making the family eligible for Family Pension. Moreover, there is no minimum qualifying service required for earning an Ordinary Family Pension and the family of a person with even a single day of service is entitled to Family Pension. In fact, despite clear cut directions from the Government of India time and again, many authorities are under the misconception that families of deserters are not eligible to Ordinary Family Pension despite fully knowing that the master-servant/employer-employee relationship between a soldier and the Government does not cease during desertion/unauthorised absence till the time a person is dismissed from service for desertion.

The service of a deserter is also not forfeited for the purposes of pension unless such a deserter is apprehended and convicted and consequently dismissed for the offence of desertion under Section 38 of the Army Act through a Court Martial and the same is amply clarified in Regulation 123 of the Pension Regulations, 1961 reproduced hereunder:

Forfeiture of Service for certain offences and its restoration

123. (a) A person who has been guilty of any of the following offences:

i. Desertion, vide Section 38 of the Army Act.
ii. Fraudulent enrolment, vide Section 34 (a) of the Army Act,

shall forfeit the whole of his prior service towards pension or gratuity upon being convicted by court martial of the offence.

(b) A person who has forfeited service under the provisions of the preceding clause

> but has not been dismissed shall, on completion of any period of three years further service in the colours and/or service in the reserve with exemplary conduct and without any red ink entry, be eligible to reckon the forfeited service towards pension or gratuity.

Hence, as per Regulation 123, the service of even a living soldier is not forfeited unless he is convicted of desertion after a court martial, but there are cases where Family Pension has been refused to widows even when the soldier had died very much in harness, before dismissal and before a court martial. Moreover, in accordance with Regulation 376 of the Regulations for the Army, a deserter does not cease to be a member of the organisation:

> **376. Deserters From The Regular Army: A person subject to Army Act who is declared absent under Army Act Section 106, does not thereby cease to belong to the corps in which he is enrolled though no longer shown on its returns,** and can, if subsequently arrested, be tried by court-martial for desertion. When arrested he will be shown on returns as rejoined from desertion.

Further, Army Instruction 51 of 1980 clearly provides that Family Pension shall only be refused to a person if he dies by way of execution of a death sentence:

> "AI 51/80: ....Family pensionary benefits......will be admissible to the widows and children of all commissioned Officers, OR and NCs(E) who were in service on 01-01-1964 or who joined/join service thereafter and who died/die while in service or after retirement with a retiring, disability or invalid/special pension, **on account of causes which are neither attributable to, nor aggravated by service except the categories enumerated below:**
>
> (a) to (i) *****
>
> **(j) Persons who are executed on being convicted to a death sentence awarded by any Court."**

The Courts have held time and again that death during desertion does not disqualify the family from getting Family Pension and other pensionary benefits. Important decisions in this regard are by the Delhi High Court in CW 3799/1995 **Smt Harnandi Vs Union of India** decided on 27-03-2001, by the Chandigarh Bench of the Armed Forces Tribunal in OA 2759/2012 **Jabita Devi Vs Union of India** decided on 22-01-2014 and OA 596/2010 **Harpreet Kaur Vs Union of India** decided on 01-02-2011.

Chapter-21

Restoration of Pension on Release from Imprisonment

Some Records Offices and also certain staff-members of the Defence Accounts Department are under the misconception that in case a person is convicted and is sentenced to imprisonment and his/her appeal is still pending, the pension needs to be suspended.

This is absolutely incorrect and is not only against rules but also against the law laid down by the Supreme Court.

The thumb rule in this regard is that irrespective of the pendency of appeal, the pension can only be discontinued after issuance of a show-cause notice, and that too, restricted to the period when the person remains imprisoned after conviction, and only till his release. The pension is supposed to be restored on release from imprisonment, and not acquittal, if the appeal is pending.

The procedure for withholding and suspending pension is provided in Paragraph 73.1 of Pension Payment Instructions (2005 version, now replaced with *pari materia* Instructions of 2013), which provides that a pensioner is supposed to apply for restoration of pension on "release" from imprisonment. The point to be noted here is that the person has to apply for restoration on "release" from imprisonment and not "acquittal". Similar provisions are available in Regulation 82 of the Pension Regulations for the Army, Part-II, 1961.

The matter was dealt with in detail by the Chandigarh Bench of the AFT in OA 159/2013 **Chander Singh Vs Union of India** decided on 10-09-2013, wherein the tribunal deliberated all rules on the subject and observed the following:

> *"...The word used in the Regulation is "Release" and not "Acquittal". These are two entirely different words having different meaning. One cannot be equated with the other. If the word 'Release' is equated with the word 'Acquittal' then it would mean that if the hearing in the appeal does not take place for 20 years, the petitioner will not get the pension for 20 years till his acquittal. That cannot be the intention of the framers of the Regulations. The word 'Release' has consciously been used in Para 82(b) which means if a person is released on bail, his pension should be restored..."*

In any case, the law in this regard has been well settled by the Supreme Court. The Apex Court has gone a step further to hold that even the pension during the time of imprisonment cannot be suspended mechanically. A Three Judge Bench in WP(C) 400 of 1987 **Rameshwar Yadav Vs Union of India**, decided on 10-01-1989, had observed as under:

> *"...Regulation 119 confers power on the competent authority to withhold in whole or in part the pension of a pensioner, who is convicted of a serious crime by a court of law. Para 29.1 of Pension Payment Instructions (1973) also confers power on the Disbursing Officer to forthwith suspend the payment of pension payable to a pensioner, if he is sentenced to imprisonment.* ***On the release of the pensioner from imprisonment, the Disbursing Officer is required to restore his pension...*** *These provisions require the competent authority to apply its mind to the question as to whether the pension should be suspended in whole or in part. While determining this question the Disbursing Officer has to consider the nature of the offence, the circumstances in which offence might have been committed and other allied matters. The officer has also to consider the hardship on the dependants of the person, if the payment of pension is suspended. In the instant case, the impugned order does not show that the competent authority applied its mind to the question as to whether the whole or a part of the pension should be suspended, instead, the authority mechanically issued orders for the suspension of the entire amount of pension for the period of imprisonment of the petitioner..."*

Hence, not only is the suspension of pension beyond the date of release from imprisonment incorrect, but also withholding of the entire amount even for the period of imprisonment is improper, as held by the Supreme Court in *Rameshwar Yadav's* case (supra).

Chapter-22

Pensionary Issues Related to Short Service and Non-Regular Officers

There are some unique issues related to Short Service Commissioned Officers and other Non-Regular Officers such as Emergency Commissioned Officers.

Such officers are naturally not entitled to the grant of Retiring Pension since they do not complete 20 years of service (unless they have pre-commissioned service to their credit). However, the officers remain fully entitled to all casualty pensionary awards (such as Disability Pension, War Injury Pension, Special Family Pension, Liberalised Family Pension, etc) and their families also remain entitled to Ordinary Family Pension in case of death in harness on account of non-service related causes, irrespective of length of service.

However, there is an exception to the above. Short Service Officers who are commissioned from the ranks are entitled to pension after completion of 12 years of combined pre and post commissioned service [See Para 6.1(b) of letter dated 03-02-1998, Chapter 29.1]. As far as Disability Pension is concerned, all non-regular officers are now governed by the same provisions as applicable to Permanent Commissioned Officers. Earlier, though the provisions of the Pension Regulations for Disability Pension were fully applicable to non regular officers, due to a grey area accentuated by specific provisions dealing with Non-Regular Officers, they were being refused the grant of Service Element of Disability Pension at par with regular officers. In fact, the system was such that Service Element was only being paid in 'attributable' cases and not in 'aggravation' cases. The latter were only being paid Disability Element alone. Further, the Service Element, in a strangely conceptualised stipulation, was not being paid for full service but only for the service length calculated from the date of joining service till the date of sustaining the disability.

The above anomaly came under sharp criticism by the Supreme Court in Civil Appeal 4474/2005 **Union of India Vs CS Sidhu** decided on 31-03-2010, which directed the Government to pay the officer full Service Element for his entire spell (10 years in that case) of service. The following were the observations of the Supreme Court:

> *"...Before parting with this case, we regret to say that the army officers and army men in our country are being treated in a shabby manner by the Government. In this case, the respondent, who was posted at a high altitude field area and met with an accident during discharge of his duties, was granted a meagre pension as stated in Annexure-P3 to this appeal. This is a pittance (about Rs 1,000/- per month plus D.A.). If this is the manner in which the army personnel are treated, it can only be said that it is extremely unfortunate. The army personnel are bravely defending the country even at the cost of their lives and we feel that they should be treated in a better and more humane manner by the Governmental authorities, particularly, in respect of their emoluments, pension and other benefits..."*

The Government had also issued a letter on 30-08-2006 (Chapter 23.19) authorising full Service Element to such officers who are in low medical category at the time of relese from the serv for the entire length of service at par with Regular Officers but again created an anomaly by providing that while post-2006 and pre-2006 'attributable disability' cases would be entitled to full Service Element with effect from 30-08-2006, in case of officers with 'aggravated disability', the benefit would only be available to post-2006 cases.

The above micro-classification, however, was again set-aside by judicial intervention and it was held that pre as well as post-2006 cases of both categories – attributable as well as aggravated disabilities, would be entitled to full Service Element for the entire length of service at par with Permanent Commissioned Officers.

In compliance of the above, the MoD later issued a fresh letter dated 23-03-2015 (Chapter 23.20).

Hence, as on date, all Short Service and other Non-Regular Officers released with a disability that is declared attributable to or aggravated by service (or deemed to be attributable/aggravated), are entitled to proper disability pension, including full Service Element at par with Permanent Commissioned Officers. Full modalities of the concept of Disability Pension are available in Chapter 2. Those who are not being released the above must claim so based upon the above mentioned letters and provisions.

Part II

Provisions

Chapter-23

Provisions Related to Disability, Casualty and Liberalised Benefits

23.1

Entitlement Rules for Casualty Pensionary Awards, 1982

(These also form a part of Pension Regulations as Appendix II)

(Ministry of Defence letter No 1(1)/81/Pen-C, dated 22.11.1983, as amended vide Corrigendum No 1(1)/81/Pen-C dated 21.08. 1984)

1. The Entitlement Rules set out below apply to service personnel who become non-effective on or after 1st January, 1982. The cases arising on or after 1st January, 1982 may be considered under these rules provided that such a case is still outstanding on the date of issue of these rules. For the purpose of defining whether a case will be treated as outstanding or not, it may be clarified that where such a case has already been decided even at the initial stage the same will be treated as having been decided. Such cases will not be reopened. These rules shall be read in conjunction with the Guide to Medical Officers (Military Pensions) 1980; as amended.

2. Pending decision on a general case to give pay and allowances to probationary nurses and cadets undergoing training at NDA/IMA and other pre-commissioned and probationary commission training institutions/academies of the Defence Services, they will continue to be governed under the existing instructions for casualty pensionary awards.

3. These rules do not apply to the cases where disablement or death, on which the claim to casualty pensionary award is based, took place-

i. during the period from 3.9.1939 to 31.3.1948, which will be dealt with in accordance with the entitlement criteria laid down in Annexure I.

ii. during the period from 1.1.1948 to 31.12.1981, which will be dealt with in accordance with the entitlement rules promulgated vide Ministry of Defence (Pensions Branch) letter No. 138999/1/PC dated 18th April 1950, amended from time to time;

iii. during the post 1948 periods of emergency, which will be dealt with in accordance with Annexure-II.

4. Invaliding from service is necessary condition for grant of disability pension. An individual who, at the time of his release under the Release Regulations, is in a lower medical category than that in which he was recruited, will be treated as invalidated from service. JCO/OR and equivalents in other services who are placed permanently in a medical category other than 'A' and are discharged because no Alternative or Shelter Appointment can be provided, as well as those who having been retained in alternative employment but are discharged before the completion of their engagement, will be deemed to have been invalidated out of service.

5. The approach to the question of entitlement of casualty pensionary awards and evaluation of disabilities shall be based on the following presumptions:

Prior to and During Service

a. Member is presumed to have been in sound physical and mental condition upon entering service except as to physical disabilities noted or recorded at the time of entrance.

b. In the event of his subsequently being discharged from service on medical grounds, any deterioration in his health which has taken place is due to service.

6. Disablement or death shall be accepted as due to military service provided it is certified by appropriate medical authority that:

a. The disablement is due to a wound, injury or disease which

   i. is attributable to military service, or

   ii. existed before or arose during military service and has been and remains aggravated thereby. This will also include the precipitating/hastening of the onset of a disability.

b. The death was due to or hastened by –

   i. a wound, injury or disease which was attributable to military service; or

   ii. the aggravation by military service of a wound, injury or disease which existed before or arose during military service.

7. Where there is no note in contemporary official records of a material fact on which the claim is based, other reliable corroborative evidence of that fact may be accepted.

8. Attributability/Aggravation shall be conceded if causal connection between death/disablement and military service is certified by appropriate medical authority.

Onus of Proof

9. The claimant shall not be called upon to prove the conditions of entitlements. He/she will receive the benefit of any reasonable doubt. This benefit will be given more liberally to the claimants in field/afloat service cases.

Post Discharge Claims

10. Cases in which a disease did not actually lead to the member's discharge from service but arose within 10 years thereafter, may be recognized as attributable to service if it can be established medically that the disability is a delayed manifestation of a pathological process set in motion by service conditions occurring prior to discharge and that if the disability had been manifest at the time of discharge the individual would have been invalided out of service on this account.

11. In cases where an individual is in receipt of a disability pension dies at home and it cannot, from a strictly medical point of view, be definitely established that the death was due to the disablement in respect of which the disability pension was granted:

a. the benefit of doubt in determining the attributability should go to the family of the deceased, if death occurs within 10 years from the date of his invalidment from service unless there are other factors adversely affecting the claim; and

b. if death takes place more than 10 year after the date of the man's invalidment from service, the benefit of doubt will go to the State.

Duty

12. A person subject to the disciplinary code of the Armed Forces is on "duty"-

a. When performing an official task or a task, failure to do which would constitute an offence, triable under the disciplinary code applicable to him.

b. When moving from one place of duty to another place of duty irrespective of the mode of movement.

c. During the period of participation in recreation and other unit activities organized or permitted by Service Authorities and during the period of traveling in a body or singly by a prescribed or organized route.

Note 1:

(a) Personnel of the Armed Forces participating in-

i. Local/national/international sports tournaments as member of service teams, or

ii. mountaineering expeditions/gliding organized by service authorities, with the approval of service HQrs, will be deemed to be "on duty" for purpose of these rules.

(b) Personnel of the Armed Forces participating in the above named sports tournaments or in privately or ganized mountaineering expeditions or indulging in gliding as a hobby in their individual capacity, will not be deemed to be "on duty" for purpose of these rules, even though prior permission of the competent service authorities may have been obtained by them

(c) Injuries sustained by the personnel of the Armed Force in impromptu games and sports outside parade hours, which are organized by, or with the approval of, the local service authority, and death or disability arising from such injuries, will continue to be regarded as having occurred while 'on duty' for purpose of these rules.

Note 2:

The personnel of the Armed Forces deputed for training at courses conducted by the Himalayan Mountaineering Institute, Darjeeling shall be treated on par with personnel attending other authorized professional course or exercise for the Defence Services for the purpose of the grant of disability/family pension on account of disability/death sustained during the courses.

d. When proceeding from his leave station or returning to duty from his leave station, provided entitled to travel at public expenses i.e. on railway warrants, on concessional voucher, on cash TA (irrespective of whether railway warrant/cash TA is admitted for the whole journey or for a portion only), in Government transport or when road mileage is paid/payable for the journey.

e. When journeying by reasonable route from one's quarter to and back from the appointed place of duty, under organized arrangements or by a private conveyance when a person is entitled to use service transport but that transport is not available.

f. An accident which occurs when a man is not strictly "on duty" as defined may also be attributable to service, provided that it involved risk which was definitely enhanced in kind or degree by the nature, conditions, obligations or incidents of his service and that the same was not a risk common to human existence in modern conditions in India. Thus for instance, where a person is killed or injured by another party by reason of belonging to the Armed Forces, he shall be deemed "on duty" at the relevant time. This benefit will be given more liberally to the claimant in cases occurring on active service as defined in the Army/Navy/Air Force Act.

Injuries

13. In respect of accidents or injuries, the following rules shall be observed:

a. Injuries sustained when the man is "on duty" as defined, shall be deemed to have resulted from military service, but in cases of injuries due to serious negligence/misconduct the question of reducing the disability pension will be considered.

b. In case of self-inflicted injuries whilst on duty, attrubutability shall not be conceded unless it is established that service factors were responsible for such action, in cases where attributability is conceded, the question of grant of disability pension at full or at reduced rate will be considered.

Diseases

14. In respect of diseases, the following rule will be observed:

a. Cases in which it is established that conditions of Military Service did not determine or contribute to the onset of the disease but influenced the subsequent courses of the disease, will fall for acceptance on the basis of aggravation.

b. A disease which has led to an individual's discharge or death will ordinarily be deemed to have arisen in service, if no note of it was made at the time of the individual's acceptance for military service. However, if medical opinion holds, for reasons to be stated, that the disease could not have been detected on medical examination prior to acceptance for service, the disease will not be deemed to have arisen during service.

c. If a disease is accepted as having arisen in service, it must also be established that the conditions of military service determined or contributed to the onset of the disease and that the conditions were due to the circumstances of duty in military service.

15. The onset and progress of some disease are affected by environmental factors related to service conditions, dietary compulsions, exposure to noise, physical and mental stress and strain. Disease due to infection arising in service, will merit an entitlement of attributability. Nevertheless, attention must be given to the possibility of pre-service history of such conditions which, if proved could rule out entitlement of attributability but would require consideration regarding aggravation. For clinical description of common disease, reference shall be made to the Guide to Medical Officers (Military Pensions) 1980, as amended from time to time. The classification of diseases affected by environmental factors in service is given in Annexure III to these rules.

Communicable Diseases and Diseases Due to Infection

16. Death or disablement resulting from such diseases, other than venereal diseases, contracted during service shall be regarded as attributable to military service. Where the disease may have been contracted prior to enrolment or during leave, the question of determining the incubating period in a particular case will arise and an opinion on this point should be expressed.

Miscellaneous Rules

17. **Medical Opinion:** At initial claim stage medical views on entitlement and assessment are given by the IMB/ RMB. Normally these views shall prevail for decisions in accepting or rejecting the claim. In case of doubt the Ministry/CCDA (Pensions) may refer such cases for second medical opinion to MA (Pensions) sections in the office of the DGAFMS/

Office of CCDA(P), Allahabad, respectively. At appeal stage, appropriate appellate medical authorities can review and revise the opinion of the medical boards on entitlement and assessment.

18. **Predisposition:** "Predisposition" or "inherent constitutional tendency" in itself is not disease and if there is a precipitating or causative factor in service which produces the disease, then it is attributable to service notwithstanding the inherent disposition.

19. **Aggravation:** If it is established that the disability was not caused by service, attributability shall not be conceded. However aggravation by service is to be accepted unless any worsening in his condition was not due to his service or worsening did not persist on the date of discharge/claim.

20. **Conditions of Unknown Aetiology:** There are a number of medical conditions which are of unknown aetiology. In dealing with such conditions, the following guiding principles are laid down:

a. If nothing at all is known about the cause of the disease, and presumption of the entitlement in favour of the claimant is not rebutted, attributability should be conceded.

b. If the disease is one which arises and progresses independently of service/environmental factors, then the claim may be rejected.

Delay in Diagnosis/Adverse Effects of Treatment

21. The question as to whether, through the exigencies of service, the diagnosis and/or treatment of the wound, injury or disease was delayed, faulty or otherwise unsatisfactory, including the adverse/unforeseen effects of treatment, shall also be considered. The entitlement for any ill-effects arising as a complication from such factors shall be conceded as attributable.

Assessment

22. Assessment of degree of disability is entirely a matter of medical judgment and is the responsibility of the medical authorities. The degree of disablement due to service/duty of a member of the military forces shall be assessed by making a comparison between the conditions of the member so disabled and the condition or a normal healthy person of same age and sex, without taking into account the earning capacity of the member in his disabled condition in his own or any other specific trade or occupation and without taking into account the effects of any individual factor or extraneous circumstances.

Where disablement is due to more than one disability, a composite assessment of the degree of disablement shall also be made by reference to the combined effect of all such disabilities in addition to separate assessment for each disability.

In other than paired organs, conditions may co-exist which through interaction may give rise to the need for consideration under the greater disablement principle. One of the simplest examples is the pensioner with entitlement for bronchitis who also suffers from coronary atherosclerosis and as a consequence of acute bouts of coughing claims increasing frequency of attacks of angina. In such cases it is a matter of clinical judgement as to the extent to which the assessment for bronchitis should be increased to cover the greater disablement arising from the interaction between that condition and the coronary atherosclerosis. The pensioner is not entitled to the total assessment of disablement for the coronary atherosclerosis which might well be in the regions of 30 to 40% but only to that portion of that assessment which it is reasonable to add to cover greater disablement. Depending on the increased frequency in the attacks of angina due to severe bouts of coughing, a greater disablement addition in the less than 20% range might well be appropriate.

a. The assessment of a disability is the estimate of the degree of disablement it causes, which can properly be ascribed to service as defined below.

b. The disablement properly referable to service will be assessed as under:

  i. At the time of discharge from Forces:

  Normally, the whole of the disablement then caused by the disability. This will apply irrespective of whether the disability is actually attributable to service, or is merely aggravated thereby.

  ii. On Resurvey of Disability after discharge from service:

  The whole of the disablement then caused by the disability, less the following:

  1. The part due to non-service factors, such as individual's habits, occupation in civil life, accident after discharge, climatic environment after discharge.

  2. Any worsening due to natural progress of the disability since discharge, apart from the effect of service.

Note: Deduction (1) will be made in all cases, while deduction (2) will apply only in cases where the disability is accepted as aggravated by, but not attributable to service.

APPEALS

23. **Right of Appeal:** Where entitlement is denied by the Pension Sanctioning Authority on initial consideration of the claim, the claimant has a right of appeal against decision on entitlement and assessment. Whereas for decision on entitlement, all concerned authorities have to give opinion, assessment of degree of disablement is entirely a matter of medical judgement and is the responsibility of appropriate medical authority.

24. Detailed procedure to be followed for appeals shall be issued by Ministry of Defence from time to time. However, to avoid in-ordinate delay in taking final decisions on the disability/family pensionary claims, suitable time limits at each stage of the claim shall be laid down.

Appellate Bodies

25. (a) **Defence Minister's Appellate Committee on Pensions**: DMACP shall deal with second appeal on claim for casualty pensionary awards. This committee consists of –

Chairman	RM/RPM
Members	URM
	Chief of Staff (Army, Navy & Air Force)
	Defence Secretary
	Financial Advisor (DS)
	DGAFMS
	JAG (Three Services)

(b) **Appellate committee for first appeals:** ACFA shall deal with claims for casualty pensionary awards on first appeals. This committee consists of:

Chairman DS (Pensions), Ministry of Defence dealing with pension cases

Members Director Personnel Services, Army HQ and his counterparts in Naval and Air HQ dealing with pension cases

Deputy Director General (Pensions) of office of DGAFMS

Deputy Financial Advisor (Pensions)

Decision of Appellate Committee for Appeal

26. After consideration of all relevant issues involved in a case, the appellate body shall give decision of upholding or rejecting the appeal by consensus.

Functions and Responsibilities

27. (a) **Service HQ**: Appropriate Service Authority shall be responsible for giving their views on matters relating to relevant service factors.

(b) **Judge Advocate General (JAG)**: He shall be responsible for giving opinion on legal matters.

(c) **Medical Authority**: Assessment of disablement and entitlement in case of disabilities other than injuries are purely medical issues. Views on such medical issues shall be given by the appropriate medical authorities as under:

i. Medical Board shall give findings and recommendations on entitlement and assessment in case of all disabilities. They are, however, not statutory bodies and their recommendation can be reviewed and revised by the medical authorities viz DGAFMS.

ii. DDG (Pensions), Office of the DGAFMS shall be the medical authority dealing with medical issues at first appeal stage of the claim.

iii. DGAFMS will be the final medical authority for giving views on medical issue at final stage to the DMACP.

ANNEXURE I NOT PUBLISHED
ANNEXURE – II

Entitlement Rules for the Disability and special family pensionary awards in respect of all ranks of the Armed forces during emergency

Period of emergency	Period of emergency
8 Sep 62 to 9 Jun 68	A/01927/AG/PS-4(a)/9948/Pen-C dated 26 Dec 62
3 Dec 71 to 31 Mar 72 25 Mar 71 to 31 Mar 72 (Op Cactus Lily)	A/01927/AG/PS-4(d)/11130/Pen-C dated 16 Dec 71
15 Aug 71 to 31 Mar 72 (Naval Personnel)	PN/3948/1191/Pen-C, Dated 1 Feb 71

1. Entitlement to disability or family pensionary awards in respect of all ranks of the Armed Forces eligible for pension under Military Rules, disablement or death shall be accepted as due to service, if –

   a. The disablement is due to a wound, injury or disease, which-

      (i) is attributable to service; or

      (ii) existed before or arose during service and has been, or remains aggravated thereby

   b. The death was due to or hastened by –

      (i) a wound or injury or disease which was attributable to service or

      (ii) the aggravation by service of a wound, injury or disease which existed before, or arose during service.

2. In dealing with these cases, the benefit of reasonable doubt will be given to the claimant. The entitlement shall be denied only if it can be established beyond reasonable doubt that the conditions mentioned above are not fulfilled.

3. Where an injury or disease, which led to discharge or death during service, was not noted in a medical report or the appropriate enrolment papers prepared at the time of commencement of the individual's service, fulfillment of the conditions mentioned in para 1 above may be accepted unless there is a positive evidence to the contrary.

4. Where there is no note in contemporary official records of a material fact on which the claim is based, other reliable corroborative evidence of the fact may be accepted.

N.B.- "Service" means service in the Armed Forces during emergency rendered anywhere in India

ANNEXURE III TO APPENDIX II
Classification of Diseases

A. Disease Affected by Climatic Conditions

1. Pulmonary Tuberculosis
2. Pulmonary Oedema
3. Pulmonary Tuberculosis with pleural effusion
4. Tuberculosis Non Pulmonary
5. Bronchitis
6. Pleurisy, emphysema, lung abscess, and Bronchiectasis
7. Lobar pneumonia
8. Nephritis (acute and chronic)
9. Otitis Media
10. Rheumatism (acute and chronic)
11. Arthritis
12. Mylegia
13. Lumbago
14. Local effects of severe cold climate – i.e. frost bite, trench foot and chilblains
15. Effects of hot climate - i.e. heat stroke and heat exhaustion

B. Disease Affected by Stress and Strain

1. Psychosis and Psychoneurosis
2. Hypertension (BP)
3. Pulmonary Tuberculosis
4. Pulmonary Tuberculosis with pleural effusion
5. Tuberculosis (Non-pulmonary)
6. Mitral Stenosis
7. Pericaditis and adherent pericardium
8. Endocarditis

9. Sub-acute bacterial endocarditis including infective endocarditis

10. Myocarditis (acute and chronic)

11. Valvular disease

12. Myocardial infarction and other forms of IHD

13. Cerebral hemorrhage and cerebral infarction

14. Peptic ulcer

C. <u>Disease Affected by Dietary Compulsions</u>

1. Infective hepatitis (Jaundice)

2. Disease of stomach and duodenum.

3. Worm infestation and particularly guinea worm and round worm infections

4. Gastritis

5. Food poisoning, especially due to tinned food

6. Gastric ulcer

7. Duodenal ulcer

8. Nutritional Disorders

D. <u>Disease Affected by Training, Marching, Prolonged Standing etc.</u>

1. Tetanus, erysipelas, septicemia and pyaemia etc. resulting from injuries

2. Alkalosis and acquired deformities resulting from injuries

3. Post traumatic epilepsy and other mental changes resulting from head injuries

4. Internal derangement of knee joint

5. Deformities of feet

6. Osteoarthritis of spine and lower limb joints

7. Burns sustained through petrol, fire, kerosene oil leading to scars and various deformities and disabilities

8. Hernia

9. Varicose veins

E. Environmental Disease

1. Disease contracted in the course of official duty of attending to a Venereal or septicaemic patient or while conducting a postmortem examination

2. Disease contracted on account of handling infectious material, poisonous chemical and radioactive substance

F. Disease Affected by Altitude

1. High altitude pulmonary oedema and pulmonary hypertension

2. Acute mountain sickness

3. Psychosis, Psychoneurosis, suicide

4. Thrombosis

G. Disease Affected by Service in Submarines and in Diving

1. Acoustic trauma resulting from continuous noise and vibrations

2. Effects of exposure to high levels or toxic gases

3. Droplet infections

4. Neurosis and psychosomatic disorders

5. Effects of barotraumas

6. Decompression sickness

7. Dysbaricosteo-necrosis

H. Disease Affected by Service in Flying Duties

1. Otitic barotraumas

2. Altitude decompression sickness

3. Hypoxia

4. Explosive decompression

5. Long duration G

I. Diseases not Normally Affected by Service

1. Malignant diseases (Cancer and Carcinoma)

2. Sarcoma (except in case of Sarcoma of bone with a history of injury due to service, on the site of development of the growth)

3. Epithelioma

4. Rodent ulcer

5. Lymphosarcoma

6. Lymph adenoma except of viral aetiology

7. Leukemia (except radiation effect)

8. Pernicious anemia (Addison's disease)

9. Osteitisdeformas (Paget's disease)

10. Gout

11. Acromegaly

12. Cirrhosis of the liver, if alcoholic

EYES

13. Error of refraction

14. Hypermetropia

15. Myopia

16. Astigmatism

17. Preshyopia

18. Glaucoma, acute or chronic, unless there is a history of injury due to service or of disease due to service

23.2

Pension Regulations related to Disability Pension

Pension Regulations for the Army, Part-I, 1961, as they relate to Disability Pension for Commissioned Officers

Disability Pension when admissible

48. a. Unless otherwise specifically provided, a disability pension consisting of service element and disability element may be granted to an officer who is invalided out of service on account of a disability which is attributable to or aggravated by military service in non-battle casualty cases and is assessed at 20 percent or more.

b. The question whether a disability is attributable to or aggravated by military service shall be determined under the rules in Appendix II.

Reassessment of disability permanently below pensionable degree at the time of invalidation

48-A In cases where an Officer's disability or its aggravation at the time of invalidation is permanently below the pensionable degree, he may claim to be brought before a medical board within a period of ten years from the date from which he was retired. If the disability is still assessed as permanently below the pensionable degree, no claim for re-assessment shall be considered.

Officers who retire voluntarily

50. An officer who retires voluntarily shall not be eligible for any award on account of any disability.

Provided that officer who is due for retirement on completion of tenure or on completion of service limits or on completion of the terms of engagement or on attaining the prescribed age of retirement and who seeks pre-mature retirement for the purpose of getting higher commutation value of pension, shall remain eligible for disability element.

(Note: Regulation 50 stands abrogated with effect from 01-01-2006, for pre-2006 as well as post-2006 retirees)

Refusal to undergo medical treatment

51. Cases where an individual suffering from a disability accepted as attributable to or aggravated by military service refuses to undergo an operation, or other medical treatment, which in the opinion of the service medical authority would cure the disability or reduce the degree of disablement, shall not be treated as those of "aggravation or "retardation of cure" under regulation 118, but shall be dealt with as follow:

a. If the refusal to undergo treatment of an operation is reasonable, full disability pension normally admissible under the regulations shall be granted.

b. If the refusal to undergo treatment or an operation is unreasonable, pensionary award be regulated as under:

i. In case where the pension sanctioning authority in consultation with the Medical Adviser (Pensions) where necessary, decides that an operation or medical treatment will cure the disability, the disability element shall be withheld but the service element as per regulation 61, shall be granted.

ii. In case where the pension sanctioning authority in consultation with the Medical Advise (Pensions), where necessary, decides that an operation or medical treatment will reduce the disability to a lower percentage, the disability element of pension shall be restricted to that element which is appropriate to the lower percentage of disablement. If that lower percentage is less than 20 percent, then only the normal service element admissible as per regulation 61, shall be granted.

c. The question whether an individual's refusal to undergo medical treatment or an operation for his disability is reasonable or unreasonable shall be decided in accordance with the criteria contained in Appendix V to these Regulations.

Officers compulsorily retired on account of age or on completion of tenure

53. (1) An officer retired on completion of tenure or on completion of terms of engagement or on attaining the age of 50 years (irrespective of the period of engagement), if found suffering from a disability attributable to or aggravated by military service and recorded by service Medical Authorities, shall be deemed to have been invalided out of service and shall be granted disability pension from the date of retirement, if the accepted degree of disability is 20 percent or more, and service element if the degree of disability is less than 20 percent. The retiring pension/ retiring gratuity, if already sanctioned and paid, shall be adjusted against the disability pension/service element as the case may be.

(2) The disability element referred to in clause (1) above shall be assessed on the accepted degree of disablement at the time of retirement/discharge on the basis of the rank held on the date on which the wound/injury was sustained or in the case of disease on the date of first removal from duty on account of that disease.

Note: In the case of an officer discharged on fulfilling the terms of his retirement, his unwillingness to continue in service beyond the period of his engagement should not affect his title to the disability element under the provisions of the above regulation.

Manifestation of a disability after retirement

54. An officer who is retired otherwise than at his own request with a retiring pension or gratuity, but who, within a period of ten years from the date of retirement is found to be suffering from a disease which is accepted as attributable to his military service, may, at the discretion of the competent authority, be granted, in addition to his/her retiring pension/gratuity, a disability element at the rate appropriate to the accepted degree of disablement and the rank last held, with effect from such date as may be decided upon in the circumstances of the case.

(Note: The bar on disability pension for "own request"/voluntary retirement cases, stands abrogated with effect from 01-01-2006 for pre-2006 as well as post-2006 retirees)

Refusal to appear before a re-survey medical board

56. In case a pensioner who has been asked under any rule or order to appear before a resurvey medical board for reassessment of his disability, refuses to do so, the disability element of his pension shall be suspended from the date of such refusal. He shall, however, continue to draw service element.

Officers who have suffered from pulmonary tuberculosis or leprosy but are retained in service

57. An officer suffering from pulmonary tuberculosis or leprosy attributable to or aggravated by military service, who rejoins duty having been found fit for retention in service on completion of leave, but is retired therefrom on account of relapse of the disability during a period of five years from the date of rejoining, shall be eligible for a disability element appropriate to the degree of disablement as accepted on the date he/she was found medically fit for retention in service in addition to -

a. the service element of disability pension admissible if he/she had been invalided on the date immediately prior to that of rejoining duty, if more favourable.

b. the retiring pension based on the total length of qualifying service rendered upto the date of retirement.

If however he/she is retired from service on account of the relapse or the disability after a period of five years from the date of rejoining, the disability pension admissible shall be regulated by the normal regulations.

Period of grant of disability pension when the invaliding disability is *incapable* of improvement

60.A (a) If the disability is certified on the basis of an invaliding or resurvey medical board to be incapable of improvement, disability pension shall be granted for a period of 10 years in the first instance. During this period, the pensioner will have a right to claim re-assessment of his pension on the basis of aggravation, if any. Where the disability pension is modified as a result of reassessment, the pension shall again be granted for a period of 10 years from the date of the revised award provided the disability is still regarded as incapable of improvement. Each successive assessment at a higher or lower rates will be for a 10 years period during which the pensioner will be given an opportunity to have his pension reassessed on the basis of further aggravation.

(b) When the percentage of disablement has remained unmodified for period of 10 years, the pensioner shall be brought before Re-survey Medical Board at the end of ten years and in the event of the disability still being regarding by the pension sanctioning authority as incapable of improvement, his pension shall be sanctioned for life. Thereafter, no revision of pension will be admissible.

(c) In case where the invaliding disability is loss of limb, total loss of sight, loss of one eye, amputation, etc, and where the question of improvement/worsening of its physical conditions does not arise, the award shall be sanctioned for life in the first instance itself.

Period of grant of disability pension when the invaliding disability is *capable* of improvement

60.B Where the disability whether attributable to or aggravated by military service of an officer is considered as capable of change (improvement or deterioration), the period of the first award calculated with reference to the date of the medical board will be in the range of one to five years. The actual period of award in such cases will, however, be decided by the Medical Board having due regard to the circumstances/conditions of each case. The period of the award on resurvey will also be for a period ranging from one to five years and will be decided after taking into account the circumstances of each case.

When the disability is accepted at the same percentage on the basis of three consecutive medical boards including the release/invaliding medical boards, the disability will be normally accepted as incapable of improvement and regulated under the provision of Regulation 60-A and the award of disability pension/disability element shall then be sanctioned for a period of 10 years in the first instance.

Provided that, if in any case where the degree of disablement has been assessed at the percentage by the successive boards, but the medical authorities are not in a position to recommend that the disability is of permanent nature, the same may be continued to be assessed on temporary basis for such shorter periods as may be considered judicious on the merits of each case.

When disability is (or falls) below 20 percent

61. (1) An individual who is invalided out of service with a disability attributable to or aggravated by service but assessed at below 20 percent, shall be entitled to service element only.

(2) An individual who was initially granted disability pension but whose disability is re-assessed at below 20 percent subsequently shall cease to draw disability element of disability pension from the date it falls below 20 percent. He shall, however, continue to draw the service element of disability pension.

(Note: There is no minimum qualifying service requirement for 'service element' with effect from 01-01-1973. Even a single day's service qualifies for grant of service element)

Pension Regulations for the Army, Part-I, 1961, as they relate to Disability Pension for Ranks other than Commissioned Officers

Primary conditions for grant of disability pension

173. Unless otherwise specifically provided, a disability pension consisting of service element and disability element may be granted to an individual who is invalided out of service on account of a disability which is attributable to or aggravated by military service in non-battle casualty cases and is assessed at 20 per cent or over.

The question whether a disability is attributable to or aggravated by military service shall be determined under the rules in Appendix II.

Individuals discharged on account of their being permanently in Low Medical Category (LMC)

173-A. Individuals who are placed in a lower medical category (other than 'E') permanently and who are discharged because no alternative employment in their own trade/category suitable to their low medical category could be provided or who are unwilling to accept the alternative employment or who having retained in alternative appointment are discharged before completion of their engagement, shall be deemed to have been invalided from service for the purpose of the entitlement rules laid down in Appendix II to these Regulations.

Note: The above provision shall also apply to individuals who are placed in a low medical category while on extended service and are discharged on that account before the completion of the period of their extension.

Serious negligence or misconduct

175. If the disability of an individual is wholly or partly due to his serious negligence or misconduct, the amount of disability pension otherwise admissible may be reduced at the discretion of the competent authority.

Refusal to undergo medical treatment

177. Cases where an individual suffering from a disability accepted as attributable to or aggravated by military service refuses to undergo an operation, or other medical treatment which in the opinion of the service medical authority, would cure the disability or reduce the degree of disablement, shall not be treated as those of "aggravation" or "retardation of cure" under Regulation 118, but shall be dealt with as follows:

a. If the refusal to undergo treatment or an operation is reasonable, the full disability pension normally admissible under the regulations shall be granted.

b. If the refusal to undergo treatment or an operation is unreasonable, pensionary award be regulated as under:

    i. In case where the Pension sanctioning authority in consultation with the Medical Advisor (Pensions) where necessary, decides that an operation or medical treatment will cure the disability, the disability element shall be with held but the service element as per regulation 186 shall be granted.

ii. In cases where the pension sanctioning authority in consultation with the Medical Advisor (Pensions) where necessary decides that an operation or medical treatment will reduce the disability to a lower percentage, the disability element of pension shall be restricted to that element which is appropriate to the lower percentage of disablement. If that lower percentage is less than 20 per cent, then only the normal service element admissible as per regulations 186, shall be granted.

c. The question whether an individual's refusal to undergo medical treatment or an operation for his disability is reasonable or unreasonable shall be decided in accordance with the criteria published in Appendix V to these Regulations.

Manifestation of a disability after an individual is retired/discharged from service

178. An individual who is retired/discharged from Service, otherwise than at his own request, with a pension or gratuity, but who, within a period of ten years from the date of retirement/discharge, is found to be suffering from a disease which is accepted as attributable to his military service may, at the discretion of the competent authority, be granted, in addition to his pension/gratuity, a disability element at the rate appropriate to the accepted degree of disablement and the rank last held, with effect from such date as may be decided upon in the circumstances of the case.

(Note: The bar on disability pension for "own request"/voluntary retirement cases, stands abrogated with effect from 01-01-2006 for pre-2006 as well as post-2006 retirees)

Reassessment of the disability which is permanently below 20 per cent at the time of invaliding

178-A. In cases where an individual's disability or its aggravation at the time of invaliding is permanently below pensionable degree, he may claim to be brought before a medical board within a period of 10 years from the date of his discharge. If the disability is still assessed as permanent below the pensionable degree, no claim for re-assessment shall be considered.

Disability at the time of retirement/discharge

179. (1) An individual retired, discharged on completion of tenure or on completion of service limits or on completion of terms of engagement or on attaining the age of 50 years (irrespective of the period of engagement), if found suffering from a disability attributable to or aggravated by military service and recorded by Service Medical Authorities, shall be deemed to have been invalided out of service and shall be granted disability pension from the date of retirement, if the accepted degree of disability is 20 per cent or more, and service element if the degree of disability is less than 20 per cent. The service pension/service gratuity, if already sanctioned and paid, shall be adjusted with the disability pension/service element, as the case may be.

(2) The disability element referred to in clause (1) above shall be assessed on the accepted degree of disablement at the time of retirement/discharge on the basis of the rank held on the date on which the wound/injury was sustained or in the case of disease on the date of first removal from duty on account of that disease.

Note: In the case of an individual discharged on fulfilling the terms of his retirement, his unwillingness to continue in service beyond the period of his engagement should not affect his title to the disability element under the provision of the above regulation.

(Note: The bar on disability pension for "own request"/voluntary retirement cases, stands abrogated with effect from 01-01- 2006 for pre-2006 as well as post-2006 retirees)

Rank for assessment of disability pension

180. The rank for the purpose of assessment of service element and disability element of disability pension, shall be the substantive rank or higher paid acting rank if any, held by the individual, on any of the following dates, whichever is most favourable:

a. the date of discharge/invalidment from service, or

b. the date on which he/she sustained the wound or injury or was first removed from duty on account of a disease causing his disablement, or

c. if he/she rendered further service, and during and as a result of such service suffered aggravation of disability, the date of the later removal from duty on account of the disability.

Note: In the case of an individual who on account of misconduct or inefficiency is reverted to a lower rank subsequent to the date on which the would or injury was sustained or disability contracted, the rank for assessment of service and disability elements of pension shall be the rank held on the date of invaliding from service.

Recruits and young soldiers and boys

181. Recruits and young soldiers, and Boys, shall be eligible for disability pension at the rates and under the conditions applicable to a sepoy of the lowest group.

Individuals remustered from a higher to a lower group

182. The service element of disability pension in respect of an individual other than officer who was remustered from a higher to a lower group on being declared surplus after rendering 15 years or more of qualifying service may be assessed, where more favorable than the service element of disability pension otherwise admissible, on the rank and group held on the date he was declared surplus and the qualifying service rendered upto that date.

Period of grant of disability pension when the invaliding disability is *incapable* of improvement

185. (a) If the disability is certified on the basis of an invaliding or resurvey medical board to be incapable of improvement, disability pension shall be granted for a period of 10 years in the first instance. During this period, the pensioner will have a right to claim re-assessment of his pension on the basis of aggravation, if any. Where the disability pension is modified as a result of reassessment, the pension shall again be granted for a period of 10 years from the date of the revised award provided the disability is still regarded as incapable of improvement. Each successive assessment at a higher or lower rates will be for a 10 years period during which the pensioner will be given an opportunity to have his pension reassessed on the basis of further aggravation.

(b) When the percentage of disablement has remained unmodified for a period of 10 years, the pensioner shall be brought before Re-survey Medical Board at the end of ten years and in the event of the disability still being regarded by the pension sanctioning authority as incapable of improvement, his pension shall be sanctioned for life. Thereafter, no revision of pension will be admissible.

(c) In cases where the invaliding disability is loss of limb, total loss of sight, loss of one eye, amputation, etc. and where the question of improvement/worsening of its physical conditions does not arise, the award shall be sanctioned for life in the first instance itself.

Period of grant of disability pension when invaliding disability is *capable* of improvement

185-A. Where the disability whether attributable to or aggravated by military service of an individual is considered as capable of change (improvement or deterioration), the period of the first award calculated with reference to the date of the medical board will be in the range of one to five years. The actual period of award in such cases will, however, be decided by the Medical Board having due regard to the circumstances/conditions of cash case. The period of the award on resurvey will also be for a period ranging from one to five years and will be decided after taking into account the circumstances of each case.

When the disability is accepted at the same percentage on the basis of three consecutive medical boards including the release/invaliding medical board, the disability will be normally accepted as incapable of improvement and regulated under the provision of Regulation 143 and the award of disability pension/disability element shall then be sanctioned for a period of 10 years in the first instance.

Provided that, if in any case where the degree of disablement has been assessed at the same percentage by the three successive boards, but the medical authorities are not in a position to recommend that the disability is of permanent nature, the same may be continued to be assessed on temporary basis for such shorter periods as may be considered judicious on the merits of each case.

When disability is (or falls) below 20 percent

186. (1) An individual who is invalided out of service with a disability attributable to or aggravated by service but assessed at below 20 percent, shall be entitled to service element only.

(2) An individual who was initially granted disability pension but whose disability is re-assessed at below 20 percent subsequently shall cease to draw disability element of disability pension from the date it falls below 20 percent. He shall, however, continue to draw the service element of disability pension.

(Note: There is no minimum qualifying service requirement for 'service element' with effect from 01-01-1973. Even a single day's service qualifies for grant of service element)

Grant or re-assessment of disability pension when the degree of disablement increases

187. If, at any time, an increase which is properly referable to service factors occurs in the degree of disablement, a disability pension may be granted, or the pension already granted may be increased, to the appropriate higher rate, with effect from the date of the medical board on the basis of whose findings the competent authority accepts the higher degree of disablement.

Refusal to appear before a re-survey medical board

188. In case a pensioner who has been asked under any rule or order to appear before a re-survey medical board, for re-assessment of his disability, refuses to do so, the disability element of his pension shall be suspended from the date of such refusal. He shall, however, continue to draw service element.

23.3

Government of India, Ministry of Defence Letter No 1(2)/97/D (Pen-C) dated 7th February 2001

Sub: Modalities for implementation of the recommendations of the fifth central Pay Commission contained in Paras 164.10 and 164.22 of the report regarding the findings of the Medical Boards

Sir,

The undersigned is directed to state that in pursuance of the Government's decisions on the recommendations of the Fifth Central Pay Commission, as contained in paras 164.10 and 164.22 of the Report, sanction of the President is hereby accorded to the modifications, to the extent specified in this letter, in the rules and regulations concerning the findings of the Medical Board, attributability/aggravation and adjudication of cases for disability pension.

Injury cases

2. **Attributability:** Decision regarding attributability would be taken by the authority next to the commanding officer which in no case shall be lower than a brigade/sub area commander or equivalent.

3. **Assessment:** The assessment with regard to the percentage of disability as recommended by theMedical Board/ Release Medical Board as approved by the next higher medical authority, would be treated as final unless the individual himself requests for review.

4. **Approving Authority for Medical Boards:** Medical Board proceedings in respect of the personnel of the three Services will be approved by the next higher medical authority than the one which constituted the board as heretofore.

In case where disability is abnormally high or low, approving authority will refer the proceeding back to the medical boards for reconsideration. If required, he may physically examine/get the individual re-examined to ascertain the correct position.

Disease Cases

5. **Attributability/Aggravation:** Attributability in respect of cases pertaining to invalidment owing to various diseases/retirement with various diseases shall continue to be adjudicated by MA (P) in respect of Personnel Below Officer Rank (PBOR) and by MOD in case of Commissioned Officers as hithertofore.

6. **Assessment:** The assessment with regard to percentage of disability as recommended by the invaliding Medical Board/ReleaseMedical Board and as adjudicated byMA (P) in respect of PBOR and MOD in case of Commissioned Officers would be treated as final and for life unless the individual himself requests for review, except in cases of disabilities which are not of a permanent nature. In the event of substantial difference of opinion between the initial award given by the Medical Boards and MA (P), the case will be referred to a Review Medical Board. The opinion of the Review Medical Board, which will be constituted by DGAFMS as and when required shall be final.

7. **Re-assessment:** There will be no periodical reviews by the Resurvey Medical Boards for re-assessment of disabilities. In cases of disabilities adjudicated as being of a permanent nature, the decision once arrived at will be final and for life unless the individual himself requests for a review. In cases of disabilities which are not of a permanent nature, there will be only one review of the percentage by a Reassessment Medical Board, to be carried out later, within a specified time frame. The percentage of disabilities assessed/recommended by the Re-assessment Medical Board will be final and for life unless the individual himself asks for a review. The review will be carried out by Review Medical Board constituted by DGAFMS. The percentage of disabilities assessed by the Review Medical Board will be final.

8. There will be no charges in the procedure for handling appeal cases and post discharges claims.

9. The attributability/aggravation aspect for adjudication of Special Family Pension claim will be dealt with as follows:

   a. Injury Cases: As per provisions contained in Para 2 above

   b. Disease Cases: As per provisions contained in Para 5 above

10. The provisions contained in this letter will be applicable to service personnel who were in service on or after 1 Jan 96. The cases which have been finalized prior to issue of this letter will not be re-opened. As regards pre 1 Jan 96 disability pensioners, the assessment made by the Reassessment Medical Board held on or after the date of issue of this letter will be considered as final and for life unless the individual himself asks for a review. This review will be carried out by Review Medical Board constituted by DGAFMS. The percentage of disability assessed by the Review Medical Board will be final.

11. These rules will be read in conjunction with Pension Regulations of the three Services, Entitlement Rules to Casualty Pensionary Awards to the Armed Force Personnel, 1982 and Guide to Medical Officers (Military Pensions) 1980, as amended from time to time.

12. Paras 8.2 and 11.5 of this Ministry's letter of even number dated 31st Jan 2001 so far as these relate to reckoning disability actually assessed by the approved Release Medical Board/Invaliding Medical Board for computing war injury element, stand modified as per the provisions contained in this letter.

13. This issues with the concurrence of the Finance Division of this Ministry vide their U.O. No. 137/DFA (Pen-C) dated 1.2.2001.

Yours faithfully,
Sd/-
(Sudhaker Shukla)
Director (Pensions)

23.4

Government of India, Ministry of Defence, Department of Ex-Servicemen Welfare Letter No 1(2)/2002/D (Pen-C) dated 1st September 2005

(Note: Also see the amendment to this letter, that is, Chapter 23.5)

Sub: Restructuring of the stages of decision making for grant of disability pension/special family pension to Armed Forces Personnel/NOKs

Sir,

In continuation of this Ministry letter No. 1(2)/97-D(Pen-C), dated the 7th February, 2001 according sanction to the modifications to the rules and regulations concerning findings of the Medical Board, attributability/aggravation and adjudication of cases of disability/special family pension cases, I am directed to convey the sanction of the president to the following modifications to the said letter as indicated below:

Sl. No	Para No.	Existing Provisions	Modified Provisions
1.	2.	**Injury cases (attributability):** Decision regarding attributability would be taken by authority next higher to the commanding Officer who in no case shall be lower than a brigade/sub area commander or equivalent.	Decision regarding attributability would be taken by the following authorities: a. AG in Army and equivalent rank in Navy and Air Force in respect of disability pension of Brigadier and equivalent and above b. ADGPS in Army and equivalent in Navy and Air Force in respect of officers upto the level of Colonel and equivalent rank. c. OIC Records in Army, Navy and Air Force in respect of PBOR.
2.	3.	**Assessment**: The assessment with regard to percentage of disability as recommended by the IMB/RMB as approved by the next higher medical authority, would be treated as final unless the individual himself requests for a review.	No change

Continued...

3.	4.	**Approving Authority for Medical Boards:** Medical Board proceedings in respect of the personnel of the three Services will be approved by the next higher medical authority than the one which constituted the board as heretofore. In case where disability is abnormally high or low, approving authority will refer the proceedings back to the medical board for reconsideration. If required he may physically examine/get the individual re-examined to ascertain the correct position.	No change
4.	5.	**Disease Cases – Attributability/ Aggravation:** Attributability/Aggravation in respect of cases pertaining to invalidment owing to various diseases/retirement with various diseases shall continue to be adjudicated by MA(P) in respect of Personnel Below Officer Rank (PBOR) and the Service Headquarters in case of Commissioned Officers as hithertofore. The power for grant of disability pension to Commissioned Officers has been delegated to SHQ vide MoD Order No. 4684/Dir (Pen)/2001 dated 14th August, 2001.	Decision regarding attributability would be taken by the following authorities: a. AG in Army and equivalent rank in Navy and Air Force in respect of disability pension of Brigadier and equivalent and above. b. ADGPS in Army and equivalent rank in Navy and Air Force in respect of officers upto the level of Colonel and equivalent rank c. OIC, Records in Army, Navy and Air Force in respect of PBOR.
5.	6.	**Assessment:** The assessment with regard to percentage of disability as recommended by the IMB/RMB and as adjudicated by MA(P) in respect of PBOR and MoD in case of Commissioned Officers would be treated as final and for life unless the individual himself requests for review except in the cases of disabilities which are not of a permanent nature. In the event of substantial difference of opinion between the initial award given by the medical boards and MA(P), the case will be referred to a Review Medical Board. The opinion of the Review Medical Board, which will be constituted by DGAFMS as and when required shall be final.	Assessment with regard to percentage of disability as recommended by the IMB/RMB and as approved by the next higher medical authority in respect of PBOR and Service HQrs in case of Commissioned Officers would be treated as final unless the individual himself requests for a review except in cases of disabilities which are not of permanent nature. In the event of substantial difference of opinion between the initial award given by the medical board and approving authority, the case will be referred to Review Medical Board. The opinion of the Review Medical Board which will be constituted by DGAFMS as and when required shall be final.

6.	7.	**Reassessment of disability:** There will be no periodical reviews by the Resurvey Medical Boards for reassessment of disability. In case of disabilities adjudicated as being of a permanent nature, the decision once arrived at will be final and for life unless the individual himself requests for a review. In case of disabilities which are not of a permanent nature, there will be only one review of the percentage by a Reassessment Medical Board, to be carried out later within a specified time frame. The percentage of disability assessed/recommended by the Reassessment Medical Board will be final and for life unless the individual himself asks for a reviews. The reviews will be carried out by a Review Medical Board constituted by DGAFMS. The percentage of disability assessed by the RMB will be final.	No change
7.	8.	There will be no changes in the procedure for handling appeal cases and post discharge claims	The appeal shall be referred to the respective Service HQrs by the Record Offices for a decision.
8.	9.	The attributability/aggravation aspect for adjudication of special family pension claim will be dealt with as follows: a. Injury cases as per provisions contained in para 2 above. b. Disease cases as per provisions contained in para 5 above.	No change

Continued...

9.	10.	The provision contained in this letter will be applicable to service personnel who were in service on or after 1st January 1996. the cases which have been finalized prior to issue of this letter will not be reopened. As regards pre 1st January 1996 disability pensioners, the assessment made by the Reassessment Medical Board held on or after the date of issue of this letter will be considered as a final and for life unless the individual himself asks for a reviews. This review will be carried out by Review Medical Board constituted by DGAFMS. The percentage of disability assessed by the Review Medical Board will be final.	No change
10.	11.	These rules will be read in conjunction with Pension Regulations of the three Services, Entitlement Rules to Casualty Pensionary Awards to the Armed Force Personnel, 1982 and Guide to Medical Officers (Military Pension) 1980 as amended from time to time.	These rules will be read in conjunction with Pension Regulations of the three Services, Entitlement Rules to Casualty Pensionary Awards to the Armed Force Personnel 1982 and Guide to Medical Officers (Military Pensions) 2002 as amended from time to time. The said rules will be amended in due course.
11.	12.	Para 8.2 and 11.5 of this Ministry's letter of even no. dated 31st January 2001 so far as these relate to reckoning disability actually assessed by the duly approved Release Medical Board/Invaliding Medical Board for computing war injury element, stand modified as per the provisions contained in this letter.	No change

2. The decision in respect of disability and special family pension in respect of officers will be taken by AG/ADGPS, and their equivalent in Navy and Air Force, in consultation with Defence (Finance).

3. The next higher medical authority for the purpose of para 3, 4 & 6 mentioned at Sr. No. 2, 3 & 5 will be the authority other than the one which constituted the Board. In case where disability is abnormally high or low, the approving authority will refer the proceedings back to the Medical Board for reconsideration. If required, he may physically examine/get the individual re-examined to ascertain the correct position.

4. In all cases (excluding invalidment, war injury and corresponding pension to family members) the decision on the disability pension should be finalized before the terms of engagement of the official is completed or the official retires/discharged. Should the individual choose to appeal, the first appeal should also be finalized before the terms of engagement of the official is completed or the official retires/discharged. In all such cases, the appeal should be finalized within six months from the date of receipt of the appeal.

5. Disability/Special Family Pension claims arising in the following contingencies shall be referred to DGAFMS by Record Office/Service HQrs, for adjudication by Review Medical Board constituted by DGAFMS and the findings of the Board will be final:

i. Cases of substantial increase in the Invaliding Disease.

ii. Manifestation of Invaliding Disease after discharge/retirement within 10 years

iii. Claims for Special Family Pension arising after the death occurring other than on duty.

6. The provisions contained in this letter are applicable from the date of issue of this letter. The cases finalized prior to the issue of this letter will not be re-opened.

7. This issues with the concurrence of Defence (Finance) vide their U.O. No. 3490/Fin (P) dated 22nd August, 2005.

Yours faithfully,
Sd/-
(P.J. Mathew)
Deputy Secy to the Govt. of India

23.5

Government of India, Ministry of Defence, Department of Ex-Servicemen Welfare Letter No 1(2)/2002/D (Pen-C) dated 31st May 2006

(Note: This is an amendment to the letter in the last Chapter, that is, Chapter 23.4)

CORRIGENDUM

The following amendments are made to MOD letter No. 1(2)2002/D (Pen-C), dt.1-9-2005 regarding restructuring of the stages of decision making for grant of disability pension/special family pension to Armed Force personnel/NOKs:

i. Sl. No. 1 Para No. 2
In the column relating to "Modified Provisions" after the "following authorities", add the words" for the purpose of grant of war injury/disability pension or lumpsum compensation in lieu of disability/war injury element". In Para (a) after in respect of "War injury/disability pension or lumpsum compensation in lieu of disability/war injury element" should be added.

ii. Sl. No. 2 Para No. 3
In the column relating to "Modified Provision" replace to words "No Change" with the following "the assessment with regard to percentage of disability as recommended by the IMB/RMB and as approved by the next higher medical authority, would be treated as final unless the individual himself requests for a reviews. The approving authorities mentioned in para 2 above can also get the individual reexamined by a Review Medical Board, in consultation with DGAFMS, if in their opinion the assessment of percentage of disability made by IMB/RMB is abnormally high or low".

iii. Sl. No. 4, Para No. 5

a. In the column relating to "Modified Provisions" after the words "following authorities" add the words "for the purpose of grant of war injury/disability pension or lumpsum compensation in lieu of disability/ war injury element". In para (a) after in respect of "war injury/disability/war injury element should be added.

b. In the column relating to "Modified Provisions" after sub para (c) add the words "In case of doubt, the case will be referred to DGAFMS for advice".

iv. Sl. No. 5 Para No. 6

In the column relating to "Modified Provisions" the existing provisions be replaced by the following.

"The assessment and period of assessment with regard to percentage of disability as recommended by the IMB/RMB and as approved by next higher medical authority will be final unless the individual himself requests for a review except in cases of disabilities which are not of a permanent nature or approving authorities mentioned in para 5 have any doubt. In both the cases the individual will be re-examined by a Review Medical Board to be constituted by DGAFMS. The opinion of the Review Medical Board will be final."

v. Sl. No. 7 Para No. 8

In the column relating to "Modified Provisions" the existing para be substituted by the following.

"The first appeals shall be referred to the respective Service Headquarters by the Records Office for a decision by Appellate Committee on First Appeals. There will be no change in the procedure for handling second appeals and post discharge claims".

vi. Sl. No. 11 Para No. 12

In the column relating to "Modified Provisions" before the words "war injury element", add the words "disability element and."

vii. Main Para No. 4

The existing para 4 be substituted by the following:

"In all cases (excluding invalidment and corresponding pension to family members) the decision on the disability pension should be finalized before the terms of engagement of the official is completed or the official retires/is discharged from service"

viii. Main Para No. 5

The existing para 5 be substituted by the following:

"Disability/Special family Pension claims arising in the following contingencies shall be referred to DGAFMS by Records Office/Service HQrs for adjudication by a Medical Board constituted by DGAFMS and the findings of the Board will be final:

a. Cases of substantial increase in the disability claimed by an individual after invalidment/retirement/discharge.

b. Manifestation of any disability within 10 years of retirement/discharge".

2. This issues with the concurrence of Defence (Finance) vide their U.O.No. 112/DFA(P), Dated 30.5.2006.

Sd/-

(M.M. Singh)

Deputy Secretary to the Govt. of India

23.6

Government of India, Ministry of Defence Letter No 200847/Pen-C/72 dated 24th February 1972

Sub: Liberalised pensionary awards for war widows and war disabled servicemen.

Sir,

In partial modification of the existing rules and orders relating to the grant of special family pensionary awards and disability pension, I am directed to convey the sanction of the President to payments being made, as indicated in Annexures I and II to this letter, in the case of officers and personnel, as well as NCsE, of the armed forces (including the Army Postal Service and the embodied units of the Territorial Army) and officers and personnel of the Defence Security Corps, killed in action or disabled on account of injuries sustained in the recent operations against Pakistan commencing from 3rd December, 1971. The awards sanctioned in this letter will be admissible also in the case of the above categories of personnel killed in action or disabled on account of injuries sustained –

i. In the international wars of 1965 (including Kutch and Kargil operations), 1962 and 1947-48 (Kashmir operations), as well as the Goa and Hyderabad operations,

ii. (a) As a result of fighting in war-like operations or border skirmishes either with Pakistan on the cease-fire line or any other country,

(b) While fighting against armed hostiles like Nagas and Mizos,

(c) During fighting in service with peace-keeping Missions abroad,

(As per Min of Defence letter No. 195163/Pen-C, dated 16th Sept 1966)

iii. During laying or clearance of mines including enemy mines, as also mine-sweeping operations, between one month before the commencement and three months after the conclusion of the operations, as per Ministry of Defence letter No. A/14670/VII/AG/PS-4 (d)/142-S/Pen-C, dated the 2nd September, 1970, and

In operation 'Cactus Lily' beginning from 25th March, 1971, and the associated Naval operations beginning from 15th August, 1971 as per Ministry of Defence letters No. A/42128/AG/PS-3 (a)/1047/S/D (Pay/Services), dated 30th November 1971 and No. PA/3819/NHQ/1101/S/D (Pay/Services), dated the 10th December, 1971

Extended to clearance of mines including enemy mines and also mine sweeping operations occurring till 31st Dec 1977 vide Ministry of Defence Letter No A/42859/AG/PS4(d)/14/S/Pen- dated 31st Jan 1977

Extended to clearance of mines, including enemy mines occurring from 01 Jan 1978 to 31 Dec 1980 in J&K Hills Sector vide Ministry of Defence Letter No A/42859/AG/PS4(d)/29/S/Pen-C dated 18th April 1979

Extended to mine casualties occurring till 31 Dec 1983 vide Ministry of Defence Letter No A/42859/AG/PS4(d)/29/S/Pen-C letter dated 21st Oct 1981.

2. The benefits will be admissible with effect from 1st February, 1972 or the date of death or disablement of the serviceman, as the case may be, whichever is later.

3. Payments already made on account of pensionary awards only in respect of any period following the casualties otherwise than in accordance with this letter, will be adjusted against payments admissible thereunder.

4. The awards sanctioned in this letter are in the nature of a special dispensation and will not be subject to alteration as a result of any revision of the pay and pension structure that may be sanctioned in future. Temporary and/or ad-hoc increase in pension, sanctioned from time to time, will not be admissible in addition to these special awards. However, where and for long as awards admissible under the existing rules and orders happen to be more favourable than those sanctioned hereunder, the higher entitlements will be payable.

5. This issues with the concurrence of the Ministry of Finance (Def) vide their U.O. No. 565/Addl. F.A. (D) of 1972.

Yours faithfully,
Sd/-
(N.S.S. Rajan)
Deputy Secretary to the Govt. Of India

23.7

Government of India, Ministry of Defence Letter No 1(1)/85/Pen-C dated 26th March 1985

Sub: **Grant of Liberalized Pensionary Awards in respect of causalities of Operation "Meghdoot".**

Sir,

I am directed to say that the president is pleased to decide that the provisions contained in this Ministry's letter No 200847/Pen-C/71, dated the 24th February 1972, as amended from time to time will be applicable to the troops employed in Operation 'Meghdoot' in respect of casualties occurring on account of the following in addition to those occurring due to enemy action-

a. Avalanches.

b. Climatic and terrain conditions.

2. The provisions of this letter shall have effect from 28th March, 1984.

3. This issues with the concurrence of Finance Division of this Ministry, vide their U.O. No. 400/DFA/AC of 1985.

Yours faithfully
Sd/-
O.P. Bhatia
Under Secretary to the Govt. of India

23.8

Special Army Order 8/S/85

(Note: Also see the Chapters 23.9 and 23.38)

Casualties occurring between 1985 and 2003 are dealt with by Special Army Order 8/S/85, the relevant extract of which is reproduced hereunder:

Paragraph 4: Battle Casualties: Battle Casualties are those sustained in action against enemy forces or whilst repelling enemy air attacks. Casualties of this type consist of the following categories:

a. Killed in Action

b. Died of wounds or injuries (other than self-inflicted)

c. Wounded or Injured (other than self-inflicted)

d. Missing

Notes

1. Air raid casualties are those sustained as a direct or indirect result of enemy air raid. These will be treated as battle casualties.

2. Casualties in fighting against armed hostiles and those whilst in aid of civil power to maintain internal security are classified as physical for statistical purposes but are treated as battle casualties for financial purposes.

3. Casualties due to encounter with troops or armed personnel or border police of a foreign country, or during fighting in service with peace keeping missions abroad under Government orders will be classified as battle casualties.

4. Accidental injuries and deaths occurring in action in an operational area will be treated as battle casualties.

5. Accidental injuries which are not sustained in action and are not in proximity to the enemy, if these have been caused by fixed apparatus (e.g, land mines, booby traps, barbed wire or any other obstacle) laid as defences against the enemy, as distinct from those employed for training purposes and if the personnel killed, wounded or injured were on duty and are not to blame will be classified as battle casualties notwithstanding the place of occurrence or agency laying those, viz, own troops or enemy, provided the casualties occur within the time limits laid down by the Government.

6. Saboteurs, even of own country will be treated as enemy for the purposes of classifying their actions as enemy action, and encounters against them as encounters against the enemy.

7. All casualties during peace time as a result of fighting in war like operations or border skirmishes with a neighbouring country will be treated as battle casualties.

8. Accidental deaths/injuries sustained due to natural calamites (such as floods, avalanches, land slides and cyclones) or drowning in river crossings at the time of performance of operational duties/movements whilst in action against enemy forces will be treated as battle casualties.

9. Reports regarding personnel wounded or injured in action will specify the nature of the wound or injury and will also state whether the personnel remained on duty.

10. Reports on personnel missing in action will indicate if possible, their likely fate, e.g, believed killed, believed prisoner of war, believed drowned.

11. Casualties occurring while operating on the international border or line of control due to natural calamities and illness caused by climatic conditions will be treated as physical casualties for statistical purposes and battle casualties for financial purposes (Added vide Corrigendum to SAO 8/S/85 on 15 May 1991).

12. Casualties taking place while carrying out battle inoculation/training will be treated as physical casualties for statistical purposes and battle casualties for financial purposes. (Added vide Corrigendum to SAO 8/S/85 on 15 May 1991).

23.9

Army Order 01/2003

(Note: Also see the Chapters 23.8 and 23.38)

Casualties occurring after the year 2003 are dealt with by Army Order 1/2003, the relevant extract of which is reproduced hereunder:

Paragraph 4: Battle Casualties: Battle Casualties are those casualties sustained in action against enemy forces or whilst repelling enemy air attacks. Casualties of this type consist of the following categories:

a. Killed in Action

b. Died of wounds or injuries (other than self-inflicted)

c. Wounded or Injured (other than self-inflicted)

d. Missing

Paragraph 5: Circumstances for classification of Physical/Battle Casualties are listed in Appendix 'A'.

Appendix A to AO 1/2003

Battle Casualties

1. The circumstances for classifying personnel as battle casualties are as under:

    a. Casualties due to encounter with troops or armed personnel or border police of a foreign country or during operations while in service with peace keeping missions abroad under Government orders.

    b. Air raid casualties sustained as a direct or indirect result of enemy air action.

    c. Casualties during action against armed hostiles and in aid to civil authorities to maintain internal security and maintenance of essential services.

    d. Accidental injuries and deaths which occur in action in an operational area.

    e. Accidental injuries which are not sustained in action and not in proximity to the enemy but have been caused by fixed apparatus (e.g., land mines, booby traps, barbed wire or any other obstacle) laid as defences against the enemy, as distinct from those employed for training purposes, and if the personnel killed, wounded or injured were on duty and are not to blame, will be classified as battle casualties, notwithstanding the place of occurrence or agency laying those, viz, own troops or enemy, provided the casualties occur within the period laid down by the Government.

    f. Casualties during peace time as a result of fighting in war like operations, or border skirmishes with a neighbouring country.

    g. Casualties occurring while operating on the International Border or Line of Control due to natural calamities and illness caused by climatic conditions.

    h. Casualties occurring in aid to civil authorities while performing relief operations during natural calamities like flood relief and earthquake.

i. Casualties occurring while carrying out battle inoculation/training or operationally oriented training in preparation for actual operations due to gun shot wounds/explosion of live ammunition/explosives/mines or by drowning/electrocution.

j. Casualties occurring while carrying out battle inoculation/training or operationally oriented training in preparation for actual operations due to gun shot wounds/explosion of live ammunition/explosives/mines or by drowning/electrocution.

k. Army personnel killed/wounded unintentionally by own troops during course of duty in an operational area.

l. Casualties due to vehicle accidents while performing bonafide military duties in war/border skirmishes with neighbouring countries including action on line of control and in counter insurgency operations.

m. Casualties occurring as a result of IED/bomb blasts by saboteurs/ANEs in trains/buses/ships/aircrafts during mobilization for deployment in war/war like operations.

n. Casualties occurring due to electrocution/snake bite/drowning during course of action in counter insurgency/war.

o. Accidental death/injuries sustained during the course of move of arms/explosives/ammunition for supply of own forces engaged in active hostilities.

p. Death due to poisoning of water by enemy agents resulting in death/physical disabilities of own troops deployed in operational area in active hostilities.

q. Accidental deaths/injuries sustained due to natural calamities such as floods, avalanches, land slides, cyclones, fire and lightening or drowning in river while performing operational duties/movements in action against enemy forces and armed hostilities in operational area to include deployment on international border or line of control.

r. Army personnel killed/wounded by own troops running amok in an operational area.

s. Army personnel killed/wounded due to spread of terror during leave/in transit because of their being army personnel.

Physical Casualties

2. Deaths caused due to natural causes/illness/accident/suicide/murder due to family disputes in operational and non- operational areas will be treated as physical casualties.

Miscellaneous Aspects

3. a. Saboteurs, even of own country, will be treated as enemy for the purpose of classifying their actions as enemy action and encounters against them as encounters against the enemy.

b. Report regarding personnel wounded or injured in action will specify the nature of the wound or injury and will also state whether the personnel remained on duty.

c. Reports on personnel missing in action will indicate, if possible, their likely fate, eg, "believed killed", "believed prisoner of war", of 'believed drowned' etc.

d. Any casualty occurring during deployment/mobilization of troops for taking part in war or war like operation, will be treated as battle casualty.

23.10

Additional Directorate General Manpower (Policy & Planning)/MP5(D) Adjutant General's Branch, Integrated HQ of Ministry of Defence (Army) Letter No 12861/MP-5-D dated 1st April 2013

CLASSIFICATION OF CASUALTIES

1. Refer the following:

    a. GOI letter No 1(2)/G7/D(PEN-C) dt 31 Jan 01.

    b. GOI letter No 1(11)/2006-D(PEN-C)/PC dt 08 Sep 09.

    c. GOI letter No 2(1)/2011-D(Pen/Policy) dt 03 Feb 11.

    d. AO 1/2003/MP.

2. Classification of casualties occurring in any circumstances are guided by the provisions of the GOI letter, referred above and AO 1/2003/MP.

3. Troops are operating in difficult and adverse conditions and a large number of casualties are occurring. While it is the endeavour to ensure that the Next of Kin (NOK) are suitably compensated, there are a large number of cases where the PCDA (P) does not sanction liberalized family Pension, despite the fact that death occurred while performing bonafide operational duties. These are primarily because of misinterpretations & the Court of Inquiry does not include sufficient details. Certain instances which have come to light are as under:

    a. An area domination patrol out for more than 24 hours needs to establish a temporary operational base, patrol base or harbor for rest. Any casualties in the harbor would be a Battle Casualty. However, in the Court of Inquiry of one such case it was brought out that the individuals were sleeping in a dhok.

    b. Any operation terminates only once the troops are back in the barracks. However, many times the reports or Court of Inquirymention "returning after completion of operation", thereby giving the impression that the operation was over.

    c. All vehicle movement in Counter Insurgency Areas is tactical. However, in many instances words like Administrative QRT or such, give the impression that the movement is non-operational and only administrative.

    d. There are cases where an individual falls/slips while occupying a defiladed position. However this issue is not highlighted, thereby denying many such casualties their correct entitlements.

    e. All casualties in OP MEGHDOOT due to climatic and terrain conditions are entitled Battle Casualty status. However, this issue is not highlighted, thereby denying many such casualties their correct entitlements.

4. In case of any casualties, the following will be ensured:

    a. Correct and timely reporting.

    b. Speedy completion of Court of Inquiry, if required.

    c. Court of Inquiry is scrutinized by PCDA (P)/MoD, hence using authorized terminology is essential, it will be ensured that only technical terms are used while describing an operation.

d. Contact ADG MP/MP-5 for clarification of issues to be included in the Court of Inquiry.

5. ADG MP/MP-5 is the only authorized office to classify a battle casualty. Units/formation will only recommend the classification.

6. For strict compliance please.

Sd/-
(Udai Jawa)
Col
Dir MP-5 & 6
For Adjutant General

23.11

Government of India, Ministry of Personnel, Public Grievances & Pensions, Department of Pension and Pensioners' Welfare Letter No 45/22/97-P&PW(C) dated 3rd February 2000

OFFICE MEMORANDUM

Sub: Special benefits in cases of death and disability in service- payment of disability pension/ family pension- recommendations of the Fifth Central Pay Commission.

The undersigned is directed to say that the Fifth Central Pay Commission inter alias recommended that for determining the compensation payable for death or disability under different circumstances, the case could be broadly categorized in five distinct categories as under:

Category-'A'

Death or disability due to natural causes not attributable to Government service Examples would be chronic ailments like heart and renal diseases, prolonged illness, accidents while not on duty, etc.

Category-'B'

Death or disability due to causes which are accepted as attributable to or aggravated by Government service. Diseases contract because of continued exposure to a hostile work environment, subjected to extreme Weather conditions or occupational hazards resulting in death or disability would be examples.

Category-'C'

Death or disability due to accidents in the performance of duties. Some examples are accidents while travelling on duty in Government vehicles or public transport, a journey on duty is performed by service aircraft, mishaps at sea, electrocution while on duty etc.

Category-'D'

Death or disability attributable to acts of violence by terrorists, anti-social elements, etc, whether in their performance of duties or otherwise. Apart form cases of death or injury sustained by personnel of the Central Police Organizations while employed in aid of the civil administration in quelling agitation, riots or revolt by demonstrators, other public servants including police personnel etc. bomb blasts in public places or transport, indiscriminate shooting incidents in public, etc, would be covered under this category.

Category-'E'

Death or disability arising as a result of (a) attack by or during action against extremists, anti social element. etc. and (b) enemy action in international war or border skirmishes and war like situations, including cases which are attributable to (i) extremists acts, exploding mines etc. while on way to an operational area; (ii) kidnapping by extremists; and (iii) battle inoculation as part of training exercises with live ammunition.

2. The Fifth Central pay Commission recommended various relief packages for the above categories, in modification of the existing provision on the subject.

3. The recommendations of the Commission have been under consideration of the Government for some time.

Orders have already been issued regarding ex-gratia payment in case of death in service vide this Deptt. OM. No. 45/55/97- P&PW(C) dated 11.09.98. In respect of disability pension/family pension the President is now pleased to decide as under:

i. Cases covered under the Category (A) would continue to be covered under the normal existing provision of CCS (Pension) Rules.

ii. In cases covered under categories (B), (C), (D) & (E) the Scales of the family pension/disability pension would be as under:

I. FAMILY PENSION-FOR CATEGORIES 'B' & 'C'

(1) Distinction between widows without children or those with children, for determination of the quantum of Extra-ordinary family Pension shall stand abolished. The quantum of monthly extra -ordinary family pension for all categories of widows shall be:

a. Where the deceased Government servant was not holding a pensionable post-

40% of basic pay subject to a minimum of Rs 1,650/-

b. Where the deceased Government servant was holding a pensionable post-

60% of basic pay subject a minimum of Rs 2500/-

(2) In case where the widow dies or remarries, the children shall be paid family pension at the rates mentioned at (a) or (b) above, as applicable, and the same rate shall also apply to fatherless/motherless children. In both cases, family pension shall be paid to children for the period during which they would have been eligible for family pension under the CCS (Pension) Rules. Dependent parents/brothers/sisters etc. Shall be paid family pension one half the rate applicable to widows/fatherless or motherless children.

II. FAMILY PENSION UNDER CATEGORY 'D' & 'E'

(1) Family pension in cases, falling under categories D & E shall be determined under the existing provision of Liberalised Pensionary Awards Scheme.

(2) If the Government servant is not survived by widow but is survived by Child/children only, all children together shall be eligible for family pension at the rate of 60% of basic pay subject to a minimum of Rs 2500/- Children allowance, as admissible now, shall stand abolished.

(3) When the Government servant dies a bachelor or as a widower without children, dependent pension will be admissible to parent without reference to pecuniary circumstances, at the rate of 75% of pay last drawn if both parents are alive and at the rate of 60% if only one of them is alive.

III. DISABILITY PENSION - FOR CASES COVERED UNDER CATEGORY 'B' & 'C'

(1) Normal pension and gratuity admissible under the-CCS (Pension) Rules, 1972 plus disability pension equal to 30% of basic pay, for 100% disability.

(2) For lower percentage of disability, the monthly disability pension shall be proportionately lower as at present, provided that where permanent disability is not less than 60% the total pension (i,e, pension or service gratuity admissible under the ordinary pension rules plus disability pension as indicated at (1) above shall not be less than 60% of basic pay subject to a minimum of Rs 2500/-

IV. DISABILITY PENSION - FOR CASES COVERED UNDER CATEGORY 'D'

(1) Disability pension comprising a service element equal to the retiring pension and gratuity to which the employee would have been entitled to on the basis of his pay on the date of invalidation but counting service upto the date on which he would have retired in the normal course and disability element equal in amount to normal family pension subject tot he the condition that the aggregate of the service and disability element shall not be less than 80% of the pay last drawn, for 100% disability.

(2) For lower percentage of disability, the disability element shall be proportionately lowered as at present.

V. DISABILITY PENSION - FOR CASES COVERED UNDER CATEGORY 'E'

(1) Disability pension, comprising a service element equal to the retiring pension and gratuity to which the employee would have been entitled to on the basis of his pay on the date of invalidation but counting service upto the date on which he would have retired in normal course and disability element equal in amount to the pay last drawn subject to the condition that the aggregate of the service and disability elements shall not exceed the pay last drawn, for 100% disability.

(2) For lower percentage of disability, the disability element shall be proportionately lower as at present.

4. Other terms and conditions in the CCS (EOP) Rules and Liberalised Pensionary Awards Scheme which are not specifically modified by these orders shall continue to remain operative.

5. The Fifth Central Pay Commission also suggested certain procedural changes. These have also been considered by the Government. The President is now pleased to decided as under:

i. The extent of disability or functional incapacity shall be determined in the following manner for purpose of computing the disability element forming part of benefits:

Percentage of disability assessed by Medical Board	**Percentage to be reckoned for Computation of disability element**
Less than 50	50
Between 50 and 75	75
Between 76 and 100	100

ii. The findings of the Medical Board on the extent of disability would be treated as final and binding unless the employee himself seeks a review by preferring an appeal to an Authority immediately superior to the one who had constituted the Board. In case the appeal is accepted and a reviewMedical Board is constituted the findings of the Board would be binding on all parties. The extent of disability as determined and accepted would be treated as final and the employee would not be required to appear before Medical Board periodically for the purpose of obtaining a certificate that the disability continues to persist.

iii. Different department and offices shall have the powers to grant disability/family pension covered under the Government orders and instructions issued on the subject. They shall exercise these powers, wherever necessary, in consolation with the Financial Advisers. Only in cases not covered strictly in terms of the Government guidelines and instructions, reference to Department of Pension and Pensioner's Welfare shall be made.

6. These orders will be effective from 01.01.1996. The past cases of pre-1996 pensioners/family pensioners will be revised under this Dept's OM No. 45/86/97-P&PW(A)-Part-II dated 27.10.1997. Such consolidated pension, shall however, be subject to the provisions of the Deptt's OM No. 45/10/98-P&PW(A) dated 17.12.1998.

7. This issues with the concurrence of the Ministry of Finance, Department of Expenditure vide their U.O.NO. 20/E.V/ 2000 dated 6.1.2000.

8. In so far as employees of India Audit and Accounts Department are concerned, these orders have been issued after consultation with the C & AG of India. Sd/- (P.K. BRAHMA) Additional Secretary to the Government of India.

Sd/-
(P.K. Brahma)
Additional Secretary to the Government of India

23.12

Government of India, Ministry of Defence Letter No 1(2)/97/I/D (Pen- C) dated 31st January 2001

Sub: **Implementation of the Government Decisions on the Recommendations of the fifth Central Pay Commission regarding disability pension/war injury pension/special family pension/ liberalised family pension/dependent pension/liberalised dependent family pension for the armed forces officers and personnel below officer rank retiring, invaliding or dying in harness on or after 1-1-96.**

Sir,

The undersigned is directed to state that in pursuance of Government decisions on the recommendations of the Fifth Central Pay Commission, sanction of the President is hereby accorded to the modification, to the extent specified in this letter, in the rules/regulations concerning above mentioned pensionary benefits of the Commissioned Officers (including MNS) and Personnel Below Officer Rank (PBOR) including NCs (E) of the three Services, Defence Security Corps and the Territorial Army (hereinafter collectively referred to as Armed Forces Personnel).

1.2 The provision of the Pension regulations of the three Services and various Service instructions/Government orders which are not affected by the provisions of this letter, will remain unchanged.

PART-I
DATE OF EFFECT AND DEFINITIONS

2.1 The provisions of this letter shall apply to the Armed Forces personnel who were in service on 1.1.1996 or joined/ join service thereafter unless otherwise specified in this letter.

2.2 Where pension has already been sanctioned provisionally or otherwise in cases occurring on or after 1.1.1996 the same would be revised in terms of these orders. In cases where pension has been finally sanctioned under the pre revised orders and if it happens to be more beneficial than the pension becoming due under, these orders, the pension already sanctioned shall not be revised to the disadvantage of the pensioners.

Definitions:

3. *Reckonable Emoluments:*

3.1 Unless otherwise specified in this letter, the term 'Reckonable Emoluments' shall mean.

a. **For Officers:** Pay including Rank Pay, Non-practising Allowance, Stagnation Increment, if any, last drawn by the officer (Ref SAI 2/S/98, SNI 2/S/98 and SAFI 1/S/98).

b. **For Personnel Below Officer Rank(PBOR):** Pay including Classification allowance, Stagnation Increment, if any, last drawn by the individual. (Ref SAI 1/S/98, SNI 1/S/98 and SAFI 1/S/98).

3.2 In the case of individuals who opt/opted to continue to draw pay in the pre-revised scales beyond 31.12.95 and remain/remained in that scale till retirement/discharge/invalidment/death in harness pension/family pension and retirement/death gratuity shall be regulated in terms of Para 3.3 and 3.4 of Ministry of Defence letter No. 1(6)/98/D (Pen/Ser) dated 03 Feb 98.

PART-II
PENSIONARY BENEFITS ON DEATH/DISABILITY IN ATTRIBUTABLE/AGGRAVATED CASES

4.1 For determining the pensionary benefits for death or disability under different circumstances due to attributable/ aggravated causes, the cases will be broadly categorised as follows:

Category A

Death or disability due to natural causes neither attributable to nor aggravated by military service as determined by the competent medical authorities. Examples would be ailments of nature of constitutional diseases as assessed by medical authorities, chronic ailments like heart and renal diseases, prolonged illness, accidents while not on duty.

Category B

Death or disability due to causes which are accepted as attributable to or aggravated by military service as determined by the competent medical authorities. Diseases contracted because of continued exposure to a hostile work environment, subject to extreme weather conditions or occupational hazards resulting in death or disability would be examples.

Category C

Death or disability due to accidents in the performance of duties such as:

i. Accidents while traveling on duty in Government Vehicles or public/private transport.

ii. Accidents during air journeys

iii. Mishaps at sea while on duty.

iv. Electrocution while on duty, etc.

v. Accidents during participation in organised sports events/adventure activities/expeditions/training.

Category D

Death or disability due to acts of violence/attack by terrorists, anti social elements, etc, whether on duty other than operational duty or even when not on duty. Bomb blasts in public places or transport, indiscriminate shooting incidents in public, etc, would be covered under this category, besides death/disability occurring while employed in the aid of civil power in dealing with natural calamities.

Category E

Death or disability arising as a result of:

a. enemy action in international war.

b. action during deployment with a peace keeping mission abroad.

c. border skirmishes.

d. during laying or clearance of mines including enemy mines as also minesweeping operation.

e. on account of accidental explosions of mines while laying operationally oriented mine-field or lifting or negotiating minefield laid by enemy or own forces in operational areas near international borders or the Line of Control.

f. War like situations, including cases which are attributable to/aggravated by:

   i. extremist acts, exploding mines etc. while on way to on way to an operational area.

   ii. battle inoculation training exercises or demonstration with live ammunition.

   iii. kidnapping by extremists while on operational duty.

g. An act of violence/attack by extremists, anti-social elements, etc.

h. Action against extremists, antisocial elements, etc. Death/disability while employed in the aid of civil power in quelling agitation, riots or revolt by demonstrators will be covered under this category.

i. Operations specially notified by the Govt. from time to time.

(Note: See Chapters 23.13, 23.14, 23.15, 23.16 and 23.37 for additions to the above categories)

4.2 Cases covered under category 'A' would be dealt with in accordance with the provisions contained in the Ministry of Defence letter No. 1(6)/98/D (Pen/Services) dated 3.2.98 and cases under category 'B' to 'E' will be dealt with under the provisions of this letter.

Notes:

i. The illustrations given in each category are not exhaustive. Cases not covered under these categories will be dealt with as per Entitlement Rules to casualty pensionary awards in vogue.

ii. The question whether a death/disability is attributable to or aggravated by military service will be determined as per provisions of the Pension Regulations for the Armed Forces and the Entitlement Rules in vogue as amended from time to time.

iii. In case of death while in service which is not accepted as attributable to or aggravated by Military Service or death after retirement/discharge/invalidment, Ordinary Family Pension shall be admissible as specified in Min of Def letter No 1 (6)/98/D(Pen/Ser) dated 03 Feb 98 as modified vide Ministry of Defence letter No. 1(1)99/D(Pen/Ser) dated 7.6.99.

iv. Where an Armed Forces personnel is invalided out of service due to non-attributable/non-aggravated causes, Invalid Pension/Gratuity shall be paid in terms of Para 9 of Ministry of Defence letter No 1(6)/98/D(Pen/Ser) dated 03 Feb 98 as amended/modified vide Ministry of Defence letter No. 1(1)/99/D(Pen/Ser) dated 07.06.99

PART-III
FAMILY PENSIONARY BENEFITS IN ATTRIBUTABLE/AGGRAVATED CASES

5. Special Family Pension(SFP)

5.1 In case of death of an Armed Forces Personnel under the circumstances mentioned in category "B" or "C" of Para 4 above, Special Family Pension shall continue to be admissible to the families of such personnel under the same conditions as in force hitherto fore. There shall be no condition of minimum service on the date of death for grant of Special Family Pension.

5.2 The Special Family Pension shall be calculated at the uniform rate of 60% of Reckonable Emoluments as defined in Para 3 above subject to a minimum of Rs 2,550/- irrespective of whether widow has child(ren) or not. There shall be no maximum ceiling on Special Family Pension. Ministry of Defence order No. F. PC 1(2)/97/D(Pen-C) dated 22.9.99 stands amended accordingly.

5.3 In case the children become the beneficiary, the Special Family Pension at same rate (i.e, 60% of Reckonable Emoluments) shall be admissible to the senior most eligible child till he/she attains the age of 25 years or up to the date of his/her marriage whichever is earlier. Thereafter Special Family Pension shall pass on to next eligible child.

Notes:

1. Widowed/divorced daughters up to the age of 25 years or marriage whichever is earlier shall also be included in the definition of family for the purpose of Special Family Pension.
2. In case the eligible child is physically or mentally handicapped and unable to earn a livelihood, the Special Family Pension would be admissible for life to such a child subject to same conditions as in force hitherto fore.

5.4 In case of personnel below officer rank, the existing provisions of nominating anyone from the eligible members of the family (except dependent brothers/sisters) for the first life award of Special Family Pension and of transferring the same in full to the widow regardless of her financial position in the event of death of parents, where they were nominated as the original awardees, shall continue.

5.5 Families of SSCOs and ECOs who die under circumstances mentioned in categoy "B" & "C" of Para 4.1 above shall also be entitled to Special Family Pension as per Para 5.1 above.

5.6 Dependant Pension in respect of Officers (including MNS Officers, IA Officers & ECOs/SSCOs): Dependent pension shall be admissible to the parent(s)/eligible brothers and sisters (in the absence of parents) of the deceased Officers, who die under circumstances as mentioned in Para 5.1 above as a bachelor or widower without children, at a rate equal to 50% of notional Special Family Pension that would have been admissible as per Para 5.2 above.

Notes:

1. Condition as laid down in Para 5.3 above regarding age limit and marriage shall equally apply to dependant brothers/sisters for grant of dependent pension which shall be paid to the senior most eligible brother/sister at a time.
2. The condition regarding means limit was dispensed with vide MOD letter No. 1(5)/87/D(Pen/Ser) dt. 30.10.87. Status-quo ante will continue.

5.7 **Second life award in respect of PBOR including NCs(E)**

Second Life Awards (Special Family Pension) shall be admissible to the parent(s) of the deceased irrespective of single or both and in the absence of the parents, to the eligible brothers and sisters of the deceased, at the rates specified in Para 5.6 above and the condition specified in the note there under.

5.8 **Special Family Pension on Remarriage of Widow**: Special Family Pension on remarriage of widow, shall be regulated as follows:

(a) Commissioned Officers:

(i) If she has children:

(a.a)	If she continues to support children after remarriage	Full Special Family Pension to continue to widow
(a.b)	If she does not support children after remarriage	Ordinary Family Pension (OFP) equal to 30% emoluments last drawn to the remarried widow; 50% of the Special Family Pension to the eligible children

(ii) If widow has no children: Full Special Family Pension to Continue to widow

(b) PBOR:

(i) **If Special Family Pension is sanctioned to the widow-**
Same provisions as applicable to officers

(ii) **Where first life award is sanctioned to parents-**

(a.a)	If widow continues to support children after remarriage or has no issues	50% of SFP to parents 50% of SFP to widow
(a.b)	If widow does not support children after re-marriage but the children are supported by the parents	Full SFP to parents Ordinary Family Pension to widow
(a.c)	If children are not supported either by the re-married widow or the parents	50% of SFP to parents 50% of SFP to eligible children Ordinary Family Pension to widow
(a.d)	On death or disqualification of parents and the widow supports the children or has no issues	Full SFP to widow
(a.e)	On death or disqualification of parents and the widow does not support the children	Full SFP to eligible children Ordinary Family Pension to widow

6. Liberalised Family Pension (LFP):

6.1 In case of death of an Armed Forces Personnel under the circumstances mentioned in category "D" & "E" of Para 4.1 above, the eligible member of the family shall be entitled to Liberalised Family Pension equal to reckonable emoluments last drawn as defined in Para 3.1 above, both for officers and PBOR. Liberalised Family Pension at this rate shall be admissible to the widow in the case of officers and to the nominated heir in the case of PBOR until death or disqualification.

6.2 If the Armed Forces Personnel is not survived by widow but is survived by child/children only, all children together shall be eligible for Liberalised Family Pension at the rate equal to 60% reckonable emoluments as defined in Para 5.2. Liberalised Family Pension shall be payable to the child/children for the period during which they would have been eligible as in the case of Special Family Pension. The Liberalised Family Pension shall be paid to the senior most eligible child at a time. On his/her death/disqualification it will pass on to next eligible child. The provision of Para 5.3 (except rates) will be applicable here also.

Note: In view of the rationalization of Liberalised Family Pension and provisions on re-marriage of widow, Children Allowance will not be payable in addition to Liberalised Family Pension.

6.3 Families of SSCOs and ECOs who die under circumstances mentioned in category "D" and "E" of Para 4.1 above shall also be entitled to Liberalised Family Pension as per Para 6.1 above.

6.4 **Dependent pension (Liberalised) in respect of Commissioned Officers (including MNS Officers, TA officers and ECOs/SSCOs):** Where an officer dies as a bachelor or as a widower without children under the circumstances mentioned in Para 4.1 'D' & 'E' above. Dependent Pension (liberalized) shall be admissible to parents without reference to their pecuniary circumstances at the rate of 75% of Liberalised Family Pension for both parents and at the rate of 60% of Liberalised Family Pension for single parent. On the death of one parent, dependent pension at the latter rate shall be admissible to the surviving parent. In the absence of parents, dependent pension shall be admissible to dependent brother(s)/sister(s) if otherwise eligible at the rate of 60% of LFP.

Note: Condition as laid down in Para 5.3 above regarding age limit and marriage shall equally apply to dependent brother/sister for grant of dependant pension which shall be paid to the senior most eligible brother/sister at a time.

6.5 **Second life award (Liberalised Family Pension) in respect of PBOR including NCs(E):** Second Life Award in respect of personnel below officer rank who die under the circumstances mentioned in Para 4.1 'D' & 'E' above shall be regulated as under:

a. If the first recipient (other than the parents) of the family pensionary award dies/is disqualified earlier than 7 years (counting from the date of casualty), the award will be continued at the same rate to the parents as second life award, if still alive, for the balance of 7 years without any reduction. After the initial period of 7 years, the second life award will be continued at the rate of 60% of the Liberalised Family Pension.

b. Where the first life award was given to a parent and the widow remarries, the Liberalised Family Pension shall be regulated depending upon the period of widow's remarriage as follows:

   i. **If widow continues to support the children or has no children**: Widow will get family pension equal to Special Family Pension (i.e. 60% of liberalized family pension or reckonable emoluments) from the date of remarriage and the parents will also get family pension at the rate of 60% of liberalized family pension for the balance of 7 years if the remarriage of widow takes place during 7 years of casualty. After the period of seven years or where remarriage of widow took place after seven years, widow will get family pension @ 60% liberalised family pension and parents will get family pension at the rate of 30% of liberalised family pension. On death or disqualification of parents, widow will get family pension equal to the liberalised family pension for life.

ii. **If widow does not support the children**: Widow will get Ordinary Family Pension (i.e. 30% of reckonable emoluments) for life from the date of remarriage and the parents will continue to get first life award at the same rate (i.e. full liberalised family pension) for balance of seven years where remarriage takes place within 7 years of casualty, provided they support the children. Otherwise, the entitlement of parents will be equally divided between the parents and children. After the period of 7 years or where remarriage of widow takes place after seven years of casualty, parents will get family pension at the rate of 60% of liberalised family pension provided they support the children, otherwise it will be divided equally between the parents and the children. On death/disqualification of parents of deceased service personnel, the senior most eligible child will get family pension at the rate of 60% of liberalised family pension.

Note: Wherever children become beneficiary, the award will be continued for a period and subject to conditions as applicable for grant of Special Family Pension. Provisions of Para 5.3 above shall also apply.

6.6 **Liberalised Family Pension on re-marriage of widow**: Liberalised Family Pension on remarriage of widow, shall be regulated as follows:

(a) Commissioned Officers:

(i) If she has children:

(aa)	If she continues to support children after re-marriage	Full Liberalised Family Pension to continue to widow
(ab)	If she does not support children after re-marriage	Ordinary Family Pension at 30% to widow. Special Family Pension at 60% to eligible children.

(ii) If widow has no children- Full Liberalised Family Pension to continue to widow.

(b) PBOR

i. **If Liberalised Family Pension is sanctioned as first life award to the Widow**: same provisions as at (a) above shall be applicable.

ii. **Where first life award is sanctioned to parents**: The admissibility of Liberalised Family pension in such cases would be regulated as mentioned in Para 6.5(b) above.

PART-IV
DISABILITY/WAR INJURY PENSIONARY AWARDS

7. Disability pension on invalidment:

7.1 Where an Armed Forces Personnel is invalided out of service under circumstances mentioned in category "B" & "C" of Para 4.1 above which is accepted as attributable to or aggravated by Military Service, he/she shall be entitled to disability pension consisting of service element and disability element as follows:

(I) **Service Element**:

i. **Commissioned Officers**: The amount of service element shall be equal to the retiring pension determined as per Para 6.1(c) of this Ministry's letter No. 1(6)/98/D(Pen/Ser) dated 03 Feb 98. For this purpose the reckonable qualifying service shall mean the actual service rendered by the officer plus the full weightage appropriate to the rank held at the time of invalidment (except in the case of TA officers) as given in Para 5(b) of the Ministry's above said letter dated 03 Feb 98. There shall be no condition of minimum qualifying service having been actually rendered for earning this element, if otherwise due.

ii. **PBOR**: Service element will be determined as follows:

Length of actual qualifying service rendered (without weightage)	Entitlement of Service Element
15 years or more (20 years or more in the case of NCs(E)	Equal to normal service pension relevant to the length of qualifying service actually rendered plus weightage of service as given in Para 5 and 6 of Ministry's letter dated 03 Feb 98 *ibid*.
Less than 15 years (20 years in case of NCs(E)	Equal to service pension as determined as per Para 6.2(b) of Ministry's letter dated 03 Feb 98 but it shall in no case be less than 2/3rd of the minimum service pension admissible to the rank/pay group.

Note: The existing provisions in the case of PBOR regarding grant of service element equal to minimum service pension appropriate to the rank and pay group in case where service is less than 15 years (20 years in the case of NCs(E) and the disability is sustained in flying/Parachute jumping duty or while being carried on duty in an aircraft under proper authority shall continue.

(II) . (a) **Disability Element**: The rates of Disability Element for 100% disability for various ranks shall be as follows:

	Other Ranks	Amount p.m.
(i)	Commissioned Officers and Honorary Commissioned Officers of the three services, MNS, TA and DSC	Rs 2,600/-
(ii)	Junior Commissioned Officers and equivalent ranks of the three services, TA and DSC	Rs 1,900/-
(iii)	Other Ranks of the three services, TA and DSC	Rs 1,550/-

(b) Disability lower than 100% shall be reduced with reference to percentages as laid down in Para 7.2 below. Provided that where permanent disability is not less than 60%, the disability pension (i.e. total of service element plus disability element) shall not be less than 60% of the reckonable emoluments last drawn.

7.2 Where an Armed Forced personnel is invalided out under circumstances mentioned in Para 4.1 above, the extent of disability or functional incapacity shall be determined in the following manner for the purposes of computing the disability element:

Percentage of disability as assessed by invaliding medical board	**Percentage to be reckoned for computing of disability element**
Less than 50	50
Between 50 and 75	75
Between 76 and 100	100

8. Disability Element on retirement/discharge:

8.1 Where an Armed Forces Personnel is retained in service despite disability arising/sustained under the circumstances mentioned under category 'B' & 'C' in Para 4.1 above and is subsequently retired/discharged on attaining age of retirement or on completion of tenure, he/she shall be entitled to disability element at the rates prescribed at Para 7.1.II(a) above for 100% disablement.

8.2 For disabilities less than 100% but not less than 20% the above rates shall be proportionately reduced. No disability element shall be payable for disabilities less than 20%. Provisions contained in Para 7.2 above shall not be applicable for computing disability element. Disability actually assessed by the duly approved Release Medical Board/ Invaliding Medical Board as accepted by the Pension Sanctioning Authority, shall reckon for computing disability element.

8.3 Retiring/Service pension or Retiring/Service Gratuity as admissible as per Ministry of Defence letter No. 1(6)/98/D(Pen/Services) dated 03 Feb 98 shall be payable in addition to disability element from the date of retirement/ discharge.

Note: An Armed Forces Personnel who retires voluntarily/or seeks discharge on request shall not be eligible for any award on account of disability. Provided that Armed Forces Personnel who is due for retirement/discharge on completion of tenure, or on completion of service limits or on completion of the terms of engagement or on attaining the prescribed age of retirement, and who seeks pre-mature retirement/discharge on request for the purpose of getting higher commutation value of pension shall remain eligible for disability element.

9. Lumpsum Compensation in lieu of Disability Element:

9.1 In case a person belonging to the Armed Forces is found to have a disability which is sustained under the circumstances mentioned under category "B" & "C" in Para 4.1 above which is assessed at 20% or more for life but the individual is retained in service despite such disability, he/she shall be paid a compensation in lump sum (in lieu of disability element) equal to the captialised value of disability element on the basis of disability actually assessed (i.e. provisions of Para 7.2 above shall not apply). The rates of disability element for calculating capitalized value shall be as laid down in Para 7.1 (II)(a). The above rates shall be proportionately reduced for lesser percentage of disability. The age next birthday will be reckoned with reference to the date of onset of disability with loading of age, if any, recommended by the Disability Compensation Medical Board. Once a compensation has been paid in lieu of the disability element, there shall be no further entitlement to the disability element for the same disability under the provisions of Para 8 above. Such disability shall also not qualify for grant of any pensionary benefits or relief subsequently.

9.2 The provision contained in Para 9.1 above shall be applicable to casualties on or after 01 Jan 96.

10. **War Injury Pension on Invalidment:**

10.1 Where an Armed Forces Personnel is invalided out of service on account of disabilities sustained under circumstances mentioned in category 'E' of Para 4.1 above, he/she shall be entitled to War Injury Pension consisting of Service element and War Injury element as follows:

a. **Service Element**: Equal to Retiring/Service Pension to which he/she would have been entitled on the basis of his/her pay on the date of invalidment but counting service upto the date on which he/she would have retired in that rank in normal course including weightage as admissible. Provisions of Para 6 of Ministry of Defence letter No. 1(6)/98/D(Pen/Ser) dated 3.2.98 shall apply of calculating Retiring/ Service Pension. There shall be no condition of minimum qualifying service for earning this element.

b. **War Injury Element**: Equal to reckonable emoluments last drawn for 100% disablement. However, in no case the aggregate of Service Element and War Injury element should exceed last pay drawn. For lower percentage of disablement, War Injury element shall be proportionately reduced.

10.2 Provisions contained in Para 7.2 shall equally apply to individuals invalided out under the circumstances mentioned in category 'D' and 'E' of Para 4.1 above for calculating War Injury element of War Injury Pension.

10.3 Retirement gratuity admissible on invalidment due to war injury shall be calculated on the basis of reckonable emoluments on the date of invalidment but counting service upto the date on which he/she would have normally retired in that rank plus weightage as applicable (total not exceeding 33 years). Other provisions of Retirement Gratuity contained in Para 12.1 of Min. of Def. Letter No. 1(6)/98/D(Pen/Ser) dated 03 Feb 98 shall equally apply.

11. War Injury Pension on Retention in Service:

11.1 Armed Forces personnel who are retained in service despite the disability due to war injury sustained under circumstances mentioned in Category 'E' of Para 4.1 above, and retire subsequently will have an option as follows to be exercised with in a period as prescribed by the Government from time to time:

a. to draw lump sum compensation in lieu of War Injury element foregoing war injury element at the time of subsequent retirement/discharge, or

b. to draw war injury element at the time of retirement in addition to retiring/service pension admissible on retirement/discharge foregoing lump sum compensation.

11.2 **Lumpsum Compensation in lieu of War Injury Pension:**

In case an Armed Forces Personnel is found to have a disability which is sustained under the circumstances mentioned in category 'E' in Para 4.1 above which is assessed at 20% or more for life but the individual is retained in service despite such disability and opts for lumpsum compensation, he shall be paid the lump sum compensation in lieu of war injury element. The rates for calculation of lumpsum compensation in lieu of war injury element for 100% disability for life will be as under:

(a)	Commissioned Officers and Hony. Commissioned Officers of the three services, MNS, TA & DSC.	Rs 5,200/-
(b)	JCOs and equivalent ranks of the Air Force, Navy, TA and DSC.	Rs 3,800/-
(c)	Other Ranks/NCs(E) and equivalent rank of Air Force, Navy, TA and DSC.	Rs 3,100/-

For disability due to war injury of less than 100% the rates shall be proportionately reduced. The one time compensation in lump sum in lieu of War Injury element will be equal to the capitalized value of War Injury element which shall be calculated in accordance with Regulation 344 of the Pension Regulations for the Army (and similar corresponding provisions in the Pension Regulations for the Air Force and the Navy) and will be equal to the capitalized value of war injury element for the actual percentage of the disability at the appropriate rate mentioned in Para 11.2 above. For this purpose, the rank shall be the rank held at the time of injury sustained by the individual due to war. Age next birthday will be reckoned with reference to the date of onset of disability with loading to age if any, recommended by the competent Medical Board.

Compensation in lieu of war injury element will be payable provided the degree of disablement is equal to or more than 20%. Once the compensation in lieu of war injury element due to disability for life has been paid, there shall be no further entitlement on account of such a disability at the time of retirement/discharge from the Armed Forces. Since this is one time payment on account of compensation, no restoration will be permitted.

11.3 The provision contained in Para 11.2 above shall be applicable to causalities occurring on or after 01 Jan 96.

11.4 **War Injury Element on subsequent retirement**: Where an Armed Forces personnel is retained in service despite injury/disability sustained under the circumstances mentioned in category 'E' of Para 4.1 above and does not opt for lump sum compensation in lieu of war injury, he/she shall be entitled to the payment of war injury element on a monthly basis at the rates prescribed under Para 11.2 above on subsequent retirement/discharge or on completion of the term of engagement.

11.5 For disabilities less than 100% but not less than 20%, the above rates shall be proportionately reduced. No war injury element shall be payable for disabilities less than 20%. Provisions contained in Para 7.2 above shall not be applicable for computing war injury element. Disability actually assessed by the duly approved Release Medical Board/ invaliding Medical Board shall reckon for computing war injury element.

11.6 Retiring/Service Pension or Retiring/Service Gratuity as admissible as per Ministry of Defence letter No. 1(6)/98/D(Pen/Services) dated 03 Feb 98 shall be payable in addition to war injury element from the date of retirement/discharge.

Note: An Armed Forces Personnel who retires voluntarily/or seeks discharge on request shall not be eligible for any award on account of disability. Provided that Armed Forces Personnel who is due for retirement/discharge on completion of tenure, or on completion of service limits or on completion of the terms of engagement or on attaining the prescribed age of retirement, and who seeks pre-mature retirement/discharge on request for the purpose of getting higher commutation value of pension, shall remain eligible for disability element.

12. **Liberalised Disability Pension in respect of Armed Forces Personnel sustaining disability under the circumstances mentioned in Category 'D' of Para 4.1 above:**

Armed Forces Personnel sustaining disability under the circumstances mentioned in category "D" of Para 4.1 above shall be entitled to same pensionary benefits as admissible to war injury cases on invalidment/retirement/ discharge including lumpsum compensation in lieu of disability as mentioned in Paras 10 and 11 above. However, on invalidment they shall be entitled to disability element instead of war injury element in addition to service element. The service element will be equal to retiring/service pension to which he/she would have been entitled on the basis of his/her pay on the date of invalidment but counting service upto that date on which he would have retired in that rank in the normal course including weightage as admissible. Provisions of Para 6 of Ministry of Defence letter No. 1(6)/98/D(Pen/Services) dated 3.2.98 shall apply for calculating retiring/service pension. There shall be no condition of minimum qualifying service for earning this element. This disability element would be admissible as laid down in Para 7.1(II)(a) above. For lower percentage of disablement, this amount shall be proportionately reduced. However, in no case aggregate of service element and disability element shall be less than 80% of reckonable emoluments last drawn.

Note: Armed Forces personnel sustaining disability under the circumstances mentioned in Category 'D' of Para 4.1 above shall not be treated as War Disabled. Hence, they will not be entitled to any special concession/dispensation otherwise available to war disabled.

Constant Attendance Allowance:

13. Constant Attendance Allowance shall continue to be admissible under the conditions as hitherto fore. However, it shall be admissible at a uniform rate of Rs 600/- pm, irrespective of the rank.

PART-V
GENERAL

Rounding off of Pensionary Awards:

14. The amount of various pensionary awards admissible as per this letter shall be rounded off to the next higher rupee by the Pension Sanctioning Authorities.

Minimum/Maximum Pension:

15. If the amount of any monthly pension (excluding Constant Attendance Allowance) admissible under the provisions of this letter works out to less than Rs 1,275/- p.m., it shall be stepped up to Rs 1,275/- pm and authorized for payment at this rate. Disability element shall not be taken into account for the purposes of stepping up of service element to the minimum level of Rs 1,275/- pm. In cases where disability element is paid in isolation, it shall not be stepped up to the minimum level of Rs 1,275/- pm. There will be no maximum ceiling on the amount of pension.

Dearness Relief:

16. Dearness Relief shall be admissible only beyond average CPI 1510 on the revised pattern introduced vide Ministry of Personnel, Public Grievances and Pension, Department of Pension and Pensioners' Welfare Office Memorandum No. 42/2/97-P&PW(G) dated 27 Oct 97 on various types of pension/family pension admissible under the provisions of this letter.

Procedure for sanction of Revised Pension in respect of those who already retired:

17. The procedure for revision of pensionary awards as per provisions of this letter, in respect of those who have already retired on or after 1.1.96 and in whose cases pensionary benefits at pre-revised rate have already been notified will be prescribed by the Pension Sanctioning Authority and intimated to service Headquarters and Record Offices.

18. Pension Regulations of the three Services will be amended in due course.

19. This issue with the concurrence of the Finance Division of this Ministry vide their U.O. No. 299/Pen/2001 dated 31.1.2001.

20. Hindi version will follow.

Yours faithfully,
Sd/-
(Sudhaker Shukla)
Director (Pensions)

23.13

Government of India, Ministry of Defence, Department of Ex-Servicemen Welfare Letter No 1(11)/2006-D (Pen-C) PC dated 8th September 2009

Sub: Implementation of Government decision on the recommendations of the fifth CPC regarding disability pension/war injury pension/special family pension/liberalized family pension/ dependent pension/Liberalized dependent pension for the Armed Forces Officers and Personnel below Officer Rank.

Sir,

The undersigned is directed to refer to this Ministry's letter No 1(2)/97/D (Pen-C) dated 31.1.2001 in terms of Para 4.1 of which various categories have been enumerated for determining the pensionary benefits for death or disability under different circumstances due to attributable or aggravated cases. One of the circumstances enumerated under Category E (f) (ii) of the said Para is "Battle inoculation including exercises or demonstration with live ammunition". However, a doubt has been raised in regard to the nature of cases to be covered under battle inoculation training exercises. The matter has been examined in this Ministry and it has been decided that the term "Battle Inoculation Training Exercises" will cover the following two categories:

a. Flying operation involved in rehearsing of war plans and implementation of OP instructions inclusive of international exercises.

b. All Combat and Tactical sorties in preparation of war.

2. Cases already settled prior to date of issue of this letter will not be reopened.

3. This issues with the concurrence of Defence (Finance) vide UO No. 2360/Fin(Pen) dated 7.9.2009.

Yours faithfully,

Sd/-

(Harbans Singh)

Deputy Secretary to the Government of India

23.14

Government of India, Ministry of Defence, Department of Ex-Servicemen Welfare Letter No 1(11)/2006-D (Pen-C)/PC dated 15th March 2010

Sub: **Implementation of Government decision of the recommendations of the Fifth CPC regarding disability pension/war injury pension/special family pension/liberalized family pension/ dependent pension/Liberalized dependent pension for the Armed Forces Officers and Personnel below Officer Rank.**

Following four clauses may be added below Para 1 (b) to this Ministry's letter No 1(11)/2006-D (Pen-C)/PC dated 8th September, 2009-

c. Valley flying and missions involving operating at Ultra Low Levels.

d. All operational missions undertaken during peace like Special operations, Live ORP, Recce, Elint, Survey and Induction trials of new weapons.

e. Missions undertaken in support of troops and security forces deployed in forward areas.

f. Flying missions involving landings on the ALGs.

2. All other entries remain unchanged.

3. This issues with the concurrence of Defence (Finance) vide UO No. 30/Fin(Pen) dated 5.3.2010.

Yours faithfully,

Sd/-

(Malathi Narayanan)

Deputy Secretary to the Government of India

23.15

Government of India, Ministry of Defence, Department of Ex-Servicemen Welfare New Delhi Letter No 2(1)/2011-D (Pen/Policy) dated 3rd February 2011

Sub: **Implementation of Government decision on the recommendations of the Fifth CPC regarding disability pension/war injury pension/special family pension/liberalized family pension/dependent pension/Liberalized dependent pension for the Armed Forces Officers and Personnel below Officer Rank.**

Sir,

The undersigned is directed to refer to this Ministry's letter No 1(2)/97/D (Pen-C) dated 31.1.2001 in terms of Para 4.1 of which various categories have been enumerated for determining the pensionary benefits for death or disability under different circumstances due to attributable or aggravated cases. Certain references were received in this Ministry from Services HQs and Pension Sanctioning Agencies for clarifying various circumstances required to be covered under Category 'D' & 'E' of Para 4.1 of this Ministry's letter dated 31.1.2001. The matter has been examined in this Ministry and it has been decided to cover following circumstances under Category 'D' and 'E' of Para 4.1 of this Ministry letter dated 31.1.2001, as mentioned below:

Under Category 'D'

Death or disability arising as a result of-

i. Unintentional killing by own troops during the course of duty in an operational area.

ii. Electrocution/attacks by wild animals and snake bite/drowning during course of action in counter insurgency/war.

iii. Accidental death/injury sustained due to natural calamities such as flood, avalanches, landslides, cyclone, fire and lightening or drowning in river while performing operational duties/movement in action against enemy forces and armed hostilities in operational area to include deployment on international border or line of control.

Under Category 'E'

i. Death or disability arising as a result of poisoning of water by enemy agents while deployed in operational area in active hostilities.

2. Cases already settled prior to date of issue of this letter will not be reopened.

3. This issues with the concurrence of Finance Division of this Ministry vide UO No. 107/F/P/10 dated 28.1.11.

Yours faithfully,
Sd/-
(Malathi Narayanan)
Under Secretary (Pension/Policy)

23.16

Government of India, Ministry of Defence, Department of Ex-Servicemen Welfare Letter No 2(3)/2012/D (Pen/Policy) Vol-II dated 7th March 2018

Sub: **Inclusion of accidental death/injury due to natural calamities while performing operational duties/movements during deployment on line of Actual Control (LAC) under Category D of Para 1 Clause (iii) of Ministry of Defence letter No 2(1)/2011/D(Pen/Policy) dated 3rd February 2011.**

Sir,

The undersigned is directed to refer to this Ministry's letter No 2(1)/2011/D (Pen/Policy) dated 03.02.2011 vide which it was inter-alia decided to cover three new circumstances under category D of Para 4.1 of this Ministry's letter No 1(2)/97/D (Pen-C) dated 31.01.2001.

2. Following amendments are carried out under Category 'D' of Para 1 Clause (iii) of Ministry of Defence letter No 2(1)/2011/D (Pen/Policy) dated 3rd February 2011.

For: Accidental death/injury sustained due to natural calamities such as flood, avalanches, landslides, cyclone, fire and lightening or drowning in river while performing operational duties/movement in action against enemy forces and armed hostilities in operational area to include deployment on international border or Line of Control.

Read: Accidental death/injury sustained due to natural calamities such as flood, avalanches, landslides, cyclone, fire and lightening or drowning in river while performing operational duties/movement in action against enemy forces and armed hostilities in operational area to include deployment on international border or Line of Control or Line of Actual Control.

3. Cases already settled prior to date of issue of this letter will not be reopened.

4. This issues with the concurrence of Finance Division of this Ministry vide their ID No. 10(4)/2010/fin/Pen dated 01.03.2018.

Yours faithfully,

Sd/-

(Manoj Sinha)

Deputy Secretary to the Government of India

23.17

Government of India, Ministry of Personnel, Public Grievances & Pensions, Department of Pensions & Pensioners' Welfare Letter No 45/22/97-P&PW(C) dated 11th September 2001

OFFICE MEMORANDUM

Sub: **Special Benefits in cases of death and disability in service- payment of disability pension/ family pension- recommendations of the Fifth Central Pay Commission.**

The undersigned is directed to refer to this Department's OM of even number dated 3.2.2000 on the above subject. In para 6 of the above mentioned OM, it has been provided that the past cases of pre-1996 pensioners/family pensioners will be revised under this Departments OM dated 27.10.97 and such consolidated pension will also be subject to the provision of this Department's OM dated 17.12.1998.

2. The question of modified parity between past and present pensioners, covered under the Central Civil Services (Extraordinary Pension) Rules/Liberalised Pensionary Award Scheme, on the lines of benefits sanctioned for ordinary pensioners/family pensioners, has been under the consideration of the Government. It has now been decided that the revision of pre-1996 pensioners/family pensioners coming under this category would be done as under:

A. The past cases of pre-1996 pensioners/family pensioners will be revised under this Department's OM No.45/86/97-P&PW(A) (Part-II) dated 27.10.1997 as is being done hithertofore and the revised pension on the basis of the provisions of this OM worked out.

B. The benefits under this Department's OM No.45/86/97-P&PW(A) (Part-III) dated 10.2.1998 shall also be extended in the case of pensioners/family pensioners of these categories. In other words, the pay of the employee would be updated from one Central Pay Commission to the subsequent one, etc, and fixed notionally as on 1.1.1986, as if he was in service in that day, as per the procedure laid down in the OM dated 10.2.'1998. The pension/family pension on such notionally fixed emoluments would now be calculated by applying the rates applicable for each category of Extra Ordinary Pensioner/Family Pensioner and this would be further consolidated for fixation of pension as on 1.1.1996 by applying the usual procedure.

C. The pension/family pension shall also be calculated as on 1 1.1996 by applying the following procedure.

I. <u>Family Pension for Categories B & C</u>

a. Where the deceased Government servant was not holding a pensionable post:

40% of minimum basic pay in the revised scale, applicable from 1.1.1996, of the post last held by the employee, subject to a minimum of Rs 1,650/-

b. Where the deceased Government servant was holding a pensionable post:

60°/of minimum basic pay in the revised scale, applicable from 1.1.1996, of the post last held by the employee, subject to a minimum of Rs 2,500/-

In case where the widow dies or remarries, the children shall be paid family pension at the rates mentioned at (a) or (b) above, as applicable, and the same rate shall also apply to fatherless/motherless children. In both cases, family pension shall be paid to children for the period during which they would have been eligible for family pension under the CCS (Pension) Rules. Dependent parents/brothers/sisters, etc, shall be paid family pension one-half the rate applicable to widows/fatherless or motherless children.

II. Family Pension under Categories D & E

Family pension shall be calculated as the minimum pay in the revised scale of pay, applicable from 1.1.1996, of the last post held by the employee.

a. If the Government servant is not survived by his widow but is survived by child/children only, all children together shall be eligible for family pension at the rate of 60% of minimum basic pay in the revised scale, applicable from 1.1.1996, of free post last held by the employee, subject to a minimum of Rs 2,500/- .

b. When the Government servant dies as a bachelor or as a widower without children, dependent pension will be admissible to parent without reference to pecuniary circumstances, at the rate of 75% of minimum basic pay in the revised scale applicable from 1.1.1996, of the post last held by the employee, if both parents are alive, and at the rate of 60% if only one of them is alive.

III. Disability Pension for Categories B & C

a. Disability pension calculated as 50% of the minimum basic pay in the revised scale, applicable from 1.1.1996, of the post last held by the employee, to be reduced proportionately, if the employee did not have required qualifying service for full pension, plus disability pension equal to 30% of the same minimum basic pay, for 100% disability.

b. For lower percentage of disability, proportionate reduction would be made in the same manner as provided in the OM dated 3.2.2000.

IV. Disability Pension for Category D

a. Disability pension would comprise of a service element equal to 50% of the minimum basic pay in the revised scale, applicable from 1.1.1996, of the post last held by the employee subject to proportionate reduction in case his qualifying service up to the deemed date of retirement falls short of full qualifying service and disability element equal to 30% of the same minimum basic pay, subject to the condition that the aggregate of service and disability element shall not be less than 80% of the minimum basic pay in the revised scale, applicable from 1.1.1996, of the post last held by the employee, for 100% disability.

b. For lower percentage of disability proportionate reduction shall be made as provided in OM dated 3.2.2000

V. Disability Pension for Cases under Category E

a. Disability pension would comprise of a service element equal to 50% of the minimum basic pay in the revised scale applicable from 1.1.1996 of the post last held by the employee subject to proportionate reduction in case his qualifying service up to the deemed date of retirement falls short of full qualifying service and a disability element equal to the same basic day, subject to the condition that the aggregate of service and disability elements shall not exceed the minimum basic pay in the revised scale, applicable from 1.1.1996, for the post last held by the employee, for 100% disability.

b. For lower percentage of the disability, proportionate reduction would be made as provided in OM dated 3.2.2000.

3. After the revised pension/family pension has been calculated in accordance with the methods indicated in (A), (B) and (C) above, the highest of the three shall be granted as revised pension w.e.f. 1.1.1996.

4. All other terms and conditions contained in OM dated 3.2.2000 shall remain unchanged.

5. This issues with the concurrence of the Ministry of Finance, Department of Expenditure vide their UO No.355/E.V/2001 dated 26.06.2001.

6. In so far as employees of the Indian Audit and Accounts Department are concerned, these orders are issued in consultation with the Office of the Comptroller & Auditor General of India.

Sd/-

Sujit Datta
Director (PW)

23.18

Government of India, Ministry of Defence Letter No 3/57/2001/D (Pen A&AC) dated 11th April 2002

Sir,

It has been brought to our notice that Ex-Servicemen discharged/released from military service before completion of service tenure on medical grounds being in low medical category are not being considered as invalided out of military services and consequent benefits are denied to him, in case it is true, it is against the spirit of the rules and will cause undue avoidable hardship to the concerned. As per Regulation 173A of PRA 1961, Personnel below officer ranks who are placed permanently in lower medical category (other than 'E') and who are discharged because no alternative employment in their own trade/category suitable to their low medical category could be provided or who are unwilling to accept the alternative employment or who having been retained in alternative appointment are discharged before completion of their engagement shall be deemed to have been invalided out of service. It is clear from the above quoted rule that Ex-servicemen who are discharged/released from military service before completion of service tenure on medical grounds being in low medical category are to be considered as invalided out of military service. The following two specific cases are referred herewith wherein they have not been considered as invalided out of military service:

i. Ex Sepoy Raj Pal Singh of Jat Regt. No. 3177311, Your case No. G-3/VI/Misc/Jat/02 dt. 22.3.2002.

ii. Ex Sep. Suraj Mal No. 01099753H of Armoured Corps, the case was referred to your office vide our DO letter No. 3(58)/2001/D (Pen A &AC) dt. 12.7.2001.

Both these cases fall under the above category and they were discharged/released from military service before completion of service tenure on medical grounds being in low medical category. As such, they are to be considered as invalided out from military service and consequent benefits are to be given to them. The above two cases may kindly be reviewed and a report in this regard to be sent immediately by fax. These two cases are required to be submitted to Raksha Mantri.

Sd/-

(Parhlad Rai)

Under Secretary to the Govt. of India

23.19

Government of India, Ministry of Defence, Department of Ex-Servicemen Welfare Letter No 1(9)/2006/D (Pen-C) dated 30th August 2006

Sub: **Grant of disability pension in respect of non-regular officers released in low medical category.**

Sir,

I am directed to say that the issue relating to counting of full length of service rendered by Emergency Commissioned Officers/Short Service commissioned Officers in determining service element of disability pension to them has been under consideration of the government for quite some time. The President is pleased to decide that non-regular officer viz. Emergency commissioned Officers, Short Service Regular Commissioned Officers and Short Service Commissioned Officers, who are found in lower medical category at the time of release than the one in which they were recruited and whose disability is accepted as attributable to or aggravated by military service, will be entitled to service element of disability pension after taking into account the full commissioned service rendered by them as in the case of Regular Commissioned Officers. The rate of service element will be the same as admissible to the Regular Commissioned Officers. Since, non-regular officers have been brought at par with the Permanent Regular Commissioned Officers in the matter of grant of Disability Pension, there will be no requirement of exercising option by non-regular commissioned officers as earlier prescribed under Para 1 of this Ministry's letter No F. 210795/74/ Pen-C dated 30.11.1977. The Special Army Instruction No 6/S of 1965 and this ministry's letter No F 210795/74/ Pen-C dated 30th November 1977 will stand modified to that extent.

2. Service element of disability pension in respect of non-regular commissioned offices retired before the date of issue of these orders shall be revised prospectively in accordance with these orders. In the case of aggravation, the benefit of service element as per these orders will be applicable only to those who retire on or after the date of issue of this letter. Past cases will not be re-opened.

3. The PSAs concerned shall be required to work out service element of disability pension notionally as admissible from the date of commencement of pension and will be further revised/updated under various orders issued by the Government from the date of issue of these orders. No arrears, however, will be payable due to notional fixation of revised pension for the period prior to the effective date of these orders. No commutation will be admissible on account of additional amount of pension accruing as a result of revision under these orders. There will be no change in the amount of retirement gratuity already paid to the pensioners.

4. The pensioners shall apply for revision of service element of disability pension in terms of these orders as per enclosed proforma, to their respective PDAs, who will refer the cases to PSAs concerned for notification of the modified award.

5. These orders will be applicable from the date of issue.

6. This issue with the concurrence of Def (Finance) vide their U.O. No 01/fin/P/06 dated 30.8.2006.

Sd/-

(M.M. Singh)

Deputy Secretary to the Govt. of India

23.20

Government of India, Ministry of Defence, Department of Ex-Servicemen Welfare Letter No 16(01)/2002-D (Pen/Pol) dated 23rd March 2015

Sub: **Grant of Service element to pre-30.08.2006 released Non Regular officers in aggravation cases.**

Sir,

The undersigned is directed to refer to Para-2 of this Ministry's letter No 1(9)/2006-D (Pen-C) dated 30.08.2006 in which the benefit of service element of disability pension in respect of non-regular officers in aggravation cases was allowed only to those who retired on or after the date of issue of letter i.e. 30.08.2006 and past cases were not to be re-opened.

2. In partial modification of above provisions, the President is now pleased to decide that in the case of aggravation too, service element of disability pension in respect of non-regular officers would be calculated after taking into account the full commissioned service rendered by them as calculated in the case of Regular Commissioned Officers. As such, they would also be allowed the benefit of revision with effect from 30th August 2006 as allowed to attributable cases as per Government letter under reference. Para 2 of the said letter may be deemed to have been amended to this extent.

3. Terminal gratuity already paid shall be refunded as per existing orders.

4. All other conditions of the impugned letter remain unchanged.

5. This issue with the concurrence of Finance Division of this Ministry vide their ID Note No. 10(10)/2002 Fin/Pen dated 7th October 2014.

6. Hindi Version will follow.

Yours faithfully,

Sd/-

(Prem Parkash)

Deputy Secretary to the Government of India

23.21

Government of India, Ministry of Defence, Department of Ex-Servicemen Welfare Letter No 16(6)/2008/D (Pension/Policy) dated 5th May 2009

Sub: Implementation of Govt. decision on the recommendations of the sixth Central Pay Commission-revision of provisions regulating Pensionary Awards relating to disability pension/war injury pension/special family pension/liberalized family pension/dependent pension (Special/dependent pension (Liberalized)/special pension/invalid pension for the Armed Forces Officers and Personnel Below Officer Rank (PBOR) retiring/discharged/ invalided out from service or dying in harness on or after 01.01.2006.

Sir,

The undersigned is directed to state that in pursuance of Government decisions on the recommendations of the sixth Central Pay commission, sanction of the President is hereby accorded to the modification, to the extent specified in this letter, in the rules/regulations concerning above mentioned pensionary benefits of the Commissioned Officers (including MNS, Territorial Army officers, Emergency Commissioned Officers, Short Service Commissioned Officers and Personnel Below Officer Rank (PBOR) of three Services including NCs (E) of Air Force, Defence Security Corps and the Territorial Army (hereinafter collectively referred to as Armed Forces Personnel).

1.2 The provisions of the Pension Regulations for the three services and various Service instructions/government orders, which are not affected by the provisions of this letter, will remain unchanged.

2. **Date of effect**

2.1 The provisions of this letter shall apply to the Armed Forces personnel who were in service on 1.1.2006 or joined/ join service thereafter unless otherwise specified in this letter.

2.2 Where pension has already been sanctioned provisionally or otherwise in cases occurring on or after 1.1.2006, the same would be revised in terms of these orders. In cases where pension has been finally sanctioned under the pre revised orders and if it happens to be more beneficial than the pension becoming due under these orders, the pension already sanctioned shall not be revised to the disadvantage of the pensioners.

DEFINITIONS

3. **Reckonable Emoluments**

3.1 Unless otherwise specified in this letter, the term "Reckonable Emoluments" shall mean:

a. **For Officers.** Pay means pay in the pay band, grade pay, military service pay and Non-practicing allowance where applicable, last drawn by the officer (Ref SAI 2/S/08, SNI 2/S/08 and SAFI 2/S/08).

b. **For Personnel Below Officers Rank (PBOR)**. Pay means pay in the pay band, grade, military service pay, 'X' Group pay where applicable and classification allowance, if any, last drawn by the individual (Ref SAI 1/S/08, SNI 1/S/08 and SAFI 1/S/08).

3.2 In the case of individuals who opt/opted to continue to draw pay in the pre-revised scales beyond 31.12.2005 and remain/remained in that scale till retirement/discharge/invalidment/death in harness, pension/family pension and retirement/death gratuity shall be regulated in terms of Para 3.4 of Ministry of Defence letter No 17(4)/200892)/D (Pen/Policy) dt 12.11.2008.

4. War Injury Pension/Liberalized Family Pension shall also be admissible to such armed Forces personnel who die or are invalided out of service on sustaining injury during trials of indigenously developed weapon system and ammunition.

5. SPECIAL/INVALID PENSION

5.1 Special Pension to PBOR

The minimum service required for grant of special pension shall continue to be 10 years in case of Combatants and 15 years in the case of NCs(E). Where the service is less than 10 years in the case of combatants and less than 15 years in the case of NCs(E), special gratuity will continue to be admissible.

5.2 Invalid Pension

The minimum service required for grant of Invalid pension will continue to be 10 years and shall be computed as per Para 6 of this Ministry's letter dated 12.11.2008. Where service is less than 10 years, invalid gratuity will be admissible.

6. DISABILITY/WAR INJURY/LIBERALIZED DISABILTY PENSION ON INVALIDMENT

6.1 As hithertofore, Disability/War Injury/Liberalized Disability pension in invalidment cases will consist of service element and disability/war injury element and shall continue to be admissible under the provisions laid down in Para 7, 10 and 12 of this Ministry's letter No 1(2)/97/D (Pen-C) dated 31.1.2001 respectively, subject to the amount to be arrived at in the manner and at the rates specified in the succeeding paras.

6.2 Service Element of Disability/Liberalized Disability/War Injury Pension.

The amount of service element shall be equal to retiring/service pension determined as per Para 6 of this Ministry's letter No 17(4)/200892)/D (Pension/Policy) dated 12.11.2006 subject to minimum of Rs 3,500/- per month. There shall be no condition of minimum qualifying service having been actually rendered for earning this element, if otherwise admissible.

6.3 Disability Element of Disability Pension/Liberalized Disability Pension.

The rates of disability element for 100% disability for various ranks shall be 30% of emoluments last drawn subject to minimum of Rs 3,500/- per month for 100% disability. For disability less than 100%, it shall be reduced proportionately. In cases of disability pension where permanent disabilty is not less than 60%, the disability pension (i.e. total of service element plus disability element) shall not be less than 60% of the reckonable emoluments last drawn subject to a minimum of Rs 7,000/- per month.

6.4 War Injury Element of War Injury Pension

The rates of War Injury Element for 100% disability for various ranks shall be equal to the reckonable emoluments last drawn which would be proportionately reduced where disability is less than 100%. However, in no case aggregate of service element and war injury element should exceed the emoluments last drawn.

6.5. The provisions of Para 7.2 of this Ministry's letter No 1(2)/97/D (Pen-C) dated 31.1.2001 for reckoning of disability or functional incapacity shall continue for the purpose of computing disability element/war injury element.

7. DISABILITY/WAR INJURY ELEMENT/LIBERALIZED DISABILITY ELEMENT ON RETIREMENT/ DISCHARGE

7.1 Disability Element/War Injury Element/Liberalized Disability Element on retirement/discharge from service shall continue to be regulated under the provisions of Para 8, 11 and 12 respectively of this Ministry's letter No. 1(2)/97/D (Pen-C) dated 31.1.2001 at the rates given below:

a. Disability Element/Liberalized Disability Element shall be admissible at the rate mentioned in Para 6.3 above; and

b. War Injury shall be admissible @ 60% of reckonable emoluments last drawn subject to minimum of Rs 6,200/- per month for 100% disability. For disability of less than 100%, the War Injury Element shall be proportionately reduced.

7.2 Retiring/Service Pension or Retiring/Service Gratuity, as admissible, will be paid in addition to disability element/ War Injury element from the date of retirement/discharge.

7.3 The aggregate of service element and liberalized disability element shall not be less than 80% of the reckonable emoluments last drawn.

7.4 However, in no case the aggregate of service element and war injury element should exceed emoluments last drawn.

8. CONSTANT ATTENDANCE ALLOWANCE

Constant Attendance Allowance shall continue to be admissible under the conditions as hithertofore. However, it shall be admissible at a uniform rate of Rs 3,000/- per month, irrespective of the rank. Further this rate be increased by 25% every time the dearness allowance payable on revised pay band goes up by 50%.

9. SPECIAL/LIBERALIZED FAMILY PENSION/DEPENDENT PENSION (SPECIAL)/DEPENDENT PENSION (LIBERALIZED)

9.1 Special Family Pension, Liberalized Family Pension, Dependent Pension (Special)/Dependent Pension (Liberalized)/2nd life award (in respect of PBOR including NCs(E), shall continue to be regulated at the rates and under the conditions laid down in this Ministry's letter No. 1(2)/97/D (Pen-C) dated 31.01.2001 subject to the reckonable emoluments as defined under Para 3 of this Ministry's letter No 1794)/2008(2)/D (Pen/Policy) dated 12.11.2008.

9.2 The amount of special family pension admissible to the families of Armed Forces personnel under the circumstances prescribed under category 'B' & 'C' of Para 4.1 of this Ministry's letter dated 31.1.2001, will be subject to a minimum of Rs 7,000/- per month.

9.3 The amount of liberalized family pension, admissible to the child/children of armed Forces personnel under the circumstances prescribed under category 'D' & 'E' of Para 4.1 and 6.2 of this Ministry's letter dated 31.1.2001, will be subject to a minimum of Rs 7,000/- per month.

GENERAL

10. Rounding off of Pensionary Awards

The amount of various pensionary awards admissible as per this letter shall be rounded off to the next higher rupee by the Pension Sanctioning Authority.

11. MINIMUM/MAXIMUM PENSION

If the amount of any monthly pension (excluding Constant Attendance Allowance) admissible under the provisions of this letter works out to less than Rs 3,000/- p.m., it shall be stepped up to Rs 3500/- pm and authorized for payment at this rate. Disability element shall not be taken into account for the purpose of **stepping up of service element to** the minimum level of Rs 3,500/- pm. There will be no maximum ceiling on the amount of pension determined under these orders.

12. **DEARNESS RELIEF**

Dearness relief shall be admissible only beyond average AICPI 536 (Base year 1982 = 100) on the revised pattern introduced vide Ministry of Personnel, public Grievances and Pension, Department of pension and Pensioners, Welfare Office Memorandum No. 42/2/2008-P&PW(G) dated 12.09.2008 on various type of pension/family pension admissible under the provisions of this letter.

13. **Procedure for sanction of Revised Pension in respect of those already retired.**

The procedure for revision of pensionary awards as per provisions of this letter, in respect of Armed Forces personnel who have already retired/discharged/invalided out/died on or after 1.1.2006 and in whose cases pensionary benefits at pre-revised rates have already been notified, the Record Offices concerned in case of PBOR and CDA (O), Pune/ Naval pay Office Mumbai/AFCAO, New Delhi, as the case may be, in respect of Commissioned Officers, will initiate and forward revised LPC-Cum-Data sheet as prescribed by PCDA (Pension) Allahabad to their respective Pension Sanctioning Authorities (PSAs) for issue of corrigendum PPOs notifying the revised pensionary awards. Further implementation instructions to all concerned will be issued by PCDA (Pensions) Allahabad immediately on receipt of these orders.

14. Relevant provisions of the Pension Regulations for the three Services will be amended in due course.

15. This issue with the concurrence of the Finance Division of this Ministry vide their UO No. 1527/09/D (Fin/Pen) dated 27.4.2009.

Yours faithfully,
Sd/-
(Harbans Singh)
Deputy Secretary to the Government of India

23.22

Government of India, Ministry of Defence, Department of Ex-Servicemen Welfare Letter No 17(4)/2008/(I)/D (Pen/Policy)/-Vol-V dated 15th February 2011

Sub: Rationalization of Casualty Pensionary Awards for the Armed Forces Officers and Personnel Below Officer Rank (PBOR) – Special benefits in cases of death and disability in service prior to 1.1.2006 – reg.

Sir,

The undersigned is directed to refer to this Ministry letter No 17(4)/2008(1)/D (Pen/Policy) dated 11.11.2008 and No 16(6)/2008(1)/D (Pen/Policy) dated 4.05.2009, issued in implementation of the Government decision on the recommendations of Sixth CPC for revision of Disability/Liberalized Disability/War Injury pension and Special Family Pension/Dependent pension (special)/Liberalized family pension/Dependent pension (Liberalized)/2nd life award (in case of PBOR) for the Armed Forces Officers and Personnel Below Officer Rank (PBOR) retired/discharged/died/ invalided out from service prior to 1.1.2006.

2. The question of grant of modified parity between pre-2006 and post-2006 armed Forces pensioners drawing pension under casualty pensionary awards has been under consideration of the Government for quite some time. the President is pleased to decide the following provisions mentioned in succeeding Paragraphs for revision of pension/ family pension for pre-2006 Armed Forces pensioners/family pensioners drawing pension under casualty pensionary awards:

<u>Special Family Pension</u>

3. The special family pension revised in terms of this Ministry's letter dated 11.11.2008 read with letter dated 4.5.2009, shall not be less than 60% of the minimum of the pay in the pay band plus Grade pay, Military service pay, 'X' Group pay where applicable/minimum of pay in case of HAG and above pay scales, in the revised pay structure introduced from 1.1.2006 corresponding to the pre-revised scale held by the deceased Armed Forces personnel at the time of death, subject to a minimum of Rs 7,000/- per month.

<u>Dependent Pension (Special)</u>

4. The dependent pension (special) revised in terms of this Ministry's letter dated 11.11.2008 read with letter dated 4.5.2009, shall not be less than 50% of the special family pension worked out based on 60% of the minimum of the pay I the pay band plus Grade pay, Military Service pay, 'X' Group pay where applicable/minimum of pay in case of HAG and above pay scales, in the revised pay structure introduced from 1.1.2006 corresponding to the pre-revised scale held by the deceased Armed Force personnel at the time of death, subject to a minimum of Rs 3,500/- per month.

<u>Second Life Award (Special Family Pension) in respect of PBOR including Non combatants (Enrolled)</u>

5. The second life award (special family pension) revised in terms of this Ministry's letter dated 11.11.2008 read with letter dated 4.5.2009, shall not be less than 50% of the special family pension worked out based on 60% of the minimum of the pay in the pay band plus Grade pay, Military Service pay, 'X' Group pay where applicable in the revised pay structure introduced from 1.1.2006 corresponding to the pre-revised scale held by the deceased Armed Force personnel at the time of death, subject to a minimum of Rs 3,500/- per month.

Liberalized Family Pension

6. The liberalized family pension revised in terms of this Ministry's letter dated 11.11.2008 read with letter dated 4.5.2009, shall not be less than the minimum of the pay in the pay band plus Grade pay, Military Service pay, 'X' Group pay where applicable/minimum of pay in case of HAG and above pay scales, in the revised pay structure introduced from 1.1.2006 corresponding to the pre-revised scale held by the deceased Armed Forces personnel at the time of death.

6.1 In case where child/children of an Armed Force personnel is in receipt of liberalized family pension, the revised pension of all children together in terms of this Ministry's letter dated 11.11.2008 read with letter dated 4.5.2009, shall not be less than 60% of the minimum of the pay in the pay band plus Grade pay, Military Service pay, 'X' Group pay where applicable/minimum of pay in case of HAG and above pay scales, in the revised pay structure introduce from 1.1.2006 corresponding to the pre-revised scale held by the deceased Armed Force personnel at the time of death, subject to a minimum of Rs 7,000/- per month.

Dependent Pension (Liberalized)

7. The dependent pension (liberalized) revised in terms of this Ministry's letter dated 11.11.2008 read with letter dated 4.5.2009, shall not be less than 75% (in case both parents are alive) and 60% (in case of single parent/dependent brother (s) and sister(s)) of the minimum of the pay in the pay band plus Grade pay, Military Service pay, 'X' Group pay where applicable/minimum of pay in case of HAG and above pay scales, in the revised pay structure introduced from 1.1.2006 corresponding to the pre-revised scale held by the deceased Armed Force personnel at the time of death.

Second Life Award (Liberalized family pension) in respect of PBOR including Non combatants (Enrolled)

8. The second life award (liberalized family pension) revised in terms of this Ministry's letter dated 11.11.2008 read with letter dated 4.5.2009, shall not be less than 60% of the Liberalized family pension worked out based on the minimum of the pay in the pay band plus Grade pay, Military Service pay, 'X' Group pay where applicable/minimum of pay in case of HAG and above pay scales, in the revised pay structure introduced from 1.1.2006 corresponding to the pre-revised scale held by the deceased Armed Force personnel at the time of death.

Disability Pension

9. The disability element in terms of Para 2.2. of this Ministry's letter dated 4.5.2009, shall not be less than 30% of minimum of the pay in the pay band plus Grade pay, Military Service pay, 'X' Group pay where applicable in the revised pay structure introduced from 1.1.2006 corresponding to the pre-revised scale held by the deceased Armed Force personnel at the time of retirement/discharge/invalidment for 100% disability.

9.1 For disability less than 100%, the disability element shall be proportionately reduced as per the period and degree of disability already accepted.

9.2 In cases where permanent disability is not less than 60%, the disability pension i.e. total of service element revised in terms Para 2.1 of this Ministry's letter dated 4.5.2009 plus disability element shall not be less than 60% of minimum of the pay in the pay band plus Grade pay, Military Service pay, 'X' Group pay where applicable/minimum of pay in case of HAG and above pay scales, in the revised pay structure introduced from 1.1.2006 corresponding to the pre-revised scale held by the Armed Force personnel at the time of retirement/discharge/invalidment, subject to minimum of Rs 7,000/- per month.

Liberalized Disability Pension

10. The disability element in terms of Para 2.2. of this Ministry's letter dated 4.5.2009, shall not be less than 30% of minimum of the pay in the pay band plus Grade pay, Military Service pay, 'X' Group pay where applicable/minimum of

pay in case of HAG and above pay scales, in the revised pay structure introduced from 1.1.2006 corresponding to the pre-revised scale held by the Armed Forces personnel at the time of retirement/discharge/invalidment for 100% disability.

10.1 For disability less than 100%, the disability element shall be proportionately reduced as per the period and degree of disability already accepted. However, in no case the revised liberalized disability pension (i.e. aggregate of service element revised in terms Para 2.1 of this Ministry's letter dated 4.5.2009 plus disability element) shall be less than 80% of the minimum of the pay in the pay band plus Grade pay, Military Service pay, 'X' Group pay where applicable/minimum of pay in case of HAG and above pay scales, in the revised pay structure introduced from 1.1.2006 corresponding to the pre-revised scale held by the Armed Forces personnel at the time of retirement/ discharge/invalidment.

War Injury Pension

11. The rates of war injury element revised in terms of Para 2.3 of this Ministry's letter dated 4.5.2009, shall not be less than 100% in case of invalidment and 60% in case of retirement/discharge, of minimum of the pay in the pay band plus Grade pay, Military Service pay, 'X' Group pay where applicable/minimum of pay in case of HAG and above pay scales, in the revised pay structure introduced from 1.1.2006 corresponding to the pre-revised scale held by the Armed Forces personnel at the time of retirement/discharge/invalidment for 100% disability.

11.1 For disability less than 100%, the disability element shall be proportionately reduced as per the period and degree of already accepted.

11.2 However, the aggregate of service element revised in terms Para 2.1 of this Ministry's letter dated 4.5.2009) and war injury element shall not exceed the minimum of the pay in the pay band plus Grade pay, Military Service pay, 'X' Group pay where applicable/minimum of pay in case of HAG and above pay scales, in the revised pay structure introduced from 1.1.2006 corresponding to the pre-revised scale held by the Armed Forces personnel at the time of retirement/discharge/invalidment. The ceiling on aggregate of war injury pension with reference to minimum of the pay in the revised pay structure, applicable from 1.1.2006, as stated above shall stand removed with effect from 1.7.2009.

12. All other terms and conditions for revision of pension/family pension in respect of pre-2006 Armed Forces pensioners/family pensioners drawing pension under Casualty Pensionary Awards which are not affected by the provisions of this letter will remain unchanged.

13. The actual benefit accrued on account of these orders shall be payable with effect from 1.1.2006.

14. All Pension Disbursing Agencies (PDAs) handling disbursement of pension to the Defence pensioners are hereby authorized to pay revised disability/liberalized disability/war injury pension/special/liberalized family pension to the existing pensioners under these orders without any further authorization from the concerned pension Sanctioning authorities. However, PCDA (Pension) Allahabad will issue further suitable implementation instructions while circulating these orders to all the PDAs concerned. Action as prescribed in Para 16.4 of this ministry's letter dated 11.11.2008 may also be taken by the PDAs in the cases covered under these orders.

15. This issues with the concurrence of Finance Division of this Ministry vide their U.O. No. 553/Fin/Pen/2011 dated 15.02.2011.

Yours faithfully,

Sd/-

(Malathi Narayanan)

Under Secretary (Pen/Policy)

23.23

Government of India, Ministry of Defence, Department of Ex-Servicemen Welfare Letter No 16(5)/2008/D (Pen/Policy) dated 29th September 2009

Sub: Implementation of Government decision on the recommendations of the Sixth Central Pay Commission. Revision of provisions regulating Pensionary Awards relating to disability pension/war injury pension, etc, for the armed Forces Officers and Personnel Below Officer Rank (PBOR) on voluntary retirement/discharge on own request on or after 1.1.2006.

Sir,

The undersigned is directed to refer to Note below Par 8 and 11 of this Ministry's letter No 1(2)/97/D (Pen-C) dated 31.1.2001, wherein it has been provided that Armed Forces personnel who retire voluntarily or seek discharge on request, shall not be eligible for any award on account of disability.

2. In pursuance of Government decision on the recommendations of the Sixth Central Pay Commission vide Para 5.1.69 of their report, President is pleased to decide that Armed Forces personnel who are retained in service despite disability, which is accepted as attributable to or aggravated by Military Service and have foregone lump-sum compensation in lieu of that disability, may be given disability element/war injury element at the time of their retirement/discharge whether voluntary or otherwise in addition to Retiring/Service Pension or Retiring/service Gratuity.

3. The provisions of this letter shall apply to the Armed Forces personnel who are retired/discharged from service on or after 1.1.2006.

4. Pension Regulations for the three Services will be amended in due course.

5. This issues with the concurrence of Ministry of Defence (Fin) vide their UO No 3545/(Fin/Pen) dated 29.9.2009.

Yours faithfully,

Sd/-

(Harbans Singh)

Director (Pen/Policy)

23.24

Government of India, Ministry of Defence, Department of Ex-Servicemen Welfare Letter No 16(05)/2008/D (Pension/Policy) dated 19th May 2017

Sub: **Grant of Disability Element to Armed Forces Personnel who were retained in service despite disability attributable to or aggravated by Military Service and subsequently proceeded on pre-mature/voluntary retirement prior to 01.01.2006.**

Sir,

The undersigned is directed to refer to this Ministry's letter No. 16(5)2008/D(Pen/Policy) dated 29th September, 2009 wherein disability element/war injury element has been allowed to such Armed Forces Personnel who were retained in service despite disability and retired/discharged voluntarily or otherwise in addition to retiring/service pension or retiring/service gratuity, subject to condition that their disability was accepted as attributable to or aggravated by military service and had foregone lump sum compensation in lieu of that disability.

2. In terms of Para-3 of the above referred letter, the provisions stated above are applicable to the Armed Forces Personnel who were retired/discharged from service on or after 01.01.2006. Armed Forces Tribunal (Principal Branch) New Delhi in OA No. 336 of 2011 vide their order dated 07.02.2012 have struck down Para-3 of this Ministry's above letter.

3. The issue of extension of above benefit to the Pre-2006 retired/discharged Armed Forces Personnel who were retained in service despite disability attributable to or aggravated by military service, was under active consideration of Government. Now, the President is pleased to decide that all Pre-2006 Armed Forces Personnel who were retained in service despite disability and retired voluntarily or otherwise will be allowed disability element/war injury element in addition to retiring/service pension or retiring/service gratuity, subject to the condition that their disability was accepted as attributable to or aggravated by military service and had foregone lump sum compensation in lieu of that disability. Further, concerned Armed Forces Personnel should still be suffering from the same disability which should be assessed at 20% or more on the date of effect of this letter.

4. Implementation of these orders is expected to be arduous and challenging. Documents like Medical Board Proceedings, retention of the personnel in service despite disability option of individual foregoing lump sum compensation and non-payment of lump sum compensation would be required in all cases which may not be available at the end of Pay Accounting Authorities/Record Offices and Pension sanctioning authorities readily in such cases, pensioners/family pensioners may be asked to produce the copies of relevant documents to the Executive authorities in support of their claims.

5. The claim for grant of disability element/war injury element in affected cases will be submitted to the PSA concerned by PCDA (O) Pune/NPO/AFCAO/Record office along with copy of medical board/fresh medical board proceedings showing extent of disability applicable as on date of effect of this letter in respect of Commissioned Officers/JCOs/OR. It will be responsibility of PCDA(O) Pune/NPO/AFCAO and Record office to confirm payment/ non-payment of lump sum-compensation in lieu of disability element to Commissioned officers and JCOs/OR. A sanction showing extent of disability and its attributability/aggravation due to Military service in terms of MOD letter No 4684/DIR(PEN)/2001 dated 14.08.2001 would be issued by the service HQrs in case of Commissioned Officers and sanction would be issued by O I/C Record office in case of JCOs/OR.

6. The corrigendum PPOs granting disability element/war injury element in all affected cases will be issued by respective Pension Sanctioning Authorities.

7. The provisions of this letter shall take effect from 01.01.2006.

8. Pension Regulation of all the three services will be amended in due course.

9. This issues with the concurrence of Finance Division of this Ministry vide their I.D. No. 10(3)/2012/FIN/PEN dated 19th May 2017.

Yours faithfully,
Sd/-
(R.K. Arora)
Under Secretary to the Government of India

23.25

Government of India, Ministry of Defence, Department of Ex-Servicemen Welfare Letter No 10(01)/D (Pen/Pol)/2009/Vol.II dated 19th January 2010

Sub: **Revision of Disability/War Injury Element of pension in respect of Armed Forces Officers and PBOR pensioners based on the recommendations of Cabinet Secretary Committee Report.**

Sir,

The undersigned is directed to state that in order to consider various issues on pension of Armed Forces Pensioners, Government had set up a Committee headed by the Cabinet Secretary. The recommendations of the said Cabinet Secretary's Committee on disability/war injury pension have been considered by the Government and the President is pleased to decide that with effect from 1.7.2009, the concept of broad banding of percentage of disability/war injury, as provided in Para 7.2 of this Ministry's letter No 1(2)/97/D (Pen-C) dated 31.01.2001, shall be extended to Armed Forces Officers and PBOR who were invalided out of service prior to 1.1.1996 and are in receipt of disability/war injury pension as on 1.7.2009. Wherever, the disability element/war injury element of pension in pre-1.1.1996 cases was not allowed for disability being accepted as less than 20% at initial stage or subsequent stage on, reassessment of disability, the same will continue to be disallowed and such, cases will not be re-opened.

2. Further, the President is also pleased to decide that the cap on war injury pension with reference to emoluments last drawn in the case of disabled pensioners belonging to category 'E' of Para 4.1 of this Ministry's above mentioned letter dated 31.1.2001, shall stand removed with effect from 1.7.2009 for Armed Forces Officer and PBOR pensioners. The provision contained in Para 8 of this Ministry's letter No. PC 1(2)/97/D (Pen-C) dated 16.5.2001, Para 10.1 (b) of this Ministry letter No 192)/97/D (pen-C) dated 31.1.2001 and Para. 6.4 & 7.4 of this Ministry's letter No 16(6)/2008 (2)/D (pen/Pol) dated 5.5.2009, shall stand modified to that extent.

3. The disability/war injury element of pension in all such cases shall be recomputed accordingly under these orders by the Pension Sanctioning Authorities (PSAs) concerned for regulating payment under this Ministry's letter No 16(6)/2008(I)/D(Pen/Policy) dated 4.5.2009 and letter No. 16(6)/2008(2)/D(Pen/Policy) dated 5.5.2009, for this purpose, each affected Armed Forces pensioner who is in receipt of disability/war injury element of pension as on 1.7.2009 will submit an application in the format enclosed as Annexure to this letter to the PSAs concerned through their Pension Disbursing Agencies and Record Office in the case of PBOR and through Pension Disbursing Agencies in the case of Commissioned Officers to PSAs concerned for revision of disability/war injury element of pension in terms of Para 1 and 2 above, as the case may be. Further, Implementation instructions to all concerned will be issued by PCDA (Pensions) Allahabad immediately on receipt of these orders.

4. Revision of War injury element of pension in respect of those who have been retired/discharged/invalided out of service on or after 1.7.2009 under category 'E' and in whose case war injury pension has already been notified in terms of this Ministry's above mentioned letter dated 5.5.2009, will be carried out suo-moto by the PSAs concerned by issue of corrigendum PPOs without any application from the concerned pensioners.

5. This issues with the concurrence of Finance Division of this Ministry vide their U.O. No. 51/Fin/Pen dated 08.01.2010.

Yours faithfully,

Sd/-

(Harbans Singh)
Director (Pension/Policy)

23.26

Government of India, Ministry of Defence, Department of Ex-Servicemen Welfare Letter No 12(16)/2009/D (Pen/Policy) dated 15th September 2014

Sub: **Rationalization of casualty Pensionary Awards for the Armed Forces and Personnel below officer Rank (PBOR) Invalided out from service prior to 1.1.1996; Extension of benefit of broad banding of percentage of disability/war injury.**

Sir,

The undersigned is directed to refer to the provisions stipulated in Para 7.2 of this Ministry's letter No 1(2)/97/D(Pen-C) dated 31.1.2001 through which the concept of broad banding of percentage of disability/war injury was introduced in respect of those Armed Forces Officers and personnel Below Officer Ranks who were invalided out of service on or after 1.1.1996 on account of disability/war injury accepted as attributable to or aggravated by Military Service. **The said provision for determining extent of disability/war injury was also extended to pre- 1.1.1996 invalided out cases from 1.7.2009** vide this Ministry's letter No 10(01)/D(Pen/Policy) 2009/Vol II dated 19.1.2010 provided that the Armed Forces personnel were in receipt of disability element/war injury element for disabilitymore than 20% as on 1.7.2009.

2. Consequent upon receipt of reference fromvarious Pensioners' Associations for extending the provisions regarding broad banding of percentage of disability to such pre- 1.1.1996 Armed Forces pensioners from 1.1.1996 itself, the matter has been suitably examined in this Ministry. **In partial modification of this Ministry's above said letter dated 19th January 2010, the President is now pleased to decide that with effect from 1.1.1996, the benefit of broad banding of percentage of disability/war injury element shall be allowed to Armed Forces Officers and PBOR pensioners who were invalided out of service prior to 1.1.1996 and were in receipt of disability element/War injury element as on 1.1.1996.** In such cases where the pensioner was not in receipt of disability element as on 1.1.1996 but became entitled at a later stage due to reassessment of disabilitymore than 20%, this benefit shall be allowed from the same date. Similarly, in those cases where the pensioners were in receipt of disability element/war injury element as on 1.1.1996 but the same was discontinued at a later stage due to reassessment of disability as less than 20%, the disability element/war injury element shall be discontinued from the later date as hithertofore. However, in those pre-1.1.1996 cases where the disability element/war injury element was not allowed for disability being accepted as less than 20% at initial stage or subsequent stage on reassessment of disability, the same will continue to be disallowed an such cases will not be re-opened. **(Note- See amendment of clerical error- Chapter 23.27)**

3. The disability element/war injury element of pension in all such cases shall be recommended accordingly under these orders by the Pension Sanctioning Authorities (PSAs) concerned for regulating payment under this Ministry's letters No. PC. 1(2)/97/D (Pen-C) dated 16.5.2001, No 16(6)/2008(1)/D (Pen/Policy) dated 4.5.2009 and letter No 12(4)/2008(1)/D (Pen/Policy)/Vol. V dated 15.2.2011. For this purpose, each affected Armed Forces pensioner who were invalided out of service prior to 1.1.1996 and were in receipt of disability element/war injury element on 1.1.1996 or thereafter, shall submit an application in the format enclosed as Annexure to this letter to the PSAs concerned through their Pension Disbursing Agencies and Record Offices in the case of PBOR and through Pension Disbursing Agencies in the case of Commissioned Officers to PSAs concerned for revision of disability element/war injury element. PSAs may, however, also identify the affected cases from the corrigendum PPOs issued by them based on the application received in terms of this Ministry's above said letter dated 19.1.2010 and for issue of corrigendum PPO.

4. If a pensioner, to whom benefit accrues under the provisions of this letter had already died on or after 1.1.1996 but before date of issue of this letter, the application for revision shall be submitted by the family pensioners or by his heir, as the case may be. Payment of LTA shall, however, be regulated as per the extant Government orders on the subject matter.

5. All other terms and conditions for grant/revision of disability element/war injury element of pension in respect of Armed Force pensioners invalided out of service prior to 1.1.1996, which are not affected by the provisions of this letter, will remain unchanged.

6. This issues with the approval of Ministry of Defence (Finance) vide their I.D. No. 10(22)/2009/FIN/PEN dated 19/08/2014.

Yours faithfully,
Sd/-
(Chanan Ram Saini)
Deputy Secretary (Pension)

23.27

Government of India, Ministry of Defence, Department of Ex-Servicemen Welfare Letter No 12(16)/2009/D (Pen/Pol) dated 21st December 2015

(Note: This letter is an amendment to Chapter 23.26)

Sub: Amendment to GOI, MOD letter No. 12(16)/2009/D(Pen/Policy) dated 15th September, 2014.

Sir,

The undersigned is directed to refer to this Ministry's letter No. 12(16)/2009/D(Pen/Policy) dated 15th September, 2014. The following amendment are made in said letter.

Last line of Para-1.

For: for disability 'more than 20%' as on 1.7.2009.

Read: for disability '20% or more' as on 1.7.2009.

10th line of Para-2.

For: entitled at a later stage due to reassessment of disability 'more than 20%'

Read: entitled at a later stage due to reassessment of disability for disability '20% or more'.

2. All other terms and conditions shall remain unchanged.

3. The provisions of this letter shall take effect from 01.01.1996.

4. Pension Regulation for three Services will be amended in due course.

5. This issues with the concurrence of Finance Division of this Ministry vide their I.D. No. PC to 10(22)/2009/Fin/Pen dated 04.12.2015.

Yours faithfully,
Sd/-
(Manoj Sinha)
Under Secretary to the Government of India

23.28

Government of India, Ministry of Defence, Department of Ex-Servicemen Welfare Letter No 2(2)/2011/D (Pen/Pol)/dated 26th December 2011

Sub: Payment of Ex-gratia lump-sum compensation to Defence Service Officers and Personnel Below Officer Rank who are invalided out of service on account of disability attributable to or aggravated by military service – regarding.

Sir,

The undersigned is directed to say that families of the Defence Service personnel who die in performance of their bonafide duties and the Armed Forces personnel who sustain injuries and are disabled or incapacitated on account of causes which are accepted as attributable to or aggravated by military service, are eligible for pensionary benefits under the Casualty pensionary Awards notified vide this Ministry's letter No 1(2)/97-D (Pen-C) dated 31.01.2001 read with letter No 16(6)/200892)/D (Pen/Pol) dated 5th May, 2009. Further, in terms of this Ministry's letter No 20(1)/98/D (Pay/Services) dated 22nd September, 1998 read with letter No 20(5)/2009/D (Pay/Services) dated 4th June, 2010 and dated 17th August, 2010, families of Defence Service personnel who dies in harness in the performance of their bonafide official duties under various circumstances are eligible for en Ex-gratia lump sum compensation.

2. Considering the hardship being faced by the disabled defence Service personnel, the question of grant of Ex-gratia lump sum compensation to the Defence service personnel who are invalided out of service on account of disability attributable to or aggravated by military service, has been under consideration of the Government.

3. The President is pleased to decide that such Defence Service personnel, who are disabled, incapacitated in the performance of their bonafide official duties under various circumstances and are boarded out from service on account of disability/war injury attributable to or aggravated by military service, shall be paid Ex-gratia lump sum compensation amounting to Rs 9 lakhs for 100% disability. For disability/war injury less than 100% but not less than 20%, the amount of Ex-gratia compensation shall be proportionately reduced. No Ex-gratia compensation shall be payable for disability/war Injury less than 20%. The proportionate compensation would be based on actual percentage of disability as certified by the Invaliding Medical Board, without applying broad banding provision as contained in Para 7.2 of this Ministry's above mentioned letter dated 31.01.2001.

4. The other terms and conditions for admissibility of Ex-gratia lump sum compensation pertaining to the circumstances, specified in this Ministry's letter No 20(1)/98/d (Pay/Services), dated 22nd September, 1998 and letter No 20(5)/2009/D (Pay/services) dated 4th June, 2010 will be applicable to decide such individual case by the Pension Sanctioning Authorities concerned.

5. The provisions of this letter shall apply to all the eligible Defence Service personnel who are invalided out of service on or after 1.4.2011 i.e. the date from which similar benefits are allowed to the personnel of Central Armed Police forces (CAPF).

6. This issues with the concurrence of Finance Division of this Ministry vide their U.O. No. 4143/Fin/Pen/2011, dated 24.10.2011.

Yours faithfully,
Sd/-
(Malathi Narayanan)
Under Secretary (Pen/Policy)

23.29

Government of India, Ministry of Defence, Department of Ex-Servicemen Welfare Letter No 1(17)/2012/D (Pen/Policy) dated 17th January 2013

Sub: Implementation of Government decision on the recommendations of the Committee of Secretaries 2012 on the issues related to Defence service Personnel and Ex-servicemen – revision of provisions regulating Casualty Pensionary awards for post-2006 JCOs/OR.

Sir,

The undersigned is directed to refer to this Ministry's letter No 16(6)/2008(2)/D (Pen/Policy) dated 5th May 2009, issued in implementation of Government decision on the recommendations of 6th CPC for revision of provisions regulating Pensionary/awards relating to Special Family pension, Liberalized Family Pension and 2nd Life awards in respect of JCO/OR discharged/invalided out from service or died in harness on or after 1.1.2006.

2. A Committee of Secretaries headed by Cabinet Secretary was constituted by the government to consider various issues on pension of Armed Forces personnel and Ex-servicemen, who have recommended establishing a linkage in the rate of the family pension of post-2006 JCO/OR family pensioners with the pension. the above recommendations of the committee has been accepted by the government and the President is pleased to decide that based on the rank, group, length of service and nature of award sanctioned to the deceased JCO/OR pensioner, the revised service pension/service element of disability/liberalized disability/war injury pension as the casemay be, shall be determined in terms of this ministry's letter No 1(13)/2012/D (Pen/Pol) dated 17.01.2013 on notional basis. In cases of JCO/OR died while in service, the entitlement of revised notional pension shall be determined by considering the individual as deemed invalided out of service under the same circumstance in which the casualty was occurred. With effect from 24.09.2012, the rates of Special Family Pension & Liberalized family pension in respect of post-2006 JCO/OR family pensioners including honorary commissioned Officers and Non combatants (enrolled), shall be worked out as 120% and 200% respectively of the revised notional pension determined as per above provisions. The 2nd life awards of family pension shall also be worked out as per the rates prescribed vide Para 6.7 & 6.5 of this Ministry's letter No 1(2)/97/D (Pen-C) dated 31.1.2001 in terms of the rates of special/Liberalized family pension determined as above.

3. The post-2006 JCO/OR family pensioners drawing Special/Liberalized family pension/2nd Life awards of Special/ Liberalized family pension in terms of Para 9 of this Ministry above mentioned letter dated 5.5.2009, happens to be more than the family pension determined in terms of these orders, the family pensioners shall continue to draw the beneficial award.

4. The other terms and conditions prescribed vide Para 9 of this Ministry's abovementioned letter dated 5.5.2009 read with provisions contained in Para 5 & 6 of this ministry's above said letter dated 31.1.2001, which are not affected by the provisions of this letter, shall remain unchanged.

5. These orders shall take effect from 24.09.2012 and shall also cover cases of post-1.1.2006 retiree/death in service cases. The financial benefit in past cases shall, however, be granted from 24.09.2012 only.

6. The Special/Liberalized family pension and 2nd Life awards of Special/Liberalized family pension of all JCO/OR including honorary commissioned Officers and Non combatants (enrolled) who were discharged/invalided out/died while in serviced on or after 1.1.2006, shall be re-calculated in terms of these orders by the pension Sanctioning Authorities concerned. Necessary implementation instructions to all concerned shall be issued by Pr. CDA (Pension) Allahabad on receipt of these orders.

7. Pension Regulations of the three Service shall be amended in due course.

8. This issues with the concurrence of Finance Division of this Ministry vide their I.D. No. PC 2/10(12)/2012/FIN/PEN dated 10.01.2013.

Yours faithfully,
Sd/-
(Malathi Narayanan)
Under Secretary to the Government of India

23.30

Government of India, Ministry of Defence, Department of Ex-Servicemen Welfare Letter No 1(16)/2012/D (Pen/Policy) dated 17th January 2013

Sub: **Implementation of Government decision on the recommendations of the Committee of Secretaries 2012 on the issues related to Defence service Personnel and Ex-servicemen – Improvement in Casualty Pensionary awards for Pre-2006 Armed Forces Officers and JCO/OR.**

Sir,

The undersigned is directed to refer to this Ministry's letter No 17(4)/2008(a)/D (Pen/Policy)/-Vol-V dated 15th February 2011, issued in implementation of Government decision on the recommendations of 6th CPC, which prescribe minimum guaranteed rates of various casualty pensionary awards for pre-2006 Armed Forces Officers and JCO/OR.

2. In order to consider various issues on pension of Armed Forces personnel and Ex-Servicemen, the Government had constituted a Committee of Secretaries headed by Cabinet Secretary. The committee in its Report have recommended the following to improve the family pension of Armed Forces pensioners:

2.1 The minimum guaranteed family pension of pre-2006 armed Forces Family pensioners should be determined with reference to minimum of the fitment table for the rank in the revised pay structure issued for implementation of recommendations of sixth CPC instead of the minimum of the pay band; and

2.2 A linkage should be established in the rate of the family pension with the pension of JCO/OR.

3. The above recommendations of the committee have been accepted by the Government and the President is pleased to decide that with effect from 24.09.202, the minimum guaranteed Special Family pension, Dependent Pension (special), Liberalized Family Pension, Dependent Pension (Liberalized) and 2nd Life awards (in case of JCO/ OR) in respect of pre-2006 family pensioners of commissioned officers & JCO/OR including honorary commissioned Officers and Non combatants (enrolled), shall be determined with reference to the minimum of the fitment table for the rank in the revised pay band as indicated under fitment tables annexed with SAI 1/S/2008, SAI 2/S/2008 & SAI 4/S/2008 as amended and equivalent instructions for Navy & Air Force, plus the grade pay corresponding to the pre-revised scale from which the pensioner had retired/discharged/invalided out/died including Military Service pay, 'X' Group pay wherever applicable, under the same rates and conditions as prescribed vide Para 3 to 8 of this Ministry's above quoted letter dated 15.2.2011.

4. In order to establish linkage in the rate of the family pension with the pension of JCO/OR, the President is also pleased to decide that based on the rank, group, length of service and nature of award sanctioned to the deceased JCO/OR pensioners, the revised service pension/service element of disability/liberalized disability/war injury pension as the case may be, shall be determined in terms of this Ministry's letter No 1(13)2012-D (PEN/POL) dated 17.01.2013 on notional basis. In cases of JCO/OR died while in service, the entitlement of revised notional pension shall be determined by considering the individual as deemed invalided out of service under the same circumstance in which the casualty was occurred. The rates of Special family pension & Liberalized family pension in respect of pre-2006 JCO/OR family pensioners including honorary commissioned Officers and Non combatants (Enrolled), shall be worked out as 120% and 200% respectively of the revised notional pension determined as per above provisions. The 2nd life awards of family pension shall also be worked out as per the rates prescribed vide Para 5 & 8 of this Ministry's above quoted letter dated 15.2.2011 in terms of the rates of/special/Liberalized family pension determined as above.

4.1 With effect from 24.09.2012, the Special/Liberalized family pension and 2nd Life awards of family pension to pre-2006 JCO/OR family pensioners shall be granted on the basis of family pension worked out as per the formulation at Para 4 above or the minimum guaranteed pension determined as per the provisions contained in Para 3 above, whichever is more beneficial.

5. All other terms and conditions for revision of family pension in respect of pre-2006 armed Forces family pensioners drawing pension under casualty pensionary awards, which are not affected by the provisions of this letter, shall remain unchanged.

6. In case a pre-2006 family pensioner drawing Special/Liberalized family pension/Dependent pension (special/ dependent pension (Liberalized)/2nd life awards of special/Liberalized family pension in terms of provisions contained in Para 3 to Para 8 of this Ministry above mentioned letter dated 15.2.2011, happens to be more than the family pension determined in terms of these orders, no revision shall be carried out to the disadvantage of the family pensioner and he/she shall continue to draw the beneficial award.

7. The actual benefit accrued in terms of these orders shall be payable with effect from 24.09.2012. No arrears on account of revision of family pension shall be admissible for the past period. However, if a family pensioner to whom the benefits under these orders accrues has died/dies before receiving the payment on account of arrears, the life time arrears (LTA) will be disposed off as per the extant orders.

8. All Pension Disbursing Agencies (PSAs) handling disbursement of pension to Defence pensioners are hereby authorized to pay revised Special Family Pension, dependent Pension (special), Liberalized Family pension, Dependent Pension (Liberalized) and 2nd Life awards in respect of pre-2006 family pensioners of commissioned Officers & JCO/ OR including honorary commissioned Officers and Non combatants (Enrolled), in terms of these orders without calling for any application from the family pensioner and without any further authorization from the concerned Pension Sanctioning Authorities PCDA (Pensions) Allahabad will issue further implementation instructions while circulating these orders to all the PDAs concerned.

9. This issues with the concurrence of Finance Division of this Ministry vide their I.D. No. PC 2/10(12)/2012/FIN/ PEN dated 10.01.2013.

Yours faithfully,

Sd/-

(Malathi Narayanan)

Under Secretary to the Government of India

23.31

Government of India, Ministry of Defence, Department of Ex-Servicemen Welfare Letter No 12(28)/2010-D (Pen/Pol) dated 10th February 2014

Sub: **Grant of Service element of disability pension to pre 1.1.1973 invalided out JCOs, OR and NCs(E)/Sailors/Airmen when the accepted degree of disablement re-assessed as less than 20%-Reg.**

Sir,

The undersigned is directed to refer to Regulation 186 of Pension Regulations for the Army Part-1 (1961) and equivalent provisions in the Pension Regulations for the Navy & Air Force, which provides that in case of personnel below officer rank granted disability pension on invalidment due to disabilities attributable to or aggravated by military service but whose accepted degree of disability subsequently falls below 20%, the service element of disability pension was made permanent provided the qualifying service rendered by the individual was 10 years or more (15 years in case of NCs(E). The requirement of rendering stipulated qualifying service for continuance of service element was further relaxed to 5 years for the individuals who were invalided out of service on or after 1.3.1968 vide this Ministry's letter No. 1(4)/68/1035-A/S/D (Pension/Services) dated 30.10.1968. In implementation of the Government decisions on the recommendations of Third Pay Commission vide SAI 4/S/75, the condition of having minimum service for continuance of service element, when disability was assessed as less than 20% was abolished in those cases where the invalidment occurred on or after 1.1.1973. Due to the abovesaid stipulation of having prescribed service for continuation of service element, pre- 1.1.1973 invalided out cases erstwhile in receipt of disability pension, were disallowed service element of disability pension and subsequently family pension also, where the disability was accepted as less than 20% in subsequent re-assessment(s).

2. Based on various representations from such personnel and their families for continuance of service element of disability pension and/or grant of family pension, the matter has been considered by the Government. The President is now pleased to decide that condition prescribed prior to 1.1.1973 for continuance of service element with reference to minimum stipulated qualifying service, in cases where the accepted degree of disability subsequently fell below 20%, shall be dispensed with from 1.1.1973 or the date from which the accepted degree of disability fell below 20%, whichever is later. The NOK of such invalided out personnel who at the time of invalidment were in receipt of disability pension and subsequently died, shall also be entitled for family pension from the date following the date of death of individual.

3. The service element of disability pension/family pension in terms of these orders shall accordingly be notified by the Pr. CDA (Pension), Allahabad. For this purpose, each affected personnel below officer rank who was invalided out prior to 1.1.1973 and initially granted disability pension but the same discontinued as their accepted degree of disability fell below 20% at the time of re-assessment, shall submit an application in the format enclosed as annexure to this letter to the PSAs concerned through their Pension disbursing Agencies and Record Office. In cases where the pensioner was alive as on 1.1.1973 or date of discontinuance of disability pension which is later and died subsequently, his heir(s) shall be paid life time arrears on account of service element of disability pension accrued in terms of these orders as per the prevailing instructions on the subject. For this purpose, eligible heir(s) of the deceased pensioner may also apply to the Pension Disbursing Agencies of the deceased pensioner.

4. The Record Offices may, however, also identity the affected cases and take necessary action after obtaining relevant information required from the pensioners for notification of their awards.

5. Further implementation instructions to all concerned will be issued by Pr. CDA (Pension), Allahabad, immediately on receipt of these orders.

6. This issues with the approval of Ministry of Defence (Finance) vide their I.D. No. 10(4)/2012/FIN/PEN dated 16.01.2014.

Yours faithfully,
Sd/-
(Malathi Narayanan)
Under Secretary to the Government of India

23.32

Government of India, Ministry of Defence, Department of Ex-Servicemen Welfare Letter No 16(01)/2014-D (Pension/Policy) dated 10th April 2015

Sub: Minimum Guaranteed Pension for Disability/War Injury element as per CSC 2012 recommendation.

Sir,

The undersigned is directed to refer to this Ministry's letter No. 17(4)2008(1)/D(Pen/Pol)/Vol-V dated 15th February 2011 issued in implementation of the Government decision on the recommendations of 6th CPC, which prescribe minimum guaranteed rate of various casualty pensionary awards for pre-2006 Armed Forces Offices and Personnel Below Officer Ranks (PBOR).

2. Further, orders were issued as per recommendation of CSC 2012 for determining the minimum guaranteed pension in respect of Pre-2006 pensioners/family pensioners. The minimum guaranteed pension has been stepped up to 50% and 30% in respect of Service Pension and Family Pension respectively of the minimum of the fitment table for the rank in the revised pay structure issued for implementation of recommendations of 6th CPC instead of the minimum of the pay band. The question of extending this benefit to disability element in respect of Pre-2006 Armed Forces Pensioners was under consideration of the Government. Now, the President is pleased to decide that the minimum guaranteed disability/War Injury Element of Pre-2006 Armed Forces Personnel should be determined with reference to the minimum of the fitment table for the rank in the revised pay structure issued for implementation of recommendations of 6th CPC instead of the minimum of the pay band, subject to consideration that the rate of disability element/war injury element of lower rank may not exceed that of higher rank. The Disability/War Injury Element of Pre-2006 shall be further stepped up as under:

Disability Pension

3. The disability element revised in terms of Para 2.2 of thisMinistry's letter dated 4.5.2009 as amended from time to time shall not be less than 30% of the minimum of the fitment table, for the rank in the revised pay structure issued for implementation of recommendation of 6th CPC instead of the minimum of the pay band corresponding to prerevised scale held by Armed Forces personnel at the time of retirement/discharge/invalidment for 100% disability.

3.1 For disability less than 100%, the disability element shall be proportionately reduced as per the period and degree of disability accepted.

3.2 In cases where permanent disability is not less than 60%, the disability pension (i.e. total of service element revised in terms Para 2.1 of this Ministry's letter dated 4.5.2009 as amended from time to time plus disability element) shall not be less than 60% of minimum of the fitment table for the rank in the revised pay structure issued for implementation of recommendation of 6th CPC instead of minimum of the pay band corresponding to the prerevised scale held by Armed Forces personnel at the time of retirement/discharge/invalidment, subject to minimum of Rs 7,000/- per month.

Liberalized Disability Pension

4. The disability element revised in terms of Para 2.2 of this Ministry's letter dated 4.5.2009 as amended from time to time shall not be less than 30% of the minimum of the fitment table for the rank in the revised pay structure issued for implementation of recommendation of 6th CPC instead of minimum of the pay band corresponding to pre-revised scale held by Armed Forces Personnel at the time of retirement/discharge/invalidment for 100% disability.

4.1 For disability less than 100%, the disability element shall be proportionately reduced as per the period and degree of disability already accepted. However, in no case the revised disability pension (i.e. aggregate of service element revised in terms of Para 2.1 of this Ministry's letter dated 4.5.2009 as amended from time to time plus disability element) shall be less than 80% of the minimum of the fitment table for the rank in the revised pay structure issued for implementation of recommendation of 6th CPC instead of the minimum of the pay band corresponding to prerevised scale held by Armed Forces personnel at the time of retirement/discharge/invalidment.

War Injury Pension

5. The War Injury element revised in terms of Para 2.3 of this Ministry's letter dated 4.5.2009 as amended from time to time shall not be less than 100% in case of invalidment and 60% in case of retirement/discharge, of the minimum of the fitment table for the rank in the revised pay structure issued for implementation of recommendation of 6th CPC instead of minimum of the pay band corresponding to pre-revised scale held by Armed Forces Personnel at the time of retirement/discharge/invalidment for 100% disability.

6. All Pension Disbursing Agencies (PDAs) handling disbursement of pension to Defence pensioners are hereby authorized to pay revised Disabilty/War Injury Element in respect of Pre-2006 retired/discharged/invalided out pensioners fromservice, in terms of these orders without calling for any application from the Defence pensioners and without any further authorization from the concerned Pension Sanctioning Authorities (PSAs). PCDA (Pension) Allahabad will issue further implementation instructions while circulating these orders to all the PDAs concerned.

7. This order will take effect from 24th September 2012. There will be no change in the amount of revision of disability element/war injury element paid during the period 01.01.2006 to 23.09.2012, therefore, no arrears shall be allowed for this period.

8. All other terms and condition shall remain unchanged.

9. Pension Regulation of all the three services will be amended in due course.

10. This issues with the concurrence of Finance Division of this Ministry vide their I.D. No. PC-3 to MF 10(12)/2012/FIN/PEN dated 23.03.2015.

Yours faithfully,
Sd/-
(Prem Parkash)
Under Secretary (Pen/Pol)

23.33

Government of India, Ministry of Defence, Department of Ex-Servicemen Welfare Letter No 16(01)/2014-D (Pension/Policy) dated 18th May 2016

Sub: **Revision of Casualty Pensionary Awards in respect of Pre-2006 Armed Forces Officers and JCOs/OR Pensioners/Family Pensioners.**

Sir,

The undersigned is directed to refer to this Ministry's letter No. 17(4)2008(1)/D(Pen/Pol)/Vol-V dated 15.02.2011 issued in implementation of the Government decision on the recommendations of 6th CPC, under which minimum guaranteed rates of various casualty pensionary awards for pre-2006 Armed Forces Offices and JCOs/OR on the basis of the minimum of the pay in the pay band plus Grade pay,Military Service Pay & 'X' Group Pay where applicable have been provided. After issue of GOI, Ministry of Defence letters No. 1(11)/2012/D (Pen/Pol) dated 17.1.2013, No. 1(04)/2015(1)-D (Pen/Pol) dated 03.09.2015 and No. 1(04)/2015(II)-D (Pen/Pol) dated 03.09.2015 the basis of the minimum of the fitment table for thee rank in the revised pay structure issued for implementation of recommendation of 6th CPC instead of the minimum of the pay band.

2. Further, in respect of disability pensioners, the minimum guaranteed rates of Disability Element/Liberalized Disability Element/War Injury Element were already revised w.e.f. 24.09.2012 vide GOI, MoD letter No 16(01)/2014/D (Pen/Pol) dated 10.04.2015 at the rates of the minimum of the fitment table for the Rank in the revised pay structure issued for implementation of recommendation of 6th CPC instead of minimum of the pay band. Similarly, the minimum guaranteed Special Family Pension, Dependent Pension (special), Liberalized Family Pension, Dependent Pension (Liberalized) & Second Life Awards in case of JCOs/ORs) in respect of pre-2006 family pensioners of commissioned Officers and JCO/OR were also revised with reference to minimum of the fitment table for the rank in the revised pay band w.e.f. 24.09.2012 vide GOI, MoD letter No 1(16)/2012/D (Pen/Policy) dated 17.01.2013.

3. Now, President is pleased to decide that the rates of Casualty pensionary Awards of all Pre-2006 Disability Pensioners/Family Pensioners shall be revised with effect from 01.01.2006 on the basis of the minimum of fitment table for the Rank in the revised Pay Band as indicated under fitment tables annexed with SAI 1/S/2008, SAI 2/S/2008 & SAI 4/S/2008 as amended and equivalent instructions for Navy and Air Force.

4. Pension Disbursing Agencies (PDAs) are hereby authorized to take following action-

a. To step up the minimum guaranteed rates of Disability Element, Liberalized Disability Element,War Injury Element/Special Family Pension, Dependent Pension (special), Liberalized Family Pension,Dependent pension (Liberalized) & Second Life wards in case of JCOs/Ors) in respect of pre- 2006 Disability/Family pensioners of Commissioned Officers and JCOs/OR in the affected cases, in respect of Pre-2006 pensioners with effect from 01.01.2006 instead of from 24.09.2012, and arrears, if any, on account of these Casualty Pensionary Awards shall be paid accordingly.

b. The minimum guaranteed rates of Disability Element, Liberalized Disability Element, War Injury Element on the basis of minimum of fitment tables for the various Ranks in the revised pay Band shall be reckoned from Annexure 1 to 7 appended with this letter.

c. Further, the minimum guaranteed rates of Special Family Pension, Dependent Pension (Special), Liberalized Family Pension, Dependent Pension (Liberalized) & Second Life wards in case of JCOs/Ors) in respect of pre-2006 Family Pensioners of Commissioned Officers and JCO/Ors on the basis of the minimum of fitment table for the Rank in the revised Pay Band shall be reckoned from Annexure "A", "B", "C" & "D" appended with this letter.

d. Therefore, if any arrears, in respect of Casualty Pensionary Awards due to difference in rates as per this Ministry's letter No 17(4)/2008(1)/D (Pen/Policy)/Vol-V dated 15.02.2011 and as envisaged in GOI, MoD letter No 16(01)/2014/D (Pen/Pol) dated 10.04.2015 and rates indicated in Annexure 1 to 7, "A", "B", "C"& "D" attached with this letter shall be paid accordingly.

e. However, in respect of Casualty family Pensionary Awards where revised pension in terms of GOI, MoD letter No 1916)/2012/d (Pen/Pol) dated 17.01.2013 is higher than the rates indicated in annexure attached with this letter, the same shall be continued.

f. Similarly, the minimum guaranteed rates of Disability Element/Liberalized Disability Element/War Injury Element revised w.e.f. 24.09.2012 vide GOI,MoD letterNo 16(01)/2014/D (Pen/Pol) dated 10.04.2015, the same shall be continued where beneficial.

g. The Service element of Disability Pension and War Injury Pension will be revised as per MoD letter No 1(04)/2015(I)-D(Pen/Pol) dated 03.09.2015 and letter No 1(04)/2015(II)-D (Pen/Pol) dated 03.09.2015 read with MoD letter No 17(4)/2008/(I)D (Pen/Pol) dated 11.11.2008 and other Government order on the subject modifying the provision of these orders issued from time to time.

h. Service element of War Injury Pension in Invalidment case will be given for the maximum of terms of engagement for the rank of Armed Force Personnel from which he had invalided out.

5. However, the aggregate of Service Element (revised in terms of Para 2.1 of GOI, MoD letter No 16(6)/2008(1)/D (Pension/Policy) dated 04.05.2009 as amended from time to time) and War Injury Element shall not exceed the minimum of the fitment table for the rank in the revised pay structure issued for implementation of recommendations of 6th CPC introduced from 01.01.2006 corresponding to the pre-revised Pay scale held by the Armed Force Personnel at the time of retirement/discharge/Invalidment. This ceiling of aggregate of War Injury Pension (Service element plus War Injury Element) with reference to minimum of fitment table in the revised pay structure, applicable from 01.01.2006, as staged above shall stand removed with effect from 01.087.2009 vide GOI, MoD letter No 10(01)/D (Pen/Pol)/2009/Vol.II dated 19.01.2010. Therefore, the arrears in respect of War Injury Pension shall be calculated in two phases viz, w.e.f. 01.01.2006 to 30.06.2009 with the ceiling as staged above and w.e.f. 01.07.2009 to 23.09.2012 with ceiling after removal of Cap. However, in no case the revised Liberalized disability pension (i.e. aggregate of service element revised in termof Para 2.1 of this Ministry letter dated 04.05.2009 as amended from time to time plus disability element) shall be less than 80% of minimum of the fitment table.

6. In cases where pensioner was alive on 01.01.2006 and died/dies subsequently before receiving payment, his legal heir/heirs is/are entitled to the LTA with effect from 01.01.2006 till death of the pensioner or 23.09.2012 whichever is earlier. In such cases, the payment will be made to Legal heir/heirs.

7. Any over payment of pension coming to the notice or under process of recovery shall be adjusted in full by the Pension Disbursing Agencies (PDAs) against the arrears becoming due on revision of Casualty pensionary Award on the basis of these orders.

8. This order will take effect from 01.01.2006 and arrears, if any, shall be payable from 01.01.2006 to 23.09.2012.

9. All other terms and condition shall remain unchanged.

10. Pension Regulation of all the three services will be amended in due course.

11. This issues with the concurrence of Finance Division of this Ministry vide their I.D. No. PC-3 to NO. 10(12)/2012/ Fin/Pen dated 12.05.2016.

Yours faithfully,
Sd/-
(R.K. Arora)
Under Secretary to the Government of India

23.34

Government of India, Ministry of Defence, Department of Ex-Servicemen Welfare Letter No 16(3)/2017/D (Pen/Policy) dated 29th January 2019

Sub: **Implementation of Government decision on the recommendations of the Seventh Central pay Commission- Provisions regulating Casualty Pensionary Awards for Defence Forces Pensioners/ family pensioners- regarding.**

Sir,

I am directed to refer to the provisions for revision of various kinds of pensionary awards notified in implementation of the Government decision on recommendations of Seventh CPC vide this Ministry's letters No 17(01)/2016-D (Pen/Pol) dated 29th Oct, 2016 amended vide this Ministry's letter No 17(01)/2017/(01)/D(Pension/Policy) dated 4th Sept, 2017 read with letter No 17(01)/2017/(02)/D(Pension/Policy) dated 5th Sept, 2017 for pre-1.1.2016 Armed Forces pensioners/family pensioners and vide letter No 17(02)/2016-D(Pen/Pol) dated 4th Sept, 2017 for post 1.1.2016 Armed Forces pensioners/family pensioners.

2. In partial modification of above said orders, it has now been decided that following minimum ceiling shall be applied to the under mentioned casualty pensionary awards:

2.1 The Disability/Liberalized Disability/War Injury pension (i.e. total of service element plus disability/liberalized disability/war injury, element as the case may be), shall be subject to minimum of Rs 18,000/- per month irrespective of degree of disability of the personnel.

2.2 In cases of disability pension where permanent disability is not less than 60%, the disability pension (i.e. total of service element plus disability element) shall not be less than 60% of the reckonable emoluments as defined in above mentioned orders, subject to a minimum of Rs 18,000/- per month.

2.3 The amount of special family pension, admissible to the families of Armed Forces Personnel, shall be subject to a minimum of Rs 18,000/- per month.

2.4 The amount of liberalized family pension, admissible to child/children of Armed Forces personnel, shall be subject to a minimum of Rs 18,000/- per month.

3. All other provisions stipulated in above mentioned Government orders which are not affected by the provisions of this letter, shall remain unchanged.

4. The provisions of this letter shall take effect from 1.1.2016.

5. This issue with the concurrence of Finance Division of this Ministry of vide their ID No. 10(16)/2018/Fin/Pen dated 26.12.2018.

Yours faithfully

Sd/-

(Manoj Sinha)

Under Secretary to the Government of India

23.35

Government of India, Ministry of Defence, Department of Ex-Servicemen Welfare Letter No 17(01)/2017(01)/D (Pension/Policy) dated 4th September 2017

Sub: Implementation of Government decision on the recommendations of the 7th Central pay Commission (CPC) – Revision of pension of pre-1.1.2016 Defence Force pensioners/family pensioners, etc.

Sir,

The undersigned is directed to refer to this Ministry's letter No. 17(01)2016/D(Pen/Pol) dated 29th October 2016 for revision of pension of pre-2016 Defence Forces pensioners/family pensioners in implementation of the Government decisions on the recommendations of the 7th CPC. As per para 9 of this Ministry's and order dated 29th October 2016 the revision of disability element of disability pension was held in abeyance pending decision of National Anomaly Committee to whom matter was referred by MoD to decide methodology for calculation of disability element of disability pension under 7th CPC. The National Anomaly committee has recommended that parity with civilians for grant of Disability element which was granted to Defence Forces under 6th CPC, shall be maintained.

2. The recommendations of the National Anomaly Committee have been considered by the Government. In partial modification of Ministry's order dated 29th October 2016, the President is now pleased to decide that Disability element of disability pension for Defence Forces Pensioners shall also be reviewed by multiplying the existing rate of disability element as had been drawn on 31.12.2015 by factor of 2.57 to arrive at revised rate of disability element as on 1.1.2016. The amount of revised disability element so arrived shall be rounded off to next higher rupee.

3. Para 13 of this Ministry's above quoted letter dated 29.10.2016 regarding "Ex-gratia awards to Cadets in cases of disablement" shall be replaced with the following:

> 13. EX GRATIA AWARDS TO CADET (DIRECT) The ex-gratia award payable to Cadet (direct)/NOKs in cases of disablement/death shall be payable subject to the same conditions as hitherto in force in the event of invalidment on medical ground/death of a Cadet (Direct) due to causes attributable to or aggravated by military service
>
> i. Monthly Ex-gratia amount of Rs 9,000/- per month.
>
> ii. In cases of disablement, Ex-gratia disability award @ Rs 16,200/- per month shall be payable in addition for 100% of disability during period of disablement subject to prorata reduction in case degree of disablement is less than 100%. No ex-gratia disability award shall be payable in cases where the degree of disablement is less than 20%.

4. The dearness relief sanctioned by the Government from 1.1.2016 and thereafter shall also be paid on rates of disability element and monthly ex-gratia award to Cadet (Direct), revised in accordance with the provision of this letter.

5. Vide para 10(ii) of MoD order dated 29.10.2016, it was ordered to pay the constant Attendance Allowance (CAA) at the existing rate since matter regarding grant of Allowances was under examination by the Committee on Allowances (CAA). In this regard, Ministry of Finance vide Resolution dated 6th July 2017 (Appendix II item 37 has accepted the recommendation of 7th CPC to enhance the existing Constant Attendance Allowance @ 4500/- p.m. by 60%. DoP&PW vide O.M. No 1/4/2017-P&PW(F) dated 2.8.2017 has issued orders in this regard for civilian pensioners. Accordingly, for armed Forces personnel the Constant Attendant Allowance shall continue to be admissible under the condition as hitherto fore at the existing rate from 1.1.2016 to 30.06.2017. However, it shall now be admissible at the enhanced uniform rate of Rs 6,750/- per month. Irrespective of the rank with effect from 1.7.2017.

6. With reference to the provision contained in Para 5.4 of this Ministry's letter dated 29th October, 2016, it is further clarified that the maximum ceiling shall be applicable only in the case of Service/Retiring Pension, Service element of Disability/liberalized disability/War Injury Pension and Ordinary family pension. The said ceiling is not applicable in the cases of Disability/Liberalized disability/War Injury element. Special Family/Liberalized family pension, etc, applicable under casualty pensionary awards.

7. The provisions of this Ministry's letter dated 29th October, 2016, which are not affected by the provisions of this letter, shall remain unchanged.

8. The provisions of this letter shall take effect from 1.1.2016.

9. This issues with the concurrence of Finance Division of this Ministry vide their UO. No. Part file (1) to (30) (01)/2016/Fin/Pen dated 14th August, 2017.

Yours faithfully,
Sd/-
(Manoj Sinha)
Under Secretary to the Government of India

23.36

Government of India, Ministry of Defence, Department of Ex-Servicemen Welfare Letter No 16(01)2009-D(Pen/Pol) dated 10th November 2010

Sub: **Grant of disability pension for the intervening period between the date of expiry of the initial award and recommendations of Fresh Medical Board-reg.**

Sir,

The issue regarding grant of disability pension for the intervening period between the initial award and recommendation of the fresh Medical Board has been under consideration for sometime past. On expiry of the award given by the medical board in respect of disability pension, it is discontinued till a fresh Medical Board recommends the same. The findings of the Appeal Medical Board are effected from the date of institution of this Board. The individual is denied disability pension for the intervening period. After considering the matter at length, it has been decided to address the award during the intervening period in the manner mentioned below:

i. After the claim is made by the pensioner for an award during the intervening period, the admissibility of such a claim may be decided first by the Administrative Authority and when required, opinion of DGAFMS may be sought who will either decide the case on the basis of available records or by holding fresh medical board to physically examine the individual and recommend clearly the assessment for the intervening period.

   Fresh cases- In future all cases of appeals while deciding for disability pension, entitlement for intervening period also will be recommended by the Competent Medical Authority.

ii. It should be made mandatory for the Medical Boards to clearly state the admissibility of the award in the intervening period in all cases in Column in Notes below S.No.7 of AFMSF-17 at page No.3 in future by issuing clear cut instructions in this regard at the earliest.

2. All such cases may be dealt with accordingly.

3. This issues with the concurrence of the Finance Division of this Ministry vide their U.O.No. 3581/F/P dated 02.11.10.

4. Hindi version will follow.

Sd/-
Malathi Narayanan
Under Secretary (Pen/Pol)

23.37

Government of India, Ministry of Defence, Department of Ex-Servicemen Welfare Letter No 2(3)/2012/D(Pen/Pol)/Vol-II dated 2nd September 2021

Sub: **Implementation of the Government decision on the recommendations of the fifth CPC regarding casualty pensionary awards for the Armed Forces Officers and JCOs & Other Ranks.**

The undersigned is directed to refer to this Ministry's letter No. 1(2)/97/D(Pen-C) dated 31st January, 2001. In terms of Para 4.1 of this letter, various categories have been enumerated for determining the pensionary benefits for death or disability under different circumstances due to attributable or aggravated by military service causes. One of the circumstances enumerated under Category "E" (f) (ii) of the said para of the above mentioned MoD letter is "battle inoculation training exercises or demonstration with live ammunition".

2. Subsequently, it was decided vide MoD letters No. 1(11)/2006-D(Pen-C)/PC dated 8th September, 2009 and No. 1(11)/2006-D(Pen-C)/PC dated 5th March, 2010 that the term 'Battle Inoculation Training Exercises' would cover the following six categories :

i. Flying operation involved in rehearsing of war plans and implementation of OP instructions inclusive of international exercises.

ii. All combat and Tactical Sorties in preparation of war.

iii. Valley flying and missions involving operating at ultra low levels.

iv. All operational missions undertaken during peace like Special operations, Live ORP, Recce, Elint, Survey and induction trials of new weapons.

v. Missions undertaken in support of troops and security forces deployed in forward areas.

vi. Flying missions involving landings on the ALGs.

3. Para 2 of the MoD letter dated 8th September, 2009 states that "cases already settled prior to the date of issue of this letter will not be reopened".

4. The matter has been examined in this Ministry and it has been decided that the flying accidents cases that occurred on or after 01.01.1996 and which fall strictly under six categories mentioned at para 2 above may also be considered for grant of pensionary benefits in terms of MoD letter No. 1(2)/97/D(Pen-C) dated 31.01.2001. Accordingly, Para 2 of the MoD letter No. 1(11)/2006/D(Pen-C)/PC dated 8th September, 2009 stands removed.

5. Service Hqrs./Record Offices concerned are advised to re-examine each such case strictly in accordance with six categories mentioned at para 2 above in consultation with PCDA without any deviation.

6. This issues with the concurrence of MoD(Fin/Pen) vide their UO No. 10(4)/2010/FIN/PEN dated 30.06.2021.

7. Hindi version will follow.

Yours faithfully

Sd/-

(Ashok Kumar)

Under Secretary to the Govt of India

23.38

Army Order 05/2020

(Note: Also see the Chapters 23.8 and 23.9)

Casualties occurring after the year 2020 are dealt with by Army Order 05/2020, the relevant extract of which is reproduced hereunder:

Appendix A to AO 5/2020/MP

Battle Casualties

1. The casualties as a result of following will be considered as battle casualties:

   a. Enemy action in international war or any other operation.

   b. Border skirmishes.

   c. During deployment with a peace keeping mission abroad or any foreign assignment.

   d. During laying or clearance of mines including enemy mines as also mine-sweeping operations or caused by fixed apparatus (e.g. land mines, booby traps, barbed wire or any other obstacle) laid as defence against the enemy.

   e. On account of accidental explosions of mines while laying operationally oriented mine-field or lifting or negotiating mine-field laid by the enemy or own forces in operational areas near international borders or the lines of control (LC/LAC/ AGPL).

   f. War like situations, including cases which are attributable to extremist acts, exploding mines etc, while on way to an operational area.

   g. Battle inoculation, duly notified operationally oriented training exercises or demonstration with live ammunition.

   h. Flying operation involved in rehearsing of war plans and implementation of op instructions inclusive of international exercises.

   j. All combat and tactical sorties in preparation of war.

   k. Valley flying and missions involving operating at ultra-low levels.

   l. All operational missions undertaken during peace like special operations, live ORP recce, ELINT, survey and induction trials of new weapons.

   m. Missions undertaken in support of troops and security force deployed in forward areas.

   n. Flying missions involving landings on the ALGs.

o. Death or injury by own troops during the course of duty in any operational area if the personnel killed or wounded are not to blame.

p. An act of violence/attack by extremists, anti-social elements etc while on operational duty.

q. Action against extremists, anti-social elements, etc. Death/injury while employed in the aid of civil power in quelling agitation, riots or revolt by demonstrators will be covered under this category.

r. Poisoning by any means by enemy agents whether on duty or even when not on duty.

s. Kidnapping by extremists while on operational duty or even when not on duty because of being an army personnel.

t. Injuries and deaths which occur in action in an operational area.

u. Electrocution/attacks by wild animals and snake bite/drowning during the course of action in counter insurgency/war.

v. Death or injury due to acts of violence/attack by terrorists, anti-social elements, etc whether on duty other than operational duty or even when not on duty. Bomb blasts in public places or transport, indiscriminate shooting incidents in public. etc would be covered under this category.

w. Death/ injury occurring while employed in the aid to civil authority in dealing with natural calamities.

x. Accidental death/injury sustained due to natural calamities such as flood, avalanches, land slide, cyclone, fire and lightening or drowning in river while performing operational duties/ movement in action against enemy forces and armed hostilities in operational area to include deployment on IB/LC/LAC.

y. Blast of any kind of explosive during operational duty on IB/ LC/ LAC and in counter insurgency (CI)/ counterterrorism (CT) operations and in ammunition storage echelons for operational purpose.

z. Casualties due to illness caused by terrain/climatic conditions while operating along IB/LC/LAC and CI/CT operations.

aa. Specialised vehicles/ MT /Plant equipment accidents while performing bonafide military duty in war/border skirmishes with neighbouring countries and during operations near IB/LC/LAC and in counter insurgency (Cl)/ counterterrorism (CT).

ab. Falls/slipping while on patrols/ambush/operational duty near IB/LC/LAC and CI/CT operations including long range patrols.

ac. Casualties under any other circumstances not covered above will be considered on a case to case basis with the approval of COAS.

Physical Casualties

2. Death caused due to natural causes/illness/accident/suicide/murder in operational and non-operational areas will be treated as Physical Casualties.

Miscellaneous Aspects

3. (a) Saboteurs, even of own country, will be treated as enemy for the purpose of classifying their actions as enemy action and encounters against them as encounters against the enemy.

   (b) Reports regarding personnel wounded or injured in action will specify the nature of the wound or injury and will also state whether the personnel remained on duty.

   (c) Reports on personnel missing in action will indicate, if possible, their likely fate, e.g "believed killed", "believed prisoner of war" or "believed drowned" etc.

   (d) Any casualty occurring during deployment/mobilisation of troops, for taking part in war or war like operations, will be treated as battle casualty.

Chapter-24

Provisions Related to Ex-Gratia Compensation

24.1

Government of India, Ministry of Defence Letter No 20(1)/98/D(Pen/Sers) dated 22nd September 1998

Sub: **Special benefits in cases of death and disability in service-Payment of Ex-Gratia lumpsum compensation to families of the Defence service personnel who die in harness-recommendations of Vth Central Pay Commission.**

Sir,

I am directed to refer to Govt. of India Ministry of Personnel, Public Grievances and Pension, Dept. of Pension & Pensioners' Welfare O.M. No. 45/55/97-P&PW dated 11.09.98 and state that the President is pleased to decide that the families of defence service personnel who die in harness in the performance of their bonafide official duties shall be paid the following ex-gratia lump sum compensation:

a. Death occurring due to accidents in the course of performance of duties - Rs 5.00 lakhs

b. Death occurring in the course of performance of duties attributable to acts of violence by terrorists, anti social elements – Rs 5.00 lakhs.

c. Death occurring during (i) Enemy action in International war or border skirmishes and (ii) Action against militants, terrorists, extremists etc. – Rs 7.50 lakhs.

2. The graded structure of ex-gratia lumpsum compensation takes into account the hardships, and risks involved in certain assignments, the intensity and magnitude of the tragedy and deprivation that families of Govt. servants experience on the demise of bread winner in different circumstances, the expectations of the employer from the employees to function in extreme and security to employees who are required to function under trying circumstances and are exposed to different kinds of risks in the performance of their duties.

3. Powers were delegated in the Ministry of Finance O.M. No. 19(18)-EV(A)/66 dated Feb., 26th 1966 to the appointing authorities to sanction awards under the relevant Extraordinary Pension Rules in those cases in which the proposed pension or gratuity is held to be clearly admissible under the rules. However, any awards proposed to be granted on ex-gratia basis were to continue to be referred to the Ministry of Finance as usual. In partial modification of those orders, in so far as they relate to ex-gratia awards, the admissibility of and entitlement to ex-gratia lumpsum compensation in the circumstances in these orders may be decided in each individual case by the CCDA (P) Allahabad as amended vide corrigendum No. 20(1)/98/D/Services) dated 12th April, 1998.

4. The conditions and guidelines to be observed governing the payment of ex-gratia compensation in terms of these orders are indicated in the annexure.

5. The orders shall apply to all cases of death in harness occurring on or after August 1, 1997. These shall be regulated and finalised in terms of the orders and instructions in force prior to the issue of these orders.

6. These orders supersede earlier orders issued on the subject vide Ministry of Defence Letter No. B/39902/XXII/AG/PS-4(d)/2069/D (Pay/Services) dated October 8, 1996 and amendment issued vide letter of even number dated June 4, 1997.

7. These orders are issued with the concurrence of Defence (Finance) vide their U.O. No. 1869/Addl. FA (d)/98 dated 11.09.1998.

Yours faithfully,
Sd/-
(B. Brahma)
Director (AG)

ANNEXURE

Annexure of Letter No. 20(1)/D/(Pay/Sers) Dated 22nd September, 1998

Conditions governing the payment of ex-gratia lumpsum compensation and guidelines to be observed.

1. The main condition to be satisfied for the payment of the ex-gratia lumpsum compensation in the specified circumstances in that the death of the employee concerned should have occurred is the actual performance of bonafide official duties. In other words a causal connection should be established between the occurrence of death and Government service.

2. Powers having been delegated to the Administrative Ministries to sanction ex-gratia payments under these orders, it shall be their responsibility as well as that of the financial Advisers to satisfy themselves that the death of the Service personnel to be compensated by the payment of the lumpsum ex-gratia to the family in fact occurred in the actual performance of bonafide official duties and to establish its causal connection and nexus with Government service. This could be done on the basis of medical and other documents relating to the case.

3. Even if a Defence personnel had died in such circumstances that a medical report could not be secured, the nexus and causal connection with Government service would need to be adequately established in determining the entitlement to the ex-gratia lumpsum payment. In deciding this issue, all evidence (both direct and circumstantial) shall be taken into account and the benefit of reasonable doubt given to the claimant. The benefit of reasonable doubt will be extended more liberally in field service cases, as provided in the guidelines for conceding attributability of disablement of death to Government service forming part of the Liberalised Pension Award Scheme, Pension Regulations for Defence Services.

4. In cases of accidents of commercial aircraft resulting in the death of passengers, compensation is payable to next of kin by the national or private airline concerned in term of international conventions. The ex-gratia lumpsum compensation in terms of these orders will, therefore, not be admissible, In addition, in the event of death due to accidents while travelling on duty by commercial aircraft shall be restricted only to those cases where death occurs in an accident while travelling on duty by service aircraft. The payment of ex-gratia in these cases will be without prejudice to the bond required to be executed by the Service personnel, if any, indemnifying the Government against any claims on account of death while travelling by service aircraft.

5. Railways also pay compensation to the next of kin of passengers killed in train accidents. Therefore, the ex-gratia compensation admissible in terms of clause (a) of para 1 of these orders shall be reduced by the compensation, if any, received by the next of kin of service personnel killed in train accidents while travelling on duty.

6. Ex-gratia compensation under the clause (b) of para 1 will be admissible to service personnel killed while employed in aid of the civil administration in quelling agitations Protest demonstrations, riots, etc, regardless of whether such agitations, demonstrations, etc, are resorted to by members of the public, political parities, etc, or by other public servants, including police Personnel. In addition, in the context of a perceptible increase in violence related incidents over the years, service personnel on duty could become unwitting victims of bomb blast in public places or vehicles, indiscriminate shooting incidents in public, etc, often resorted to by terrorists, antisocial elements, etc, The compensation under clause (b) will also, therefore, be admissible in cases of death in such incidents, provided the service personnel concerned were actually on duty at the relevant time.

7. Cases of death resulting from acts of violence or assault by terrorists, anti-social elements, etc, against a service personnel with the intention of deterring or preventing him from performing duties or because of any act done or attempted to be done by such service personnel in the lawful discharge of his duties; or because of his official position will also be covered under clause (b).

8. Ex-gratia compensation under clause (c) of para 1 will generally be restricted only to those cases where the death of the Service personnel is directly caused by actual field operations. In addition, families of service personnel killed after being kidnapped by militants, terrorist, extremists, etc, because of their official position or with, a view to spreading terror, will also be entitled to the compensation under this clause.

9. Few illustrative examples of cases to be covered under the different clauses of para 1 are contained in the Appendix for the guidance of sanctioning authorities. In cases of any doubt in regard to the applicability of the ex-gratia compensation scheme, such cases will be referred to the department of pension and pensioners Welfare for appropriate decision in consultation with the Department of Expenditure.

10. The ex-gratia compensation in the circumstances specified in these orders shall be admissible in addition to such other benefits as may be admissible under the liberalised pensionary award scheme as the case may be. This will also be mutually exclusive of such other benefits as may be admissible under the group Insurance Scheme of the respective Defence services fund, etc, and will be payable in addition to such benefits.

11. In determining the admissibility of the ex-gratia compensation payable from Central Government Funds, ex-gratia payments, if any, made to families of the deceased service personnel from state funds of the State Government concerned shall not be taken account and shall be excluded.

12. In certain cases, relief is also provided to families of deceased Service personnel from sundry Govt. sources, such as the Prime Minister's Relief Funds, etc, In such cases, it should be insured of the relief/ex-gratia compensation paid from different sources does not exceed Rs 10 lakhs in each individual cases.

13. In view of the fact that the ex-gratia compensation in terms of those orders is payable to the families of the deceased Service personnel, default contributory negligence, if any, on the part of the service personnel concerned shall not be taken into account in sanctioning the compensation.

14. Any related issue not specifically covered in these orders shall be decided in terms of the relevant provisions in this regard contained in the Liberalised pensionary award scheme as amended from time to time and the instructions issued there under.

15. Where any doubt arises as to the interpretation of the provisions of these orders, it shall be referred to the Department of Pension & Pensioners' Welfare for decision.

EXAMPLES

Clause (a): Death Attributable to accidents while on duty:

1. Death, as result of an accident while travelling in public, private or official vehicle or otherwise, of a Group 'D' employee, Despatch Rider, Messenger, Postman, Notice server etc. deputed to distribute dak, notices, etc., or of personnel on field duties.
2. Death occurring due to an accident while traveling on bonafide duties in a service aircraft.
3. Accidents during test flights of aircraft and non Scheduled flights, of chartered aircraft resulting in death of Service Personnel traveling on duty in public interest in such flights.
4. Dearth, in accidents of personnel undertaking official journeys on duty.
5. Accidents to ships, river steamers, etc. resulting in death of Service Personnel undertaking journeys on duty by these modes of travels.
6. Death, as a result of accidents, of Service personnel while proceeding on raids against anti-social elements, etc.
7. Death, due to contact with live electric/power lines, of personnel deployed on flood/cyclone relief activities.
8. Death due to electrocution, of Service Personnel engaged in rectification of defects in generation and distribution of electricity.
9. Accidents while engaged in rectification of defects in machinery and equipments.
10. Death due to accidental explosion of boilers, storage tanks of inflammable materials, chemicals, etc.
11. Death due to fire accidents while on duty.
12. Death of Fire Fighting Staff engaged in fire fighting operations.

Clause (b): Death attributable to acts of violence by the terrorists, anti-social elements, etc:

1. Death resulting from acts of violence of assault by terrorists smugglers, dacoits, anti-social elements etc. against individual Service Personnel.
   (a) With the intention of deterring or preventing him from performing his duties; or
   (b) Because of any act done or attempt to be done in the lawful discharge of his duties or
   (c) Because of his official position.
2. Service personnel killed in the course of performance of their duties as a result of violence or attack by armed hostile extremists, terrorists, anti-social elements, etc.
3. Service Personnel on duty, killed in an incident or terrorists violence in Jammu & Kashmir, the North Eastern Region, Punjab etc. other than in actual operations and encounters.
4. Death due to stone throwing, use of weapons and other violent acts by demonstrators, anti-social elements etc. Service personnel while employed in aid of the civil administration in quelling agitations, protest demonstrations, riots etc.
5. Death of Service personnel while proceeding on raids against anti social elements etc. attributable to attacks by the parties so raided, including anti social elements.
6. Death while on duty, as unwitting victims of bomb blast in public or vehicle, indiscriminate shooting incidents in public, etc.

Clause (c): Death occurring during wars or Border skirmishes and action against militants, terrorists and extremists:

The ex-gratia compensation under clause (c) of para 1 will be restricted only to those cases where service Personnel are killed, in actual field operations. A higher rate of compensation has been prescribed in these cases having regard to the magnitude of the hardships and risks involved in field operations including combing operations against terrorists, militants, etc. This will generally be applicable only to the service personnel deployed along the borders, Line of control, etc, as well as those engaged in combing terrorism, The condition of being actually involved in field operations will, therefore, have to be satisfied before the higher ex-gratia compensation of Rs 7.50 lakhs is sanctioned.

As indicated in para 1 of the letter, compensation under this clause will be admissible to families of Service personnel killed:

i. in action in international wars

ii. while fighting in war-like situations or border skirmishes with any country.

iii. in action against armed hostile militants, terrorists and extremists;

iv. during laying or clearance of mines, including those laid by enemies, militants, terrorists etc, as well as in the course of mine sweeping operations;

v. as a result of exploding mines enroute to an operational area;

vi. during battle inoculation as part of prescribed training exercise involving the use of live ammunition.

In addition, families of service personnel killed after being kidnapped by militants, terrorists, extremists, etc, because of their official position or with a view to spreading terror will also be entitled to the compensation under this clause.

Yours faithfully,
Sd/-

24.2

Government of India, Ministry of Defence, Letter No 20(1)/98/(Pay/Services) dated 12th April 1999

CORRIGENDUM

Sub: **Special benefits in cases of death and disability in service – Payment of Ex-Gratia lumpsum compensation to families of the Defence Service Personnel who die in harness – Recommendations of the Fifth Central Pay Commission.**

Reference this Ministry's letter No. 20(1)/98/D(Pay/Services), dated the 22nd September, 1998 on the above subject.

2. The competent Authority has approved the delegation of power to CCDA(P), Allahabad to sanction/adjudicate matters relating to the grant of ex-gratia payment to the families of the Defence Service personnel who die in harness. In the last two lines of para 3 of this Ministry's letter referred to above, the words "by the Ministry of Defence in consultation with Financial adviser (Defence Services)" may be omitted and replaced by "by the CCDA(P) Allahabad.

3. This issues with the concurrence of Ministry of Defence (Finance) vide their UO No. 329/AG/PA/99 dated 1.4.99.

Yours faithfully,

Sd/-

(R.K. Grover)

Under Secretary to Government of India

24.3

Government of India, Ministry of Defence Letter No 20(1)/98/D (Pensions/ Services) dated 3rd August 1999

CORRIGENDUM

Sub: **Special benefits in cases of death and disability in service – Payment of Ex-Gratia lumpsum compensation to the families of the defence Service Personnel who die in harness – Recommendations of the Fifth Central Pay Commission.**

This Ministry's letter No. 20(1)/98/D/(Pay/Services) dated 22 Sept 98 as amended vide letter of even number dated 12 April 1999 is further amended as follows:

Existing Para 1(c) may be deleted and substituted by the following:

(b) Death occurring (i) during border skirmishes and (ii) action against militants, terrorists, extremists etc. - Rs 7.50 lacs

(c) Death occurring during enemy action in international war or such war like engagements which are specifically notified by Ministry of Defence - Rs 10.00 lacs

2. This letter takes effect from 1st May, 1999

3. This issues with the concurrence of Finance Division of this Ministry vide their UO No. 787/PA dated 3rd August, 1999.

Yours faithfully,

Sd/-

(R.K. Grover)

Under Secretary to Government of India

24.4

Government of India, Ministry of Defence Letter No 20(5)/2009/D(Pay/Services) dated 4th June 2010

Sub: **Special benefits in cases of death and disability in service-Payment of Ex-Gratia lumpsum compensation to the families of the Defence Service personnel who die in harness-Recommendations of the Sixth Central Pay Commission**

Sir,

I am directed to refer to this Ministry's letter No. 20/1/98/D(Pay/Services) dated 22.9.1998 as amended vide letter of even number dated 12th April, 1999, 3rd August, 1999, 19th May, 2000 and 21st October, 2008 on the above subject.

2. Vide para 1 of the above mentioned letter dated 21st October, 2008, the existing rates of ex-gratia lump sum compensation to the next of kin of the deceased defence personnel have already been revised as follows:

(a)	Death occurring due to accidents in course of duties	Rs 10.00 lakhs
(b)	Death in the course of duties attributable to acts of violence by terrorists, etc.	Rs 10.00 lakhs
(c)	Death occurring during enemy action in war or border skirmishes or in action against militants, terrorists, etc.	Rs 15.00 lakhs
(d)	Death occurring during enemy action in International war or war like engagements specifically notified.	Rs 20.00 lakhs

3. A new clause (d) shall be added to para 1 of aforesaid letter dated 21st October, 2008 as follows and existing clause (d) may be renumbered as (e):

(e)	Death occurring while on duty in the specified high altitude, inaccessible border posts, etc. on account of natural disasters, extreme weather conditions.	Rs 15.00 lakhs

4. In certain cases, relief is also provided to the families of deceased Armed Forces personnel from sundry Government sources, such as the Prime Minister's Relief Fund, Chief Minister's Relief Fund, etc. In such cases, it should be ensured that the aggregate of the relief/ex-gratia compensation paid from different sources does not exceed Rs 20 lakhs in each individual case. Para 12 of Annexure to this Ministry's letter No. 20/1/98/D(Pay/Services) dated 22nd September 1998 stands modified to that extent.

5. The amendment made at para 3 above is in extension of the provisions of Ministry of Personnel, Public Grievances and Pensions (Department of Pension and Pensioners' Welfare) O.M. No.38/37/08-P&PW (A) dated 2nd September, 2008 while the amendment at para 4 is in extension of the provisions of the Ministry of Personnel, Public Grievances and Pensions (Department of Pension and Pensioners' Welfare) O.M. No.45/7/2008-P&W(F) dated 16th March, 2009 to Armed Forces personnel.

6. The provisions of ex-gratia payments to the families of Defence Forces personnel, as contained in MoD letter dated 22.9.1998 as amended vide MoD letter dated12.4.1999, 3.8.1999, 19.5.2000 and 21.10.2008 not affected by the amendments mentioned in para 3 and 4 above, shall remain unchanged.

7. The amendments mentioned in para 3 and 4 above take effect from 1st January, 2006.

8. This Ministry's Letters No. (i) PC.20(1)/98/D(Pay/Services) dated 30.4.2009 and (ii) 20/2/2009/D(Pay/Services) dated 13.7.2009 are hereby cancelled.

9. This issues with the concurrence of Finance Division of this Ministry vide their F.No.PC-8(15)/2004-AG(242-PA) dated 2.6.2010.

Sd/-
PS Walia
Under Secretary to Govt of India

24.5

Government of India, Ministry of Defence Letter No 20(5)/2009/D (Pay/Services) dated 17th August 2010

Sub: **Special benefits in cases of death and disability in service-payment of Ex-Gratia lumpsum compensation to the families of the Defence Service personnel who die in harness-Recommendations of the Sixth Central pay Commission.**

Sir,

I am directed to refer to para 4 of this Ministry's letter of even number dated 4th June, 2010 on the above subject which provide that the aggregate of the relief/ex-gratia compensation paid from different sources should not exceed Rs 20 Lakhs in each individual case.

2. The matter has been reviewed in terms of Ministry of Personnel Public Grievances and Pension, Department of Pension and Pensioners Welfare O.M. No 45/7/2008-P&PW(F) dated 12th, July, 2010. It has been decided that there will be no ceiling for grant of ex-gratia lump sum compensation in terms of this Ministry's letter No. 20/1/98/D (Pay/services) dated 22.9.98 as amended.

3. The above revised provision will be effective from 1.1.2006.

4. All other terms and condition of this Ministry's letter No 20(1)/98/D (Pay/Services) dated 22.9.98 as amended shall remain unchanged.

5. This issues with the concurrence of Finance Division of this Ministry vide their U.O. No. PC 8 (15)/2004-AG/PA (370-PA) dated 13.08.2010.

Yours faithfully,

Sd/-

(P.S.Walia)

Under Secretary to the Government of India

24.6

Government of India, Ministry of Defence Letter No 20(2)/2016/D (Pay/Services) dated 2nd November 2016

Sub: Ex-gratia lump sum compensation – Recommendations of the Seventh Central Pay Commission.

Sir,

I am directed to refer to this Ministry's letter No. 20(1)98/D(Pay/Services) dated 22.09.1998 as amended vide letter of even number dated 12.04.1999, 03.09.1999, 19.05.2000, 21.10.2008 and letter No 20(5)/2009/D (Pay/Services) dated 4.6.2010 on the above subject and to say that in pursuance of Government's decision on the recommendations of the Seventh Central Pay Commission, the existing rate of ex-gratia lump sum compensation to the Next of Kin of the deceased Defence Forces Personnel is revised as follows:

(a)	Death occurring due to accidents in course of duties	Rs 25 Lakhs
(b)	Death in the course of performance of duties attributable to acts of violence by terrorist, anti social elements, etc.	Rs 25 Lakhs
(c)	Death occurring in border skirmishes and action against militants, terrorists, extremists, sea pirates.	Rs 25 Lakhs
(d)	Death occurring during while on duty in the specified high altitude, inaccessible border posts, on account of natural disasters, extreme weather conditions.	Rs 35 Lakhs
(e)	Death occurring during enemy action in war or such war like engagements, which are specifically notified by Ministry of Defence and death occurring during evacuation of India Nationals from a war-torn zone in foreign country.	Rs 45 Lakhs

2. This letter takes effect from 01.01.2016.

3. The other terms and conditions contained in the Ministry's letter dated 22.09.1998 as amended shall remain unchanged.

4. This issues with the concurrence of Finance Division of this Ministry vide their UO. No. 8(1)/2016-AG (414-PA) dated 27.10.2016.

Yours faithfully,

Sd/-

(Prashant Rastogi)

Under Secretary to the Government of India

24.7

Government of India, Ministry of Defence Letter No. 20(1)2017/D(Pay/Services) dated 14th July 2021

Sub: Ex-Gratia lumpsum compensation - Clarification.

I am directed to refer to this Ministry's letter No. 20(1)98/D(Pay/Services) dated 22.9.1998 as amended vide letter of even number dated 12.4.1999, 3.8.1999, 19.5.2000, 21.10.2008, letter No. 20(5)2009/D(Pay/Services) dated 4.6.2010 Number No. 20(2)2016/D(Pay/Services) dated 2.11.2016 on the above subject and to say that following has been clarified for better interpretation of the aforementioned letters regarding grant of Ex-gratia lump sum compensation to the next of kin of the Defence Service personnel who die in harness in the performance of their bonafide official duties:

(a) A person subject to the disciplinary code of the Armed Forces shall be treated on 'Bonafide Official duty':

a. When performing an official task or a task failure to do which would constitute an offence, triable under the disciplinary code applicable to him.

b. When moving from one place of duty to another place of duty irrespective of the mode of journey.

c. During the period of participation in recreation and other unit/sports activities organized or approved by service authorities and during the period of traveling in relation thereto.

Note 1: Personnel of the Armed Forces participating in local/national/international sports tournaments as member of service teams or mountaineering expeditions/ gliding organized by service authorities, with the approval of Service HQs, shall be deemed to be 'on bonafide duty' for the purpose of grant of ex-gratia lump sum compensation.

Note 2: Personnel of Armed Forces participating in sports tournaments or in privately organized mountaineering expeditions of indulging in gliding as a hobby in their individual capacity, shall not be deemed to be 'on bonafide duty' for the purpose of grant of ex-gratia lump sum compensation, even though prior permission of the competent service authorities may have been obtained by them.

Note 3: Injuries sustained by personnel of the Armed Forces in impromptu games and sports which are organized by or with the approval of the local service authority and death or disability arising from such injuries, wil be regarded as having occurred 'on bonafide duty' for the purpose of grant of ex-gratia lump sum compensation.

Note 4: The personnel of the Armed Forces deputed for training at courses conducted by the Himalayan Mountaineering Institute, Darjeeling and other similar institutes shall be treated at par with personnel attending other authorized professional courses or exercise for the Defence Services for the purpose of grant of ex-gratia lump sum compensation on account of death sustained during the courses.

d. When proceeding on leave/valid out pass from his duty station to his leave station or returning to duty from his leave station on leave/valid out pass.

Note 1: An Armed Forces personnel while travelling between his place of duty to leave station and vice-versa is to be treated on duty irrespective of whether he has availed railway warrant/concession vouchers/cash TA etc or not for the journey. This would also include journey pertormed from leave station to duty station in case the individual returns early.

Note 2: The occurrence of death should have taken place in reaching the leave station from duty station or vice versa using the commonly available/adopted route and mode of transpart.

e. When travelling by a reasonable route from one's official residence to and back from the appointed place of duty, irrespective of the mode of conveyance (whether private or provided by the Government).

f. Death which occurs when an individual is not strictly 'on duty' e.g. on leave, including cases of death as a result of attack by or action against extremists or anti-social elements may also be considered attributable to service, provided that it involved risk which was due to his belonging to the Armed Forces and that the same was not a risk faced personal by a civilian. Death due to enmity is not admissible.

Note 1: For the purpose of grant of ex-gratia lump sum compensation leave shall include all types of leave granted by Competent authority. Leave/Casual Leave shall not be treated as 'Duty' except in situations mentioned above.

2. This letter takes effect from the date of issue of this letter.

3. The other terms and conditions contained in the Ministry's letter dated 22.9.1998 as amended shall remained unchanged.

4. This issues with the concurrence of Finance Division of this Ministry vide their U.O. No. 8(15)/2004-AG/PA dated 13.7.2021.

(T Johnson)
Gp Capt
Director (Pay/Services)

24.8

Government of India, Ministry of Defence, Department of Military Affairs ID No 20(1)/2017/D(Pay/Services) dated 23rd September 2021

Sub: Ex-Gratia lump sum compensation - clarification.

Reference MoD letter No. 20(1)/2017/D(Pay/Services) dated 14.07.2021 on the subject noted above.

2. In this regard, the following points may be taken care of while dealing with Ex-gratia cases, in order to avoid cases, coming up through Courts.

a. All sporting events duly approved by SHQ shall be treated as bonafide duty. Similarly all impromptu games and sports which are organised by or with the approval of the local service authority will also be treated as bonafide duty.

b. Journey from duty station to leave station and vice versa will be treated as bonafide duty. So if the leave station is abroad the journey upto the leave station and back will be treated as bonafide duty.Any injury/ death during the leave period whether in India or abroad will not be treated as bonafide duty.

c. Service personnel participating in high risk activity like sky diving, rafting, motor cycle expeditionor Iron Man competition on their own accord in a private capacity to pursue their hobby even if they have taken prior permission, any injury or death will not be treated as bonafide duty.

Sd/-
(T Johnson)
Gp Capt
Director (Pay/Services)

Chapter-25

Provisions Related to Pension to Families of Missing Personnel

25.1

Government of India, Ministry of Defence Letter No 12(16)/86/D (Pension Service) dated 3rd June 1988

Sub: **Release of DCRG, leave Encashment and family Pension in respect of Armed Forces personnel who are missing.**

Sir,

A number of cases have been referred to this Ministry for grant of terminal and other pensionary benefits to the families of service personnel who have suddenly disappeared while in operational and non-operational service and whose whereabouts are not known. At present all such cases are considered on merits. In the normal course unless a period of 7 years has elapsed from the date of disappearance of the employee, he cannot be deemed to be dead and therefore the retirement benefits cannot be paid to the family. This principle is based on Section 108 of the Indian Evidence Act which provides that when the question is whether the man is alive or dead and it is proved that he had not been heard of for 7 years by those who would naturally have heard of him had he been alive, the burden of proving that he is alive is shifted to the person who affirms it. This has resulted in grant hardship and distress to the families who have to wait for 7 years before any terminal benefits could be paid to them.

2. The president is therefore pleased to decide that when a member of the 'Indian Armed' Forces is declared missing while in service, the family will be paid the following benefits subject to adjustment of outstanding dues in respect of the missing personnel, if any:

a. **Immediately after the date of declaration of disappearance:**

The amount of salary due, leave encashment due and DSOF/AFPP Fund amount subject to nomination made by the missing personnel.

b. **After the lapse of one year from the date of declaration of disappearance/presumption of death:**

Family pension/DCRG etc. as admissible in normal conditions.

3. The above benefits may be sanctioned after observing following formalities:

i. The family must lodge a report with the concerned Police Station and obtain a report that the employee has not been traced after all efforts had been made by the police.

ii. The claimant will be required to furnish an indemnity bond with two solvent sureties to the effect that all payments thus made will be recovered from the amount due to the person if he/she reappears and makes any claims.

4. The family can apply to the concerned authority for grant of family pension and DCR Gratuity after one year from the date of declaration of disappearance of the service personnel in accordance with the procedure for sanction of family pension and DCR Gratuity. In case the disbursement of DCR Gratuity is not effected within 3 months of the date of application, the interest shall be paid at the rates applicable and responsibility for the delay fixed.

5. In the case of officers, the respective Branch/Dte at Service HQrs and in the case of JCOs/OR and equivalent in Navy and Air Force, their respective Records Offices will process such cases with CDA(O)/PAO/CDA(P)/CDA(Navy)/CDA(Air Force).

6. The provisions of this letter take effect from 29th August, 1986.

7. This issues with the concurrence of the Finance Division of this Ministry vide their u.o. No. 802- Pen of 1988.

Yours faithfully,
Sd/-
(Y.K. Talwar)
Desk Officer

25.2

Government of India, Ministry of Defence Letter No 12(16)/86/D (Pension Service) dated 23rd March 1992

Sub: Grant of family pension and gratuity to the families, etc, of Armed Forces personnel/pensioners who disappear suddenly and whose whereabouts are not known.

Sir,

I am directed to refer to this Ministry's letters of even number dated 3rd June, 1988 and 20th March, 1990 and to say that the guidelines contained in the succeeding paragraphs will regulate payment of the benefits grants under the above noted letters.

2. The date of disappearance of the serving Armed Forces personnel/pensioners will be reckoned from the date the First Information Report is lodged with the, police by the family and the period of one year after which the benefits of family pension and gratuity are to be sanctioned, will be reckoned from this date. However, the benefits to be sanctioned to the family, etc, of the missing personnel will be based on and regulated by the emolument drawn by him and the rules/orders applicable to him as on the last date he/she was on duty including authorised periods of leave. Family pension at normal/enhanced rates, as may be applicable in individual cases, will be payable to the family of missing personnel. Family pension where sanctioned at pre-1.1.986 rates will be revised and consolidated w.e.f. 1.1.1986 in terms of the Govt of India, letter No. 1(4)/87/D(Pens/Sers) dt. 27th July 1987, as amended from time to time.

3. In the case of missing pensioners, the family pension at the rates indicated in the PPO will be payable and authorised by the Pension Sanctioning Authority. Where the PPO does not contain this information, the Pension Sanctioning Authority will take necessary action to sanction the family pension as due, as provided in para 2 above.

4. Death gratuity will also be payable to the families, but not exceeding the amount which would have been payable as Retirement gratuity if the person had retired. The difference between retirement gratuity and death gratuity shall be subsequently payable after the death is conclusively established or on the expiry of seven years period from the date of missing.

5. An indemnity bond will be obtained for the above purpose from the family members, etc, in the formats unclosed as Appendix 'A' (for missing personnel) and as Appendix 'B' (for missing pensioners) to this letter, which have been prepared by the Deptt of Pension & Pensioners, which are in consultation with Deptt of Legal Affairs.

6. Cases already settled otherwise, than in accordance with this letter need not be reopened, unless such a opening will be to the advantage of the beneficiaries.

7. This issues with the concurrence of Finance Division of this Ministry vide their U.O.285/Pen of 1992.

8. Hindi version will follow.

(Based on Deptt of Pension & Pensioners Welfare O.M. No. 1/17/86-P&PW (C) dt. 25.1.1991)

Yours faithfully,
Sd/-
(Diwan Chand)
Desk Officer

25.3

Government of India, Ministry of Defence Letter No 12(16)/85/D (Pension Service) dated 26th August 1993

Sub: **Grant of family Pension and gratuity to the families of Armed Forces personnel/pensioners who disappear suddenly and whose whereabouts are not known.**

Sir,

I am directed to refer to this Ministry's letter of even number dated 23rd March 1992 on the above subject and to say that in accordance with the provisions contained therein the date of disappearance of the serving Armed Forces personnel/pensioners is reckoned from the date the First Information Report is lodged with the police by the family and the period of one year after which the benefits of Family pension and Gratuity are be sanctioned, is reckoned from this date. At present the Family Pension is sanctioned and paid to the eligible member of the family one year after the date of lodging the FIR with the police and no Family Pension is paid for the intervening period of one year from the date the F.I.R. is lodged to the date the family pension can be sanctioned.

2. The above practice is causing hardship to the families. It has, therefore, been decided that the Family Pension, which in pursuance of the earlier orders, will continue to be sanctioned and paid one year after the date of lodging the F.I.R. will accrue from the date of lodging the F.I.R. or expiry of leave of the service personnel who has disappeared whichever is later. At the time of issue of sanction of family pension, the payment of pension from the date of accrual will be authorized. The usual procedure of obtaining the Indemnity Bond, etc, will continue to the followed while sanctioning payment of family pension as laid down in Govt. letter of even number dated 23 March, 1992. It will be ensured by the concerned authorities that Family Pension is not authorised for any period during which payment of pay and allowances in respect of the disappeared service personnel has been made.

3. The provisions of this letter take effect from 18th February, 1993, based on Deptt. of Pension & Pensioners Welfare OM No. 1/17/P&PW/86-E dated 18th February, 1993.

4. This issues with the concurrence of Finance Division of this Ministry vide their U.O. NO. 1793/Pen- 93 dated 25.8.93.

Yours faithfully,

Sd/-

(Diwan chand)

Desk Officer

25.4

Indemnity Bonds for Missing Personnel and Pensioners

(IN THE CASE OF MISSING SERVING PERSONNEL)
INDEMNITY BOND

KNOW ALL MEN by these presents that we (a) ____________________ (b) the wife/son/brother/nominee etc. of (c) ____________________ who was holding the rank of ____________________ in the Unit/Corps ____________________ is reported to have been missing since__________________(thereinafter referred to as missing service person) resident of ____________________ hereinafter called "the, obligor") and (d) ____________________ son/wife/daughter of Shri ____________________ resident of ____________________ the sureties for and on behalf of the obligor (hereinafter celled "the Sureties") are held family bound to the president of India (hereinafter called "the Govt") in the sum of Rs ____________________ (in words) ____________________ equivalent of the amount on account of payment of salary, leave encashment, Retirement/Death Gratuity and each and every sum being the monthly family pension will and truly to be paid to the Govt on demand and without a demur together with simple interest @ ____________________ % p.a. from the date of payment thereof until repayment for which payment who bind ourselves and our respective heirs, executors, administrators, legal representatives, successors and assigns by these presents.

Signed this ____________________ day of ____________________ one thousand nine hundred and ____________________
WHEREAS (c) ____________________ was at the time of his disappearance in the employment of the Govt. receiving a pay at the rate of Rs ____________________ (in words) ____________________ only per month from the Government.

AND WHEREAS the said (c) ____________________ disappeared on the ____________________ day of ____________________ 19 ____________________ and there was due to him at the time of his disappearance the sum equivalent of (i) salary due/(ii) leave encashment (iii) Defence Service Officers Provident Fund/Armed Forces Personnel Provident Fund and (iv) Retirement/Death Gratuity.

AND WHEREAS the obligor is entitled to family pension at Rs ____________________ (Rupees ____________________ only) plus admissible Dearness Relief thereon.

AND WHEREAS the obligor has represented that he/she is entitled to the aforesaid sum and approached the Govt. for making payment thereof to avoid undue delay and hardship.

AND WHEREAS the Govt. has agreed to make payment of the said sum of Rs ____________________ (in words) ____________________ and monthly family pension Rs ____________________ (in words) ____________________ ____________________ and The Dearness relief thereon to the Obligor upon the Obligor and the Sureties entering into a Bond in the above mentioned sum to indemnify to Govt. against the claims to the amount so due to the aforesaid missing serving person.

AND WHEREAS the Obligor and at his/her request the Surety/Sureties have agreed to execute the Bond in the terms and manner her in after contained.

NOW THE CONDITION OF THIS BOND is such that if after payment has been made to the Obligor, the Obligor and/or Surety/Sureties shall in the even of a claim being made, by any other person or the missing employee on appearance, against the Govt, with respect to the aforesaid sum of Rs ____________________ (in words) ____________________ and the sum paid by the Govt. as monthly pension and relief as aforesaid the refund to the Govt. the said sum of Rs ____________________ (in words) ____________________ and each and every sum paid by Govt. as monthly pension and Dearness relief together with simple interest @ ____________________ % per annum and shall, otherwise, indemnify and keep the Govt. harmless and indemnified against and from all liabilities in respect of the aforesaid sums and all costs incurred in the consequence of the claim there to THEN the above written Bond or obligation shall be void and of no effect but otherwise, it shall remain in full force, effect and virtue.

AND THESE PRESENTS ALSO WITNESS that the liability of the Surety/Sureties hereunder shall not be impaired or discharged by reason of time being granted by or any forbearance set or omission of the Govt whether with or without the knowledge or cannot of the Surety/Sureties in respect of or in relation to the obligations or conditions to be performed or discharged by the Obligor or by any other method or thing whatsoever which under the law relating to the sureties would but for this provision shall have no effect of so releasing the Surety/Sureties from such liability nor shall it be necessary for the Govt. to sue the obligor before suing the Surety/Sureties either of them for the amount due hereunder and the Govt. agrees to bear the stamp duty, if any chargeable on those presents.

IN WITNESS WHEREOF the Obligor and the Surety/Sureties hereto have set and subscribed their respective hands hereunto on the day, month and year above written.

Signed by the above named 'Obligor' in the presence of

1. ______________________________

2. ______________________________

Signed by the above named "Surety/Sureties"

1. ______________________________

2. ______________________________

Accepted for and on behalf of the President of Indian by ________________ (Name and designation of the Officer directed or authorised in Pursuance of Article 299(1) of the Constitution, to accept the Bond for end on behalf of the President) in the present of ________________

(Name and designation of witness)

Note I

(a) Full name of claimant referred to as the 'Obligor'

(b) State relationship of the 'Obligor' to the missing serving person

(c) No and Name of the 'missing serving person'

(d) Full name of names of the Sureties with name of names of the father(s) husband(s) and place of residence

Note II

The Obligor as well as the Sureties should have attained majority so that the bond may have legal effect or force.

Note III

The rate of simple interest will be as prescribed by the Govt from time to time. It is 6% p.a. the date of issue of the O.M.

APPENDIX 'B'
(IN THE CASE OF MISSING PENSIONERS)
INDEMNITY BOND

KNOW ALL MEN by these presents that we (a) __________________ (b) the widow/son/brother/nominee etc. of (c) __________________ who had retired/was discharged in the rank of __________________ from __________________ Unit/Corps and who was in receipt of Pension from controller of Defence Accounts (Pensions) in reported to have been missing since __________________ (thereinafter referred to as 'missing pensioner' resident of __________________ hereinafter called "the obligor") and (d) __________________ son/wife/daughter of Shri __________________ resident of __________________ and __________________ son/wife/daughter of __________________ resident of __________________ the sureties for and on behalf of the Obligor (hereinafter celled "the Sureties") are held family bound to the President of India (hereinafter called "the Govt") in each and every sum being the arrears of pension and monthly family pension and Dearness relief thereon well and truly to be paid to the Govt on demand and without a demur together with simple interest @ __________________ % p.a. from the date of payment thereof until repayment for which payment who bind ourselves and our respective heirs, executors, administrators, legal representatives, successors and assigns by these presents.

Signed this __________________ day of __________________ one thousand nine hundred and __________________
WHEREAS (c) __________________ was at the time of his disappearance in the employment of the Govt. receiving a pay at the rate of Rs __________________ (in words) __________________ only per month from the Government.

AND WHEREAS the said (c) __________________ disappeared on the __________________ day of __________________ 19 __________________ and there was due to him at the time of his disappearance the sum equivalent of arrears of pension due.

AND WHEREAS the Obligor is entitled to family pension at Rs __________________ (Rupees __________________ only) plus admissible Dearness Relief thereon.

AND WHEREAS the Obligor has represented that he/she is entitled to the aforesaid sum and approached the Govt. for making payment thereof to avoid undue delay and hardship.

AND WHEREAS the Govt. has agreed to make payment of the said sum of Rs __________________ (in words) __________________ only and the monthly family pension Rs __________________ (in words) __________________ __________________ and The Dearness relief thereon to the Obligor upon the Obligor and the Sureties entering into a Bond in the above mentioned sum to indemnify to Govt. against the claims to the amount so due to the aforesaid missing person.

AND WHEREAS the Obligor and at his/her request the Surety/Sureties have agreed to execute the Bond in the terms and manner her in after contained.

NOW THE CONDITION OF THIS BOND is such that if after payment has been made to the Obligor, the Obligor and/or Surety/Sureties shall in the even of a claim being made, by any other person or the missing pensioner on appearance, against the Govt. with respect to the aforesaid sum of Rs __________________ (in words) __________________ and each and every sum paid by Govt. as monthly family pension and relief together with simple interest @ __________________ % per annum and shall, otherwise, indemnify and keep the Govt. harmless and indemnified against and from all liabilities in respect of the aforesaid sums and all costs incurred in the consequence of the claim there to THEN the above written Bond or obligation shall be void and of no effect but otherwise, it shall remain in full force, effect and virtue.

AND THESE PRESENTS ALSO WITNESS that the liability of the Surety/Sureties hereunder shall not be impaired or discharged by reason of time being granted by or any forbearance set or omission of the Govt whether with or without the knowledge or cannot of the Surety/Sureties in respect of or in relation to the obligations or conditions to be performed or discharged by the Obligor or by any other method or thing whatsoever which under the law relating to the sureties would but for this provision shall have no effect of so releasing the Surety/Sureties from such liability nor shall it be necessary for the Govt. to sue the obligor before suing the Surety/Sureties either of them for the amount due hereunder and the Govt. agrees to bear the stamp duty, if any chargeable on those presents.

IN WITNESS WHEREOF the Obligor and the Surety/Sureties hereto have set and subscribed their respective hands hereunto on the day, month and year above written.

Signed by the above named 'Obligor' in the presence of

1. ______________________________

2. ______________________________

Signed by the above named 'Surety/Sureties'

1. ______________________________

2. ______________________________

Accepted for and on behalf of the President of Indian by ____________________ (Name and designation of the Officer directed or authorised in Pursuance of Article 299(1) of the Constitution, to accept the Bond for end on behalf of the President) in the present of ____________________

(Name and designation of witness)

Note I (a) Full name of claimant referred to as the 'Obligor'

(a) State relationship of the 'Obligor' to the missing serving person

(b) No and Name of the 'missing serving person'

(c) Full name of names of the Sureties with name of names of the father(s) husband(s) and place of residence

Note II The Obligor as well as the Sureties should have attained majority so that the bond may have legal effect or force.

Note III The rate of simple interest will be as prescribed by the Govt from time to time. It is 6% p.a. the date of issue of the O.M.

25.5

Extract of Army Order 01/2003 dealing with Missing Personnel

Section 3
Missing Personnel

* * *

55. During operations, some personnel will inevitably be reported missing and some time must necessarily elapse before information is available as to their probable fate. It is the duty of every person who comes into possession of information regarding missing Officers/JCOs/OR to bring this to the notice of appropriate authorities without delay.

56. It is also likely that officers, JCOs and OR who are separated from their units might subsequently be able to join another unit. It will be the responsibility of the latter unit to immediately intimate Army Headquarters, Adjutant General's Branch, MP 5 (d), Record Offices and parent unit by OP IMMEDIATE signal, giving full particulars of the individual concerned.

57. Subsequent information regarding missing personnel, i.e. confirmed killed, confirmed prisoner or rejoined, will be reflected in battle casualty reports.

58. Army personnel may be found missing when there are no operations/hostilities. Great care must be exercised in dealing with such cases. They would be reported as deserters only after conclusive evidence is obtained. A few examples are cited below:

a. A person may have drowned in a river and his dead body may not been recovered or seen by a reliable witness.

b. A person may have been abducted.

c. A person may have been on board an aircraft or a ship which is missing, and consequently no trace has been found of it.

d. A person involved in a skirmish whilst in aid of civil authorities to maintain internal security and fighting against armed hostilities, may have been killed but his dead body may not have been recovered or seen by a reliable witness.

e. A person having gone on Annual Leave or in transit through a disturbed area does not report back from Annual Leave or goes missing while in transit. Such a person may have been killed/rendered incapable of reporting in time and as such should be reported missing till conclusive evidence of desertion is found.

Rules for Reporting Personnel Missing:

59. Following instructions will be observed whilst reporting personnel as missing:

a. A person will be regarding as missing with effect from the day following on which he was last seen.

b. A "missing" casualty will not be reported until 72 hours from the date he was missing i.e. 96 hours after he was seen, e.g. a man last seen on 17 Nov. will be reported on 21 Nov as missing with effect from 18 Nov.

* * *

25.6

Government of India, Ministry of Defence, Department of Ex-Servicemen Welfare Letter No 1(1)/2010/D (Pen/Pol) dated 15th February 2011

Sub: Grant of family Pension and gratuity to the families of Armed Forces personnel/pensioners who disappear suddenly and whose whereabouts are not known.

Sir,

The undersigned is directed to refer to this Ministry's letter No 12(16)/86/D (Pen/Sers) dated 3rd June 1988 as amended vide letters of even No dated 20th March 1990 dated 23rd March 1992 and dated 26th August 1993, concerning grant of family pension to the eligible family members of the Armed Forces personnel/pensioners who have suddenly disappeared and whose whereabouts are not known, after one year from the date of lodging FIR or expiry of authorized leave of the Armed Forces Personnel who has disappeared whichever is later.

2. While considering the demand of Staff side of the national council (CM), concerning withdrawal of the mandatory condition of one year prescribed in regard to sanction of family pension to the eligible family member of the civilian Government servant/pensioners Ministry of Personnel, Public Grievances & Pension, Department of Pension & Pensioners' Welfare, New Delhi vide their OM No 1/28/04-P&PW(E) dated 2nd July 2010 has decided in consultation with the Ministry of Finance (Department of Expenditure) that the family pension/retirement or death gratuity to the eligible family members of a Government pension/retirement or death gratuity to the eligible family members of a Government servant/pensioners reported missing and whose whereabouts are not known, may be sanctioned after a period of six months from the date of registration of an FIR with the Police subject to fulfillment of other conditions.

3. This provisions of Ministry of Personnel, Public Grievances & Pension, Department of Pension & Pensioners, Welfare, New Delhi above said OM dated 2nd July 2010 shall mutatis mutandis apply to Armed Forces Personnel.

4. This issues with the concurrence of Finance Division of his Ministry vide their UO No 172/F/P/2011 dated 14.2.11.

Yours faithfully,
Sd/-
(Malathi Narayanan)
Under Secretary to the Government of India

25.7

Government of India, Ministry of Personnel, Public Grievances & Pensions, Department of Pension & Pensioners' Welfare Letter No F No 1/17/2010-P&PW(E) dated 2nd January 2012

Sub: **Grant of Family Pension to next eligible member in the family in the case of missing family pensioner.**

Sir,

The under signed is directed to state that as per extant instructions of the Government, conditional provisions have been made in the case of a missing employee/pensioners, as a measure of social security, to cut short the period of 7 years, as given in Section 107 and 108 of Indian Evidence Act, 1872, after which the presumption of a missing person being no longer alive may be raised, and enable the family pensioner to receive family pension after a period of six months from the date of filing FIR. However, there is no such provision in the case of a missing family pensioner that the next eligible member of the family of the employee/pensioner may be granted family pension.

2. The Department of Pension and Pensioner's Welfare has been receiving requests to issue a clarification where family pension to eligible child/children of a family pensioner who has been declared missing can be granted.

3. The matter has been considered in this Department in consultation with the Department of Expenditure, Ministry of Finance. It has been decided to make similar provisions to mitigate the hardships of the family caused by the deprivation of his rightful family pension as a consequence of disappearance of the family pensioner. The administrative Departments/Ministries may grant family pension to the next eligible members in the family subject to fulfillment of conditions as prescribed from time to time for dealing with the cases of missing employees/ pensioners.

4. The Indemnity Bond prescribed for missing pensioners has been suitably modified to include the name and relationship of the next eligible family member as well as the deceased employee/pensioner and the missing family pensioner(s).

5. These provisions would also be applicable in case a person, who is eligible for family pension, goes missing before the family pension is actually sanctioned to him/her. In such cases, family pension will be sanctioned to the next eligible person.

6. This issues with the concurrence of Department of Expenditure vide their I D No. 380/E.V/2011, dated 22.11.2011.

Sd/-
(K.K. Mittal)
Director

25.8

Government of India, Ministry of Defence, Department of Ex-Servicemen Welfare Letter No 1(1)/2012-D (Pension/Policy) dated 5th June 2013

Sub: Grant of Family Pension to next eligible member in the family in the case of missing family pensioner.

I am directed to state that it has been decided to extend the provision of Government of India, Ministry of Personnel Public Grievances & Pensions, Department of Pension & Pensioners' Welfare F. No 1/17/2010-P&PW(E) dated 2nd January, 2012 on the above subject matter regarding "Grant of Family Pension to next eligible member in the family in the case of missing family pensioner", to the families of Defence Service Personnel, mutatis mutandis, with effect from 2nd January, 2012. No arrear on account of this shall be paid.

2. This issues with the concurrence of Ministry of Defence (Finance) vide their I D No. 10(3)/2010/Fin/Pen dated 28.05.2013.

Sd/-

(Malathi Narayanan)

Under Secretary to the Government of India

25.9

Government of India, Ministry of Defence, Department of Ex-Servicemen Welfare Letter No (1)/2010-D(Pension/Policy) dated 23rd December 2014

Sub: **Grant of Family Pension and gratuity to the eligible member of the family of an employee/ pensioner/family pensioner reported missing-consolidated instructions regarding**

Sir,

The Provisions for grant of Ordinary family pension and DCRG to the eligible members of families of the deceased Armed Forces Personnel/Pensioners are contained in AI 51/80 and AI 8/S/70 as modified from time to time. The instructions regarding grant of family pension and gratuity to the eligible member of the Family of an Armed Forces Personnel/Pensioner reported missing have been issued vide this Ministry's letter No 12 (16)86/D(Pen/Ser) dated 03.06.1988 and No 12 (16)/86/D(Pen/Ser) dated 23.03.1992. Clarifications/amendments in this regard have also been issued vide letter No. 12 (16)/85/D(Pen/Ser) dated 26.08.1993, letter No. 1 (1)/2010/D(Pen/Pol) dated 15.02.2011 and MoD letter No. 1 (1)/2012/D(Pen/Pol) dated 05.06.2013.

2. It has now been decided to issue consolidated instructions in supersession of previous instructions as mentioned above regarding grant of family pension to the eligible members of family of the Armed Forces Personnel/pensioner/ family pensioner reported missing and whose whereabouts are not known. It includes those kidnapped by insurgents/ terrorists but does not include those who disappear after committing frauds/crime/desertion etc.

3. In the case of a missing Armed Forces Personnel/pensioner/family pensioner, the family can apply for the grant of family pension, amount of salary due, leave encashment due and the amount of DSOP/AFPP fund and gratuity (whatever has not already been received) to the IHQ/Record office concerned, where the officers and JCOs/ORs. in Army and equivalent in Navy and Air Force, had last served, six months after lodging of police report. The family pension and/or retirement gratuity may be sanctioned by the respective Pension Sanctioning Authority's (PSAs) after observing the following formalities:

i. The family must lodge a report with the concerned Police station and obtain a report from the police,that the Armed Forces Personnel/pensioner/family pensioner has not been traced despite all efforts made by them. The report may be a First Information report or any other report such as a Daily Diary/General Diary Entry, filed by the Police authorities concerned, as per the practice prevalent in the state/UT.

ii. An indemnity bond should be taken from the nominee/dependents of the Armed Forces Personnel/ pensioner/family pensioner that all the payments will be adjusted against the payments due to the Armed Forces Personnel/pensioner/family pensioner in case she/he appears on the scene and makes any claim.

4. In the case of a missing Armed Forces Personnel, the family pension, at the ordinary or enhanced rate, as applicable, will accrue from the expiry of leave or the date up to which pay and allowances have been paid or the date of the police report, whichever is later. In the case of a missing pensioner/family pensioner, it will accrue from the date of the police report or from the date immediately succeeding the date till which pension/family pension had been paid, whichever is later.

5. The retirement gratuity will be paid to the family within three months of the date of application. In case of any delay, the interest shall be paid at the applicable rates and responsibility for delay shall be fixed. The difference between the death gratuity and retirement gratuity shall be payable after the death of the employee is conclusively established or on the expiry of the period of seven years from the date of the police report.

6. Before sanctioning the payment of gratuity, Service HQrs/Records Offices will assess all Government dues outstanding against the employee/pensioner and affect their recovery in accordance with instruction in force.

7. The amount of salary due, leave encashment due and the amount of DSOP/AFPP fund will be paid to the family in the first instance as per the nominations made by the Armed Forces Personnel/pensioner on filing of a police report and submission of an indemnity bond as indicated above.

8. The benefits to be sanctioned to the family/nominee of the missing Armed Forces Personnel/pensioner will be based on and regulated as per the emoluments drawn by him/her as on the last date he/she was on duty including authorized periods of leave.

9. Formats of separate Indemnity Bonds to be used in the case of missing Armed Forces Personnel, missing pensioners and missing family pensioners are available at the official website of PCDA (Pension) Allahabad.

10. This issues with the concurrence of Ministry of Defence (Finance) vide their ID No. 10(3)/2010/Fin/Pen dated 08/12/2014.

11. Hindi version will follow.

Sd/-

(Prem Parkash)

Under Secretary (Pension/Policy)

Chapter-26

Provisions Specifically Concerning Family Pension

26.1

Army Instruction 3/SPECIAL/1977

GRANT OF ORDINARY FAMILY PENSION TO WIDOWS/CHILDREN OF O.R. RESERVISTS

The widows and children of OR reservists (other than those transferred to the reserve after earning a pension in respect of their colour service) who were on the reserve strength on 31st December 1972 or those who died on that date as well as those who were/are transferred to the reserve thereafter and who died/die on or after 1st January 1973 while in the reserve or after retirement with a reservist pension on account of causes which are neither attributable to nor aggravated by service, will be granted ordinary family pension at a rate of Rs 44/- per month.

2. The conditions of eligibility and payment of ordinary family pension in such cases will be as laid down in para 4, 5 and 6 of AI 2/S/64, as amended from time to time.

3. Pension Regulations for the Army Part I, (1961) will be amended in due course.

Case No 30(1)/74/D (Pension/Services)

M of F (Def) UO No 4373/Pen of 1977

26.2

Army Instruction 03/1995

AI 3/1995: Amendment in A1 51/80

Army Instruction 51/80 regarding grant of ordinary Family Pension to widow/children of Army personnel (including those in DSC) governed by Military rules, is amended as under:

Insert the following as Para 9 (c) after Para 9 (b):

"9 (c)- Children born out of a void marriage in terms of Sec 11 of Hindu Marriage Act 1955 shall be entitled to share the Ordinary Family Pension if otherwise eligible though their mother would not have been eligible for the same had she been alive at the time of death of her husband on account of her marriage being null and void under Section 11 of Hindu Marriage Act 1955".

Case No A/4960/AG/PS-4(a)/780/B/D (Pen/Ser)

M of D (Fin) U.O. No 921/DFA(P) of MOD

Sd/-
(R.K. Kataria)
Deputy Secretary

26.3

Employees' Provident Fund Organization Letter No 11/3(1)97/KD/Double Pension dated 15th January, 2002

Sub: Admissibility of Military Family Pension/Govt. Family Pension to those who are entitled for Family Pension from Employees Provident Fund Organisation (EPFO) - amendment in Govt. Pension Rules - Regarding.

It was brought to the notice of this office that in certain cases, where Family Pension Scheme 1971/Employees Pension Scheme was granted to family of Ex-Servicemen or retired Central Government Employees by virtue of their membership under Employee's Family Pension Scheme 1971/Employee's Pension Scheme 1995, family pension from the Military Service/Central Government service was denied to them on the plea that only one family pension is payable as per the CCS Pension Rules/Military Pension Rules, etc.

In this connection, several application/references have also been received seeking individual exemption from Employees' Family Pension Scheme 1971/Employees' Pension Scheme 1995 on the plea that their family will be given family pension by the former employer (Central Government/Military Service) only after the exemption granted by Central Provident Fund Commission Consequently the Employee's Family Pension Scheme 1971 has been replaced by Employees' Pension Scheme, 1995 in which there is no provision to grant individual exemption. Some of the members instead desired to have option to continue as a member of Employees' Provident Fund Scheme 1952 without being enrolled as member of Employees' Pension Scheme 1995. Since exemption is not possible under Employees' 1995 being linked to the membership under Employees' Provident Fund Scheme, 1952, no such option is permitted under the Statutory Scheme framed under EPF & MP Act. 1952.

Whereas there is no bar/prohibition in getting family pension from EPFO irrespective of the fact that they are also getting family pension from some other authorities, as both the entitlement are on account of different spells of service under different employers. As the Employees' Pension Scheme, 1995 is a Social Insurance Scheme and funded by the employers/employees, there cannot be any discrimination among the spouses for family pension. Since the pensionary benefits under the Statutory Scheme (EPS 95) is largely based on the membership & contribution under the scheme, EPFO has no other option but to release pensionary benefits as per the Employees' Pension Scheme, 1995. In other words, EPS 95 is a separate statutory scheme which applies on its own force to the covered establishment under EPF & MP Act. 1952.

Accordingly, the matter relating to admissibility of double family pension (i.e. one from the Military Service Rules/ CCS Pension Rules and the other from EPFO under Employees Family Pension Scheme 1971/Employees' Pension scheme 1995) was taken up with the Central government. The Ministry of Labour has now informed vide their letter No. R-15025/5/97-SS.II dated 10.12.2001 that necessary rules in this regard have since been amended by the Department of Pension and Pensioners Welfare permitting family pension under Govt. Pension Rules, in addition to pension under Employees' Family Pension Scheme 1971/Employees' Pension Scheme 1995 [Reference Department of Pension & Pensioners Welfare letter No. 1/19/96 P&PW (E) dated 2.11.2001 along with their notification date 27.7.2001]. The extract is reproduced as under:

In the CCS (Pension) Rules 1972, in Rule 54 Sub-rule 13B after the first proviso, the following proviso shall be inserted, namely:

"Provided further that family pension admissible under the Employees Pension Scheme, 1995 and the Family Pension Scheme, 1971, shall however, be allowed in addition to the Family Pension admissible under these Rules."

You are aware that Govt. has already removed the restriction regarding drawl of civil pension in addition to Military Pension vide O.M. No. 28//7/99-PN&PW(Vol.-II) dated 11.4.2001 issued by Deptt. of Pension & Pensioners' Welfare.

In order words, in the case of re-employment of a Military Pensioner in Civil Services, the pensionary benefits for 2nd shell of service shall not be subject to any limitation as per CCs Pension Rules, 1972.

You may accordingly inform the above important changes in the Government Pension Rules to all Employees' Unions/ employers' Associations/family pensioners under Employees' Family Pension Scheme, 1971/Employees' Pension Scheme, 1995 and all managements of Public Sector Undertakings for circulation among their absorbed Central Govt. Employees, re-employed Ex-Servicemen, etc.

While highlighting the comprehensive benefit package available under Employees' Pension Scheme. 1995, it may also be reiterated that all those who are covered under the Employees' Provident Fund Scheme 1952 are necessarily to become members of Employees' Pension Scheme, 1995 and there is no provision for individual exemption from Employees' pension Scheme, 1995. Govt. employees who were/are absorbed in Public Sector Undertakings, who may not complete 10 years of "eligible service" for member pension, may also be enlightened about the provision of "Withdrawal benefit" or the "family pension" benefits available under the Employees' Pension Scheme, 1995. This will help us to avoid such avoidable references/applications seeking exemption from the Pension Schemes.

Sd/-

(A. Vishwanathan)

Addl. CPF Commissioner (P)

26.4

Government of India, Ministry of Defence, Department of Ex-Servicemen Welfare Letter No 1(1)/2001/D (Pen-C) dated 24th June 2005

Sub: **Grant of Liberalised Family Pension to Widows Who Remarried Before 01.01.1996 - Instructions Regarding**

Sir,

In continuation of this Ministry's letter No PC 1(2)/97-D (Pen-C) dated the 15th May, 2001 on the subject mentioned above. I am directed to convey the sanction of the President to grant Liberalized family pension to a widow whose liberalized family pension was stopped on her remarriage before 01.01.1996 with a person other than the real brother of the deceased. Such pension may be regulated in terms of para 6.5 of this Ministry's letter No 1(2)/97/D (Pen-C) dated 31.01.2001.

2. The actual benefit arising out of this order will be payable from the date of issue of this letter.

3. Pension Regulations of the three Services will be amended in due course.

4. This issues with the concurrence of Defence (Finance) vide their UO No 2907/Fin/Pen dated 24.6.05.

Yours faithfully,
Sd/-
(P.J. MATHEW)
Deputy Secretary to the Government of India

26.5

Government of India, Ministry of Defence, Department of Ex-Servicemen Welfare Letter No 1(1)/2001/D (Pen-C) dated 20th January 2009

Sub: **Grant of special family pension to widows who remarried before 01.01.1996- Instructions regarding**

Sir,

In continuation of this Ministry's letter No PC 1(2)/97-D (Pen-C) dated the 15th May, 2001 on the subject mentioned above, I am directed to convey the sanction of the President to grant Special Family Pension to a widow whose Special Family Pension was stopped on her remarriage before 01 January 1996. Such Pension may be regulated in terms of Para 5.8 of this Ministry's letter No 1(2)/97/D (Pen-C) dated 31 January 2001.

2. The actual benefit arising out of this order will be payable from the date of issue of this letter. No arrears shall be admissible.

3. Pension Regulations of the three Services will be amended in due course.

4. This issues with the concurrence of Defence (Finance) vide their UO No 200/Fin/Pen dated 07.01.2009.

Yours faithfully,
Sd/-
(Ajay Saxena)
Under Secretary to the Government of India

26.6

Government of India, Ministry of Personnel, Public Grievances & Pensions, Department of Pension & Pensioners Welfare Letter No 1/16/2008-P&PW (E) dated 17th August 2009

Sub: **Family Pension– Extension of the scope of Family Pension to the Dependent disabled siblings (i.e. brothers/sisters) of Central Government Servants/Pensioners- reg**

Sir,

The undersigned is directed to say that as per the existing provisions in Rule 54 (14) of the CCS (Pension) Rules, 1972, read with various orders/instructions issued by this Department in this regard from time to time, the following are presently covered in the definition of family in relation to a Government servant/Pensioner for the purpose of eligibility for family pension-

a. Wife in the case of a male Government servant, or husband in the case of a female Government servant.

b. A judicially separated wife or husband, such separation not being granted on the ground of adultery and the person surviving was not held guilty of committing adultery.

c. Son/Daughter upto the date of his/her marriage or till the date he/she starts earning, or till the age of 25 years, whichever is the earliest.

d. Unmarried/widowed/divorced daughter, upto the date of marriage/remarriage or till the date she starts earning, whichever is earliest;

and

e. Parents who were wholly dependent upon Government servant when he/she was alive provided the deceased employee has left behind neither a widow nor a child.

f. Further, the dependency criteria for the purpose of family pension has been revised and fixed as the minimum family pension, alongwith the dearness relief thereon, vide this Department's O.M. No. 38/37/08-P&PW(A) dt.2.9.2008.

2. Representations have been received in this Department from various quarters requesting for extension of the scope of family pension so as to cover the dependent disabled siblings (i.e. brothers/sisters) of Government servants/pensioners within the ambit of "family" for the purpose of eligibility for family pension. The arguments advanced by the representationists in support of their request are that the dependent disabled siblings (i.e. brother/sisters) are left to fend for themselves after the death of the Government servant/pensioner on whom they were fully dependent before his/her death. They need to be taken care of by the society and the Government as they are helpless and without any means to manage their lives.

3. These representations have been sympathetically examined in this Department in consultation with other Ministries/Departments concerned. It has now been decided to include the dependent disabled siblings (i.e. brothers/sisters) of Government servants/pensioners in the definition of "family" for the purpose of eligibility for family pension. Such disabled siblings shall be eligible for family pension for life in the same manner and following the same disability criteria, as laid down in Rule 54 of the CCS (Pension) Rules, 1972 in the case of son/daughter of Government employees/Pensioners suffering from any disorder or disability of mind (including mentally retarded) or physically crippled or disabled, so as to render him/her unable to earn a living even after attaining the age of 25 years.

4. This issues with the concurrence of Ministry of Finance, Department of Expenditure vide their U.O. No 677/E-V/2008 dt.19.2.2009.

5. These orders, in so far as their applicability relates to the employees of the Indian Audit and Accounts Department, are being issued in consultation with the Comptroller and Auditor General of India, vide their U.O. No 69- Audit Rules.26-2008 dated 17.7.2009.

6. The CCS (Pension) Rules, 1972 shall stand modified to that extent.

Sd/-

(Rajni Razdan)

Secretary (P&PW)

26.7

Government of India, Ministry of Personnel, Public Grievances and Pension, Department of Pension & Pensioners Welfare Letter No 1/11/2011-P&PW(E) dated 30th November 2011

Sub: **Interpretation of dependency criterion for grant of two family pensions under the CCS (Pension) Rules 1972- Regarding**

Sir,

The undersigned is directed to refer to this Department's O.M. No 45/86/97-P&PW(A) Part-I dated 27th October, 1997 and O.M. No 45/51/97-P&PW(E) dated 5th March, 1998 regarding eligibility of dependent parents, sons and daughters for receipt of family pension and the income/dependency criterion prescribed for that Attention is also invited to O.M. No 38/37/08-P&PW(A), dated 2nd September 2008 whereby the dependency criterion has been revised.

2. This department has been receiving communications from various quarters seeking clarification whether in the wake of the Office Memoranda referred to above, second family pension is admissible to a family pensioner who is already in receipt of an amount of family pension which is equal to or more than the dependency criterion.

3. It is hereby clarified that family pension admissible to a beneficiary in respect of one deceased employee/ pensioner is not to be counted as income for the purpose of determination of eligibility for another family pension which is admissible in connection with another deceased employee/pensioner. However, any other income/earning of the beneficiary under consideration will be counted toward income for deciding eligibility for family pension.

4. It is further clarified that the sum of amounts of family pensions admissible to a family pensioner as indicated above shall be regulated as per Rule 54 (11) (a) of the CCS (Pension) Rules, 1972 as amended from time to time.

5. This issues with the concurrence of Department of Expenditure vide their I.D No. 383/E.V/2011, dated 22nd November, 2011.

Yours faithfully,
Sd/-
(K.K. Mittal)
Director

26.8

Government of India, Ministry of Personnel, Public Grievances & Pensions, Department of Pension & Pensioners Welfare Letter No 1/16/1996-P&PW (E) (Vol.II) dated 27th November 2012

Sub: Eligibility of children from a void or voidable marriage for family pension-clarification regarding.

The undersigned is directed to refer to this Department's O.M. No 1/16/96-P&PW(E) dated 2.12.1996 whereby it was clarified that Pensionary benefits will be granted to children of a deceased Government servant/pensioner from void or voidable marriages when their turn comes in accordance with Rule 54 (8). It is mentioned in Para 4 of the O.M. that "it may be noted that they will have no claim whatsoever to receive family pension as long as the legally wedded wife is the recipient of the same."

2. The matter has been re-examined in consultation with the Ministry of Law and Justice (Department of Legal Affairs) and Ministry of Finance 9Department of Expenditure). It has been decided that in supersession of Para 4 of the O.M. *ibid*, dated 2.12.1996, the share of children from illegally wedded wife in the family pension shall be payable to them in the manner given under sub-rule 7 (c) of Rule 54 of CCS (Pension) Rules, 1972, along with the legally wedded wife.

3. It has been decided that in past cases, no recovery from the previous beneficiary should be made. On receipt of an application from eligible child/children of the deceased Government employee/pensioner born to an ineligible mother, a decision regarding division or otherwise of family pension may be taken by the competent authority after satisfying himself/herself about veracity of facts and entitlement of the applicant(s).

4. As regards pensioners/family pensioners belonging to the Indian Audit and Accounts Departments, these Orders issue after consultation with the comptroller and Auditor General of India.

5. This issues with the concurrence of Department of Legal Affairs vide their FTS No. 3036, dated 17.10.2012.

6. This issues with the concurrence of Ministry of Finance, Department of Expenditure vide their I.D No. 530/E.V/2012, dated 23.11.2012.

Sd/-
(D.K. Solanki)
Under Secretary to the Government of India

26.9

Government of India, Ministry of Defence, Department of Ex-Servicemen Welfare Letter No 01(05)/2010-D (Pen/Policy) dated 17th January 2013

Sub: **Implementation of the Government decision on the recommendations of Committee on the issues related to Defence Service Personnel and Ex-servicemen, 2012 – Grant of dual Family Pension from Military as well as civil employment**

Sir,

The undersigned is directed to refer to the provision contained in Army Instructions 51/1980 read with provisions contained in this Ministry's letter No 10(6)/92/D (Pen/Sers) dated 28.9.1992 and Regulation 78 of Pension Regulations for the Army Part-I (2008) according to which the NOK of armed Forces pensioners who got re-employed in Civil Departments/PSUs/Autonomous bodies/Local funds of Central/State governments after getting retired from military service with pension, are authorized to draw Ordinary Family Pension either from military side or from civil side in terms of provisions contained in this Ministry's above said letter dated 28.9.1992 and Rule 54 (13-A) & Rule 54 (13-B) of CCS (Pension) Rule 1972.

2. In order to consider various issues on pension of Armed Forces personnel and Ex-servicemen, the government had constituted a Committee of Secretaries headed by Cabinet Secretary. The Committee in its Report has recommended that NOK of a pensioner who gets second employment in the Government after discharge from military service would be entitled to draw two Family Pensions.

3. The above recommendation of the committee has been accepted by the Government and the President is pleased to decide that the families of Armed Forces pensioners who got re-employed in civil Departments/PSUs/ Autonomous bodies/Local Funds of Central/State governments after getting retired from military service and were in receipt of military pension till death, shall be allowed to draw Family Pension from military side in addition to the family pension, if any, authorized from the re-employed civil department subject to fulfillment of other prescribed conditions as hithertofore.

4. The provisions of this letter shall be applicable to the Armed Forces Personnel who got discharged/retired/ invalided out from service with effect from 24th September 2012 or thereafter. Benefit of these provisions shall also be allowed in past cases however the financial benefit shall be granted from 24th September 2012 only.

5. Pension Regulations of the three services shall be amended in due course.

6. This issues with the concurrence of Finance Division of this Ministry vide their I D No. PC 1/10(12)/2012/FIN/ PEN dated 10.01.2013.

Yours faithfully,

Sd/-

(Malathi Narayanan)

Under Secretary to the Government of India

26.10

Government of India, Ministry of Defence, Department of Ex-Servicemen Welfare Letter No 01(14)/2012/D (Pen/Policy) dated 17th January 2013

Sub: Implementation of the Government decision on the recommendations of Committee of Secretaries 2012 on the issues related to Defence Service Personnel and Ex-servicemen– Enhancement of Ordinary Family Pension in respect of pre-2006 JCO/OR family pensioners.

Sir,

The undersigned is directed to refer to this Ministry's letter No 17(4)/2008(1)/d (Pen/Policy) dated 11.11.2008 as amended, issued for implementation of Government decision on the recommendations of the Sixth CPC for revision of pension/family pension in respect of pre-2006 Armed Forces Pensioners/family pensioners. As per provisions contained in Para 5 of above said letter dated 11.11.2008, with effect from1.1.2006 revised ordinary family pension of all pre-2006 JCO/OR family pensioners determined in terms of fitment formula laid down I Para 4.1 therein, shall in no case be lower than thirty percent of the minimum of the pay in the pay band plus the Grade pay corresponding to the pre revised scale from which the pensioner had retired/discharged/invalided out/died including Military Service Pay and 'X' Group pay, where applicable. Accordingly, rates of minimum guaranteed ordinary family pension for JCO/OR were notified under Annexure-III (Revised) of this Ministry's letter No 17(3)/2010/D (Pen/Policy) dated 15.11.2010.

2. In order to consider various issues on pension of Armed Forces personnel and Ex-servicemen, the Government had constituted a Committee of Secretaries headed by Cabinet Secretary. The committee in its Report have recommended that the minimum guaranteed ordinary family pension of pre-2006 JCO/OR family pensioners should be determined with reference to minimum of the fitment table for the rank in the revised pay structure issued for implementation of recommendations of sixth CPC instead of the minimum of the pay band and also a linkage should be established in the rate of the family pension with the pension of JCO/OR.

3. The above recommendation of the committee has been accepted by the Government and the President is pleased to decide that with effect from 24.09.2012 the minimum guaranteed ordinary family pension in respect of pre-2006 JCO/OR including honorary commissioned officers and Non Combatants (Enrolled) of Army, Navy, Air Force, DSC & TA family pensioners shall be determined as thirty percent of the minimum of the fitment table for the rank in the revised pay band as indicated under fitment tables annexed with SAI 1/S/2008 as amended and equivalent instructions for Navy & Air Force, plus the Grade pay corresponding to the pre-revised instructions for Navy& Air Force, Plus the Grade pay corresponding to the pre-revised scale from which the pensioners had retired/discharged/ invalided out/ died including Military Service Pay and 'X' Group pay, wherever applicable.

4. The President is also pleased to decide that to establish linkage in the rates of ordinary family pension with pension of JCO/OR, the revised service pension/special pension/invalided pension as the case may be, shall be determined in terms of this Ministry's letter No 1(13)/2012/D (Pen/Pol) dated 17.01.2013 on notional basis taking into consideration the rank, group, length of service and nature of award sanctioned to the deceased JCO/ OR pensioner. Similar entitlement should also be determined in cases of JCO/OR died while in service. the rates of enhanced rate and normal rate of Ordinary family pension in respect of pr3-2006 JCO/OR family pensioners including honorary commissioned Officers and Non Combatants 9Enrolled), shall be worked out as 100% and 60% respectively of the revised notional pension determined as per above provisions.

4.1 With effect from 24.09.2012, the enhanced rate and normal rate of Ordinary family pension to pre-2006 JCO/ OR family pensioners shall be granted on the basis of family pension worked out as per the formulation at Para 4 above or the minimum guaranteed pension determined as per the provisions contained in Para 3 above, whichever is more beneficial.

5. All other benefit accrued in terms of these orders shall be payable with effect from 24.09.2012. No arrears on account of revision of family pension shall be admissible for the past period. However, if a family pensioner to whom the benefits under these orders accrues has died/dies before receiving the payment on account of arrears, the life time arrears (LTA) will be disposed off as per the extant orders.

6. The actual benefit accrued in terms of these orders shall be payable with effect from 24.09.2012. No arrears on account of revision of family pension shall be admissible for the past period. However, if a family pensioner to whom the benefits under these orders accrues has died/dies before receiving the payment on account of arrears, the life time arrears (LTA) will be disposed off as per the extant orders.

7. The provision of these orders shall not apply to UK/HKSRA/KCIO pensioners and Pakistan/Burma pensioners.

METHODOLOGY FOR IMPLEMENTATION

8. All Pension Disbursing Agencies (PDAs) handling disbursement of pension to Defence pensioners are hereby authorized to carry out revision of Ordinary Family Pension in respect of pre-2006 JCO/OR family pensioners drawing ordinary family pension as on 24.09.2012 in terms of these orders without calling for any applications from the family pensioner and without any further authorization from the concerned Pension Sanctioning Authorities (PSAs). Revision of Ordinary Family pension in respect of TA personnel and also in death in service cases where qualifying service is less than 15 years shall, however, be referred to the respective Pension Sanctioning/authorities (PSA) on ***Annexure – A*** attached to this letter for issue of corrigendum PPO.

9. Keeping in view the above decision and to quicken the process of revision of ordinary family pension, specific tables (total six tables) indicating revised rate of ordinary family pension payable from 24.09.2012 have been prepared for JCO/OR of Regular Army, Navy, Air Force and DSC who were discharged/invalided out/died in service prior to 1.1.2006 and are enclosed as Appendix to this letter. PDAs will revise and pay the ordinary family pension with reference to applicable Table for the rank and group in which the JCO/OR was pensioned with reference to the actual qualifying serviced as shown in/Column-1. In cases where ordinary family pension of an pre-2006 JCO/OR pensioner had not been commenced as the pensioner was alive on 24.09.2012, the rate of revised ordinary family pension shall be payable by the PDAs from the date following the death of the pensioner at appropriate rate.

10. The initial Pension Payment Order (PPO) in respect of JCO/OR, its corrigendum PPO indicates rank, group and qualifying serviced for which the individual has been pensioned. These information are available with PDAs as they have revised pension of all such pensioners in the recent past in terms of Government orders issued on the recommendations of Sixth CPC and Cabinet Secretary Committee (2009). In case, however, any information regarding qualifying service, rank, group, etc, is not available with Pension Disbursing Agencies, such cases may be referred to PSAs concerned on the proforma enclosed as ***Annexure – B***. The PSAs will provide the requisite information from the available records.

11. An intimation regarding disbursement of revised ordinary family pension shall be sent by the PDAs to the Office of the PCDA (P) Allahabad on monthly basis in the format prescribed as ***Annexure – C*** to these orders a copy of which shall also be provided by the PDAs to the pensioners concerned for their information. Those Public Sector Banks who are disbursing Defence pension through central pension Processing Centers (CPPC), the monthly progress report may be furnished by the CPPC of the bank directly to the office of the PCDA (Pension), Allahabad.

12. This issues with the concurrence of Finance Division of this Ministry vide their I D No. PC 2/10(12)/2012/ FIN/ PEN dated 10.01.2013.

Yours faithfully,

Sd/-

(Malathi Narayanan)

Under Secretary to the Government of India

26.11

Government of India, Ministry of Defence, Department of Ex-Servicemen Welfare Letter No 02(03)/2010-D (Pen/Policy) dated 17th January 2013

Sub: **Implementation of the Government decision on the recommendations of Committee on the issues related to Defence Service Personnel and Ex-servicemen, 2012 – Grant of Family Pension for life to handicapped children of Armed Forces Personnel.**

Sir,

The undersigned is directed to refer to the provisions in this Ministry's letter No A/49601/AG/PS-4(3)/3363/B/D(Pen/Ser) dated 27.8.1987 last modified vide this Ministry's letter No 906/A/D/(Pen/Ser)/05 dated 13.8.2008, which provides that the son or daughter of an Armed Forces Personnel who is suffering from any disorder or disability of mind or is physically crippled or disabled so as to render him or her unable to earn a living even after attaining the age of twenty five years is eligible for lifelong family pension. Such disabled son or daughter, however, becomes ineligible for Family Pension on his/her getting married or when he/she starts earning his/her livelihood.

2. A Committee of Secretaries headed by Cabinet Secretary was constituted by the Government to consider various issues on pension of Armed Forces personnel and Ex-servicemen, who have recommended for continuance of family pension to mentally/physically challenged children who drew, are drawing or may draw family pension even after their marriage. The above recommendation of the Committee has been accepted by the Government and the President is pleased to decide that the son or daughter of an Armed Forces Personnel who is suffering from any disorder or disability of mind or is physically crippled or disabled so as to render him or her unable to earn livelihood, granted family pension for life even after his/her marriage subject to fulfillment of other prescribed conditions as hithertofore.

3. These order shall take effect from 24th September 2012 and shall also cover past cases. The financial benefit in past cases shall, however,, be granted from, 24th September 2012 only.

4. Pension Regulations of the three services shall be amended in due course.

5. This issues with the concurrence of Finance Division of this Ministry vide their I D No. PC 1/10(12)/2012/FIN/PEN dated 10.01.2013.

Yours faithfully,

Sd/-

(Malathi Narayanan)

Under Secretary to the Government of India

26.12

Government of India, Ministry of Defence, Department of Ex-Servicemen Welfare Letter No 1(9)/2013-D (Pen/Policy) dated 17th November 2017

Sub: Eligibility of Widowed/Divorced daughter for grant of Family Pension- clarification.

The undersigned is directed to state that the provision for grant of family Pension to a widowed/divorced daughter beyond the age of 25 years has been made vide GOI, Ministry of Personnel, P.G. &Pensions, Department of pension & Pensioners Welfare OM No. 1/19/03- P&PW (E) dated 25.08.2004 circulated vide GOI, MoD letter No 878/A/D(Pen/Sers)/04 dated 21.09.2004 applying the same provision to the Armed Forces Personnel.

2. It was clarified vide Government of India, Ministry of Personnel, P.G. & Pensions, Department of Pension & Pensioners Welfare OM No. 1/13/09-P&PW (E) dated 11.09.2013 circulated vide MoD ID No. 1(9)/2013/D(Pen/Pol) dated 16.09.2015, the family pension is payable to the children as they are considered to be dependent on the Government servant/pensioner or his/her spouse. A child who is not earning equal to or more than the sum of minimum family pension and dearness relief thereon is considered to be dependent on his/her parents. Therefore, only those children who are dependent and meet other conditions of eligibility for family pension at the time of death of the Government servant or his/her spouse, whichever is later, are eligible for family pension. If two or more children are eligible for family pension at that time, family pension will be payable to each, child on his/her turn provided he/she is still eligible for family pension when the turn comes. Accordingly, divorced daughters who fulfill other conditions are eligible for family pension if a decree of divorce had been issued by the competent court during the life time of at least one of the parents.

3. Grievances were being received from various quarters that the divorce proceedings are a long drawn procedure which take many years before attaining finality. There are many cases in which the divorce proceedings of a daughter of Government employee/pensioner had been instituted in the competent court during the life of one or both Government employee/pensioner & spouse, but none of them was alive by the time the decree of divorce was granted by the competent authority.

4. The matter has been examined in this department and it has been decided that the clarification "grant family pension to a divorced daughter in such cases where the divorce proceedings had been filed in a competent court during the life time of the employee/pensioner or his/her spouse but divorce took place after their death-provided the claimant fulfils all other conditions for grant of family pension. In such cases, the family pension will commence from the date of divorce" given by Government of India, Ministry of Personnel, P.G. & Pensions, Department of Pension & Pensioners Welfare vide OM No 1/13/09-P&PW (E) dated 19.07.2017 would also apply mutatis mutandis to divorced daughters of Armed Forces Personnel.

5. This issues with the concurrence of Finance division of this Ministry vide their I D No. 10(09)/2015/Fin/Pen dated 17.10.2017.

Sd/-

(Manoj Sinha)

Under Secretary to the Government of India

26.13

Government of India, Ministry of Defence, Department of Ex-Servicemen Welfare Letter No PC 2(6)/2013/D (Pen/Pol) dated 8th July 2019

Sub: **Clarification regarding grant of Dual Family Pension i.e. Ordinary Family pension (OFP) from Military side as well as Special Family Pension (SFP)/Liberalized Family Pension (LFP) for re-employed Military service - reg.**

Sir,

The undersigned is directed to state that reference have been received seeking clarification as to whether Special Family Pension (SFP)/Liberalized Family Pension (LFP) is admissible on death of a military pensioner re-employed in military service, and his death is attributable to military service.

2. Prior to 17.01.2013, the NOKs of Armed Force Pensioner who got re-employed in Civil Department/PSUs/ Autonomous bodies/Local fund of Central/State Governments after getting retired from military service were authorized to draw Ordinary Family Pension (OFP) either from military side or from civil side whichever was beneficial to them in terms of GOI, MoD letter No. 10(6)/92/D (Pens/Sers) dated 28.09.1992 and regulating 78 of Pension Regulation Part-I, 2008. Subsequently, vide GOI, MoD letter no 01(05)/2010-D(Pen/Policy) dated 17.01.2013, two family pensions were allowed w.e.f. 24.09.2012 in the event of death of a re-employed military pensioner.

3. It was further clarified that dual family pension is admissible irrespective of the fact whether the re-employment was in civil or military department vide GoI, MoD letter No 10(17)/2012-D (Pen/Pol) dated 21.03.2013. Hence, the family pensioners of military personnel re-employed in military e.g. Territorial Army/Defence Security Corps (TA/ DSC) are also covered in the ambit of the GOI, MoD letter No. 01(05)/2010-d (Pen/Policy) dated 17.01.2013 for grant of dual family pension w.e.f. 24.09.2012. However, the admissibility of dual family pension was restricted to ordinary family pension (OFP).

4. Department of Pension and Pensioners Welfare vide their OM No 1/3/2016-P&PW(F) darted 24.01.2019 has clarified that the provisos of two family pensions one in respect of military/civil service and the other for civil service after re-employment, as available in terms of CCS (pension) Rules, is also applicable under CCS (EOP) Rules.

5. The matter regarding extending the admissibility of Special Family Pension (SFP)/Liberalized Family Pension (LFP) in cases of death attributable to military service in terms of GoI, MoD letter No 1(2)/97/D (Pen-C) dated 31.01.2001 in the case of dual family pension has been examined. It has been decided that Department of Pension and Pensioners Welfare OM No 1/3/2016-PP&W (F) dated 24.01.2019 would apply mutatis mutandis to military/civil pensioners re-employed in military service and it is clarified that the provisions of two family pensions, one in respect of military/ civil service and Special Family Pension (SFP)/Liberalized Family Pension (LFP) for re-employed military service is also applicable. Special Family Pension(SFP)/Liberalized Family Pension (LFP), if any, would be admissible in terms of GoI, MoD letter no 1(2)/97/D (Pen-C) dated 31.01.2001 on death of a pensioner who was re-employed in military service and if his death is attributable to military service, in addition to Ordinary Family Pension in respect of the previous military/civil service.

6. Where, however on death of the re-employed ex-serviceman if the family is eligible for special Family Pension (SFP)/Liberalized Family Pension (LFP) for first service, family pension for second spell of service would be Ordinary Family Pension.

7. Special Family Pension (SFP)/Liberalized Family Pension (LFP) shall be granted only in respect of one service and in no case, Special Family Pension (SFP)/Liberalized Family Pension (LFP) will be granted for both the services.

8. The financial benefits in the past cases will accrue with effect from 24.09.2012.

9. Pension Regulation of the three Services shall be amended in due course.

10. This issues with the concurrence of Finance Division of this Ministry vide their ID No. 10(02)/2017/FIN/PEN dated 21.06.2019.

Sd/-

(A.K. Aggarwal)

Deputy Secretary to the Government of India

26.14

Government of India, Ministry of Personnel, Public Grievances & Pensions, Department of Pensions & Pensioners' Welfare Letter No 1/24/2019-P&PW(E) dated 16th June 2021

Sub: **Suspension of family pension to a person charged with the offence of murdering or abetting in the murder of the Government servant– Allowing family pension to other eligible family member.**

In accordance with sub-rule (11-C) of rule 54 of the Central Civil Services (Pension) Rules, 1972, if a person, who is eligible to receive family pension on death of a Government servant or a pensioner, is charged with the offence of murdering the Government servant/pensioner or for abetting in the commission of such an offence, the payment of family pension remains suspended till the conclusion of the criminal proceedings instituted in this regard. In that case, family pension is neither paid to the person who is charged with the offence nor to any other eligible member of the family till the conclusion of the said criminal proceedings. If on conclusion of the criminal proceedings, the person concerned is convicted for the murder or abetting in the murder of the Government servant, he/she is debarred from receiving the family pension. In that case, the family pension becomes payable to other eligible member of the family, from the date of death of the Government servant. If, however, the person concerned is subsequently acquitted of the charge, the family pension becomes payable to that person from the date of death of the Government servant.

2. The above provisions have been reviewed in consultation with Department of Legal Affairs. Denying the payment of family pension to any other member of the family (e.g. dependent children, parents, etc.), who is not charged with the offence, till the conclusion of criminal proceedings is not considered justified, as finalisation of the criminal proceeding may take a long time and the eligible children/parents of the deceased may suffer for want of financial support by way of family pension.

3. It has, accordingly, been decided that in cases where a person eligible to receive family pension is charged with the offence of murdering the Government servant or for abetting in the commission of such an offence and the payment of family pension to him/her remains suspended under Rule 54 (11-C) of CCS (Pension) Rules, 1972, family pension may be allowed to other eligible member of the family till the conclusion of the criminal proceedings in this regard. If the spouse of the Government servant is charged with the offence of murdering the Government servant or for abetting in the commission of such an offence and the other eligible family member is a minor child of the deceased Government servant, the family pension to such minor child shall be payable through a duly appointed guardian, and the mother or father of the minor child (who is charged with the offence) shall not act as guardian for the purpose of drawal of family pension.

4. If the concerned person is subsequently acquitted of the charge, the family pension shall become payable to that person from the date of such acquittal and the family pension to other member of the family shall be discontinued from that date.

5. This will take effect from the date of issue of this Office Memorandum. In the cases where the payment of family pension has been suspended as per the provisions of Rule 54 (11-C) of CCS (Pension) Rules, 1972, before the issue of this Office Memorandum, the arrears of family pension accruing from the date following the date of death Govt. Servant/Pensioner, shall also be paid to the other eligible family member of the Govt. Servant/Pensioner.

6. The provisions of Rule 54 (11-C) of CCS (Pension) Rules, 1972, shall stand amended to the extent mentioned above. Formal amendment to the Central Civil Services (Pension) Rules, 1972 shall be notified separately.

Sd/-

(Sanjoy Shankar)

Deputy Secretary to the Government of India

26.15

Government of India, Ministry of Defence, Department of Ex-Servicemen Welfare Letter No 2(3)/2021/D(Pen/Pol) dated 5th January 2022

Sub: **Allowing family pension to other eligible family member in the event of family pensioner is charged with the offence of murdering the Government servant or for abetting in the commission of such an offence.**

The undersigned is directed to refer to the provisions contained in DoP&PW O.M. No. 1/24/2019-P&PW(E) dated 16.06.2021 allowing family pension to other eligible family member in the event of family pensioner is charged with the offence of murdering the Government servant or for abetting in the commission of such an offence.

2. In terms of Regulation No. 75 of Pension Regulations for the Army, Part- I, 2008 in the event of an eligible member to receive ordinary family pension under these Regulations is charged with the offence of murdering the service personnel or for abetting in the commission of such an offence, the claim of such a person including other eligible member or members of the family to receive ordinary family pension, shall remain suspended till the conclusion of the criminal proceedings instituted against him.

3. The above provisions have been reviewed and it has been decided that the provisions contained in above mentioned DoP&PW OM dated 16th June, 2021 shall mutatis-mutandis apply to Armed Forces Pensioners also. These provisions shall be applicable with effect from 16 June 2021.

4. The relevant provisions of Pension Regulations of the three Services shall stand modified to the extent mentioned in DoP&PW OM dated 16th June, 2021.

5. This issues with the concurrence of the Finance Division of this Ministry vide their UO Note No. 10(06)/2021/ Fin/Pen dated 08.12.2021.

6. Hindi version will follow.

Yours faithfully,

Sd/-

(Ashok Kumar)

Under Secretary to the Government of India

26.16

Government of India, Ministry of Defence, Department of Ex-Servicemen Welfare Letter No PC-1(07)/2013-D(Pension/Policy) dated 4th May 2020

Sub: **Inclusion of names of the widowed/divorced/unmarried daughter/parents/permanently disabled children/dependent disabled siblings (i.e. brothers and sisters) in the PPO- Procedure regarding.**

I am directed to refer to this Ministry's letter No. 1(07)/2013-D(Pension/Policy) dated 15.05.2015 regarding simplification of pension process for permanently disabled children and dependent parents/siblings for family pension. It has been noticed that name of divorced/widowed/unmarried daughter has not been included in MoD letter No. 1/(07)/2013/ D(Pension/Policy) dated 15.05.2015 causing delay in sanctioning of family pension to such eligible members i.e. widowed/divorced/unmarried daughter, although name of such eligible members was a part of DoP&PW OM No. 1/6/08-P&PW(E) dated 22.06.2010.

2. It is, therefore, decided to issue amendment to Gol MoD letter No. 1(07)/2013-D(Pension/Policy) dated 15.05.2015 as under-

a. **For:** "Disabled children/siblings and dependent parents"

   Read: "Permanently disabled child/children/ siblings/dependent parents and widowed/ divorced/ unmarried daughter," wherever it appears in GoI MoD letter dated 15.05.2015.

b. New clause numbered 5(iii) **"To widowed/divorced/unmarried daughters"** may be inserted below Para-5(ii) to GoI MoD letter dated 15.05.2015 as under:

   (iii) **"To widowed/divorced/unmarried daughters"**

In case the eligibility of all the above categories of claimant mentioned in para 5(i) and 5(ii) of GoI, MoD letter no. 1(7)/2013-D(Pension/Policy) dated 15.05.2015 ceases to be payable, the PDA will allow family pension to such widowed/divorced/unmarried daughter in their hierarchy of DoB after production of marriage/ re-marriage/ death certificate, as the case may be, in respect of all the categories of claimants mentioned in Sub Para - (i) and (ii) of para 5 of GoI, MoD letter dated 15.05.2015, if any.

c. After inserting above clause in GoI, MoD letter dated 15.05.2015, remaining sub clauses under para 5 may be renumbered in following manner:

   - Existing Clause 5(iii) "To the dependent parents-first mother, then father" to be renumbered as 5(iv)
   - Existing Clause 5(iv) "To the permanently disabled siblings" to be renumbered as 5(v).

3. The word "**Farther**" in first line of para 5(iii) of GoI, MoD letter no. 1(7)/2013-D(Pension/Policy) dated 15.05.2015 may be replaced by word "**Father**".

4. The renumbered para 5(iv) referred above may be amended as follows:

   For: "When claimants in (i) and (ii) die or become ineligible- on production of death certificate/ re-marriage-intimation of spouse and/ or death certificates of all permanently disabled children, family pension would be allowed by PDA to dependent parents."

Read: "When claimants in (i), (ii) and (iii) die or become ineligible- on production of death certifate/ marriage/re-marriage -intimation of spouse and/or on production/intimation of marriage/re-marriage/death certificates (as the case may be) of all the eligible dependent son(s) or daughter(s) including permanently disabled child/children and widowed/divorced/unmarried daughter, family pension would be allowed by the PDA to dependent parents."

5. All other terms and conditions shall remain unchanged.

6. This issues with the concurrence of the finance Division of this Ministry vide their ID No 10(01)/2015/Fin/Pen dated 18/02/2020.

7. Hindi version will follow.

Yours Faithfully,

Sd/-

(A K Agrawal)

Deputy Secretary to the Government of India

26.17

Government of India, Ministry of Defence, Department of Ex-Servicemen Welfare Letter No 14(02)/2019/D(Pen/Pol) dated 5th October 2020

Sub: **Revision of Regulation relating to rate of Family Pension (Normal rate & Enhanced rate) of Pension Regulations for the Army, Part-1 (2008) in the light of amendment done in Sub Rule (3) of Rule 54 of CCS Pension Rule, 1972 by DoP&PW-reg.**

The undersigned is directed to refer to the provision of Note 3 (i) & (ii) below Army Instruction 51/80 and Regulation 64 (b) in Pension Regulation for Army, Part-I (2008) under which the minimum of 7 years of continuous qualifying service is required for grant of enhanced rate of Family Pension for the Armed Forces personnel.

2. Consequent upon issue of Gazette Notification No. 550 dated 19.09.2019 of the Ministry of Personnel, Public Grievances & Pensions, Department of Pension and Pensioners' Welfare (DoP&PW), the condition of minimum requirement of 7 years of continuous service for grant of enhanced rate of Ordinary Family Pension in the sub rule (3) (a) & (b) of Rule 54 of CCS Pension Rule, 1972 has been deleted w.e.f. 1st October, 2019 and now Government servants who died in service/invalided out even with less than 7 years of qualifying service shall be eligible for enhanced rate of Family Pension. This notification also has a provision where a Government servant who died within ten years before the 1st day of October 2019 without completing continuous service of seven years, his family shall be eligible for family pension at enhanced rates in accordance with sub rule (3) with effect from the 1st day of October 2019, subject to fulfillment of other conditions for grant of family pension.

3. Now, the President is pleased to decide that the same provision shall be extended to Armed Forces Personnel also. Accordingly, the clause "after having rendered not less than 7 years continuous qualifying service" of Regulation 64(b) of Pension Regulations for the Army, Part-1 (2008) stands deleted w.e.f. 01.10.2019.

4. It has also been decided that where an Armed Forces Personnel died within ten years before the 1st October, 2019 without completing continuous service of seven years, his family shall be eligible for ordinary family pension at enhanced rate as per Regulations 64(b) of Pension Regulations for the Army Part-I(2008) with effect from the 1st October 2019 subject to fulfillment of other conditions for grant of Ordinary Family Pension.

5. Further, the provision of Army Instruction No. 51/1980 would stand modified upto this extent w.e.f. 01.10.2019. The regulation and their instructions for grant of Ordinary Family Pension in Navy and Air Force shall also be amended accordingly.

6. This issues with the concurrence of the Finance Division of this Ministry vide their ID No. 10(02)/2020/FIN/PEN dated 23.09.2020.

7. Hindi Version will follow.

Yours faithfully,

Sd/-

(Ashok Kumar)

Under Secretary to the Govt. of India

26.18

Government of India, Ministry of Defence, Department of Ex-Servicemen Welfare Letter No 1(7)/2013/D(Pen/Pol)/Vol-1 dated 28th September 2021

Sub: Amendment of income criteria for grant of family pension to children/siblings suffering from mental or physical disability.

The undersigned is directed to say that in accordance with Reguiation 69 of Pension Regulations for the Army, Part-I (2008) read with MoD letter No. PN/7995/D(Pen/Pol)/2010 dated 1.10.2010 as amended from time to time, if a child/ sibling of a deceased Armed Forces Personnel/Pensioner is suffering from a mental or physical disability, he/she is eligible for family pension for life, if the disability is of such a nature so , as to prevent him/her from earning his/her livelihood subject to fulfilling income criteria.

2. Department of Pension & Pensioner's Welfare (DoP&PW) has considered the matter regarding income criteria for determining eligibility for family pension in the case of a child/sibling, suffering from mental or physical disability DoP&PW vide their OM No. 1/17/2019-P&PW(E) dated 08.02.2021 decided that a child/sibling of a deceased Government servant/pensioner, who is suffering from a mental or physical disabi1ity, shall be eligible for family pension for life, if the appointing authority is satisfied that the disability is of such a nature so as to prevent him/her from earning his/her livelihood, as evidenced by a disability certificate obtained from a competent medical authority. Such a child shall be deemed· to be not earning his/her livelihood, if his/her overall income from sources other than family pension is less than the entitled family pension at ordinary rate and the dearness relief admissible thereon, payable on death of the Government servant/pensioner concerned.

2.1. Accordingly, a child/sibling of a deceased Government servant/pensioner, who is suffering from a mental or physical disability, shall be eligible for family pension for life, if he/she fulfils, among others, the following conditions:

i. A disability certificate is issued by the competent medical authority.

ii. The overall income of the disabled child, from sources other than family pension, remains less than the entitled family pension at ordinary rate (i.e 30% of the last pay drawn by the deceased Government servant/pensioner concerned) plus the dearness relief admissible thereon.

3. The issue has been considered in this Ministry and the President is pleased to decide that the decision taken at para 2 & 2.1 above shall also be extended for dependent children/siblings, who is suffering from a mental or physical disability, of deceased Armed Forces personnel/pensioners with effect from 08.02.2021.

4. In cases where a child/sibling, suffering from a mental or physical disability is presently not in receipt of a family pension due to non-fulfillment of the earlier income criteria, family pension may be granted to such a child/sibling, if he/ she fulfils the income criteria mentioned in para-2 above and also fulfills the other conditions for grant of family pension at the time of death of Government servant or pensioner or previous family pensioner. The financial benefits, in such cases, shall accrue with effect from 08.02.2021. All other conditions relating to grant of family pension remain unaltered.

5. The provisions of Pension Regulation for three services will be amended in due course.

6. This issues with the concurrence of the Finance Division of this Ministry vide their ID Note no. 10(03)/2021/FIN/PEN dated 15.09.2021.

7. Hindi Version will follow.

Sd/-
Yours faithfully,
(Ashok Kumar)
Under Secretary to the Govt. of India

26.19

Government of India Ministry of Personnel, Public Grievances and Pensions, Department of Pension and Pensioners Welfare Letter No.1/19/03-P&PW dated 25th August 2004

Sub: Eligibility of divorced/widowed daughter for grant of family pension.

The undersigned is directed to say that as per clauses (ii) and (iii) of sub-rule (6) of Rule 54 of the C.C.S. (Pension) Rules, 1972 read with clause (b) of Para 7.2 of this Department's O.M. No.45/86/97-P&PW (A)-Part I dated the 27th October 1997, son/daughter including widowed/divorced daughter shall be eligible for grant of family pension till he/she attains the age of 25 years or up to the date of his/her marriage/remarriage, whichever is earlier (subject to income criterion to be notified separately). The income criterion has been laid down in this Department's O.M. No.45/51/97-P&PW (E) dated the 5th March 1998 according to which, to be eligible for family pension, a son/daughter (including widowed/divorced daughter) shall not have an income exceeding Rs 2550 per month from employment in Government, the private sector, self employment etc. Further orders were issued vide this Department's O.M. No.45/51/97-P&PW (E)(Vol.II) dated 25th July 2001 regarding eligibility of disabled divorced/widowed daughter for family pension for life subject to conditions specified therein.

2. Government has received representations for removing the condition of age limit in favour of divorced/widowed daughter so that they become eligible for family pension even after attaining the age limit of 25 years. The matter has been under consideration in this Department for sometime. In consultation with the Ministry of Finance, Department of Expenditure and the Ministry of Law and Justice, Department of Legal Affairs etc., it has now been decided that there will be no age restriction in the case of the divorced/widowed daughter who shall be eligible for family pension even after their attaining 25 years of age subject to all other conditions prescribed in the case of son/daughter. Such daughter, including disabled divorced/widowed daughter shall, however, not be required to come back to her parental home as stipulated in para 2(ii) of this Department's O.M. dated 25 July 2001, which may be deemed to have beek modified to that extent.

3. This issues with the concurrence of the Ministry of Finance, Department of Expenditure vide I.D.No.98/E.V/2004 dated 13.02.2004.

4. These orders, in so far as they apply to the employees of the Indian Audit and Accounts Department, are issued in consultation with the Comptroller and Auditor General of India vide U.O. No.67 Audit (Rules)/37-99 dated 20.5.2004.

Sd/-

Chapter-27

Provisions Related to Re-Employment

27.1

Government of India, Ministry of Personnel, Public Grievances and Pensions Letter No 45/73/97-P&PW(G) dated 2nd July 1999

OFFICE MEMORANDUM

Sub: Recommendations of the 5th Central Pay Commission - Payment of Dearness Relief to re-employed pensioners and employed family pensioners - Decision regarding.

In terms of the existing orders, Dearness Relief to pensioners and family pensioners is to remain suspended during the period a pensioner/family pensioner is re-employed/employed under the Central or State Government or in a Statutory Corporation/Company/Body/Bank under them in India or abroad. These orders are also applicable to pensioners and family pensioners permanently absorbed in a Statutory Corporation/Company/Body/Bank under the Central or State Government.

1. In paragraph 138.21 of their Report, the 5th Central Pay Commission had recommended that Dearness Relief should be paid to employed family pensioners and re-employed pensioners in cases where their pay is fixed at the minimum of the pay scale of the post of re-employment ignoring the entire pension, and that, in other cases of re-employment; Dearness Relief shall be payable on pay plus the non ignorable portion of pension as was the case at present. The Commission had further recommended in paragraph 141.12 that, with a view to maintaining the original value of the pension, the payment of Dearness Relief should not be suspended where pay is fixed at the minimum of the pay scale during employment/re-employment of a family pensioner/pensioner.

2. These recommendations have been considered and accepted by the Government. The President is accordingly pleased to decide as follows:

a. In so as re-employed pensioner are concerned, the entire pension admissible is to be ignored at present only in case of those civilian pensioners who held posts below Group 'A' and those ex-servicemen who held posts below the ranks of Commissioned Officers at the time of their retirement. Their pay, on re-employment, is to be fixed at the minimum of the pay scale of the post in which they are re-employed. Such civilian pensioners will consequently be entitled to Dearness Relief on their pension in terms of the recommendation of the 5th Central Pay Commission at the rates applicable from time to time.

b. In terms of the existing orders on the subject, the pay of re-employed pensioners who held Group 'A' post or post of the ranks of Commissioned Officers at the time to their retirement is to be fixed at present:

- at the same stage as last drawn before retirement or, if there is no such stage, the stage next above the pay last drawn.
- at the maximum of the pay scale, if the pay drawn is more than the maximum of the pay scale of the post in which re-employed.

- at the minimum of the pay scale of the post in which re-employed, if is more than the pay last drawn.

  Further, the pay on re-employment is required to be fixed after ignoring only a portion of the pension (Rs 1,500) received for the previous employment. In view of the fact that (i) the pension is taken into account in such cases and is not entirely ignored; (ii) the pay in the post of re-employment is not required to be fixed at the minimum of the scale in all cases and (iii) Dearness Allowance at the rates applicable from time to time is also admissible on the pay fixed in terms of the orders on the subject, these re-employed pensioners will not be entitled, in addition, to any Dearness Relief on their pension.

c. As regards employed pensioners, since the family pension received by the eligible dependents of central Government employees is, in any case, not taken into account in determining their pay on employment, Dearness Relief at the rates applicable from time to time shall be admissible on their family pension.

d. While implementing these decisions, orders issued by the department of Personnel & Training vide OM No. 3/1/85-Estt (Pay-II) dated 31.07.1986 and as amended from time to time regarding fixation of pay of re-employed pensioners shall be duly kept in view.

These orders shall be effective from July 18, 1997.

4. (I) In accordance will the Government's decisions, referred to in the proceeding paragraph, all family pensioners, in receipt of family pension from the central Government who were/are employed under the Central Government or the State Government or a Corporation/Company/Body/Bank under them in India or abroad shall be eligible to draw dearness relief, at rates applicable from time to time, on the amount of family pension with effect from July 18, 1997. A certificate may still be necessary to determine dependency. All Pension Payment Authorities, including authorised Public Sector Banks are requested to forthwith release dearness on account of the family pensioners concerned being employed. the arrears, if any, due with effect from July 18, 1997 shall also be paid.

(II) (a) In the case of Central Government pensioners who were/are re-employed under the Central Government or the State Government or a Corporation/Company/Body/Bank or autonomous organisation, dearness relief will now be admissible to such of those re-employed pensioners who satisfy the conditions referred to in para 3(a) above. For this purpose, the central Government Department concerned, including subordinate organisations, State Government, Corporation/Company/Body/Bank etc. employing a Central Government pensioner shall be required to issue a certificate indicating the following:

i. The re-employed pensioner retired from a civil or military post in the Central Government and was holding a post not included in classified as group 'A' or a post below the rank of commissioned officer in the armed forces:

ii. The entire amount of pension sanctioned by the central Government was ignored in fixation of the pay on re-employment i.e., no part of the pension was taken into account in such fixation of pay in the pay scale of the post in which the Central Government retired/retiree officer was re-employed/absorbed; and.

iii. The pay of the re-employed/absorbee was/is fixed at the minimum of the pay scale of the post in which he had/has been initially re-employed after his retirement from the Central Government.

(b) All Central Government Ministers/Departments/Organisations shall bring these orders to the notice of all Central Government pensioners who happened to be re-employed by them as on July 18, 1997 or were/are re-employed subsequently. In cases such re-employed pensioners satisfy the conditions referred to above, the necessary certificate on the above lines shall be issued after verification from the details referred to in para 17 of the Central Civil Services (Fixation of pay of Re-employed pensioners) order 1986 issued vide Department of Personnel & Training OM No. 3/1/85 - Estt(Pay-II) dated 31.07.1986 and as amended from time to time.

(c) The Pension Disbursing Authority shall release dearness relief on pension to those re-employed pensioners who submit the Certificate referred to above.

(d) In all other cases of re-employed pensioners, no dearness relief shall be admissible on pension during the period of their re-employment. Payment of dearness relief in these cases shall become admissible only with effect from the date they cease to be re-employed.

(e) The Pension Disbursing Authority shall require such a pensioner to produce a certificate of cessation of re-employment from the office in which he had been re-employed.

5. Formal amendment to the Central Civil Services (Pension) Rules, 1972, is being issued separately.

6. CPAO may take immediate action to suitably amend the relevant provision of the Scheme for Payment of Pension to Central Government Civil Pensioners, including the proforma at Annexure- XVII and notify the same to all Public Sector Banks disbursing pension to Central Government pensioners/Family pensioners. A copy of the notification may be endorsed to this department.

7. Necessary orders in respect of re-employed Defence pensioners and family pensioners will be issued separately by the Ministry of Defence.

8. Administrative Ministries may bring these orders to the notice of all subordinate organisations autonomous bodies and Public Sector Undertaking including Nationalised banks, financial institutions etc, under them so that the eligible Central Government pensioners re-employed in these organisations do not face any difficulty in obtaining the requisite certificate.

9. This issues with the concurrence of the Ministry of Finance, Department of Expenditure.

10. In so far as these orders relates to personnel of the Indian Audit and Accounts Departments, these have been issued in consultation with the Comptroller & Auditor General of India.

11. Hindi Version will follow.

Sd/-
(Ganga Murthy)
Director

27.2

Government of India, Ministry of Defence Letter No7(1)95-D(Pension/ Services) dated 28th August 2000

Sub: Recommendations of the 5th Central pay commission - payment of dearness relief to re-employed pensioners and employed family pensioners decision regarding.

1. Recommendation of the V CPC regarding dearness relief to the employed family pensioners and re-employed ex-servicemen have been considered and accepted by the Government. Accordingly, in addition to MOD letter No. 7(1)/95/D(Pen/Sers) dated 08 Oct. 99, the President is pleased to decide the payment of Dearness Relief to Family Pensioners. Ex-servicemen re-employed in Armed Forces as follows:

a. In so far as re-employed pensioner are concerned, the entire pension admissible is being ignored at present only in the case of those ex-servicemen who held posts below the ranks of commissioned officers (PBOR) at the time of their retirement. Their pay, on re-employment, is to be fixed at the minimum of the pay scale of the post in which they are re-employed. Such pensioners will consequently be entitled to Dearness Relief on their pension in terms of the recommendations of the 5th Central Pay Commission at the rates applicable from time to time.

b. In terms of the existing orders on the subject, the pay of re-employed pensioners who held posts of the ranks of Commissioned Officers at the time of their retirement is to be fixed as last drawn before retirement or, if there is no such stage/at the stage next above the pay last drawn. In view of the fact that (i) the pension is taken into account in such cases and is not entirely ignored; (ii) the pay in the post of re-employment is not required to be fixed at the minimum of the scale in all cases; and (iii) Dearness Allowance at the rates applicable from time to time is also admissible on the pay fixed in terms of the orders on the subject, these re-employed pensioners will not be entitled to any Dearness Relief on their pension.

c. As regards employed family pensioners, since the family pension received by the eligible dependents of Armed Forces pensioners is, in any case, not taken into account at determining their pay on employment, Dearness Relief at the rates applicable from time to time shall be admissible on their family pension.

d. While implementing these decisions, orders issued by MOD vide order No. 1(48)/87/D(Pay/Services) dated 31st Jan., 1991, regarding fixation of pay of re-employed pensioners shall be duly kept in view.

2. (I) In accordance with the Government's decision referred to in the preceding paragraph al family pensioners, in receipt of family pension from the Central Government and who were/are employed under the Central Government or the State Government or a Corporation/Company/Body/Bank under them in India or abroad shall be eligible to draw dearness relief, at rates applicable from time to time. On the amount of family pension with effect from July 18, 1997. All Pension Payment Authorities, including authorised Public Sector Banks are requested to forthwith release dearness relief on family pensions in cases where this was withheld on account of the family pensioners concerned being employed. The arrears, if any, due with effect from 18 July, 1997 shall be paid.

(II) (a) In the case of Armed Forces PBOR pensioners who were/are re-employed under the Armed Forces, dearness relief will now be admissible to such of these re-employed PBOR pensioners who satisfy the conditions referred to in para 1(a) above. For this purpose, Armed Forces employing a Armed Forces pensioner shall be required to issue certificate indicating the following:

i. The re-employed pensioner retired from a military post below the rank of commissioned officer in the armed forces.

ii. The entire amount of pension sanctioned by the Central Government was ignored in fixation of the pay on re-employment i.e. no part of the pension was taken into account in such fixation of pay in the pay scale of the post in which the Armed Forces personnel was re-employed;

iii. The pay of the re-employed/retired was/is fixed at the minimum of the pay scale of the post in which he had/has been initially re-employed after his retirement from the Armed Forces.

(b) These orders will be brought to the notice of all Armed Forces pensioners who happened to be re-employed by them as on 18 July, 1997 or were/are re-employed subsequently.

(c) The Pension Disbursing Authority shall release dearness relief on pension to those re-employed pensioners who submit the Certificate referred to in para 2(II) (a) above.

(d) In all other cases of re-employed commissioned officer pensioners, no dearness relief shall be admissible on pension during the period of their re-employment, Payment of dearness relief these cases shall become admissible only with effect from the date they cease to be re-employed. The Pension Disbursing Authority shall require such a pensioner to produce a certificate of cessation of re-employment from the office in which he had been re-employed.

3. Formal amendment to the pension regulations for the Army/Navy/Air Force, is being issued separately.

4. Principal CDA(P) may take immediate action to suitably amend the relevant provision of the Scheme for Payment of Pension to Armed Forces Pensioners, notify the same to all Public Sector Banks disbursing pension to Armed Force pensioners/Family pensioners. A copy of the notification may be endorsed to this Ministry.

5. These orders shall be effective from 18 July, 1997.

6. This issues with the concurrence of the finance Division of this Ministry vide their UO No. 2940/Pen/2000 dated 29.08.2000.

7. Hindi Version will follow.

Sd/

(L.K. Haldar)

Under Secretary to the Government of India

27.3

Government of India, Ministry of Personnel, Public Grievances & Pensions, Department of Pension & Pensioners Welfare UO No 41/42/2007-P&PW(G) dated 3rd April 2008

Department of Pension & Pensioner's Welfare

Desk 'G'

Sub: **Payment of Dearness relief to re-employed pensioners and employed family pensioners-decision regarding.**

Department of Ex-Servicemen Welfare may please refer to their I.D. Note No 12(4)/03-D(Pen/Ser) dated 10th October, 2007, on the above subject.

2. The case of re-employed pensioners and family pensioners has been examined in this Department in consultation with DOPT. The DOPT has clarified that if the pay is fixed at a higher stage because of advance increments and no protection of the last pay drawn is being given, the pay should be treated as fixed at a minimum only for the purposes of ignoring the entire pension and allowing Dearness Relief on pension. They have further clarified that for availing this benefit, the ex-servicemen should have retired at post below Commissioned Officer rank (PBOR) before attaining the age of 55 years.

Sd/-
(M.P. Singh)
Director (PP)

27.4

Government of India, Ministry of Personnel, Public Grievances & Pension, Department of Personnel & Training Letter No 3/3/2016-Estt (Pay-II) dated 1st May 2017

OFFICE MEMORANDUM

Sub: Applicability of Central Civil services (Revised Pay) Rules, 2016. to persons re-employed in Government Service after retirement and whose pay is debatable to Civil Estimates.

The pay fixation of re-employed pensioners on re-employment in Central Government, Including that of Defence Forces personnel/Offices, is being done in accordance with Central Civil Service (Fixation of Pay of Re-employed Pensioners) Orders, 1986, issued vide this Department's O.M. No. 3/1/85-Estt (Pay II) dated 31 July, 1986 (as revised from time to time). Persons re-employed in Government service after retirement have been excluded from the purview of the Central Civil Services (Revised Pay) Rules, 2016 vide Rule 2 (2) (vii) thereof. The question of extension of the benefit of the revised pay rules to these persons and the procedure to be followed for fixing their pay in the revised pay structure has been considered by the Government. The President is pleased to decide that, in partial modification of the Rule 2 (2) (vii) of the Central Civil Services (Revised Pay) Rules, 2016, the provisions of these rules shall apply to such persons also who were in/came into re-employment on or after 1st January 2016, subject to the orders hereinafter contained. This decision will cover all Government servants re-employed in Central Civil Departments other than those employed on contract except where the contract provides otherwise, whether they have retired with or without a pension and/ or gratuity or any other retirement benefits, e.g. contributory fund, etc, from a civil post or from the Armed Forces.

2. Re-employed persons who become eligible to elect revised pay structure in accordance with these orders should exercise their option in the manner laid down in Rule 5 and 6 of the Central Civil Services (Revised Pay) Rules, 2016, within three months of the date of issue of these orders or in cases where the existing scales of pay of the posts held by them are revised subsequent to the issue of these orders, within three months of the date of such order.

Fixation/drawal of pay of Personnel/Officers re-employed prior to 01.01.2016 and who were in re-employment as on 01.01.2016:

3. (a) The initial pay of a re-employed Government servant who elects or is deemed to have elected to be governed by the revised pay structure from the 1st day of January, 2016 shall be fixed according to the provisions of Rule 7 of the C.C.S. (R.P.) Rules, 2016, if he/she is:

i. A Government servant who retired without receiving a pension, gratuity as any other retirement benefit and

ii. A retired Government servant who received pension or any other retirement benefits but which were ignored while fixing pay on re-employment.

3. (b) The initial pay of a re-employed Government servant who retired with a pension or any other retirement benefit and whose pay on re-employment was fixed with reference to these benefits or ignoring a part thereof, and who elects or is deemed to have elected to be governed by the revised structure from the 1st day of January, 2016 shall be fixed in accordance with the provisions contained in Rule 7 of the Central Civil Services (Revised Pay) Rules, 2016. Pension (excluding the ignorable portion of pension, if any), as defined in Para 3 (1) of CCS (Fixation of Pay of Re-employed Pensioners) Orders, 1986 admissible on relevant date, i.e. date of coming over to the revised pay structure, effective

from 1.1.2016 or later, shall be deducted from his/her pay in accordance with the general policy of the Government on fixation and subsequent drawal of pay of re-employed pensioners.

3. (c) In addition to the pay so fixed, the re-employed Government servant would continue to draw the retirement benefits he/she was permitted to draw in the pre-revised scales, as modified based on the recommendations of the Seventh Central Pay Commission, Orders in respect of which have been issued separately by the Department of Pension & Pensioners' Welfare.

3. (d) Where a re-employed Government servant elects to draw his/her pay in the existing pay structure and is brought over to revised pay structure from a date later than the 1st day of January, 2016, his/her pay from the later date in the revised scale shall be fixed in accordance with the provisions of Rule 11 of the Central Civil Service (Revised Pat) Rules, 2016.

4. Further, the existing ceiling of Rs 80,000/- for drawal of pay plus gross pension on re-employment is enhanced to Rs 2,25,000/-, the maximum basic pay prescribed for Secretary to the Government of India under Central Civil service (Revised Pay) Rules, 2016.

Ignorable part of Pension

5. The President is also pleased to enhance the ignorable part of pension from Rs 4,000/- to Rs 15,000/- (Rupees Fifteen Thousand) in the case of Commissioned Service Officers and Civil Officers holding Group "A" posts who retire before attaining the age of 55 years. the existing limits of civil and military pensions to be ignored infixing the pay of re-employed pensioners will, therefore, cease to be applicable to cases of such pensioners as are re-employed on or after 1.1.2016.

6. In the case of persons who were already on re-employment as on 01.01.2016, the pay may be fixed on the basis of these orders, with effect from the date of coming over to the new pay structure, i.e. 01.01.2016 or later, as per the option exercise by them in terms of Para 2 above. In such case, there terms would be determined afresh as if they have been re-employed for the first time from such date of coming over to the new pay structure.

Fixation/drawal of pay of employees appointed on re-employment basis on or after 1st day of January, 2016

7. Pursuant to the introduction of the system of Pay Matrix vide the Central Civil Services (Revised Pay) Rules, 2016, the President is further pleased to amend the relevant provisions of CCS (Fixation of Pay of re-employed Pensioners) Orders, 1986 in the manner indicated below:

Existing Provisions (1986 Orders read with OM dated 5th April 2010)	**Revised Provisions**
Para 4 (a): Re-employed pensioners shall be allowed to draw pay only in the prescribed pay scale/pay structure of the post in which they are re-employed. No protection of the scales of pay/pay structure of the post held by them prior to retirement shall be given *Note: Under the provisions of CCS (RP) Rules, 2008, revised pay structure comprises the grade pay attached to the post and the applicable pay band.*	Order 4 (a): Re-employed pensioners shall be allowed to drawn pay only in the Level in the revised pay structure applicable to the post in which they are re-employed. No protection of the scales of pay/pay structure of the post held by them prior to retirement shall be given. *Note: revised pay structure in relation to a post will be as define din Rule 3 (ix) of the Central Civil Services (Revised Pay) Rules, 2016.*

Para 4 (b) (i): In all cases where the pension is fully ignored, the initial pay on re-employment shall be fixed as per entry pay in the revised pay structure of the re-employed post applicable in the case of direct recruits appointed on or after 1.1.2016 as notified vide Section II, Part A of first Schedule to CCS (RP) Rules, 2008.	Order 4 (b) (i): In all cases where the pension is fully ignored, the initial pay on re-employment shall be fixed as per Rule 8 of the Central Civil Services (Revised Pay/ rules, 2016) *Note 1: The case where pension is fully ignored is given in Order 4 (d) below.* *Note 2: Pension is fully ignored means that pension is not deducted from pay.*
Para 4 (b) (ii): In cases where the entire pension and pensionary benefits are not ignored for pay fixation, the initial basic pay on re-employment shall be fixed at the same stage as the last basic pay drawn before retirement. However, he shall be granted the grade pay of the re-employed post. The maximum basic pay cannot exceed the grade pay of the re-employed post plus pay in the pay band of Rs 67,000 i.e. the maximum of the pay band PB-4. In all these cases, the non-ignorable part of the pension shall be reduced from the pay so fixed. **Illustration** A Colonel who retired with basic pay of Rs 61,700 (grade pay Rs 8,700; pay in the pay band Rs 53,000) is re-employed as a Deputy Secretary in an organization with grade pay of Rs 7,600. In this case, on re-employment, his basic pay will continue to be Rs 61,700. However, his grade pay on re-employment will be Rs 7,600 and the pay in the pay band Rs 54,100. Thereafter, the non-ignorable part of the pension will be reduced from the pay so fixed. *Note: In the revised pay structure, basic pay is pay in the pay band plus the grade pay attached to the post.*	Order 4 (b) (ii): In cases where the entire pension and pensionary benefits are not ignored for pay fixation, the initial basic pay on re-employment shall be fixed at the same stage as the last basic pay drawn before retirement, if there is no such stage in the re-employed post, the pay shall be fixed at the stage next above that pay. If the maximum pay in the level applicable to the post in which a pensioner is re-employed is less than the last basic pay drawn by him before retirement, his initial basic pay shall be fixed at such maximum pay of the re-employed post. Similarly, if the minimum pay in the level applicable to the post in which a pensioner is re-employed is more than the last basic pay drawn by him before retirement; his initial basic pay shall be fixed at such minimum pay of the re-employed post. However, in all these cases, the non-ignorable part of the pension shall be reduced from the pay so fixed. *Note 1: Revised pay structure in relation to a post will be as defined in Rule 3 9ix) of the Central Civil Services (Revised Pay) Rules, 2016.* *Note 2: "Basic Pay" in the revised Pay Structure means the pay draw mom the prescribed Level in the Pay Matrix.* *Note 3: Last pay drawn shall be as per definition of pre-retirement pay in terms of Order 3 of the CCS (Fixation of Pay of Re-employed Pensioners) Orders, 1986, read with DoPT OM No. 3/19/2009-Estt. (Pay-II) dated 8th November 2010.*

Continued...

Para 4 (c): The re-employed pensioner will, in addition to pay as fixed under Para (b) above shall be permitted to drawn separately any pension sanctioned to him and to retain any other form of retirement benefits.	Order 4 (c): No change.
Para 4 (d): In the case of persons retiring before attaining the age of 55 years and who are re-employed, pension (including PEG and other forms of retirement benefits) shall be ignored for initial pay fixation in the following extent: (i) In the case of ex-servicemen who held posts below commissioned officer rank in the Defence Forces and in the case of civilians who held posts below Group 'A' posts at the time of their retirement, the entire pension and pension equivalent of retirement benefits shall be ignored. (ii) In the case of Commissioned Officers belonging to the Defence Forces and Civilian pensioners who held Group 'A' posts at the time of their retirement, the first Rs 4,000/- of the pension and pension equivalent retirement benefits shall be ignored.	Order 4 (d): In the case of persons retiring before attaining the age of 55 years and who are re-employed, pension (including PEG and other forms of retirement benefits) shall be ignored for pay fixation to the following extent: (i) No change (ii) In the case of Commissioned service officers belonging to the Defence Forces and Civilian pensioners who held Group 'A' posts at the time of their retirement, the first Rs 15,000/- of the pension and pension equivalent retirement benefits shall be ignored.

8. Apart from the above, it is also clarified as under:

   i. **Drawal of Increments:** Once the initial pay of the re-employed pensioners has been fixed in the manner indicated above, he will be allowed to drawn normal increments as per the provisions of Rule 9 and 10 of CCS (RP) Rules, 2016 read with Order 5 of the CCS (Fixation of Pay of re-employed Pensioners) Orders, 1986.

   ii. **Treatment of Military Service Pay (MSP):** MSP is granted to Defence Forces officers/personnel while they are serving in the Defence Forces. Accordingly, on their re-employment in civilian organizations, including secret organizations under the Cabinet Secretariat umbrella, the question of grant of MSP to such officers/personnel does not arise. However, the benefit of MSP in the pension should not be withdrawn. **Accordingly, while the pension of such re-employed pensioners will include the element of MSP, they will not be granted MSP as part of pay while working in civilian organizations.** Also, in respect of all those Defence Officers/Personnel, whose pension contains an element of MSP and whose pay on re-employment is subject to deduction of pension (excluding the ignorable portion, if any), the element of MSP as contained in the pension shall be ignored while deducting the pension at the time of pay fixation. In other words, the MSP portion of the pension need not be deducted from the pay fixed on re-employment

   iii. **Fixation/drawal of pay of re-employed persons who retired prior to 1.1.2016 and who have been re-employed after 1.1.2016, and whose entire pension and pensionary benefits are not ignored for pay fixation**. The pay on re-employment will be fixed in terms of Order 4 (b) (ii) of the CCS (Fixation of Pay of Re-employed Pensioners) Orders, 1986, as amended above, after notionally arriving at their revised basic pay at the time of retirement as if they had retired under the revised pay structure, in terms of Rule 7 of the Central Civil Services (Revised Pay) Rules, 2016. In all these cases, the non-ignorable part of the pension shall be reduced from the pay so fixed. Regulation of MSP, however, shall be as per clarification in Para 8 (ii) above.

iv. **Fixation/drawal of pay in all other cases:** Pay fixation in cases not covered in Order 4 (d) will be as per the general principle of 'pay minus pension'. i.e. while the last pay drawn shall be reckoned for pay fixation, the entire pension shall be deducted from the pay so fixed. Regulation of MSP, however, shall be as per clarification in Para 8 (ii) above.

9. An undertaking may be obtained from re-employed pensioners who opt/are deemed to have opted for the revised pay structure to the effect that, they understand and agree that the special dispensation provided through this O.M. is subject to the condition of deduction of pension as admissible to them from time to time, wherever required as per extant instructions.

10. These instructions shall apply in respect of those re-employed pensioners who are re-employed against civil posts carrying pay upto Level 17 of the pay Matrix of CCS (RP) Rules, 2016.

11. In so far as the person serving in the Indian Audit & Accounts Department are concerned, these orders are being issued after consultation with the Comptroller & Auditor General of India.

12. These Orders shall take effect from 1.1.2016.

Sd/-
(Pushpender Kumar)
Under Secretary to the Government of India

Chapter-28

Provisions of the 4th Central Pay Commission

28.1

Government of India, Ministry of Defence Letter No 1(5)87/D (Pensions/Services) dated 30th October 1987

Sub: **Implementation of the Govt. decisions on the recommendations of the Fourth Central Pay Commission regarding pensionary benefits for the Armed Forces officers and personnel below officer rank retiring or dying in harness on or after 1.1.86**

Sir,

I am directed to refer to the Govt. decisions on the recommendations of the Fourth Central Pay Commission as notified vide Government of India, Ministry of Personnel, Public Grievances and Pensions, Department of Pension & Pensioners' Welfare Resolution No. 2/13/87-PIC dated 18th March 1987 and convey the sanction of the President to the modifications, to the extent specified in this letter, in the rules/regulations concerning pensionary benefits of the Commissioned Officers (including MNS and Territorial Army Officers) and personnel below officer rank (including NCs (E) of the three services, Defence Security Corps and the Territorial Army) (hereinafter collectively referred to as Armed Forces personnel).

1.1 The provisions of the Pension Regulations of the three Services and various instructions/Govt. orders which are not affected by the provisions of this letter, will remain unchanged.

PART-I

Date of Effect and Definitions

2.1 The provisions of this letter shall apply to the Armed Forces personnel who were in service as on 1.1.1986 or joined/join service thereafter.

2.2 Where pension has been sanctioned provisionally in cases occurring on or after 1.1.1986 the same should be revised in terms of these orders. In cases where pension has been finally sanctioned under the pre-revised orders and if it happens to be more beneficial than the pension becoming due under orders, the pension already sanctioned shall not revised to the disadvantage of pensioners.

DEFINITIONS

3. Reckonable Emoluments:

3.1 The term 'Reckonable Emoluments' shall mean:

Emoluments reckonable for

1	2	3
Category	Retiring/Service Pension	All types of Gratuities and Family Pension (ordinary, special and liberalized special) and war, injury pension.
Officers	Average of the pay, Non-practising allowance (NPA) and rank pay, if any, drawn by the officer during the last 10 months of his service	Pay plus NPA and rank pay, if any, last drawn by the officer
Personnel below officer rank	Maximum pay of the pay including 50% of the highest classification pay, if any, of the rank held and group in which paid continuously for at least 10 months at the time of discharge	Pay including classification pay, if any, last drawn by the individual

Pay, Non-Practising Allowance, Classification Pay and Rank Pay:

3.2 The terms 'Pay' 'NPA' Classification Pay' and 'Rank Pay' referred to in para 3.1 shall mean respectively the basic pay in the revised pay scales, Non-practising allowance, Classification pay and the rank pay introduced with effect form 1.1.86 vide the following Service Instructions:

(a) For Service Officers

AI 1/S/87 dated 26.5.87, as amended

NI 1/S/87 dated 11.6.87

AFI 1/S/87 dated 26.5.87

(b) For Personnel Below Officer Rank

AI 3/S/86 dated 13.10.86, as amended,

AI 4/S/86 dated 13.10.86

NI 1/S/86 11.10.86

AFI 1/S/86 dated 13.10.86

3.3 In the case of individuals who opt to continue to draw pay in the pre-revised scales beyond 31.12.1985 and remain in that scale till retirement/invalidment/death in harness the term "Pay" (referred to in para 3.1) will comprise of the following:

(a) Officers:

Basic pay in the pre-revised scales and appropriate Non-Practising allowance, if any, plus dearness allowance additional dearness allowance and ad-hoc dearness allowance admissible upto CPI 608 in terms of this

Ministry's letter No. 12(1)/83/D (Pay/Services) Vol. II dated 28.2.1986 appropriate to the basic pay (including NPA, if any) plus two installments of interim relief at the rates in force on 31.12.1985 appropriate to the said basic pay.

(b) **Personnel Below Officer Rank** (including NCs (E):

Basic pay in the pre-revised scales plus pre-revised rates of good service pay/badge pay/appointment pay/50% of the highest classification pay appropriate to the pay group, if any, plus appropriate dearness allowance and additional dearness allowance admissible upto average CPI 608 in terns of this Ministry's letter No. 12(1)/83/D (Pay/Services) Vol. II dated 24.2.1986 plus two installments of interim relief at the rates in force on 31.12.1985, and also the Home Saving element. For calculation of gratuity and family pension, classification pay actually drawn will be included in computing reckonable emoluments.

Notes:

(1) Where an officer immediately before his/her retirement or death while in service had been absent from duty on leave (including furlough leave) for which leave salary is/was payable or having been suspended had been re-instated without forfeiture of service, the emoluments which he/she would have drawn, had he/she not been absent from duty or not been suspend shall reckon for pensionary benefits.

Provided that any increase in pay (other than the increment referred to in Note 4 below) which is/was not actually drawn shall not form part of emoluments.

(2) Where an officer immediately before his/her retirement or death while in service had proceeded on leave for which leave salary is payable, after having held a higher paid acting rank, the emoluments drawn in such paid acting rank shall reckon for pensionary benefits only if it is certified that he/she would have continued to hold the paid acting rank but for his/her proceeding on leave.

(3) Where an officer immediately before his/her retirement or death while in service had been under suspension, or absent from duty the period where of does not count as service, the emoluments which he/she drew immediately before such absence from duty or being placed under suspension, shall reckon for pensionary benefits.

(4) Where an officer immediately before his/her retirement or death while in service, was on annual leave, or furlough leave and earned an increment which was not withheld, such increment though not actually drawn, shall form part of emoluments reckonable for pensionary benefits.

Provided that the increment was earned during the currency of such leave not exceeding 120 days or during that first 120 days of the leave where such leave was for more than 120 days.

(5) Where an officer is serving in an organization other than the Armed Forces, the actual pay and allowances drawn during such service shall not be treated as emoluments, but the basic pay (plus NPA and the rank pay, if any) which he/she would have drawn in the Armed Forces, had/she not been on such service, shall alone the treated as emoluments reckonable for pensionary benefits.

4. Average Emoluments:

4.1 Average Emoluments in the case of officers shall be determined with reference to the emoluments drawn by him during the last 10 months of his service.

4.2 In the case of officers who have opted for the revised scales of pay and have retired within 10 months of coming over to the revised pay scales, the "average pay" for 10 months period proceeding retirement shall be calculated by taking into account pay as follows:

(a)	For the period during which pay was drawn in the pre-revised scales	Basic pay and NPA, if any plus actual DA/ADA/Ad hoc DA and interim relief appropriate to the basic pay (including NPA if any) at the rates in force on 31.12.1985, drawn during the relevant period, and,
(b)	For the period during which pay is drawn in the revised scales	Basic pay in the revised scale plus NPA and rank pay, if any

Notes:

(1) If during the last 10 months of his/her service an officer had been absent from duty on leave for which leave salary is payable or having been suspended had been reinstated without forfeiture of service, the emoluments which he/she would have drawn and he/she not been absent from duty or suspended shall be taken into account for determining the average emoluments.

Provided that any increase in pay (other than the increment referred to in Note 3) which is not actually drawn shall not form part of his emoluments

(2) If during the last 10 months of the service, an officer had been absent from duty or had been under suspension the period whereof does not count as service, the aforesaid period of absence from duty or suspension, shall be disregarded in the calculation of the average emoluments and equal period before the 10 months shall be included

(3) In the case of an officer who was on annual leave or furlough leave during the last 10 months for his service and earned an increment which was not with held, such increment though not actually drawn, shall be included in the average emoluments

Provided that the increment was earned during the currency of such leave not exceeding 120 days or during the first 120 days of leave where such leave was for more than 120 days.

5. **Qualifying Service:**

(a) The term 'Qualifying Service' (QS) shall mean Qualifying service reckonable for:

Category	Pension	Death-cum-Retirement Gratuity		Retiring/Service/ Invalid/Terminal Gratuity
		Retirement Gratuity	Death Gratuity	
Officers	Actual qualifying service rendered by the officer plus a weightage (in years appropriate to the rank last held as indicated below subject to the qualifying services including weightage not exceeding 33 years.	Actual qualify-ing service plus a weightage of 5 years subject to the total qualifying ser-vice including weightage not exceeding 33 years.	Actual qualifying service rendered plus a weightage of 5 years subject to total qualifying service not exceeding 33 years. In case actual service is less than 5 years weight age shall be given	Actual qualifying service rendered
Personnel below officer rank (including NCs (E) and Honorary Commissioned officers)	Actual qualifying service rendered by the individual plus a weightage of 5 years subject to the total qualifying service including weightage not exceeding 33 years.	Same as above	Same as above	Same as above

(b) Weightage for the purpose of calculation of pension of commissioned officer will be as given below:

(i) Service officers (other than MNS)

Army	Navy	Air Force	Weightage in years
Subaltern	Sub. Lt.	Plt. Offr./Flg Offr	9
Captain	Lt.	Flt Lt.	9
Major	Lt. Cdr.	Sqn.Ldr	8
Lt. Col (TS)	Cdr (TS)	Wg. Cdr. (TS)	5

Continued...

Lt. Col (S)	Cdr. (S)	Wg. Cdr. (S)	7
Col.	Captain (with less than 3 years 10 months service)	Gp. Capt.	7
Brig.	Capt. (With 3 years 10 months service & more)	Air Cmde.	5
Maj. Gen.	Rear Admiral	AVM	3
Lt. Gen.	Vice Admiral	Air Marshal	3
Lt. Gen. (Army Commander/VCOAS)	Vice Admiral (FOC-in-C/ VCNS)	Air Marshal (AOC-in-C/ VCAS)	3
COAS	CNS	CAS	3

(ii) MNS Officers

Rank	**Weightage in years**
Captain	7
Major	6
Lt. Col.	5
Col.	5
Brig.	5
Maj. Gen.	3

Notes:

(1) There will be no weightage for officers and personnel below officer rank who retire prematurely for permanent absorption in public sector undertakings and autonomous bodies.

(2) There will be no weightage for officers and personnel below officer rank of the Territorial Army.

(3) The above weightage shall not be reckoned for determining the minimum qualifying service specified for admissibility or Retiring Officers Pension i.e. 20 years (15 years for late entrants), 15 years for personnel below officer rank and 20 years for NCs(E).

(4) Full pre-commissioned service rendered under the Central Government whether in a civil Deptt. or in the Armed Forces shall be taken into account for working out the qualifying service for earning pensionary benefits subject to fulfillment of other conditions. This will also be counted for determining the minimum qualifying service indicated in Note 3 above for earning Retiring/Service pension.

(5) In calculating the length of qualifying service, fraction of a year equal to three months and above but less than 6 months shall be treated as a completed one half year and reckoned as qualifying service

PART-II

Retiring/Service Pension/Gratuity, Invalid Pension/Gratuity, Special Pension/Gratuity, Ordinary Family Pension, Retirement/Death Gratuity

6. Retiring/Service Pension

6.1 Officers

a. The minimum period of qualifying service (without weightage) actually rendered and required for earning retiring pension shall continue to be 20 years (15 years in the case of late entrants).

b. Retiring pension in respect of the Commissioned Officers, of the three services, including MNS and TA officers, shall be calculated at 50% of the average of emoluments reckonable for pension as defined in paras 3 and 4 above. The amount so determined shall be subject to a maximum of Rs 4,500/- p.m. and shall be the retiring pension for 33 years of reckonable qualifying service as defined in para 5 above. For lesser years of reckonable qualifying service, this amount shall be proportionately reduced.

Note: The retiring pension of an officer of the rank of Lt. Col. (TS), Brigadier or Major General and equivalent, shall not be less than the pension which would have been admissible to him as a Major, Colonel or a Brigadier and equivalent as the case may be, had he not been promoted to the higher rank.

6.2 Personnel Below Officer Rank

a. The minimum period of qualifying service (without weightage) actually rendered and required for earning service pension will continue to be 15 years (20 years in the case of NCs(E)).

b. Service pension in respect of the personnel below officer rank of the three services (including those of the DSC and TA but excluding reservists) for 33 years of qualifying service shall be calculated at 50% of the emoluments reckonable for pension as defined in para 3 above, and for lesser period of qualifying service (as defined in para 5 above) it shall be reduced proportionately; the amount of service pension finally arrived at shall be subject to a minimum of Rs 375/- p.m.

Note: The existing provisions for assessing the service pension of the rank/pay group on the basis of the rank actually held continuously at least for 10 months at the time of discharge, shall continue to be applicable. This is also applicable in the case of Honorary Commissioned Officers. However, this condition will not be required to be fulfilled in the case of JCOs and equivalents who are granted Hony. Commission and who retire on completion of their tenure of appointment or are discharged on account of causes beyond their control.

c. Based on (a) and (b) above, tables of rates of service pension for various ranks/groups of personnel below officer rank and Honorary Commissioned Officers of the three services who have opted for the revised scales of pay are given in Annexure A,B, C, D and E attached to this letter. The rates of pension have been arrived at by adding a weightage of 5 years to the qualifying service actually rendered., For instance, the pension for 15 years service has bee arrived by taking into account qualifying service of 20 years (including a weightage of 5 years) Service pension in the case of TA personnel will be determined by the CDA(P) by taking into account the reckonable emoluments and qualifying service as defined in paras 3 and 5.

d. Tables showing the rates of service pension of personnel below officer rank with pre-revised scales of pay are not being prescribed, as it is considered unlikely that anybody would have opted for the pre-revised scales of pay. In odd cases where individuals might have opted for the pre-revised scales of pay, CDA(P), CDA(N) and CDA(AF) shall calculate and authorize service pension taking into account the reckonable emoluments as per para 3.3(b) ante, after getting the necessary particulars.

6.3 a. All other conditions governing the grant of retiring/service pension shall continue to be applicable as hitherto fore except that the requirement of 'satisfactory service certificate' prescribed at present shall be dispended with. However, while issuing retirement notification in the case of service officers and while submitting pension claims in respect of personnel below officer rank, the Service Headquarters/Record Officers, shall invariably indicate whether or not any disciplinary/quasi/judicial proceedings are pending against the individual. In the event of the fact of involvement of the individual in any disciplinary/quasi/judicial proceedings coming to the notice of Service Headquarters/Record Offices subsequent to the issuing of retirement notification/submission of pension claims until the date of retirement of the individual, the Service Headquarters/Record offices shall intimate immediately this fact to the Pension Sanctioning Authority.

b The existing provisions contained in Ministry of Defence letter No. 12(1) 74/S/556/D (Pens/Sers) dated 20.07.1974, as amended, regarding grant of provisional pension to Armed Forces personnel who at the time of their discharge/retirement are found to be involved in disciplinary/quasi-judicial proceedings shall continue to be applicable.

7. Retiring/Service Gratuity

7.1 The minimum period of qualifying service shall continue to be 10 years (without weightage) for earning retiring gratuity in the case of officers, and 5 years (without weightage) for earning service gratuity in the case of personnel below officer rank (including NCs(E)).

7.2 The retiring gratuity to officers and service gratuity to personnel below officer rank shall be admissible at a uniform rate of ½ a months' emoluments as defined in para 3 above for each completed six months period of qualifying service as defined in para 5 above. There shall be no deduction in the quantum of retiring service gratuity so arrived at in respect of officers and personnel below officer rank who are permitted to retire or are discharged prematurely on compassionate grounds/reasons.

8. Reservist Pension

A reservist who is not in receipt of service pension shall be granted, on completion of the prescribed combined colour and reserve qualifying service of not less than 15 years a reservist pension equal to 2/3rd of the lowest pension admissible to a Sepoy, but in no case less than Rs 375/- p.m.

9. Invalid Pension/Gratuity

When an individual is invalided out of service with a disability neither attributable to nor aggravated by service, he will be entitled to invalid pension if the service actually rendered is 10 years or more, and invalid gratuity if it is less than 10 years, at the rates indicated below:

i. Invalid pension - Amount equal to the service element of disability pension that would have been admissible in case the causes were attributable to or aggravated by service.

ii. Invalid gratuity - At half a month's emoluments as defined in para 3 above for each six monthly period of service

10. Terminal Gratuity in Respect of SSCOs

Short Service Commissioned Officers shall be entitled to Terminal Gratuity at the rate of ½ a month's emoluments as defined in para 3 above, for each completed six months period of service.

11. Special Pension and Gratuity

Special pension and gratuity to personnel below officer rank (including NCs(E)) who are not transferred to the reserve, but are discharged in large numbers in pursuance of the Govt. policy:

i. of reducing the strength of establishment of the Armed Forces; or

ii. of re-organisation; which results in disbandment of any unit/formation

shall be admissible at the following scales:

Length of actual qualifying service rendered (without weightage) **Scale of Special Pension/Gratuity**

A. Combatants		
(a)	Special pension	
	(i) 15 years or more (ii) 10 years or more but less than 15 years	Equal to normal service pension Equal to the service pension as determined as per para 6.2(b)
(b)	Special gratuity	
	(i) 5 years or more but less than 10 years (ii) less than 5 years	Equal to 1⅓ months' emoluments as defined in para- 3 above for each completed year of qualifying service Equal to 3 months' emoluments as defined in para 3 above
B. Non- Combatants (Enrolled)		
(a)	Special pension	
	(i) 20 years or more (ii) 15 years or more but less than 20 year	Equal to normal service pension Equal to the service pension as determined as per para 6.2(b)
(b)	Special gratuity	
	(i) 5 years or more but less than 15 years (ii) Less than 5 years	Equal to 1⅓ months emoluments as define in para 3 above for each completed year of qualifying service Equal to 3 months' emoluments as defined in para 3 above

12. Retirement Gratuity/Death Gratuity:

12.1 **Retirement Gratuity**

An individual who has completed 5 years qualifying service and is eligible for service/invalid gratuity or pension of any type, shall be granted on the termination of his service a retirement gratuity equal to one fourth of reckonable emoluments for each maximum of six monthly period of qualifying service subject to a maximum of 16½ times the reckonable emoluments, provided that the amount of retirement gratuity payable shall in no case exceed Rupees One Lakh. There will also be no ceiling on reckonable emoluments for calculating the gratuity. The emoluments and qualifying service for this purpose shall be as defined in paras 3 and 5 above, respectively.

12.2 **Death Gratuity:**

Death gratuity at the following rates shall be admissible in the event if death in harness:

Length of qualifying service		Rate of death gratuity	
(i)	Less than one year	2 times	of reckonable emoluments
(ii)	One year or more but less than 5 years	6 times	
(iii)	Five years or more but less than 20 years	12 times	
(iv)	20 years or more	Half of reckonable emoluments as defined in para 3 above for each completed six monthly period of qualifying service as defined in para 5 above, subject to a minimum of 12 times and a maximum of 33 times the reckonable emoluments provided that the amount of Death Gratuity shall in no case exceed Rs 1 Lakh	

Notes:

(1) Death Gratuity at the rates indicated in (i) to (iii) above will be admissible also to the families of short service/emergency commissioned officers in the event of their death while in service.

(2) The emoluments and qualifying service for this purpose shall be as defined in paras 3 and 5 above, respectively. There will be no ceiling on reckonable emoluments for calculating Death Gratuity.

13. Ordinary Family Pension:

a. Ordinary family pension shall continue to be admissible to the families of the Armed Forces personnel (excluding families of reservists) under the same conditions as in force hithetofore. This will also be admissible to the families of MNS officers. The rates of ordinary family pension shall be as follows:

Reckonable emoluments as defined in para-3	Rate of family pension p.m. including dearness relief upto CPI 608
Not exceeding Rs 1,500/- p.m.	30% of reckonable emoluments subject to a minimum of Rs 375/-p.m.
Exceeding Rs 1,500/- p.m. but not exceeding 3000/- p.m.	20% of reckonable emoluments, subject to a minimum of Rs 450/- p.m.
Exceeding Rs 3,000/- p.m.	15% of reckonable emoluments subject to a minimum of Rs 600/- p.m. and a maximum of Rs 1,250/-

b. The existing provisions for payment of ordinary family pension at enhanced rates where an individual who has rendered a minimum of 7 years of continuous qualifying service dies while in service or after retirement with pension for a period of seven years from the date following the date of death of the individual or upto the date on which the deceased would have attained the age of 65 years of enhanced ordinary family pension for this period shall be the lowest of the following amounts:

   i. 50% of the reckonable emoluments as defined in para 3 above

   ii. Twice the normal rate of ordinary family pension as determined vide (a) above

   iii. The amount of retiring/service/invalid pension/service element of disability pension/special pension

c. Families of reservist pensioners shall be entitled to a family pension at the rate of Rs 375/- p.m.

d. In case children become the beneficiaries, the family pension would be admissible upto the age 25 years in the case of sons and unmarried daughter, provided that the eligibility would cease from the date of the marriage of the daughter or if the son or daughter starts earning his or her livelihood before attaining the age of 25 years. However, in case the eligible child is physically or mentally handicapped and is unable to earn a livelihood, the family pension would be admissible for life to such a child.

PART-III
Pensionary Awards in attributable/aggravated cases other than battle Casualty cases

14. Disability Pension

14.1 As hitherto, Disability Pension will continue to consist of service element and disability element and shall continue to be admissible under the same conditions as specified in various orders/regulations. However, the amounts of these elements shall be arrived at in the manner and at the rates specified in paras 14.2 and 14.3 below

14.2 Service Element

(a) Officers: (including officers of MNS and TA)

The amount of service element shall be equal to the retiring pension determined as per para 6.1 (b) above. For this purpose the reckonable qualifying service shall mean the actual service rendered by an officer plus the full weightage appropriate to the rank held at the time of invalidment (except in the case of TA Officers) as given in para 5(b)above. There shall be no condition of minimum qualifying service having been actually rendered for earning this element, if otherwise due.

(b) Personnel below Officer Rank

Service element, will be determined as follow:

Length of actual qualifying service rendered (without weightage)	**Entitlement of service element**
15 years or more (20 years or more in the case of NCs [E])	Equal to normal service pension relevant to the length of qualifying service actually rendered, plus weightage of service as given in para 5
Less than 15 years (20 years the case of NCs [E])	Equal to the service pension as determined as per para 6.2(b), but it shall in no case, be less than 2/3rd of the minimum service pension admissible to the rank/pay group

Note: The existing provisions in the case of JCOs/OR/NCs (E) regarding grant of service element equal to minimum service pension appropriate to the rank and group in cases where the Service is less than 15 years (20 years in case of NCs (E)) and the disability is sustained while on flying/parachute jumping duty or while being carried on duty in an aircraft under proper authority, shall continue.

14.3 **Disability Element**

(a) The rates of disability element for 100% disability for the various ranks shall be as follows:

	Rank	**Amount p.m.**
(i)	Commissioned Officers and Honorary Commissioned Officers of the three Services MNS, TA and DSC	Rs 750/-
(ii)	Junior Commissioned Officers and equivalent rank of three services, TA and DSC	Rs 550/-
(iii)	Other rank/NCs (E) of the three services, TA and DSC	Rs 450/-

(b) For disabilities less than 100% but not less than 20% above rates shall be proportionately reduced.

Provided that where permanent disability is not less than 60% the disability pension (i.e. total of service element and disability element) shall not be less than the special family pension admissible vide para 15.2(b), i.e. it shall not be less than 60% of emoluments as defined in para 3 above subject to a minimum of Rs 750/- p.m

Compensation in lieu of Disability Element

14.4 In case a person belonging to the Armed Forces is found to have a disability which is (i) accepted by the competent authority as attributable to/aggravated by service factors, and (ii) assessed at 20% or more for life but the individual is retained in service, despite such disability, he shall be paid a compensation in lump sum (in lieu of the disability element) equal to the capitalised value of disability element. For this purpose, the rank for disability element shall be the rank held at the time of onset of the disability and age on next birth-day will be reckoned with reference to the date of onset of the disability with loading to age, if any, recommended by the Medical Board. Once a compensation has been paid in lieu of the disability element, there shall be no further entitlement to the disability element for the same disability. Such disability shall also not qualify for grant of any pensionary benefit or relief subsequently.

Constant Attendance Allowance

14.5 The rate of Constant Attendance Allowance will be Rs 300/- p.m. irrespective of the rank, where admissible under the conditions as heretofore.

15. Special Family Pension

15.1 The existing system of sanctioning Special Family Pension to the widow/widower/eligible heir and children allowance and children education allowance to each eligible child separately shall be discontinued. Instead, Consolidated Special Family Pension shall be payable to tile eligible/nominated heir. This will be applicable in cases where Defence personnel die on account of causes which are accepted as attributable to or aggravated by service, irrespective of the length of their service on the date of death. The families of those who die after retirement are also eligible for this if death is due to or hastened by service factors, and subject to fulfillment of existing conditions for grant of special family pension.

15.2 The rates of Special Family Pension inclusive of children allowance and children education allowance shall be as under irrespective of whether the deceased person of the Armed Forces had completed 7 years of services or not:

	Reckonable emoluments	Reckonable emoluments
(a) If the widow is childless	(i) Not exceeding Rs 1,500/-	50% of reckonable emoluments/-
	(ii) Exceeding Rs 1,500/- but not exceeding Rs 3,000/-	40% of reckonable emoluments subject to a minimum of Rs. 750/-
	(iii) Exceeding Rs 3,000/-	30% of reckonable emoluments subject to a minimum of Rs. 1200/- and maximum of Rs. 2500/-
(b) If the widow has child/children	In all cases	60% of reckonable emoluments subject to a minimum of Rs. 750/- and maximum of Rs.2500/-

Note: Reckonable emoluments for this purpose will be as defined in para 3.

15.3 Special Family Pension at the rates indicated in para 15.2(b) above shall be admissible to the widow till the child/ children attain the age prescribed under the rules and thereafter the widow shall be paid family pension at the rates indicated at 15.2(a) above. Special family pension shall be regulated similarly where parents in the case of personnel below officer rank, have been nominated as the first awardee.

15.4 In cases where Special Family pension is granted to the widow and she dies or remarries, the children shall be paid special family pension at the ratesindicated in para 15.2(a) above and the same rate shall also apply to fatherless/ motherless children. In both cases, special family pension shall be paid to the children for the period during which they would have been eligible, as in the case of ordinary family pension.

15.5 In the case of personnel below officer rank, the existing Provision of nominating anyone of the eligible nominees of the family for the first award of special family pension and of transferring the same in full to the widow regardless of her financial position in the even of death of parents, where they were nominated as the original awardees, shall continue.

15.6 Families of SSCOs and ECOs Who die on account of causes attributable to or aggravated by military service will also be entitled to special family pension as indicated in para 15.2 above.

16. Dependant Pension in Respect of Officers (Including MNS Officers), TA Officers and ECOs/SSCOs.

Dependant pension shall be admissible to the parent(s)/eligible brothers and sisters (in the absence of the parents) of the deceased officer at a rate equal to 50% of the Notional Special Family Pension that would have been admissible as per para 15.2(a) above, if they were largely dependent on the deceased officer for support and are in pecuniary need. The existing condition regarding 'means limit' is dispensed with.

Second Life Awards in Respect of Personnel Below Officer Rank including NCs(E)

17. Second Life Awards (Special Family Pension) shall be admissible to the parent(s) of the deceased and in the absence of the parents, eligible brothers and sisters of the deceased, at the rate of 50% of the special family pension determined vide para 15.2(a) above, if the claimant(s) was/were largely dependent on the deceased for support and is/are in pecuniary need.

PART-IV

Liberalised Pensionary Awards (Battle Casualty and such other cases as may be specially notified by Government)

War Injury Pension

18.1 War Injury Pay will now be known as War Injury Pension which will, henceforth not consist of service element and disability element but will be a consolidated amount. War Injury Pension for 100% disability shall be equal to the reckonable emoluments last drawn, as defined in para 3 above on the date of invalidment.

18.2 Where disability is less than 100% the amount of War Injury Pension as in para 18.1 above shall be proportionately reduced. In no case, however, the amount of War Injury Pension shall be less than 60% of the reckonable emoluments last drawn in the case of officers and 80% of the reckonable emoluments last drawn in the case of personnel below officer rank.

18.3 The minimum amounts of War Injury Pension prescribed in para 18.2 above shall be admissible in case the degree of disability is assessed at below 20% at the time of invalidment or at any subsequent reassessment stage.

18.4 In addition to the War Injury Pension, the individual shall be entitled to Retirement Gratuity as per para 12.1. Retirement Gratuity shall be calculated on the basic or reckonable emoluments on the date of invalidment but counting of service upto the date on which he would have normally retired in that rank plus weightage of 5 years (total not exceeding 33 years).

18.5 Separate orders will be issued (i) for regulating commutation of War Injury Pension and (ii) regarding the War Injury Pension that would be admissible to Armed Forces personnel who are retained in service inspite of the disability due to war injury and retire subsequently.

Liberalised Special Family Pension:

19.1 Liberalised Special Family Pension shall be equal to the reckonable emoluments last drawn, as defined in para 3 above, both for the officers and the personnel below officer rank. No children allowance or children education allowance shall be payable in addition. Liberalised Special Family Pension at this rate shall be admissible to the widow in the case of officers and to the nominated heir in the case of personnel below officer rank until death or disqualification.

Note: In the case of both officers and personnel below officer rank, if a widow re-marries her deceased husband's real brother and continues to live a communal life with and/or contributes to the support of other living eligible heirs, she will continue to be eligible to the liberalised special family pension at the rate indicated in para 19.1 above. On remarriage with any other person, she will forfeit her right to the liberalised special family pension but will be given ordinary family pension at the rates indicated in para 13 from the date following the date of her re-marriage, and from the said date children will be allowed children allowance as specified in para 22 below.

19.2 If the Government servant is not survived by a widow but is survived by child/children only, all children together shall be eligible for family pension at the rates specified in para 15.2(a) and also draw in addition the children allowance specified in para 22.

Note: Liberalised Special Family Pension shall be payable to the children for the period during which they would have been eligible as in the case of ordinary family pension. The liberalised special family pension shall be paid to the senior most eligible child at a time.

Dependent Pension in respect of Officers (including MNS Officers, TA Officers and ECOs/SSCOs)

20. Where an officer dies as a bachelor or a widower without children, Dependant Pension will be admissible to parents without reference to their pecuniary circumstances, at 3/4th of the reckonable emoluments last drawn by the deceased officer, for both parents and at 3/4th of this rate for single parent. On the death of one parent, dependant Pension at the latter rate will be admissible to the surviving parent.

Second Life Award (Liberalised Special Family Pension) in respect of Personnel below Officer Rank (including NCs (E)).

21. Second Life award in respect of battle casualties in the case of personnel below officer rank shall be regulated us under:

a. If the first recipient (other than the parents) of the family pensionary award dies or is disqualified earlier than 7 years (counting from the date of casualty), the award will be continued at the same rate to the parents if still alive, for the balance of 7 years without any reduction.

b. After the initial period of 7 years, the award to be continued will be equal to half of the Liberalised Special. Family Pension.

c. If the first award was in favour of the widow and she remarries with a person other than the real brother of her deceased husband, she would get an amount equal to ordinary family pension and the second life award will be sanctioned to a parent if still alive, at the rates mentioned in sub paras (a) and (b) above, depending upon whether the claim had arisen within 7 years or after 7 years of the casualty, subject to the provisions of sub para (d).

d. Where the first life award was given to a parent and the widow remarries with a person other than the real brother of her deceased husband, within seven years counting from the date of casualty, she would get an amount equal to the ordinary family pension, and the original recipient (parent) will continue to receive the first life award at the same rate, for the balance of 7 years without any reduction; and thereafter the award will be half of the liberalised special family pension.

e. Where the first award was give to a parent and the widow remarries with a person other the real brother of her deceased husband, after seven years counting from the date of casualty, she will get an amount equal to the ordinary family pension, and the amount to the original recipient (parent) will be reduced to half of the liberalised special family pension.

f. Children allowance if otherwise admissible will be payable at the rates specified in para 22, in cases falling under sub para (b) above.

Children Allowance and Children Education Allowance

22. The children allowance and children education allowance will be merged together. A consolidated allowance at the following rates shall be allowed in cases covered by Note under the para 19.1 and by paras 19.2 and 21(b):

i. in the case of Service Officers – Rs 150/- Pm. Per Child

ii. in the case of Personnel Below Officer Rank – Rs 100/- Pm Per Child

Constant Attendance allowance

23. Constant Attendance Allowance shall continue to be admissible under the conditions in force hitherto. However, it shall be admissible at a uniform rate of Rs 300/- p.m., irrespective of the rank.

24. Subject to fulfillment of other conditions in force hitherto fore, disability and family pensionary awards shall

continue to be granted at 90% of the notional liberalised pensionary awards in addition to the retirement/ death gratuity becoming due as per the provisions of this letter in respect of casualties occurring in battle inoculation exercises, covered by this Ministry's letter No. B/41022/AC/PS4(d)/5/S/Pen-C dated the 5th March, 1984.

PART-V
GENERAL

Rounding Off of Pensionary Awards

25. The amount of various pensionary awards admissible as per this letter shall be rounded off to the next higher rupee by the Pension Sanctioning Authorities.

Minimum Pension

26. If the amount of any monthly pension (viz. retiring/Service/Invalid/disability/Reservist/Dependants/Ordinary or Special Family pension (excluding Constant Attendance allowance) admissible under the provision of this letter works out to less than Rs 375/- p.m., it shall be stepped up to Rs 375/- and authorised for payment this rate.

Dearness Relief

27. Dearness relief shall be admissible only beyond average CPI 608 on the new pattern introduced vide Ministry of Personnel, Public Grievances and Pensions, Department of Pensions and Pensioners' Welfare Office Memorandum 2/5/87-PICdated 22nd April, 1987, on various types of pensions/family pensions admissible under the provisions of this letter. Constant Attendance Allowance shall not, however, qualify for the grant of dearness relief.

Commutation of Additional Pension

28. The additional amount of retiring/service pension becoming due under the provisions of this letter to those who have already retired shall also qualify for commutation upto the existing limits. Accordingly, in their cases commutation of additional amount of pension should be allowed by the pension Sanctioning Authorities without waiting for any application from them, on the basis of the percentage indicated in the commutation application already furnished by the individuals, and by taking into account the same age next birth-day (including loading age, if any) which was taken earlier while computing the capitalised value of a portion of prerevised pension. Medical Board for the purpose of commutation of additional amount of pension, has also been dispensed with even in cases where one had retired more than a year back, provided.

i. either one had applied for commutation of original pension within a year of retirement.

or

ii. where one had applied for commutation of original pension after a year from the date of retirement, a medical board for the purpose had already been held.

Procedure for Sanction of Revised Pension in respect of those who have already retired.

29. The procedure for revision of pensionary awards as per provisions of this letter, in respect of those who have already retired on or after 1.1.86 and in whose cases pensionary benefit at pre-revised rate have already been notified will be prescribed by the CGDA and intimated to service Headquarters and Records Offices.

30. Pension Regulations of the three Services will be amended in due course.

31. This issues with the concurrence of the Finance Division of this Ministry vide their U.O. No. 286-Pension of 1987

Sd/-

(G. Asvathanarayan)

Additional Secretary to the Govt. of India

Chapter-29

Provisions of the 5th Central Pay Commission

29.1

Government of India, Ministry of Defence Letter No 1(6)/98 D(Pension/Services) dated 3rd February 1998

Sub: **Implementation of the Government Decision on the recommendations of the Fifth Central Pay Commission regarding pensionary benefits for the armed forces officers and personnel below officer rank (PBOR) retiring or dying in harness on or after 01-01-1996.**

Sir,

The undersigned is directed to state that in pursuance of Govt's decisions on the recommendations of the Fifth Central Pay Commission announced vide Government of India, Ministry of Personnel, Public Grievances and Pension, Department of Pension and Pensioners' Welfare Resolution No. 45/86/97P & PW(A) dt 30th Sept. 97, sanction of the President is hereby accorded to the modification to the extent specified in this letter, in the rules/regulations concerning pensionary benefits of the Commissioned Officers (including MNS and Territorial Army Officers) and Personnel below Officer Rank (PBOR) including NCs(E) of the three Services, Defence Security Corps and the Territorial Army (hereinafter collectively referred to as Armed Forces personnel.)

1.2 The provisions of the Pension Regulations of the three services and various service instructions/Government orders, which are not affected by the provisions of this letter, will remain unchanged. This supercedes the provisions contained in Ministry of Defence letter No. 1(1)/92D(Pension/Service) of 02-4-1992.

PART I

DATE OF EFFECT AND DEFINITIONS

2.1 The provisions of this letter shall apply to the Armed Forces personnel who were in service as on 01-01-1996 or joined/join service thereafter.

2.2 Where Pension/Family Pension/Death Gratuity/Retirement Gratuity/Commuted Value of Pension has already been sanctioned, provisionally or otherwise, in cases occurring on or after 01-01-1996, the same should be revised in terms of these orders. In cases where pension has been finally sanctioned under the pre-revised orders and if it happens to be more beneficial than the pension becoming due under these orders, the pension already sanctioned shall not be revised to the disadvantage of the pensioners.

Definitions:

3. **Reckonable Emoluments**

3.1 'Reckonable Emoluments' will mean:

Emoluments Reckonable for

Category	Retiring/Service/Invalid Pension	Family pension	All types of gratuities
Officers	Pay including rank pay, stagnation increment and NPA, if any, last drawn.	Pay including Rank Pay, Stagnation increment and NPA, if any, last drawn	Pay including Rank Pay, Stagnation increment and NPA, if any, plus Dearness Allowance admissible on the date of retirement/ Invalidment/ death.
Personnel below officer rank	Maximum pay of the pay scale, including 50% of the highest classification allowance if any, of the rank held and group in which paid.	Pay including classification allowance stag-nation increment, if any, last drawn by the individual.	Pay including classification allowance plus Stagnation increment if any, plus Dearness Allowance admissible on the date of retirement/Invalidment/ death.

Pay, Non-Practising Allowance, Classification Allowance, Rank Pay and Stagnation Increment.

3.2 The terms Pay, 'NPA'; 'Classification Allowance', 'Rank Pay' and 'Stagnation Increment' as referred to in para 3.1 will mean respectively the basic pay in the revised pay scales, non-practising allowance, classification allowance, rank pay and stagnation increment introduced with effect from 01-01-1996 vide the following service Instruction:

a. For Service Officers: SAI 2/S/98. SNI 2/S/98, SAFI 2/S/98

b. For PBOR: SAI 1/S/98. SNI 1/S/98, SAFI/1/S/98

3.3 Those who have retired between 01-01-1996 and 31-12-1997 will have an option to retain the pre-revised scales of pay and have their pension and death-cum-retirement gratuity calculated under the rules in force immediately before coming into effect of these orders. The pension and death-cum-retirement gratuity in cases will be regulated as follows:

I. The term reckonable emoluments shall mean:

a. **Officers:** Basic Pay, Rank Pay plus Stagnation Increment plus appropriate non-practising allowance, if any, in the pre-revised scales plus actual Dearness Allowance upto AICPI 143, and Interim Relief I & II.

b. **PBORs including NCs(E)**: Maximum of scale of pay of the rank and group in the pre-revised scales plus 50% of the highest classification pay appropriate to the pay group plus actual Dearness Allowance upto AICPI 1436 and Interim Relief I &II. For calculation of gratuity and family pension. Basic Pay, Classification Pay actually drawn will be included in computing reckonable emoluments.

II. Retiring Pension for officers will be calculated at 50% of average of reckonable emoluments drawn during last 10 months and service pension for PBOR at 50% of reckonable emoluments. To the pension so calculated the difference of Dearness Relief between AICPI 1436 and AICPI 1510 allowed at the prescribed rate shall be added. The amount so arrived at will be regarded as service pension for regulating payment of Dearness Relief beyond average AICPI 1510.

III. Death cum-retirement gratuity shall be admissible with reference to emoluments at (I) above under the orders in force immediately before coming into effect of these orders. The maximum amount of gratuity shall not exceed Rs 2.5 lakhs in terms of Ministry of Defence letter No. 5(1)/95/D(Pens/Sers) dated 08 Aug. 1995.

IV. Commutation of pension shall be admissible in accordance with the orders in force immediately before coming into effect of these orders.

V. Family pension shall be allowed in accordance with the orders applicable prior to the issue to these orders and shall be calculated with reference to the reckonable emoluments in the pre-revised scale. To the family pension so calculated the difference of Dearness Relief between AICPI 1436 and AICPI 1510 allowed at the prescribed rate shall be added. The amount so arrived at will be regarded as family pension for regulating payment of Dearness Relief beyond average AICPI 1510.

3.4 In the case of persons who retain pre-revised scale and retire or die in harness subsequent to 31-12-1997, Pension Retirement Gratuity, Death Gratuity and Family Pension, as may be relevant, shall be calculated in terms of paragraph 6 to 13 of these orders. The reckonable emoluments for calculation of pensionary benefits in their case will be as follows:

a. **Officers** – Basic Pay, Rank Pay plus Stagnation Increment plus appropriate non-practicing allowance, if any, in the pre-revised scales plus actual Dearness Allowance upto AICPI 1510, and Interim Relief I & II at the rates in force on 31 Dec 1995 appropriate to the said basic pay.

b. **PBORs including NCs(E)** – Maximum of scale of pay of the rank and group in the pre-revised scales plus 50% of the highest classification pay appropriate to the pay group plus actual Dearness Allowance upto AICPI 1510 and Interim Relief I & II at the rates in force on 31 Dec 1995 appropriate to the said Basic Pay. For calculation of gratuity and family pension Basic Pay, Classification Pay actually drawn will be included in computing reckonable emoluments.

Notes:

(1) Where an officer immediately before his/her retirement or death while in service had been absent from duty on leave (including furlough leave) for which leave salary is/was payable or having been suspended had been re-instated without forfeiture of service furlough leave) for which leave salary is/was payable or having been suspended had been re-instated without forfeiture of service, the emoluments which he/she would have drawn, had he/she not been absent from duty or not been suspended will reckon for pensionary benefits.

(2) Where an Officer immediately before his/her retirement or death while in service had proceeded on leave for which leave salary is payable, after having held a higher paid acting rank, the emoluments drawn in such paid acting rank will reckon for pensionary benefits only if it is certified that he/she would have continued to hold the paid acting rank but for his/her proceeding on leave.

(3) Where an Officer immediately before his/her retirement or death while in service had been under suspension or absent from duty the period whereof does not count as service, the emoluments which he/she drew immediately before such absence from duty or being placed under suspension, will reckon for pensionary benefits.

(4) Where an officer is serving in an organization other than the Armed Forces, the actual pay and allowances drawn during such service will not be treated as emoluments, but the basic pay including Rank Pay,

Stagnation Increment plus NPA, if any, which he/she would have drawn in the Armed Forces, had he/she not been on such service, will alone be treated as emoluments reckonable for pensionary benefits.

4. Average Emoluments:

4.1 Average Emoluments in the case of officers shall be determined with reference to the reckonable emoluments drawn by him/her during the last 10 months of his/her service.

4.2 In the case of officers who have opted for the revised scales of pay and have retired within 10 months of coming over to the revised pay scales, the 'average pay' for 10 months period preceding retirement will be calculated by taking into account pay as follows:

(a) For the period during which pay was drawn in the pre-revised scales	Basic pay (including rank pay), stagnation increment and NPA, if any, plus actual DA and interim reliefs I &II appropriate to the basic pay (including rank pay and NPA, if any) drawn at the rates in force during the relevant period and
(b) For the period during which pay is drawn in the revised scales	Basic Pay (including rank pay) and stagnation increment plus NPA, if any.

Notes:

(1) If during the last 10 months of his/her service an officer had been absent from duty on leave for which leave salary is payable or having been suspended, had been re-instated without forfeiture of service, the emoluments which he/she would have drawn had he/she not been absent from duty or suspended, will be taken into account for determining the average emoluments.

(2) If during the last 10 months of the service, an officer had been absent from duty or had been under suspension the period whereof does not count as service, the aforesaid period of absence from duty or suspension, will be disregarded in the calculation of the average emoluments and equal period before the 10 months will be included.

5. Qualifying Service:

a. The term "Qualifying Service" (QS) will mean:

Qualifying Service reckonable for			
Pension	**Retirement Gratuity**	**Death Gratuity**	**Retiring/service/ Invalid/Terminal Gratuity**
Actual qualifying service rendered by the Individual plus a weightage (in years) appropriate to the last rank held as indicated in (b) below subject to the total qualifying service including weightage not exceeding 33 years.	Actual qualifying service plus a weightage of 5 years subject to the total qualifying service including weightage not exceeding 33 years	Actual qualifying service rendered plus a weightage of 5 years subject to total qualifying service not exceeding 33 years. In case actual service is less than 5 years no weightage will be given.	Actual qualifying service rendered.

Notes:

(1) QS would commence from the date of commission. In case the Short service Commission is followed by Permanent Commission, the period during which an officer holds Short Service Commission on probation will reckon for the purposes of pensionary benefits.

(2) In case of TA personnel, aggregate of qualifying embodied service shall count for service pension. Aggregate qualifying embodied service may be continuous or rendered in broken spells. For calculating the total embodied service, the breaks in embodied service due to disembodiment will be treated as condoned but the period of breaks itself will not be treated as qualifying service for pension. Where qualifying embodied service has been rendered in broken spells, five per cent cut will be imposed on the pension of those JCOs/ OR who have completed 15 years or more of aggregate embodied serve, but have not completed 20 years of aggregate embodied service.

b. Weightage for the purpose of calculation of pension will be as given below

I. Service Personnel/Officers (other than MNS)

Rank (Army)	**Rank (Navy)**	**Rank (Air Force)**	**Weightage in years**
PBOR including NCs (E) and Hon. Commissioned Officers	Equivalent Ranks	Equivalent Ranks	05
Lieutenant	Sub Lieutenant	Flying Officer	09
Captain	Lieutenant	Flt. Lieutenant	09
Major	Lt. Cdr.	Sqn Ldr	08
Lt. Col.(TS)	Cdr. (TS)	Wg. Cdr.(TS)	05
Colonel	Captain (with less than 3 years 10 months service)	Gp. Captain	07
Brig.	Captain (with 3 years 10 months service & more)	Air Cmde	05
Major General	Rear Admiral	AVM	03
Lt. General	Vice Admiral	Air Marshal	03
Lt. General (Army Cdr/ VCOAS)	Vice Admiral (FOC-in-C/VCNS)	Air Marshal (AOC-in-C/ VCAS)	03
COAS	CNS	CAS	03

II MNS Officers

Captain			07
Major			06
Lt. Col. - Brig.			05
Maj. Gen.			03

Notes:

(1) There will be no weightage for officers and PBOR who retire prematurely for permanent absorption in public sector undertakings and autonomous bodies.

(2) There will be no weightage for officers and PBOR of the Territorial Army.

(3) The above weightage will not be reckoned for determining the minimum qualifying service specified for admissibility of Service Pension, i.e. 20 years for service officers (15 years for late entrants) and 15 years for PBOR and 20 years for NCs (E).

(4) Full pre-commissioned service rendered under the Central Government whether in a civil department or in the Armed Forces, will be taken into account for working out the qualifying service for earning pensionary benefits subject to fulfillment of other conditions. This will also be counted for determining the minimum qualifying service indicated in Note 3 above for earning retiring/service pension.

(5) In calculating the length of qualifying service, fraction of a year equal to three months and above but less than 6 months will be treated as a completed one half year and reckoned as qualifying service. This will, however, not be applicable for computing minimum qualifying service for pension.

(6) All leave including study leave will count as qualifying service for pension provided that service for at least a period specified by the Government has been rendered from the date of return from the study leave last availed of. Any period of leave without pay shall not qualify unless specifically authorised by the Government.

PART-II

RETIRING/SERVICE PENSION/GRATUITY, INVALID PENSION/GRATUITY, SPECIAL PENSION/ GRATUITY, ORDINARY FAMILY PENSION, RETIREMENT/DEATH GRATUITY

6. **Retiring/Service Pension:**

6.1 **Officers:**

a. The minimum period of qualifying service (without weightage) actually rendered and required for earning retiring pension will be 20 years. In the case of late entrants (i.e., an officer who is retired on reaching the prescribed age limit for compulsory retirement with atleast 15 years commissioned service qualifying for pension but whose total service (without weightage) actually rendered and required for earning retiring pension will continue to be 15 years.

b. Serving JCOs/ORs. including corresponding ranks of the Navy and Air Force granted EC/SSC will be eligible for retiring pension after 12 years of qualifying service (without weightage) actually rendered.

c. Retiring Pension in respect of Commissioned Officers of the three Services as mentioned at sub para (a) & (b) above, including MNS and TA officers, will be calculated at 50% of average emoluments as defined at para 4 above. The amount so determined will be the retiring pension for 33 years of reckonable qualifying service as defined in para 5 above. For lesser period of reckonable qualifying service, this amount will be proportionately reduced.

Note: The retiring pension of an officer of the rank of Lt. Col. (TS), Brigadier or Major General and equivalent, shall not be less than the pension which would have been admissible to him/her as a Major, Colonel, or a Brigadier and equivalent as the case may be, had he/she not been promoted to the higher rank.

6.2 **Personnel Below Officer Rank (PBOR):**

a. The minimum period of qualifying service (without weightage) actually rendered and required for earning service pension will continue to be 15 years (20 years in the case of NCs (E)).

b. Service pension in respect of the PBOR of the three services (including those of the DSC and TA) for 33 years of qualifying service will be calculated at 50% of the emoluments reckonable for pension as defined in para 3 above. For lesser period of qualifying service (as defined in para 5 above) it will be reduced proportionately. The amount of service pension finally arrived at will be subject to a minimum of Rs 1275/- per month.

Note: The existing provisions of assessing the service pension of the rank/pay group on the basis of the rank actually held continuously at least for 10 months at the time of discharge, shall continue to be applicable. This is also applicable in the case of Honorary Commissioned Officer. However, this condition will not be required to be fulfilled in the case of JCOs and equivalents who are granted Honorary Commission and who retire on completion of their tenure of appointment or are discharged on account of causes beyond their control.

c. Based on sub paras (a) and (b) above, tables of rates of service pension for various ranks/groups of PBOR and Hony Commissioned Officers of the three services who have opted for the revised scales of pay w.e.f. 01-10-1996 and 10-10-1997 are given in Annexure A & B respectively attached to this letter. The rates of service pension have been arrived at by adding a weightage of 5 years to the qualifying service actually rendered.

   Service pension in the case of TA personnel will be determined by the CDA(P) by taking into account the reckonable emoluments and qualifying aggregate embodied service as defined in paras 3 and 5 above.

Note: Personnel discharged/invalided within ten months from 10-10-1997 will be granted pension for the group last held irrespective of the length of service rendered in the revised group.

d. Tables showing the rates of service pension of PBOR with pre-revised scales of pay are not being prescribed, as it is considered unlikely that anybody would have opted for the pre-revised scales of pay. In odd cases where individuals might have opted for the pre-revised scales of pay, Chief CDA (P)/CDA (N)/(AF) will calculate and authorize service pension taking into account the reckonable emoluments as per para 3.3 (b) ante, after getting the necessary particulars.

Disciplinary cases:

7. While issuing retirement notification in the case of service officers and while submitting pension claims in respect of PBORs, the Service headquarters/Record Offices, shall invariably indicate whether or not any disciplinary/quasi-judicial proceedings are pending against the individual. In case Service Headquarters/Record Offices come to know of any disciplinary/quasi-judicial/judicial proceedings against individual subsequent to the issuing of retirement notification/ submission of pension claims, they will intimate this fact immediately to the Pension Sanctioning Authority. The existing provisions contained in Ministry of Defence Letter No. 12(1)/74/S 556/D (Pen/Sers) dated 20th July 1974 as amended regarding grant of provisional pension to Armed Forces personnel who at the time of their discharge/retirement are found to be involved in disciplinary/quasi-judicial/judicial proceedings, will continue to be applicable.

8. Retiring/Service Gratuity:

8.1 The minimum period of qualifying service for earning retiring/service gratuity will continue to be 10 years (without weightage) in the case of permanent commissioned officers and 5 years (without weightage) in the case of PBOR including NCs (E).

8.2 The retiring/service gratuity will be admissible at a uniform rate of 1/2 a month's reckonable emoluments as defined in para 3 above for each completed six monthly period of qualifying service as defined in para 5 above.

9. Invalid Pension/Gratuity:- When an individual is invalided out of service with a disability neither attributable to nor aggravated by service, he/she will be entitled to invalid pension, if the service actually rendered is 10 years or more, and invalid gratuity if it is less than 10 years, at the rates indicated below:

a. Invalid pension:- Amount equal to the service element of disability pension that would have been admissible in case the causes were attributable to or aggravated by service.
b. Invalid Gratuity:- At half month's reckonable emoluments as defined in para 3 above for each six monthly period of qualifying service.

10. Terminal Gratuity in respect of SSCOs:- Short Service Commissioned Officer will be entitled to Terminal Gratuity at the rate of 1/2 a month's emoluments as defined in para 3 above, for each completed six monthly period of service.

11. Special Pension and Gratuity: Special pension and gratuity to PBOR including NCs (E) who are discharged in large number in pursuance of the Government policy:

i. of reducing the strength of establishment of the Armed Forces; or
ii. of re-organization, which results in disbandment of any Unit/Formation, will be admissible at the following scales:

Length of actual qualifying service rendered (without weightage) | **Scale of special pension/gratuity**

A. COMBATANTS

a. **Special Pension**

(i)	15 years or more	Equal to normal service pension
(ii)	10 years or more but less than 15 years.	Equal to the service pension as determined in para 6.2 (b)

b. **Special Gratuity**

(i)	5 years or more but less than 10 years	Equal to 1⅓ months reckonable emoluments as defined in para 3 above for each completed year of Qualifying Service
(ii)	Less than 5 years	Equal to 3 months reckonable emoluments as defined in para 3 above

B. NON-COMBATANTS (ENROLLED)

a. **Special Pension:**

(i)	20 years or more	Equal to normal service pension
(ii)	15 years or more but less than 20 years	Equal to the service pension determined in para 6.2(b)

b. **Special Gratuity:**

(i)	5 years or more but less than 15 years	Equal to 1 1/3 months reckonable emoluments as defined in para 3 above for each completed year of qualifying service.
(ii)	15 years or more but less than 20 years	Equal to 3 months reckonable emoluments as defined in para 3 above.

12. Retirement Gratuity/Death Gratuity:

12.1 Retirement Gratuity: An individual who has completed 5 years qualifying service and is eligible for service/invalid gratuity or pension of any type, shall be granted on the termination of his/her service a retirement gratuity equal to one fourth of reckonable emoluments for each completed six monthly period of qualifying service subject to a maximum of 16 ½ times the reckonable emoluments. The Reckonable emoluments and qualifying service for this purpose will be as defined in paras 3 & 5 above respectively.

12.2 Death Gratuity: Death Gratuity at the following rates will be admissible in the event of death in harness.

Length of qualifying service	Rate of Death gratuity
(a) Less than one year	Two times of reckonable emoluments
(b) One year or more but less than 5 years	Six times of reckonable emoluments
(c) Five years or more but less than 20 years	Twelve times of reckonable emoluments
(d) 20 years or more	Half of reckonable for each completed six monthly period of qualifying service subject to a minimum of 12 times and a maximum of 33 times the reckonable emoluments

Notes:

(1) Death Gratuity at the rates indicated in (a) to (c) above, will also be admissible to the families of short service/emergency commissioned officers in the event of their death while in service.

(2) The reckonable emoluments and qualifying service for this purpose shall be as defined in paras 3 and 5 above respectively.

(3) The maximum limit of Retirement/Death Gratuity will be Rs 3.5 Lakhs.

13. Ordinary Family Pension:

13.1 In case of death of an Armed Forces personnel while in service or after retirement with a service pension/ disability pension/Invalid pension/Special pension on account of causes which are neither attributable to nor aggravated by service, ordinary family pension shall continue to be admissible to the families of the Armed Forces Personnel (except families of reservists) under the same conditions as in force hithertofore. This will also be admissible to the families of MNS officers. The ordinary family pension shall be calculated at uniform rate of 30% of reckonable emoluments as defined in para 3 above subject to a minimum of Rs 1,275/- per month and a maximum of 30% of the highest pay in the Government. (The highest pay in the Government is Rs 30,000 since 01-01-1996.)

13.2 For the purpose of grant of Ordinary Family Pension, the definition of Family, shall also include:

a. Son/daughter including widowed/divorced daughter till he/she attains the age of 25 years or upto the date of his/her marriage/remarriage, whichever is earlier (subject to income criterion to be notified separately).

b. Parents who were wholly dependent on the Armed Forces Personnel when he/she was alive provided the deceased employee had left behind neither a widow nor a child (Clarificatory orders in regard to determining dependency criteria in case of parents shall be issued separately).

Note: In case the eligible child is physically or mentally handicapped and is unable to earn a livelihood the ordinary family pension would be admissible for life to such a child subject to same conditions as in force hithertofore.

13.3 The existing provision for payment of OFP at enhanced rates where an individual who has rendered a minimum of 7 years of continuous qualifying service dies while in service or after retirement with a pension, for period of seven years from the date following the date of death of the individual or upto the date on which the deceased would have attained the age of 65 years, whichever is earlier shall continue. The amount of enhanced ordinary family pension for this period shall be the lowest of the following amounts:

a. 50% of the Reckonable emoluments as defined in para 3 above.

b. The amount of retiring service/invalid pension/service element of disability pension/special pension (before commutation) admissible under this letter, in cases where the deceased was a pensioner.

13.4 Families of reservist pensioners shall be entitled to a family pension at the rate of Rs 1,275/- per month.

PART – III

GENERAL

ROUNDING OFF OF PENSIONARY AWARDS

14. The amount of various pensionary awards admissible as per this letter shall be rounded off to the next higher rupee by the Pension Sanctioning Authorities.

Minimum/Maximum Pension

15. If the amount of any monthly pension viz retiring/service pension/invalid pension/special pension/ordinary family pension admissible under the provisions of this letter works out to less than Rs 1,275/- per month, it shall be stepped up to Rs 1,275/- per month and authorized for payment at this rate. In cases where service element of disability pension fall short of Rs 1,275/- the same shall be stepped up to Rs 1,275/- p.m. There will be a maximum ceiling on the amount of service pension/Invalid pension/Special pension and ordinary family pension upto 50% and 30% respectively of the highest pay in the Government (the highest pay in the Govt. is Rs 30,000 since 01-01-1996).

Dearness Relief

16. Dearness Relief shall be admissible only beyond average CPI 1510 on the revised pattern introduced vide Ministry of Personnel, Public Grievances and pension. Department of Pension and Pensioners' Welfare Office Memorandum No. 42/2/97-P&PW(G) dated 27th October, 1997, on various types of pension/family pension admissible under the provisions of this letter.

Commutation of Additional Pension

17. The additional amount of retiring/service pension of post 01.01.1996 pensioners becoming due under the provisions of this letter to those who have already retired, will also qualify for commutation upto the existing limits. Accordingly, in their cases commutation of additional amount of pension should be allowed by the Pension Sanctioning Authorities without waiting for any application from them on the basis of the percentage indicated in the commutation application already furnished by the individuals, taking into account the same age next birthday (including loading age, if any) which was taken earlier while computing the capitalized value of a portion of pre-revised pension. Medical Board for the purpose of commutation of additional amount of pension, has also been dispensed with even in cases where one had retired more than a year back, provided:

a. Either one had applied for commutation of original pension within a year of retirement, OR

b. Where one had applied for commutation of original pension after a year from the date of retirement, a medical board for the purpose had already been held.

Procedure for sanction of Revised Pension in respect of those who have already retired.

18. The procedure for revision of pensionary awards as per provisions of this letter, in respect of those who have already retired on or after 01.01.1996 and in whose cases pensionary benefits at pre-revised rate have already been notified will be prescribed by the pension sanctioning authorities (PSAs) and intimated to service Headquarters and Record Offices.

19. Orders regarding grant of disability pension/special family pension/liberalized pensionary awards on implementation of Government decisions on the recommendations of Fifth Central Pay Commission will be issued separately.

20. The arrears on account of revision of pension would be paid in cash with the stipulation that where the amount of arrears is less than Rs 5,000/-, it should be paid in one installment and where it is in excess of Rs 5,000/- it should be paid in two installments; in the first installment, payment should be restricted to Rs 5,000/- plus 50% (fifty percent) of the balance amount of arrears. Orders regarding payment of second installment would be issued separately.

21. Pension Regulations of the three services will be amended in due course.

22. This issues with the concurrence of the Finance Division of this Ministry vide their U.O. No. 203/Pen/98 dated 28.01.1998.

23. Hindi version will follow.

Sd/-

(Sudhakar Shukla)

Deputy Secretary to the Govt of India

29.2

Government of India, Ministry of Defence Letter No 1(1)/99/D (Pension/ Services) dated 7th June 1999

Sub: **Implementation of Government's decision on the recommendation of Vth CPC relating to pensionary benefits in respect of Commissioned Officers and Personnel Below Officer Rank.**

Consequent on issue of Ministry of Personnel, Public Grievances and Pensions, Department. of Pension & Pensioners' Welfare OM No. 45/10/98 P&PW (A) dated 17.12.1998 regarding modified provisions on grant of pension/family pension in respect of civilians, the undersigned is directed to say that the president is pleased to decide that wef 1.1.96 pension of all Armed Forces pensioners irrespective of their date of retirement shall not be less than 50% of the minimum pay in the revised scale of pay introduced wef 1.1.96 of the rank, and rank Group (in case of PBOR) all held by the pensioner. However, the existing provisions in the rules governing qualifying service and minimum pension shall continue to be operative. Similarly wef 1.1.96 family pension shall not be less than 30% of the minimum pay in the revised scale introduced wef 1.1.96 of the rank, and rank and group (in case of PBOR) last the provisions contained in this Ministry' s letters:

No. 1(6)/98/D (Pen/Sers) dated 3.2.98 (Post 1.1.96 cases)

No. 1(2)/97/D (Pen/Sers) dated 24.11.97 (Pre - 1.1.96 cases)

No. 1(3)/98/D (Pen/Sers) dated 27.05.98 (Pre 1.1.96 Commissioned Officers) and No. 1 (2)/98/D (Pen/Sers), dated 14.07.98 (Pre-1.1.96 PBOR) shall be treated as modified to the extent indicated above.

2. The revision of pension/ordinary family pension shall be undertaken as follows:-

2.1 COMMISSIONED OFFICERS

POST & PRE-1.1.96 CASES

a. Pension shall continue to be calculated at 50% of the average emoluments in all cases and shall be subject to a minimum of Rs 1275/- p.m and a maximum of upto 50% of the highest pay applicable to Armed Forces personnel but the full pension in no case shall be 50% of the minimum of the revised scale of pay introduced wef 1.1.96 for the rank last held by the commissioned officer at the time of his/her retirement. However such pension shall be reduced pro-rata, where the pensioner has less than the maximum required service for full pension.

b. Ordinary family pension so calculated/consolidated under Para 8 of this Ministry's letter dated 27.05.98 shall not be less than 30% of minimum of the revised scale of pay introduced wef. 1.1.96 for the rank held by the pensioner/deceased commissioned officer.

c. In post 1.1.96 cases, PSAs will revise pension/family pension suo-moto where beneficial to the pensioner. However, in pre- 1.1.96 cases action to revise pension/family pension in terms of these orders, shall be initiated by the concerned PSA where applications have already been received in pursuance of earlier orders issued under this Ministry's letter dated 27.05.1998 regardless of whether their cases have already been finalized or are in the process of finalization. Those pensioner/family pensioner who have not so far submitted the necessary application are required to submit application (in duplicate) upto 30.06.99 as per proforma annexed hereto through usual channel.

2.2 PBOR

POST AND PRE-1.1.96 CASES

a. The revision of service pension in terms of these modified orders in respect of PBOR retirees will not be beneficial except for the rank of JCOs granted Hony Commission of Lt and Captain as the service pension is calculated at the maximum of the pay scale including 50% of highest classification allowance, if any, of the rank and group in which paid.

b. Ordinary family pension so calculated/consolidated under Para 12 of this Ministry's letter dated 14.07.98 shall not be less than 30% of the minimum of he revised scale of pay introduced wef. 1.1.96 for the rank and group held by the pensioner/deceased individual at the time of discharge/death. The revision of ordinary family pension in respect of those family pensioners who are in receipt of family pension @ 1275/- p.m. wef. 1.1.96 will not benefit further under these modified orders i.e. where the minimum reckonable emoluments in the revised scale introduced w.e.f. 1.1.96 is Rs 4250/- p.m. or less.

c. In post 1.1.96 cases revision of pension/ordinary family pension will be undertaken by the PSA concerned on receipt of a nominal roll of affected cases from the Record office concerned. However in pre-1.1.96 cases, action to revise pension/family pension in terms of these orders will be initiated by the PSA concerned on receipt of application (in duplicate) through RO concerned in the form annexed hereto. Those pensioners/ family pensioners who have not so far submitted the necessary applications to facilitate revision of their pension/family pension and are desirous of availing the benefits under these orders are required to submit application to their RO through P.D.A concerned latest by 30.06.1999.

3. The grant of enhanced family pension will be regulated in accordance with the provisions of this Ministry's letter No.6 (1)/99/D (Pen/Sers), dated 18.03.1999.

4. Where the revised and consolidated pension of pre 1.1.96 pensioners/family pensioners are not beneficial to him/ her under these orders and is either equal to or less than existing consolidated pension/family pension under this Ministry' s letter dated 24.11.97, 27.05.98 and 14.07.98 as the case may be, his/her pension/family pension will not be revised to the disadvantage of the pensioner. In such cases pensioner will be informed by the PSA in case of Commissioned officers and by R.O in the case of PBOR to this effect directly.

5. This issues with the concurrence of Finance Division of this Ministry's vide their UO No. 3136/Pen/99 dated 7.6.1999.

Yours faithfully,
Sd/-
(Amrit Lal)
Under Secretary to the Govt. of India

29.3

Government of India, Ministry of Defence Letter No 1(1)/99/D(Pension/ Services) dated 23rd June 1999

CORRIGENDUM

Sub: **Implementation of Government's decision on the recommendation of Vth Central Pay Commission relating to pensionary benefits in respect of Commissioned Officers and Personnel Below Officer Rank.**

The following amendments are made to this Ministry's letter No. 1(1)/D (Pen/Sers) dated 7th June 1999 on the above subject.

a. Para 1 line 8: For "retirement", Read "retirement/discharge/invalidment"

b. Para 2.1 (c): For "upto 30.06.99 as............ Channel", Read "upto 31.12.99 as per proforma annexed to Ministry of Defence letter No. 1(3)/98/D/(Pen/Sers) dt.27.05.1998".

c. Para 2.2 (c): For "in the form annexed hereto", Read "in the form annexed to Ministry of Defence letter No.1 (2)/98/D (Pen/Sers) dated 14.07.1998".

d. Para 2.2 (c): For "30.06.99", Read "31.12.99"

2. This issues with the concurrence of Finance Division of this Ministry vide their U.O. No. 3390/Pen/99 dated 16.06.99.

Yours Faithfully
Sd/-
(Amrit Lal))
Under Secretary to the Govt. of India

29.4

Government of India, Ministry of Defence Letter No PC/5601/ATP/LVII/1103/C/D(Pen/Sers) dated 21st June 2002

Sub: **Removal of anomaly in pension revision of Havaldars (granted Honorary rank of Nb Sub) under 5th Pay Commission recommendations.**

Sir,

As per Regulation 137 Pension Regulations for the Army 1961 (part-1), Hav. who are granted Hony rank of Nb/Sub on retirement are entitled to an additional pension at the rate prescribed from time to time. The rate was revised from Rs 45/- p.m. to Rs 100/- p.m. w.e.f. 01.10.1991. Consequently on the issue of orders for consolidation of pension under 5th CPC vide Govt. of India, Min. of Defence letter no. 1(2)/97/d/(Pen/Sers) dt. 24.11.97, the additional pension was taken as Rs 100/- p.m. for those pre-96 retirees who retired on or after 01.10.91. For pre-96 retirees who retired prior to this date the additional pension for the rank of Hony Nb/Sub continued to be Rs 45/- p.m. However, with the issue of Govt. letter no.1 (2)/98/d (Pen/Sers) dt. 14.07.98 service pension of all the pre-86 retirees was brought at par to those who retired on of after 01.01.86. While doing this, concordance tables provided in the aforesaid Govt. letter dt. 14.07.98, took into the account the additional pension of Rs 100/- p.m. for Hony Nb/Sub although this rate was applicable only w.e.f. 01.10.91. This created an anomalous situation. In the case of that Hony Nb/Sub who retired between 01.01.86 and 30.09.91, the rate of additional pension for consolidation purposes was being taken as Rs 45/- under the Govt. letter dt. 24.11.97. However for Hony Nb/Sub retiring prior to 01.01.86, the rate of additional pension of Rs 100/- had been taken under Govt. letter dt.14.07.98 as stated above.

2. The removal of this anomaly has been under consideration of the Govt. for some time. The President is now pleased to decide that for consolidation of pension of Pre-96 retirees under Govt. letter dt. 24.11.97, the rate of additional pension for the rank of Nb/Sub under Reg. 137 PRA Pt.I (1961), shall be taken as Rs 100/-p.m. as in the case of pre-86 retirees.

3. This issues with the occurrence of Min. of Defence(Fin) vide their UO No.1614/Pen/02 dt.12.06.2002.

Sd/-

Chapter-30

Provisions of the 6th Central Pay Commission

30.1

Government of India, Ministry of Defence, Department of Ex-Servicemen Welfare Letter No 17(4)/2008(1)/D(Pen/Policy) dated 11th November 2008

Sub: Implementation of Government decision on the recommendations of the Sixth Central Pay Commission – Revision of Pension of Pre 2006 Armed Forces Pensioners/Family Pensioners.

Sir,

The undersigned is directed to say that in pursuance of Government's decision on the recommendations of Sixth Central Pay Commission, notified vide Government of India, Ministry of Personnel, Public Grievances and Pension, Department of Pension & Pensioners' Welfare Resolution No 38/37/08-P&PW(A) dated 29.8.2008, sanction of the President is hereby accorded to the regulation, with effect from 1.1.2006, of pension/family pension of all Pre-1.1.2006 pensioners/family pensioners of the Armed Forces in the manner indicated in the succeeding paragraphs. Separate Orders will be issued by this Ministry in respect of Armed Forces Personnel who retired/died on or after 1.1.2006.

2. Applicability

2.1. These orders shall apply to all the Armed Forces Pensioners/Family Pensioners who were drawing pension/family Pension as on 1.1.2006 under the Pension Regulations of the three Services/State Forces and various Government orders issued from time to time.

2.2. The provisions of this letter do not apply to the following categories:

i. Gallantry awardees drawing monetary allowance attached to the award, such as Param Vir Chakra, Ashok Chakra, etc.

ii. UK/HKSRA Pensioners.

iii. Persons in receipt of Compassionate Allowance, Guzara, Reservist allowance or any other allowance on which dearness relief is not admissible.

iv. Reservists in receipt of Ex-gratia payment at Rs 600/- per month covered by Govt. of India, Ministry of Defence letter No. B/39042/AG/PS-4(a&c)/1331/C/D(Pen/Sers) dated 29th Dec 2000.

v. Families of the deceased reservists in receipt of Ex-gratia family pension at Rs 605/- per month covered by Govt. of India, Ministry of Defence letter No. B/40029/AG/PS-4(d)/1/B/D(Pension/Services) dated 7.1.1999. (Separate orders will be issued in respect of (iv) and (v) above)

3. Definitions

a. **'Existing Pensioner' or 'Existing Family Pensioner'** means a pensioner who was entitled to/drawing pension/family pension on 31.12.2005. This will also include a pensioner/family pensioner who became entitled to pension/family pension with effect from 1.1.2006 consequent upon retirement/discharge/death of Armed Force personnel on 31.12.2005. For the purpose of family pension, it also covers members of family to those who retired/discharged prior to 1.1.2006 and in whose case family pension had not commenced as the pensioner was alive on 31.12.2005.

b. **'Existing Pension'** means the basic pension exclusive of Dearness Pension but inclusive of commuted portion of pension, if any due on 31.12.2005 and covers all kinds of pension viz. retiring/service/special/reservist/invalid/disability/liberalized disability & war injury pension. This will also include pension/family pension, which became due with effect from 1.1.2006 consequent on retirement/discharge/death of a Armed force personnel on 31.12.2005.

   In the case of PBOR under the three services, the 'Existing Pension' would mean the revised pension fixed as on 1.1.2006 in terms of the provisions contained in this Ministry's letter No 14(3)/2004- D(Pen/Sers)/Vol-III dated 1.2.2006 and No. 14(3)/2004- D(Pen/Sers)/Vol-V dated 2.5.2006. This also includes additional pension sanctioned to Havildar granted Honorary Rank of Naib Subedar. It will, however, not include Adhoc Ex-gratia payment, if any.

c. **'Existing Family Pension'** means the basic family pension drawn on 31.12.2005 exclusive of Dearness pension under the Pension Regulations of the three Services/State forces and other orders issued on the subject from time to time. It also covers Liberalized and Special Family Pension and Dependent Pension sanctioned in battle and non-battle casualty cases.

d. **'Existing Dearness Relief'** means the dearness relief due to pensioners/family pensioners upto average AICPI (IW) 536 (Base year 1982=100) as on 1.1.2006 at the rate of 24% of Basic Pension/Basic Family pension plus Dearness pension as admissible vide Government of India, Ministry of Personnel Public Grievances and Pension, Department of Pension and Pensioners' Welfare Office Memorandum No. 42/2/2006-P&PW(G) dated 5.4.2006.

e. **'Dearness Pension'** means Dearness Pension as admissible vide Ministry of Finance, Deptt. of expenditure OM No. 105/1/2004/IC dated 01.03.2004.

f. **'Pension Disbursing Agency'** (PDA) means Treasury, Post Office, Pay and Accounts Office, Defence Pension Disbursing Office (DPDO), Indian Embassy Nepal and authorized Public/Private Sector Banks.

g. **'Pension Sanctioning Authority'** (PSA) means PCDA (Pension) Allahabad, PCDA (Navy) Mumbai and CDA (AF) Delhi as the case may be.

4. Consolidation of Pension

4.1 The Pension/Family Pension of existing Pre-1.1.2006 pensioners/family pensioners will be consolidated with effect from 1.1.2006 by adding together:

i. The Existing Pension (including commuted portion of pension, if any)/Existing Family Pension.

ii. Dearness Pension, if any, as applicable from 1.4.2004 to those retired/died prior to 1.4.2004.

iii. Dearness Relief upto AI CPI (IW) 536 i.e. 24% of basic pension/family pension plus dearness pension.

iv. Fitment weightage @ 40% of the Existing Pension/Existing Family Pension. Where the amount of fitment weightage works out in fraction of a rupee, it will be rounded off to the next higher rupee.

NOTE: Where the Existing Pension/Existing Family Pension includes the effect of merger of 50% of Dearness Pay in respect of those retired/died on or after 1.4.2004, the existing pension/family pension for the purpose of fitment weightage will be re-calculated after excluding the merged Dearness Pay of 50% from emoluments for computation of existing pension/existing family pension. This will be in line with the definition of "Existing Pension" and "Existing Family Pension" given in Para 3 of these orders.

4.2 The amount so arrived at in terms of Para 4.1 above will be regarded as consolidated pension/family pension with effect from 1.1.2006. **Since the consolidated pension will be inclusive of commuted portion of pension, if any, the amount of pension commuted will be deducted from the said amount while making monthly disbursements.**

5. The consolidation of pension will further be subject to the provision that the consolidated pension, in no case shall be lower than fifty percent of the minimum of the pay in the pay band plus the grade pay corresponding to the pre revised scale from which the pensioner had retired/discharged including Military Service Pay and 'X' Group pay where applicable. For example, if a pensioner had retired in the pre-revised scale of pay of 6600 – 170 – 9320, the corresponding pay band being 9300 - 34800 and the corresponding grade pay and Military Service Pay being Rs 4,600/- and Rs 2,000/- respectively, his minimum guaranteed pension would be 50% of Rs 9,300 + Rs 4,600 + 2,000 i.e. Rs 7,950 for 33 years of qualifying service. The pension so calculated will be reduced prorata, where the pensioner had less than the maximum required service of 33 years for full pension and in no case it will be less than Rs 3,500/-. In case the pension consolidated as per Para 4.1 above is higher than the pension calculated in the manner indicated above, the same (higher consolidated pension) will be treated as Basic Pension with effect from 1.1.2006.

The consolidation of family pension will be subject to the provision that the consolidated family pension, in no case, shall be lower than thirty percent of the sum of the minimum of the pay in the pay band and the grade pay thereon corresponding to the pre-revised pay scale in which the pensioner/deceased Armed Force personnel had retired/died including Military Service Pay and 'X' Group pay where applicable. In case the family pension consolidated as per Para 4.1 above is higher than the family pension calculated in the manner indicated above, the same (higher consolidated family pension) will be treated as Basic family pension with effect from 1.1.2006.

6. The following elements will continue to be paid as separate elements in addition to the pension/family pension updated under these orders. These payments will not be taken into account for purpose of consolidation as well as for applying minimum limit of Rs 3,500/-per month to pension/family pension:

i. Monetary Allowance attached to gallantry awards such as ParamVir Chakra, Ashok Chakra etc.

ii. Constant Attendance Allowance where admissible.

6.1 With effect from 01.01.2006, the amount of adhoc exgratia will cease to be paid in respect of Pre-1.1.1973 Commissioned Officer pensioners as all Pre-1986 pensioners have been brought at par with Post-1986 pensioners.

Note: The payment of adhoc exgratia for Pre-1.1.1973, PBOR pensioners stands already discontinued with effect from 1.1.2006 under this Ministry's letter No. 14(3)/2004-D (Pen/Sers) dated 2.5.2006.

7. Since the consolidated pension/family pension arrived at as per Para 4.1 above includes dearness relief upto average index level AI CPI 536, dearness relief will be admissible thereon only beyond index average 536 in accordance with the revised scheme of dearness relief for which orders have been issued separately by Department of Pension and Pensioners' Welfare vide their OM No. 42/2/2008-P&PW(G) dated 12.9.2008. The four installments of dearness relief sanctioned earlier from 01.07.2006, 1.1.2007, 1.7.2007 and 1.1.2008 in Department of P&PW's Office Memorandum No. 42/2/2006-P&PW(G) dated 15.9.2006, No. 42/2/2007-P&PW (G) dated 29.03.2007, No. 42/2/2007-P&PW(G)

dated 18.9.2007 and No. 42/2/2008-P&PW (G) dated 19.03.2008 respectively will be adjusted towards the arrears becoming due on updation of pension/family pension as in Para 4.1 and Para 5 above.

8. Where the consolidated pension/family pension in terms of paragraph 4.1 above works out to an amount less than Rs 3,500/-per month, the same will be stepped upto Rs 3,500/-per month. This will be regarded as pension/ family pension with effect from 01.01.2006.

9. Pending finalization of the rates of disability/war injury element and issue of separate Government orders in this regards, the disability pension/war injury pension consisting of service element and disability element/war injury element will be consolidated under the provisions of Para 4.1 above as an interim measure and will be treated as revised interim disability/war injury pension with effect from 1.1.2006. This interim disability/war injury pension will qualify for grant of dearness relief at the revised rates notified vide Dept. of P&PW OM No. 42/2/2008-P&PW(G) dated 12.9.2008.

9.1 Where a pensioner is in receipt of disability/liberalized disability/war injury pension, the minimum limit of Rs 3,500/- will apply to service pension/service element and disability/war injury element will be payable in addition. Where the disability element is drawn in isolation, the minimum limit of Rs 3,500/- will apply for 100% disability. For lesser degree of disability the minimum limit will be proportionately reduced.

10. The upper ceiling on pension/ordinary family pension laid down in the Department of Pension and Pensioner's Welfare Office Memorandum No. 45/86/97-P &PW(A) (Part-I) dated 27.10.1997 has been increased from Rs 15,000/- and Rs 9,000/- to Rs 45,000/- and Rs 27,000/- i.e. 50% and 30% respectively of the highest pay in the Government (The highest pay, in the Government is Rs 90,000/- since 1.1.2006).

11. In the case of pensioners in receipt of civil and military pension, the floor ceiling of Rs 3,500/- will not apply to the two pensions taken together and the individual pension will be governed by respective Pension Rules. Accordingly, the floor ceiling of Rs 3,500/- will apply individually to the civil and military pension. In case a pensioner is in receipt of pension as well as a family pension, the floor ceiling of Rs 3,500/- will apply individually to such pension and family pension.

12. Additional Pension for Pensioners 80 years age and above The quantum of additional pension/family pension available to the old pensioners/family pensioners shall be as follows:

Age of pensioner/family pensioner	Additional quantum of pension
From 80 years to less than 85 years	20% of revised basic pension/family pension
From 85 years to less than 90 years	30% of revised basic pension/family pension
From 90 years to less than 95 years	40% of revised basic pension/family pension
From 95 years to less than 100 years	50% of revised basic pension/family pension
100 years or more	100% of revised basic pension/family pension

The amount of additional pension will be paid directly by the PDA without any individual authorization where date of birth of pensioner/family pensioner is available in the PPO and shown separately in the pension scroll. For example, in case where a pensioner is more than 80 years of age and his/her revised pension in terms Para 4.1 & 5 above is Rs 10,000 p.m., the pension will be shown as (i) Basic Pension = Rs 10,000 and (ii) Additional Pension = Rs 2,000 p.m. On his/her attaining the age of 85 years, it will be shown as (i) Basic Pension = Rs 10,000 and (ii) Additional pension = Rs 3,000 p.m.

In cases where the age of pensioner/family pensioner is not available on the PPO/office records, the same shall be obtained by the concerned Records office/Service HQrs from the pensioner/family pensioner. The authenticity of the age declared by the pensioner/family pensioner shall be verified by the concerned Records office/Service HQrs before submitting the claim to the PSAs concerned for notification of date of birth through the corrigendum PPO.

13. Dearness Relief:

The consolidated pension/family pension as worked out in accordance with provisions of Para 4.1 read with Para 5 and additional pension wherever payable under Para 12 above shall be treated as final 'Basic Pension' with effect from 01.01.2006 and shall qualify for grant of Dearness Relief sanctioned thereafter by the Government.

14. Consolidation of Pension for employed/re-employed pensioners

The employed/re-employed Commissioned Officer pensioners are not getting dearness relief on pension. Further the employed/reemployed Personnel Below Officer Rank pensioners whose pay on reemployed has been fixed above the minimum of scale of pay of the reemployed post, are also not getting dearness relief on pension under the extant orders. In their case, the notional dearness relief/dearness pension which would have been admissible to them but for their employment/re-employment will be taken into account for consolidation of their pension in terms of paragraph 4.1 read with Para 5 above as if they were drawing the dearness relief/dearness pension. The consolidated pension so arrived at will be the basic pension with effect from 1.1.2006. Dearness Relief beyond 1.1.2006 will, however, not be admissible to them during the period of employment/re-employment.

15. Applicability to permanent absorbees in PSUs/Autonomous Bodies.

The cases of Armed Forces Personnel who have been permanently absorbed in public sector undertakings/autonomous bodies will be regulated as follows:

Pension

15.1 Where the Government servants on permanent absorption in public sector undertakings/Autonomous Bodies continue to draw pension separately from the Government, the pension of such absorbees will be updated in terms of these orders. In cases, where the Government servants have drawn one time lump sum terminal benefits equal to 100% of their pension and have become entitled to the restoration of 1/3rd commuted portion of pension, as per Supreme Court Judgment dated 15.12.1995, their cases will not be covered by these orders.

Family Pension

15.2 In cases where, on permanent absorption in public sector undertakings/autonomous bodies, the terms of absorption permit grant of family pension under the orders applicable to the Armed Forces, the family pension being drawn by family pensioners will be updated in accordance with these orders.

16. Methodology for Implementation and Reporting

16.1 All Pension Disbursing Agencies handling disbursement of pension to the Defence Pensioners are hereby authorized to pay pension/family pension to existing pensioners/family pensioners at the consolidated rates in terms of Paras 4.1 and 5 above without any further authorization from the concerned Pension Sanctioning Authorities.

16.2 For revision of pension/family pension in terms of Para 4.1 above, a table indicating the existing pension/ family pension with and without dearness pension, the consolidated pension/family pension and the monthly difference payable from 1.1.2006 of pension/family pension due upto 31.12.2008 is enclosed for ready reference as **Annexure-I** to these orders. Except for the category of pensioners mentioned at Para 11 above, this table may be used where the pensioner/family pensioner is in receipt of single pension only. The amount indicated under column 4 to 9 of **Annexure-I** may be used for payment of arrears upto the month upto which arrears will be paid after due check. Where a pensioner is not in receipt of dearness pension/dearness relief, the amount indicated under column 4 to 9 of the **Annexure-I,** will not be used and the PDAs will themselves workout the amount of difference payable as arrears in such cases.

16.3 For revision of pension/family pension in terms of the provisions as at Para 5 above, concordance tables as per **Annexure – II** for Pre- 1.1.2006 commissioned officers pensioners/family pensioners and **Annexure - III** for PBOR pensioners/family pensioners are enclosed. Revision of pension/family pension in all cases where fixation of pension as at Para 5 above is **more beneficial** than the pension arrived at as per Para 4.1 above, will be carried out by all the Pension Disbursing Agencies (PDAs) handling payment of pension to Armed Forces pensioners in terms of these tables and the revised pension together with arrears thereof worked out and be paid immediately. Dearness relief at the rates notified from time to time will also be admissible on such revised pension.

16.4 A suitable entry regarding revised pension with effect from 1.1.2006 fixed in terms of Paras 4.1 and 5 above as the case may be, will be recorded by the Pension Disbursing Agencies in the Pension records of the pensioners viz. Pension Payment Order, Check register/Pension Payment scroll register. An intimation regarding disbursement of revised pension may be sent by the Pension Disbursing Agencies to the Office of PCDA (P), Allahabad in format prescribed as at Annexure-IV to these orders so that the later can update its records. **A copy of the said Annexure-IV may invariably be provided by the PDAs to the pensioners concerned for their information**. An acknowledgement shall be obtained by the Pension Disbursing Agencies from Office of PCDA (Pensions), Allahabad in token of receipt of the requisite Annexure-IV sent to PCDA(P) Allahabad.

Miscellaneous Instructions

17. If a pensioner/family pensioner to whom benefit accrues under the provisions of this letter, has already died before receiving the payment of arrears, the LTA will be disbursed in the following manner:

i. If the claimant is already in receipt of Family Pension or happens to be the person in whose favour Family Pension already stands notified and the awardee has not become ineligible for any reason, the LTA under the provisions of this letter should be paid to such a claimant by the PDAs on their own.

ii. If the claimant has already received LTA in the past in respect of the deceased to whom the benefit would have accrued the LTA under the provisions of this letter should also be paid to such a claimant by the PDAs on their own.

iii. If the claimant is a person other than the one mentioned at (i) & (ii) above, payment of LTA will be made to the legal heir/heirs as per extant Government orders.

18. No commutation will be admissible for the additional amount of pension accruing as a result of this revision. The existing amount of pension commuted, if any, would continue to be deducted from the consolidated pension while making monthly disbursements.

19. Updation of pension/family pension under these orders will not affect the amount of Retirement Gratuity/ Death Gratuity already determined and paid to the pensioners/family pensioners with reference to rules in force at the time of discharge/death.

20. Any overpayment of pension coming to the notice or under process of recovery shall be adjusted in full by the Pension Disbursing Agencies against arrears becoming due on revision of pension on the basis of these orders.

21. 40% of the arrears for the period of 1.1.2006 to 31.8.2008 on account of updation of pension/family pension under these orders will be paid immediately and remaining 60% of arrears shall be payable in the year 2009-2010.

22. It is considered desirable that the benefit of these orders should reach the pensioners as expeditiously as possible. To achieve this objective, it is desired that all Pension Disbursing Agencies should ensure that the revised pension and the first installment of arrears due to the pensioners in terms of the these orders is paid to the pensioners or credited to their account immediately. Instructions regarding release of second installment of arrears will be issued in due course.

23. These orders issue with the concurrence of the Finance Division of this Ministry vide their UO 1882/ DFA(Pen)/2008 dated 20.10.2008.

24. Hindi version of these orders will follow.

Sd/-
(Harbans Singh)
Director (Pension Policy)

30.2

Government of India, Ministry of Defence, Department of Ex-Servicemen Welfare Letter No 17(4)/2008(2)/D (Pen/Pol) dated 12th November 2008

Sub: Implementation of the Government Decision on the Recommendations of the Sixth Central Pay Commission - revision of provisions regulating pension/gratuity/commutation of pension/ family pension/disability pension for the armed forces officersand personnel below officer rank (PBOR) retiring or dying in harness on or after 01-01-2006.

Sir,

The undersigned is directed to state that in pursuance of Government's decision on the recommendations of the Sixth Central Pay Commission announced vide Government of India, Ministry of Personnel, Public Grievances and Pension, Department of Pension and Pensioners' Welfare Resolution No.38/37/08 P&PW (A) dated 29.08.2008, sanction of the President is hereby accorded to the modification to the extent specified in this letter, in the rules/regulations concerning pensionary benefits of the Commissioned Officers (including MNS and Territorial Army Officers) and Personnel below Officer Rank (PBOR) of the three Services, Non-combatants (Enrolled) in the Air Force, Defence Security Corps and the Territorial Army (hereinafter collectively referred to as Armed Forces Personnel) retiring or dying in harness on or after 01.01.2006.

1.2 The provisions of the Pension Regulations of the three services and various Services instructions/Government orders, which are not affected by the provisions of this letter, will remain unchanged.

PART-1
DATE OF EFFECT AND DEFINITIONS

2.1. Save as otherwise provided in these orders, the provisions of this letter shall apply to the Armed Forces personnel who were in service as on 01-01-2006 or joined/join service thereafter.

2.2 Where Pension/Family Pension/Death Gratuity/Retirement Gratuity/Commuted Value of Pension has already been sanctioned, provisionally or otherwise, in cases occurring on or after 01-01-2006, the same should be revised in terms of these orders.

In cases where pension has been finally sanctioned under the pre-revised orders and if it happens to be more beneficial than the pension becoming due under these orders, the pension already sanctioned shall not be revised to the disadvantage of the pensioners.

DEFINITIONS

3. RECKONABLE EMOLUMENTS

3.1 Except in respect of Commissioned Officers and Personnel Below Officer Rank retired/discharged/invalided/ died between 1.1.2006 and 31.8.2008 (both dates inclusive), the term "Reckonable Emoluments" will mean:

Category	Retiring/Service/Invalid Pension	Family pension	All Types of Gratuities
Commissioned Officers	Pay in the Pay Band, Grade Pay, Military Service Pay and Non Practicing Allowance, if any last drawn	Pay in the Pay Band, Grade Pay, Military Service Pay and Non Practicing Allowance, if any last drawn	Pay in the Pay Band, Grade Pay, Military Service Pay and Non Practicing Allowance, if any plus Dearness Allowance admissible on the date of retirement/ invalidment/death.
Personnel Below officer Rank	Pay in the Pay Band, Grade Pay, Military Service Pay, 'X' Group Pay and whole of Classification allowance, if any, last drawn	Pay in the Pay Band, Grade Pay, Military Service Pay, 'X' Group Pay including Classification allowance, if any, last drawn by the individual.	Pay in the Pay Band Grade Pay, Service Pay 'X' Group pay and classification allowance, if any, plus Dearness allowance admissible on the date of discharge/ invalidment/death.

3.2 In respect of Commissioned Officers and PBOR retired/discharged/invalided/died between 1.1.2006 and 31.8.2008, the term "Reckonable Emoluments" as defined at Para 3.1 above will apply except that Military Service Pay will reckon notionally for reckonable emoluments in such cases.

PAY, GRADE PAY, MILITARY SERVICE PAY, NON-PRACTICING ALLOWANCE, 'X' GROUP PAY AND CLASSIFICATION ALLOWANCE

3.3. The term Pay in the Pay Band, Grade Pay, Military Service Pay, NPA, 'X' Group Pay and Classification Allowance as referred to in para 3.1 above will mean respectively the pay in the Pay Band, Grade Pay, MSP, Non-practicing allowance, 'X' Group Pay and classification allowance introduced with effect from 01-01-2006 vide the following Services Instructions:

a. For Service Officers: SAI - 2/S/2008, SNI- 2/S/2008, SAFI - 2/S/2008

b. For PBOR: SAI- 1/S/2008, SNI- 1/S/2008, SAFI - 1/S/2008

SPECIAL PROVISIONS FOR THOSE WHO RETAIN THE PRE-REVISED SCALE OFPAY

3.4 Those who have elected to continue to draw pay in the pre-revised scale of pay and have retired or will be retiring/ discharged/invalided out of service on or after 1.1.2006, their pension and gratuity shall be calculated under the rules in force immediately before coming into effect of these orders. The pension and death-cum-retirement gratuity in such cases will be regulated as follows:

i. The term 'Reckonable Emoluments' for this para shall mean:

a. **Commissioned Officers**: Basic Pay, Rank Pay Stagnation increment and NPA, if any, in the pre-revised scales and will include Dearness pay and DA upto average AICPI 536 (Base year 1982 = 100), which is 24%.

b. **PBOR including NCs(E)**: Maximum pay of the pay scale including 50% of the highest classification allowance, if any, of the rank continuously held during last ten months and group in which paid and will include Dearness Pay and DA up to average AICPI 536 (Base Year 1982 = 100) which is 24%.

ii. Retiring pension for Officers will be calculated at 50% of average of reckonable emoluments drawn during last 10 months and service pension for PBOR at 50% of reckonable emoluments. The amount so determined will be the pension for 33 years of reckonable qualifying service including rank weightage. For lesser period of reckonable qualifying service, this amount will be proportionately reduced.

iii. Retirement/Death gratuity shall be admissible with reference to emoluments at (i) above plus dearness allowance under the order in force immediately before coming into effect of these orders. The maximum amount of gratuity shall not exceed Rs 3,50,000/- in terms of Para 12 of this Ministry's letter NO.1(6)/98/0 (Pen/Sers) dated 03.02.1998.

iv. Commutation of pension shall be admissible in accordance with the orders in force before 02.09.2008.

v. Family pension shall be allowed in accordance with orders applicable prior to the issue of these orders and shall be calculated with reference to reckonable emoluments as defined in Para 3.1 of this Ministry's letter No. 1(6)/98/0 (Pen/Sers) dated 03.02.98 and will also include Dearness Pay. To the family pension so calculated, dearness relief upto average AICPI 536 (Base year 1982 = 100) at the rate contained in Department of P&PW's O. M. No. 42/2/2006-P&PW(G) dated 05.04.2006 which is 24% shall be added. The amount so arrived at will be regarded as the family pension for regulating payment of dearness relief beyond average AICPI 536.

NOTES:

1. Where an Officer immediately before his/her retirement or death while in service had been absent from duty on leave (including furlough leave) for which leave salary is/was payable or having been suspended had been re-instated without forfeiture of service, the emoluments which he/she would have drawn, had he/she not been absent from duty or not been suspended, will reckon for pensionary benefits.

2. Where an Officer immediately before his/her retirement or death while in service had proceeded on leave for which leave salary is payable, after having held a higher paid acting rank, the emoluments drawn in such paid acting rank will reckon for pensionary benefits only if it is certified that he/she would have continued to hold the paid acting rank but for his/her proceeding on leave.

3. Where an Officer immediately before his/her retirement or death while in service had been under suspension or absent from duty the period whereof does not count as service, the emoluments which he/she drew immediately before such absence from duty or being placed under suspension, will reckon for pensionary benefits.

4. Where an Officer is serving in an organization other than the Armed Forces, the actual pay and allowances drawn during such service will not be treated as emoluments, but the sum of the Pay in the Pay Band, Grade Pay, Military Service Pay plus NPA, if any, which he would have drawn in the Armed Forces, had he not been on such service, will alone be treated as emoluments reckonable for pensionary benefits.

4. AVERAGE EMOLUMENTS

4.1. Average Emoluments shall be determined with reference to the reckonable emoluments drawn by him/her during the last 10 months of service and shall include the Pay drawn in Pay Band plus Grade pay as admissible, Military Service Pay, whole of classification allowance and 'X' Group pay where applicable in case of PBOR and Non Practicing Allowance, if any.

4.2. In the case of Commissioned Officers and PBOR who have opted for the revised pay structure and have retired/ discharged within 10 months from the date of coming over to the revised pay structure, the 'average emoluments' for 10 months period preceding retirement/discharge will be calculated by taking into account pay as follows:

(a) For the period during which pay is drawn in the revised pay structure	Pay drawn in the prescribed pay band plus the applicable grade pay, whole of the classification allowance in case of PBOR and 'X' Group pay where applicable in case of PBOR and NPA, if any. Military Service Pay will reckon notionally in such cases.
(b) For the period during which pay was drawn in the pre-revised pay scales	(i) Pay including rank pay for Commissioned Officers and 50% of highest classification allowance in case of PBOR plus Dearness Pay, stagnation increment, NPA, if any and actual DA appropriate to the pay at the rates in force on 1.1.2006 drawn during the relevant period. (ii) Notional increase of the pay by applying the fitment benefit of 40% of the basic pay including rank pay for Commissioned Officer and 50% of highest classification allowance in case of PBOR, stagnation increment, NPA, if any, drawn in the pre-revised pay scale.

4.3 The clause of protective pension mentioned at Para 6.3 below will also be applicable in such cases.

NOTES:

1. If during the last 10 months of service, an Officer had been absent from duty on leave for which leave salary is payable or having been suspended, had been re-instated without forfeiture of service, the emoluments which he would have drawn had he not been absent from duty or suspended, will be taken into account for determining the average emoluments.
2. If during the last 10 months of the service, a person had been absent from duty or had been under suspension the period whereof does not count as service, the aforesaid period of absence from duty or suspension, will be disregarded in the calculation of the average emoluments and equal period before the 10 months will be included.

5. QUALIFYING SERVICE:

5.1 PENSION

5.1.1. COMMISSIONED OFFICERS

a. The minimum period of qualifying service actually rendered and required for earning retiring pension will be 20 years. In the case of late entrants (i.e., an Officer who is retired on reaching the prescribed age limit for compulsory retirement with at least 15 years commissioned service qualifying for pension but whose total service is less than 20 years) the minimum period of Qualifying Service actually rendered and required for earning retiring pension will continue to be 15 years.
b. Serving JCOs/ORs. of Army and corresponding ranks of the Navy and Air Force granted EC/SSC will be eligible for retiring pension after 12 years of qualifying service actually rendered.

5.1.2 PERSONNEL BELOW OFFICER RANK (PBOR)

a. The minimum period of qualifying service actually rendered and required forearning service pension will continue to be 15 years (20 years in the case of NCs (E)).

5.1.3. ADDITION TO QUALIFYING SERVICE

The benefit of adding years of qualifying service (rank weightage) as provided in Para 5(b)(l) & (II) of this Ministry's letter dated 03.02.1998 for the purpose of computation of pension shall be continued in respect of those Commissioned Officers who retired/invalided out of service during the period 1.1.2006 to 1.9.2008. In respect of Commissioned Officers retired/retiring/invalided out on or after 2.9.2008, the weightage to qualifying service for the purpose of computation of pension stands withdrawn with effect from 2.9.2008.

In the case of PBOR discharged/invalided out from service on or after 1.1.2006, the weightage to qualifying service for purpose of computation of pension stands withdrawn with effect from 1.1.2006.

5.2 The term "Qualifying Service" (QS) for computation of all kinds of gratuity will mean:

QUALIFYING SERVICE RECKONABLE FOR		
Retirement Gratuity	Death Gratuity	Retiring/Service/Invalid/Terminal Gratuity
Actual qualifying service plus a weightage of 5 years subject to the total qualifying service including weightage not exceeding 33 years	Actual qualifying service rendered plus a weightage of 5 years subject to total qualifying service not exceeding 33 years. In case actual service is less than 5 years no weightage will be given.	Actual qualifying service

NOTES:

1. Qualifying Service would commence from the date of commission. In case the Short Service Commission is followed by Permanent Commission, the period during which an Officer holds Short Service Commission on probation will reckon for the purposes of pensionary benefits.

2. In case of TA personnel aggregate of qualifying embodied service shall count for service pension. Aggregate qualifying embodied service may be continuous or rendered in broken spells. For calculating the total embodied service, the breaks in embodied service due to disembodiment will be treated as condoned but the period of breaks itself will not be treated as qualifying service for pension. Where qualifying embodied service has been rendered in broken spells, five per cent cut will be imposed on the pension of those JCOs/OR who have completed 15 years or more of aggregate embodied service, but have not completed 20 years of aggregate embodied service.

3. Full pre-commissioned service rendered under the Central Government whether in a civil department or in the Armed Forces, will be taken into account for working out the qualifying service for earning pensionary benefits subject to fulfillment of other conditions. This will also be counted for determining the minimum qualifying service.

4. In calculating the length of qualifying service, fraction of a year equal to three months and above but less than 6 months will be treated as a completed one half year and reckoned as qualifying service. This will, however, not be applicable for computing minimum qualifying service for pension.

5. All leave including study leave will count as qualifying service for pension provided that service for at least a period specified by the Government has been rendered from the date of return from the study leave last availed of. Any period of leave without pay shall not qualify unless specifically authorized by the Government.

PART-II
RETIRING/SERVICE PENSION/RETIREMENT/DEATH/SPECIAL GRATUITY/ ORDINARY FAMILY PENSION

6. RETIRING/SERVICE PENSION:

6.1. COMMISSIONED OFFICERS

a. Linkage of full pension with 33 years of Qualifying Service is dispensed with effect from 2.9.2008. The Retiring pension of Commissioned Officers retiring/invalided out on or after 2.9.2008 will be calculated at 50% of emoluments last drawn or average of reckonable emoluments drawn during last 10 months, whichever is more beneficial.

b. Grant of retiring pension to the Commissioned Officers retired/invalided out during 1.1.2006 to 1.9.2008 will continue to be governed by the Rules/Orders which were in force immediately before coming into effect of these orders.

6.2. PERSONNEL BELOW OFFICER RANK

In case of PBOR, linkage of full pension with 33 years of qualifying service is dispensed with from 1.1.2006. Service pension of PBOR will be calculated at 50% of emoluments last drawn or average of reckonable emoluments drawn during last 10 months, whichever is more beneficial.

7. MINIMUM PENSION

The amount of pension calculated as per Para 6.1 above will be subject to the provision that the pension in no case shall be lower than fifty percent of the sum of the minimum of the pay in the pay band plus grade pay and Military Service Pay from which the pensioner has retired. In case of Commissioned Officers who have retired during 1.1.2006 and 1.9.2008, the pension will be reduced pro rata where the pensioner has less than the maximum required service of 33 years for full pension and in no case it will be less than Rs 3,500/- per month.

NOTES:

The retiring pension of an Officer of the rank of Major General and equivalent,shall not be less than the pension which would have been admissible to him as a Brigadier and equivalent, as the case may be, had he not been promoted to the higher rank.

8. GRATUITY

The maximum limit of all kinds of Gratuity i.e. Retiring/Retirement/Service/Invalid/Special/Terminal/Death Gratuity shall be Rs 10 lakhs.

9. COMMUTATION OF PENSION

9.1. Armed Forces Personnel shall be entitled to commute for a lump sum payment upto 50% of their pension.

9.2. The existing Table of Commutation Value for pension Annexed to AI 85/71 shall be substituted by a new table as at 'Annexure - I' to this letter.

9.3. The revised Table of Commutation Value for Pension will be used for all commutations of pension, which become absolute on or after 02.09.2008. In the case of those pensioners, in whose case commutation of pension became absolute on or after 01.01.2006 but before 02.09.2008, the pre-revised Table of Commutation Value for commutation of pension will be used for payment of commuted value of pension based on pre-revised pay/pension. Such pensioners shall have an option to commute the amount of pension that has become additionally commutable on account of retrospective revision of pay/pension on implementation of the recommendations of the Sixth Central Pay Commission. On exercising such an option by the pensioner, the revised Table of Commutation Value for Pension will be used for the commutation of the additional amount of pension that has become commutable on account of retrospective revision of pay/pension. In all cases where the date of retirement/discharge/invalidment/commutation of pension is on or after 02.09.2008, the revised Table of Commutation Value for Pension will be used for commutation of entire pension.

10. ADDITIONAL PENSION TO OLD PENSIONERS

The quantum of pension available to the old pensioners shall be increased as follows:

AGE OF PENSIONER	ADDITIONAL QUANTUM OF PENSION
From 80 years to less than 85 years	20% of basic pension
From 85 years to less than 90 years	30% of basic pension
From 90 years to less than 95 years	40% of basic pension
From 95 years to less than 100 years	50% of basic pension
100 years or more	100% of basic pension

The Pension Sanctioning Authorities should ensure that the date of birth and the age of a pensioner are invariably indicated in the pension payment order to facilitate payment of additional pension by the Pension Disbursing Authority as soon as it becomes due. The amount of additional pension will be shown distinctly in the pension payment order. For example, in case where a pensioner is more than 80 years of age and his pension is Rs 10,000 p.m. the pension will be shown as (i) Basic pension = Rs 10,000 and (ii) Additional Pension = Rs 2,000 p.m. The pension on his attaining the age of 85 years will be shown as (i) Basic Pension = Rs 10,000 and (ii) Additional pension = Rs 3,000 p.m.

11. FAMILY PENSION

11.1 For the purpose of grant of family pension, the 'Family' shall be categorized as under:

CATEGORY-I

a. Widow or widower, upto the date of death or re-marriage, whichever is earlier;

b. Son/daughter (including widowed daughter), upto the date of his/her marriage/re-marriage or till the date he/she starts earning or till the age of 25 years, whichever is earlier.

CATEGORY-II

c. Unmarried/Widowed/Divorced daughter, not covered by Category I above, upto the date of marriage/re-marriage or till the date she starts earning or upto the date of death, whichever is earlier.

d. Parents who were wholly dependent on the Armed Forces personnel when he/she was alive provided the deceased personnel had left behind neither a widow nor a child.

Family pension to dependent parents, unmarried/divorced/widowed daughter will continue till the date of death.

Family pension to unmarried/widowed/divorced daughters in Category-II and dependent parents shall be payable only after the other eligible family members in Category I have ceased to be eligible to receive family pension and there is no disabled child to receive the family pension. Grant of family pension to children in respective categories shall be payable in order of their date of birth and younger of them will not be eligible for family pension unless the next above him/her has become ineligible for grant of family pension in that category.

11.2 The dependency criteria for the purpose of family pension shall be the minimum family pension along with dearness relief thereon.

11.3 The childless widow of a deceased personnel shall continue to be paid family pension even after her re-marriage subject to the condition that the family pension shall cease once her independent income from all other sources becomes equal to or higher than the minimum prescribed family pension in the Central Government. The family pensioner in such cases would be required to give a declaration regarding her income from other sources to the pension disbursing authority every six months.

11.4 The enhanced rate of ordinary family pension shall be payable for a period of ten years, without any upper age limit from the date following the date of death of the personnel, to the family of a personnel who dies in service. These provisions will, however, not apply in cases where the period of seven years for payment of enhanced family pension has already been completed as on 1.1.2006 and the family was in receipt of normal rate of ordinary family pension on that date. There will be no change in the period for payment of enhanced family pension to the family in the case of death of a pensioner i.e. 7 years from the date of death or till attaining the age 67 years whichever is earlier.

ADDITIONAL FAMILY PENSION TO OLD FAMILY PENSIONERS

11.5 The quantum of family pension available to the old family pensioners shall be increased as follows:

AGE OF FAMILY PENSIONER	ADDITIONAL QUANTUM OF FAMILY PENSION
From 80 years to less than 85 years	20% of basic pension
From 85 years to less than 90 years	30% of basic pension
From 90 years to less than 95 years	40% of basic pension
From 95 years to less than 100 years	50% of basic pension
100 years or more	100% of basic pension

The Pension Sanctioning Authorities should ensure that the date of birth and the age of a family pensioner is invariably indicated in the pension payment order to facilitate payment of additional family pension by the Pension Disbursing Authority as soon as it becomes due. The amount of additional family pension will be shown distinctly in the pension payment order. For example, in case where a family pensioner is more than 80 years of age and his/her family pension is Rs 10,000 p.m. the pension will be shown as-

(i) Basic family pension = Rs 10,000 and (ii) Additional pension = Rs 2,000 p.m. The family pension on his/her attaining the age of 85 years will be shown as (i) Basic Family Pension = Rs 10,000 and (ii) Additional pension = Rs 3,000 p.m.

PART -III

GENERAL

ROUNDING OFF OF PENSIONARY AWARDS

12. The amount of various pensionary awards admissible as per this letter shall be rounded off to the next higher rupee by the Pension Sanctioning Authorities.

MINIMUM/MAXIMUM PENSION

13. If the amount of any monthly pension viz retiring pension/service pension/invalid pension/special pension/ family pension admissible under the provisions of this letter works out to less than Rs 3,500/- per month, it shall be stepped up to Rs 3,500/- per month and authorized for payment at this rate. In cases where service element of disability pension falls short of Rs 3,500/- p.m. the same shall be stepped up to Rs 3,500/- p.m. There will be a maximum ceiling on the amount of Service Pension/Invalid Pension/Special Pension and Ordinary Family Pension upto 50% and 30% respectively of the highest pay in the Government (the highest pay in the Govt. is Rs 90,000 since 1.1.2006).

DEARNESS RELIEF

14. Dearness Relief shall be admissible only beyond average AICPI 536 (Base Year 1982 = 100) on the revised pattern introduced vide Ministry of Personnel, Public Grievances and pension, Department of Pension and Pensioners' Welfare Office Memorandum No. 42/2/2008-P&PW (G) dated 12.09.2008, on various types of pensions/family pension and additional pension/family pension.

COMMUTATION OF ADDITIONAL PENSION

15. The Armed Forces personnel who had already retired/discharged from service during 1.1.2006 and 1.9.2008 and have availed of the benefit of commutation of pension not exceeding maximum permissible limit (i.e. 43% & 45% in respect of commissioned officers and PBOR respectively) within one year of retirement/discharge, the benefit of commutation of additional pension as at Para 8.3 above, will be allowed with reference to the age next birthday as on the date of fresh option without medical examination. In case of Armed Forces personnel retired/discharged during 1.1.2006 to 1.9.2008 and had not availed the commutation of pension upto maximum permissible limit within one year of retirement/discharge, the benefit of commutation of additional pension as at Para 8.3 above may be allowed with reference to age next birthday as on date of fresh option after medical examination. The pensioners who have already undergone medical examination in the latter case need not be medically examined again for this purpose.

PROCEDURE FOR SANCTION OF REVISED PENSION IN RESPECT OF THOSE WHO HAVE ALREADY RETIRED

16. For revision of pensionary awards as per provisions of this letter in respect of Armed Forces personnel who have already retired/discharged/invalided out/died on or after 01.01.2006 and in whose cases pensionary benefits at pre-revised rates have already been notified, the Record Offices concerned in case of PBOR and CDA(O), Pune/Naval Pay Office Mumbai/AFCAO, New Delhi, as the case may be, in respect of Commissioned Officers, will initiate and forward revised LPC-cum-data sheet as prescribed by PCDA(Pensions), Allahabad to their respective Pension Sanctioning Authorities (PSAs) for issue of corrigendum PPOs notifying the revised pensionary awards. Further implementation instructions to all concerned will be issued by PCDA (Pensions), Allahabad immediately on receipt of these orders.

17. Orders regarding grant of disability pension/liberalized disability pension/war injury pension, admissible with effect from 1.1.2006 will be issued separately.

18. Pension Regulations of the three services will be amended in due course.

19. This issues with the concurrence of the Finance Division of this Ministry vide their UO NO.1930/DFA(Pens) dated 24.10.2008.

20. Hindi version will follow.

Sd/-
(Harbans Singh)
Director (Pension Policy)

30.3

Government of India, Ministry of Defence, Department of Ex-Servicemen Welfare Letter No 17 (4)/2008 (2)/1(Pen/Policy) dated 27th November 2008

Sub: Implementation of the Government decision on we recommendations of the Sixth Central Pay Commission – revision of provisions regulating pension/commutation of pension/gratuity/ family pension/disability pension for the armed forces officers and personnel below officer rank (PBOR) retiring or dying in harness on or after 01.01.2006.

This Ministry's letter No. 17 (4)/2008 (2)/1(Pen/Policy) Dated 27th November, 2008 is amended as follows:

i. **Para 1 Line 7:**

Word "EC/SSC," be added after word "including" appearing within bracket.

ii. **Para 4.3:**

May be deleted.

iii. **Para 5.1.2:**

"a" appearing brackets of "(a)" under this para be deleted.

iv. **Para 7 Line 1:**

Para "6.1" may be read as Para "6.1(b)"

v. **Para 9.3 may be substituted as under:**

"9.3 The revised table of Commutation value of pension will be used for all commutations of pension, which become absolute on or after 2.6.2008. In all cases where the date of retirement/discharge/Invalidment is on or after 2.9.2008, the revised Table of commutation value for commutation of pension will be used for commutation of pension.

In the case of those pensioners in whose case commutation of pension became absolute on or after 1.1.2006 but before 2.9.2008, the pre revised Table of commutation value for commutation of pension has been used for the payment of commuted value of pension based on pre-revised pension. Such pensioners shall have an option to commute the amount of pension that has become additionally commutable on account of retrospective revision of pay/pension on implementation of the recommendations of the Sixth Central Pay Commission. On exercising such an option as per Annexure – II by the pensioner, the revised Table of Commutation Value of pension will be used for the commutation of the additional amount of pension that has become commutable on account of retrospective revision of pension with reference to age next birthday already reckoned for the commutation of pre revised pension."

vi. **Para 15 may be substituted as under:**

Commutation of additional pension

"15. The Armed Forces personnel who had already retired/discharged/invalided out from service during 1.1.2006 and 1.9.2008 and have availed of the benefit of commutation of pension not exceeding maximum permissible limit (i.e. 43% & 45% in respect of Commissioned Officers and PBOR respectively) within one year of retirement/ discharge/ invalidment, the benefit of commutation of additional pension (i.e. 50% less the percentage already commuted), will be allowed with reference to the age next birthday as on the date of fresh option as per annexure II without medical examination by applying revised commutation value annexed to this letter. In case of Armed Forces personnel retired/ discharged/invalided out during 1.1.2006 to 1.9.2008 and had not availed for commutation of pension upto maximum permissible limit within one year of retirement/discharge, the benefit of commutation of additional pension as at Para

9.3 above may be allowed with reference to age next birthday as on date of fresh option after medical examination. The pensioners who have already undergone medical examination the latter case need not be medically examined again for this purpose."

This issues with the concurrence of the Finance Division of this Ministry vide their UO No. 2080/2008/DFA(P), dated 26.11.2008.

Hindi version will follow.

Sd/-

(Harbans Singh)

Director (Pension/Policy)

30.4

Government of India, Ministry of Defence, Department of Ex-Servicemen Welfare Letter No 1(8)/2008-D (Pen/Policy) dated 12th June 2009

Sub: **Notional Pay fixation of Honorary Ranks for the purpose of pension- Recommendations of the Sixth Central Pay Commission contained in Para 5.1.62.**

Sir,

I am directed to say that in pursuance of Governments decision on the recommendations of the Sixth Central pay Commission contained in Para 5.1.62 of Chapter V of the Report, the President is pleased to decide that Honorary rank of Naib Subedar granted to Havildars will be notionally considered as a promotion to the higher grade of Naib Subedar and benefit of fitment in the pay band and the higher grade pay will be allowed notionally for the purpose of fixation of pension only. Accordingly, additional element of pension of Rs 100/- pm payable to Havildars granted Hony rank of Naib Subedar as per Regn. 137 of pension Regulations for the Army Part-I (1961), amended vide this Ministry's letter No 1(1)/88/D(Pen/Sers) dated 6.11.1991 will cease to be payable. The notional fixation of pay in the rank of Naib Subedar will not be taken into account for payment of retirement gratuity, encashment of leave, composite transfer grant etc.

2. This letter takes effect from 1st January 2006.

3. This issues with the concurrence of Finance Division of this Ministry vide their UO No. 2351/Finance/Pension dated 3.6.2009.

Sd/-

(Harbans Singh)

Director (Pension/Policy)

30.5

Government of India, Ministry of Defence, Department of Ex-Servicemen Welfare Letter No 1(13)/2016/D(Pen/Policy) dated 21st February 2020

Sub: Revision of pension of Pre-01.01.2006 retiree Havildar granted Hony Rank of Nb Subedar.

Sir,

I am directed to refer to this Ministry's letter No. 1(8)/2008-D(Pen/Policy) dated 12.06.2009 according to which "Honorary rank of Naib Subedar granted to Havildars will be notionally considered as a promotion to the higher grade of Naib Subedar and benefit of fitment in the pay band and the higher grade pay will be allowed notionally for the purpose of fixation of pension only." This provision was applicable for Havildars granted Hony rank of Naib Subedar retired on or after 01.01.2006.

2. A section of Pre-2006 retiree Havildars granted Hony rank of Naib Subedar approached various courts for implementing the provision of this Ministry letter dated 12.06.2009 in their cases. Hon'ble AFT Chandigarh vide their order dated 27.10.2017 in OA No. 2755 of 2013 filed by Ex Havildar (Hony.Nb.Sub) Hoshiar Singh, allowed the benefit of Gol, MoD letter No. 1(8)/2008-D(Pen/Policy) dated 12.06.2009 to all Pre-2006 Havildars granted Hony rank of Naib Subedar w.e.f. 01.01.2006. Further, pension revision tables for Hony Naib Subedars in pursuance of Govt. policy letter dated 08.03.2010 and 17.01.2013 were also quashed and respondents were directed to prepare these tables afresh taking into account the aspect that the benefit under Gol, MoD letter dated 12.06.2009 was to be granted.

3. The issue has been examined in the Ministry and undersigned is directed to say that Government has decided to implement the Hon'ble AFT Chandigarh order dated 27.10.2017 referred above. The provision of GoI, MoD letter No. 1(8)/2008- D(Pen/Policy) dated 12.06.2009 is hereby extended w.e.f. 01.01.2006 to Pre-2006 retiree Havildars who were granted Hony rank of Naib Subedars, Further, as per the directions of Hon'ble Court the tables meant for Hony Nb Subedar for implementation of GoI, MoD letter No. PC 10(1)/2009-D(Pen/Pol) dated 08.03.2010 and GoI, MoD letter No. 1(13)/2012/D(Pen/Policy) dated 17.01.2013 circulated vide PCDA (P), Allahabad Circular No. 430 dated 10.03.2010 and Circular No. 501 dated 17.01.2013 respectively are hereby quashed. However, to extend the benefits of these Govt. orders tables are hereby prepared afresh and attached with this letter.

4. All Pension Disbursing Agencies handling disbursement of pension to Defence pensioners are hereby authorized to carry out revision of service pension/special pension/invalid pension/service element of disability pension w.e.f. 01.01.2006, 01.07.2009 and 24.09.2012 to the affected pensioners in the category of Pre-01.01.2006 retiree Havildar granted Hony rank of Naib Subedar drawing pension with 15 years or more qualifying service in terms of these orders without calling for any application from the pensioners and without any further authorization from the PCDA (Pension), Allahabad and pay the arrears on account of such revision. If rate of pension mentioned in various orders issued earlier by this Ministry in respect of Hony. Nb. Subedar happens to be more beneficial than the rates as per attached tables, then the same will not be revised to the disadvantage of the pensioners.

5. No arrears on account of revision of pension based on national fixation of pay shall be admissible for the period prior to 01.01.2006.

6. Pension of Hony.Nb.Subedars who are in receipt of Special Pension, Invalid Pension and Service Element of Disability Pension for less than 15 years of qualifying service would also need to be revised in terms of these orders. However, Pension Disbursing Agencies shall refer such cases to the PCDA (Pension), Allahabad for issuing of Corr. PPO.

7. No commutation of pension will be admissible on additional amount of pension accruing as a result of revision under these orders.

8. Notional fixation of pay in terms of these orders will not affect the entitlement of retirement Gratuity already determined and paid with reference to rules in force at the time of discharge/invalidment.

9. Any overpayment of pension coming to the notice or under process of recovery shall be adjusted in full by the Pension Disbursing Agencies against arrears becoming due on revision of pension on the basis of these orders.

10. If a pensioner to whom the benefit accrues under the provisions of this letter has died/dies before receiving the payment of arrears, the Life Time Arrears of pension (LTA) shall be paid as usual manner.

11. All other terms and conditions of this Ministry letter No.PC10(1)/2009-D(Pen/Pol) dated 08.03.2010 and No. 1(13)/2012/D(Pen/Pol) dated 17.01.2013 shall remain unchanged.

12. Ministry of Finance, Department of Expenditure has concurred the proposal with following conditions:

i. The revised pension of an honorary rank Naib Subedar who had retired before 01.01.2006 shall not exceed that of an honorary rank Naib Subedar who retired on or after 01.01.2006.

ii. The revised pension of an honorary rank Naib Subedar who had retired before 01.01.2006 shall not exceed that of a regular Naib Subedar who retired either before or after 01.01.2006.

13. This issues with the concurrence of M/o Finance, D/o Expenditure vide their ID No. 1(13)/EV/2019 dated 05.02.2020 and the Finance Division of this Ministry vide their ID No. 10(06)/2012/Fin/Pen dated 20.02.2020.

14. Hindi Version will follow.

Sd/-
Ashok Kumar
Under Secretary to the Govt of India

30.6

Government of India, Ministry of Defence, Department of Ex-Servicemen Welfare Letter No 1(04)/2015(I)-D (Pen/Pol) dated 3rd September 2015

Sub: **Revision of pension of pre-2006 Commissioned Officer pensioners/family pensioners.**

The undersigned is directed to refer to this Ministry's letter No 17(4)/2008(I)/D (Pen/Pol) dated 11.11.2008 as amended, issued in implementation of government decision on the recommendations of the Sixth CPC for revision of pension/family pension in respect of Pre-2006 Armed Forces pensioner/family pensioners. As per provisions contained in Para 5 therein, with effect from 01.01.2006 revised pension and revised ordinary family pension of all pre-2006 Armed Forces pensioners/family pensions determined in terms of fitment formula laid down in Para 4.1 above said letter dated 11.11.2008, shall in no case be lower than fifty percent and thirty percent respectively, of the minimum of the pay band plus the Grade pay corresponding to the pre-revised scale from which the pensioner had retired/discharged/invalided out/died including Military Service Pay where applicable.

2. The above minimum guaranteed pension was revised vide GOI, MOD letter No 1(11)/2012/D(Pen/Pol) dated 17.01.2013 with effect from24.09.2012, at the rate of minimum of fitment table for the Rank in the revised pay band as indicated under fitment table annexed with SAI 2/S/2008 and SAI 4/S/2008 as amended, plus Grade Pay corresponding to the pre-revised scale from which the pensioner had retired/discharged/invalided out/died including Military Service Pay.

3. Now, after issue of GOI, Ministry of Personnel, PG & Pensioners, Department of Pension & Pension Welfare OM No. 38/37/08-P & PW (A) dated 30.07.2015, it has been decided that the pension/family pension of all pre-2006 pensioners/family pensioners may be revised in accordance with Para 2 with effect from 01.01.2006 instead of 24.09.2012.

4. In case the consolidated pension/family pension calculated as per Para 4.1 of this Ministry's letter No. 17(4)/ 2008(1)/O (Pen/Pol) dated 11.11.2008 is higher than the pension/family pension calculated I the manner indicated above, the same 9higher consolidated pension/family pension) will continue to be treated as basic pension/ family pension.

5. Accordingly, revised tables indicating minimum guaranteed pension/ordinary family pension for Indian Commissioned Officers which is annexed with GOI,MOD letter No 1(11)2012-D(Pen/Policy) dated 17.01.2013, shall be effective with effect from01.01.2006 instead of 24.09.2012. Pension Disbursing Authorities are hereby authorized to step up the pension/family pension of the affected 0pre-2006 pensioners/family pensioners with effect from 01.01.2006 instead of 24.09.2012 and arrears of pension/family pension will be paid.

6. All other terms and conditions shall remain unchanged.

7. The provisions of this letter shall take effect from 01.01.2006 and arrears, if any, shall be allowed from 01.01.2006 to 23.09.2012.

8. This issues with concurrence of finance Division of this Ministry vide their ID No 22(5)/2015/fin/Pen dated 25.08.2015 and Ministry of Finance, Department of expenditure vide their ID No. 1(12)/EV/2015 dated 2.9.2015.

9. Hindi Version will follow.

Sd/-

(R.K. Arora)

Under Secretary to the Government of India

30.7

Government of India, Ministry of Defence, Department of Ex-Servicemen Welfare Letter No 1(2)/2016-D (Pen/Pol) dated 30th September 2016

Sub: Revision of pension of pre-2006 Pensioners (JCOs/OR and Commissioned Officers)- delinking of qualifying service of 33 years for revised pension.

The undersigned is directed to refer to this Ministry's letter No 17(4)/2008(I)/D (Pen/Pol) dated 11.11.2008 as amended, for implementation of government decision on the recommendations of the Sixth CPC for revision of pension/family pension in respect of Pre-2006 Armed Forces pensioner/family pensioners. As per provisions contained in Para 5 of the letter, revised pension and revised ordinary family pension of all Pre-2006 Armed Forces pensioners/family pensions determined in terms of fitment formula laid down in Para 4.1 above said letter dated 11.11.2008, should in no case be lower than fifty percent and thirty percent respectively, of the minimum of the pay band plus the Grade pay corresponding to the pre-revised scale from which the pensioner had retired/discharged/invalided out/died including Military Service Pay and 'X' Group Pay, where applicable. The pension so calculated had to be reduced pro-rata where pensioners had rendered less than 33 years of qualifying service.

2. The above minimum guaranteed pension was revised with effect from 24.09.2012 vide GOI, MOD letter No 1(11)/2012/D(Pen/Pol) dated 17.01.2013 in case of commissioned officers. As per this letter, with effect from 24.09.2012, the minimum guaranteed pension in respect of Pre-2006 commissioned officers/family pensioners should be determined as fifty and thirty percent respectively of the minimum of the fitment table for the rank in the revised pay band as indicated under fitment tables annexed to SAI 1/S/2008 as amended equivalent instructions for Navy & Air Force and SAI 4/S/2008 (for MNS Officers), plus Grade Pay corresponding to the pre-revised scale from which the pensioner had retired/discharged/invalided out/died including M.S.P. The minimum guaranteed pension/family pension in respect of Pre-96 retired EC/SSC officers should be revised w.e.f. 24.09.2012 as 50%/30% respectively of the pay in pay band corresponding to the pre revised scale of pay of Rs 10,500/- (in terms of Para 9(a) (i) of SAI 1/S/2008) plus grade pay of Rs 5,400/- and M.S.P. of Rs 6,000/-.

3. The above minimum guaranteed pension was further revised, vide Ministry's letter No. 1(04)/2015/(I)-O (Pen/Pol) dated 3rd September, 2015 (in r/o ICOs) and Letter No. 1(04)/2015(11)-D(Pen/Pol) dated 3rd September, 2015 in r/o JCO/OR. Pension/family pension in respect of Pre-2006 Armed Forces pensioners/Family pensioners, has been determined as fifty and thirty percent respectively of the minimum of the fitment table for the rank in the revised pay Band as indicated under fitment tables annexed with 1/S/2008, 2/S/2008, & 4/S/2008 as amended and equivalent instructions for navy and Air Force, plus Grade pay corresponding to the pre-revised scale from which the pensioner had retired/discharged/invalided out/died including Military Service Pay and 'X' Group pay where applicable w.e.f. 01.01.2006. However, vide Ministry's letter No 1(7)/2014-D(Pen/Pol) dated 31.07.2016, the minimum guaranteed pension in case of Medical Officers of AMC/ADC/RVC has been revised by adding NPA @ 25% of minimum of fitment table for the rank in the revised Pay band as indicated in the fitment table annexed with SAI 2/S/2008.

4. Now, GOI, Ministry of Personnel, PG & Pensions, Department of pension & Pensioners Welfare has issued O.M. No 38/37/08 P&PW (A) dated 06.04,2016 for delinking of Qualifying Service with pension for revision purpose. Therefore, it has been decided that w.e.f. 1.1.2006, revised consolidated pension and family pension of Pre-2006 armed forces pensioners shall not be lower than 50% and 30% respectively of the minimum of the pay in the Pay band plus Grade pay corresponding to the pre-revised scale from which the pensioner had retired/discharged/invalided out/died including Military Service Pay and X group pay, if any, without pro-rata reduction of pension even if they had rendered qualifying service of less than 33 years at the time of retirement. Accordingly, Para 5 of this Ministries letter dated 11.11.2008 would stand modified to this extent.

5. Revised table indicating minimum guaranteed retiring/service pension and ordinary family pension have been annexed to this letter as follows:-

Annexure A for commissioned officers (ICOs)

Annexure B for Army Pensioners (JCOs/OR)

Annexure C for Air Force Pensioners (JCOs/OR)

Annexure D for Navy Pensioners (JCOs/OR)

Pension Disbursing Agencies (PDA) are hereby authorized to step up the pension/family pension of the affected pre-2006 pensioners where the existing pension being paid to the pensioners, is less than the rate of pension indicated in above said annexure. Necessary implementation instructions to all concerned shall be issued by principal CDA (Pensions), Allahabad.

6. The provisions of this letter shall take effect from 01.01.2006 and arrears, if any shall be payable from 01.01.2006. Further, the Pension/Family Pension of the Armed Force Personnel has been revised a number of times in past vide various letters issued by this Ministry, therefore, if pension already revised w.e.f. 01.01.2006, 01.07.2009, 24.09.2012 & 01.07.2014 (OROP) under respective Govt. orders happens to be more than this amount, then Retiring/Service and Family Pension as per above orders will continue to be paid as basic pension during that period.

7. Payment of Life Time Arrears (LTA).

If a pensioner to whom the benefit accrues under the provisions of this letter has died/dies before receiving the payment of arrears, the Life Time Arrears of pension (LTA) shall be paid in the following manner:-

a. If the claimant is already in receipt of Family Pension or happens to be the person in whose favour Family Pension already stands notified and the aware has not become Ineligible for any reasons, the LTA under the provisions of this letter should be paid to such a claimant by the PDA on their own.

b. If the claimant has already received LTA in the past in respect of the deceased to whom the benefit would have accrued, the LTA under the provisions of this letter should also be paid to such a claimant by the PDA on their own.

c. If the claimant is a person other than the one mentioned at 7 (a) & 7 (b) above, payment of LTA shall be made to the legal heir/heirs as per extant Government ores on the subject.

8. Additional Pension. The rate prescribed in these orders shall be the minimum guaranteed basic pension form 1.1.2006. Additional pension as applicable to the old aged pensioners/family pensioners on attaining the relevant age 80 years and above shall also be enhanced by the PDAs, where beneficial from 1.1.2006 or the date from which the pensioners attain the age of 80 years or more, whichever is later as per the extant orders on the subject.

9. All other terms and conditions shall remain unchanged.

10. This issues with the concurrence of Finance Division of this Ministry vide their ID No 10(6)/2016/FIN/PEN dated 29.09.2016.

11. Hindi Version will follow.

Sd/-

(Manoj Sinha)

Under Secretary to the Government of India

Chapter-31

Provisions of the 7th Central Pay Commission

31.1

Government of India, Ministry of Defence, Department of Ex-Servicemen Welfare Letter No 17(01)/2016-D (Pen/Pol) dated 29th October 2016

Sub: Implementation of Government's decisions on the recommendations of the Seventh Central pay Commission, Revision of pension of pre-2016 Defence Forces Pensioners/Family Pensioners.

Sir,

The undersigned is directed to state that in pursuance of Government's decision on the recommendations of 7th Central pay Commission, notified vide Government of India, Ministry of Defence Resolution No. 17(1)/2014/D (Pen/Policy) dated 30th September 2016 based on Ministry of Personnel, Public Grievances and Pension, Department of Pension & Pensioners' Welfare Office Resolution No. 38/37/2016-P&PW(A) dated 4th August 2016 and Office Memorandum F.No. 38/37/2016-P&PW(A)(ii) dated 4th August 2016, sanction of the President is hereby accorded to regulate the Pension/Family Pension of all Pre-1.1.2016 pensioners/family pensioners of the Defence Forces with effect from 1.1.2016 in the manner indicated in succeeding Paragraphs. Separate Orders will be issued by this Ministry in respect of Defence Forces Personnel who retired/died on or after 1.1.2016 and for revision of disability element in respect of pre-2016 Defence pensioners.

2. **Applicability**

These orders shall apply to all Defence Forces pensioners/family pensioners who were drawing pension/family pension as on 1.1.2016 under the Pension Regulations of the three Services/State Forces and various Government order issued from time to time.

3. **Non-Applicability**

The provisions of this letter do not apply to the following categories.

i. Gallantry awardees drawing only monetary allowance attached to the award, such as ParamVir Chakra, Ashok Chakra etc.

ii. United Kingdom/Hong Kong & Singapore Royal Army (UK/HKSRA) Pensioners.

iii. Persons in receipt of compassionate allowance, Guzara, Reservist allowance or any other Allowance on which dearness relief is not admissible.

iv. Reservists in receipt of Ex-gratia payment at Rs 750/- per month covered under Govt. of India, Ministry of Defence letter No 1(06)/2010-D(Pen/Policy) dated 22nd Nov 2013.

v. Families of the deceased Reservists in receipt of Ex-gratia pension at Rs 645/- per month covered by Govt. of India, Ministry of Defence letter No 1(06)/2010-D(Pen/Policy) dated 22nd Nov 2013.

4. **Definitions**

a. **"Existing Pensioner" or "Existing Family Pensioner"** means a pensioner who was entitled to/drawing pension/family pension on 31.12.2015. This will also include a pensioner/family pensioner who became entitled to pension/family pension with effect from 1.1.2006 consequent upon retirement/discharge/death of Defence Forces Personnel on 31.12.2015. For the purpose of family pension, it also covers members of family to those who retired/discharged prior to 1.1.2016 and in whose case family pension had not commenced as the pensioner was alive on 31.12.2005.

b. **"Existing Pension"** means the basic pension inclusive of commuted portion of pension of any, due on 31.12.2015 and covers all kinds of pension viz Retirement/Service/Special/Reservist/Invalid pension/ Service element of Disability/Liberalized Disability Pension/War Injury Pension. This will also include Pension/Family Pension, which became due with effect from 1.1.2006 consequent on retirement/discharge/ death of Defence Force Personnel on 31.12.2015.

c. **"Existing Family Pension"** means the basic family pension drawn on 31.12.2015 under the Pension Regulations of the three Service/State Forces and other orders issued on the subject from time to time. It also covers Special Family Pension/Dependent Pension/2nd Life award of Special Family Pension and Liberalized Family Pension sanctioned in battle and non-battle casualty cases.

d. **"Pension Disbursing Agency"** (PDA) means Treasury, Post Office, Pay and Accounts Office, Defence Pension Disbursement Office (DPDO), Indian Embassy, Nepal and authorized Public Sector/Private Sector Banks.

e. **"Pension Sanctioning Authority"** (PSA) means PCDA (Pensions) Allahabad, PCDA (Navy) Mumbai, and PCDA AF) Delhi, as the case may be.

5. **Revision of Pension**

5.1 For existing pensioners, who have retired/died before 01.01.2016, the revised pension/family pension with effect from 01.01.2016 shall be determined by multiplying the Basic Pension (before commutation)/Basic Family Pension (exclusive of Dearness Relief) as had been drawn as on 31.12.2015 by 2.57 to arrive at revised pension under 7th CPC. The amount of revised pension/family pension so arrived at shall be rounded off to next higher rupee. The Disability Element will be regulated as per Para 9. Illustrations for revision of pension are annexed in Annexure-A attached to this letter.

5.2 For this purpose, the existing Pension/Family Pension will be the Basic Pension (before commutation)/Basic Family Pension only without the element of Additional Pension (referred to at Para 12) available to the old pensioners/family pensioners of the age of 80 years and above. The Additional Pension/Family Pension payable to the old pensioners/ family pensioners will be worked out in accordance with Para 12 of this order.

5.3 since the revised pension will be inclusive of commuted portion of pension, if any, the commuted portion will be deducted from the said amount while making monthly disbursements.

5.4 **Minimum and Maximum Pension:**

The minimum basic pension with effect from 01.01.2016 will be Rs 9,000/- per month (excluding the element of additional pension admissible to old pensioners). The upper ceiling of pension/family pension will be 50% and 30% respectively of the highest pay in the Government (The highest pay in the Government is Rs 2,50,000/- with effect from 01.01.2016).

5.5 The revised Pension/Family Pension in terms of Paragraph 5.1 includes dearness relief sanctioned from time to time by the Government.

6. Where the revised Pension/Family Pension in terms of Paragraph 5.1 above works out to an amount less than Rs 9,000/-, the same shall be stepped up to Rs 9000/-. This will be regarded as Pension/Family Pension with effect from 1.1.2016.

7. The existing instructions regarding regulation of Dearness Relief to employed/re-employed pensioners/family pensioners, as contained in Department of pension & Pensioner's Welfare O.M. No 45/73/97-P&PW(G) dated 02.07.1999 and as amended from time to time, shall continue to apply.

8. **Applicability to Permanent absorbees in PSUs/Autonomous Bodies**: Pension of a Defence Forces Personnel who has been permanently absorbed in Public Sector Undertaking/autonomous Body will be regulated as under:

8.1 **Pension:** Where the Defence Force Personnel on permanent absorption in Public Sector Undertaking/ Autonomous Body continues to draw pension separately from the Government, the pension of such absorbees will be revised in terms of these orders. In cases, where the Defence Forces Personnel has drawn one time lump-sum terminal benefits equal to 100% commutation of the pension and has become entitled to the restoration of 43%/45% commuted portion of pension as per the orders issued by this Ministry from time to time, such cases will not be covered by these orders. Orders for regulating pension of such pensioners will be issued separately.

8.2 **Family Pension:** In cases, where on permanent absorption in Public Sector Undertaking/Autonomous Bodies, the family pension is being drawn by the family of the PSU absorbee under the orders applicable to the Defence Forces, the same will be revised in accordance with these orders.

9. **Disability Element**

The implementation of 7th CPC recommendations relating to methodology for calculation of disability element has been referred to the Anomalies Committee. The disability element which was being paid to pre-2016 Defence Pensioners as on 31.12.2015 will continue to be paid till decision on the recommendations of anomalies Committee is taken by the Government.

10. Following elements will continue to be paid as separate elements in addition to the Pension/Family Pension revised under these orders. These payments will not be taken into account for the purpose of revision as well as for applicability with regard to the minimum limit of Pension/family Pension i.e. Rs 9,000/- per month.

i. Monetary allowance attached to Gallantry Awards such as Param Vir Chakra, Ashok Chakra etc.

ii. Constant Attendant Allowance (CAA)- Matter to be examined by Committee comprising Finance Secretary and Secretary (Expenditure) as Chairman and Secretaries of Home Affairs, Defence, Posts, Health & Family Welfare, Personnel & Training and Chairman Railway Board as members. Till a final decision is taken on the recommendations of the Committee, Constant Attendant Allowance shall be paid at the existing rates.

11. Where a pensioner is in receipt of Disability Liberalized Disability/War injury Pension, the minimum limit of Rs 9,000/- will be applicable to Service Pension/Service Element, Disability/War injury Element will be payable in addition to Service Pension/Service Element.

12. Additional Pension for Pensioners of age 80 years and above: The quantum of Additional Pension/Family Pension available to the old pensioners/family pensioners shall be as follows:

Age of Pensioner/family pensioner	**Additional quantum of Pension**
From 80 years to less than 85 years	20% of revised basic pension/family pension
From 85 years to less than 90 years	30% of revised basic pension/family pension
From 90 years to less than 95 years	40% of revised basic pension/family pension
From 95 years to less than 100 years	50% of revised basic pension/family pension
From 100 years or more	100% of revised basic pension/family pension

The amount of additional pension will be shown distinctly, For example, in case where a pensioner more than 80 years of age and his/her pension in terms of Para 5.1 above is Rs 10,000/-pm, the pension will be shown as (i) Basic pension-Rs 10,000 and (ii) Additional Pension – Rs 2,000 pm (20% of revised basic pension Rs 10,000). The pension on his/her attaining the age of 85 yrs will be shown as (i) Basic Pension – Rs 10,000 and (ii) additional pension – 3000 pm, (Note: The additional Pension will not be admissible on Disability Element/Liberalized Disability Element/War Injury Element of Disability/Liberalized Disability/War Injury Pension).

13. **Ex-gratia awards to Cadets in cases of disablement.**

The following ex-gratia award shall be payable subject to the same conditions as hitherto in force in the event of invalidment of a Cadet (Direct) on medical grounds due to causes attributable to or aggravated by military training:

i. Payment of monthly ex-gratia award of Rs 9,000/- per month;

ii. Payment of ex-gratia disability award @ Rs 16,200/- per month for 100% disability during the period of disablement. The amount will be reduced proportionately from the ex-gratia disability award in case the degree of disablement is less than 100%.

14. **Dearness Relief**

The revised Pension/Family Pension as worked out in accordance with provisions of Para 5.1 read with Para 6 and additional pension wherever payable under Para 12 above shall be treated as "Basic pension" with effect from 1.1.2016 for the purpose of calculation of dearness Relief sanctioned thereafter by the Government.

15. **Revision of Pension for employed/re-employed pensioners**

The revision of pension in respect of employed/re-employed Commissioned Officer and Personnel Below Officer Rank pensioners will also be carried out as per methodology provided in Para 5.1 i.e. their Basic Pension as on 31.12.2015 will be multiplied by 2.57 to arrive at revised Pension as on 01.01.2016. The revised pension so arrived at will be the Basic Pension with effect from 1.1.2016. However, Dearness Relief beyond 1.1.2016 will not be admissible to employed/re-employed Commissioned Officer pensioners and Personnel Below Officer Ranks pensioners, whose pay on re-employment has been fixed above the minimum of scale of pay of the re-employed post during the period of employment/re-employment.

16. **Methodology for Implementation and Reporting**

16.1 All Pension Disbursing Agencies handling disbursement of pension to the Defence Pensioners are hereby authorized to pay pension/family pension to existing pensioners/family pensioners at the revised rates in terms of Para 5.1 above without any further authorization from the concerned Pension Sanctioning authorities.

16.2 It is considered desirable that the benefit of these orders should reach the pensioners as expeditiously as possible. To achieve this objective, it is directed that all Pension Disbursing Agencies should ensure that the revised pension and the arrears due to the pensioners in terms of Para 5.1 above is paid to the pensioners or credited to their account in one Installment within two months from the date of issue of the letter.

16.3 A suitable entry regarding revised pension with effect from 1.1.2016 fixed in terms of Para 5.1 above, as the case may be, will be recorded by the pension disbursing Agencies in the Pension records of the pensioners viz, Pension Payment Order, Check Register/Pension Payment Scroll Register. An intimation regarding disbursement of revised pension may be sent by the Pension Disbursing Agencies to the Office of PCDA (P) Allahabad in prescribed Annexure to these orders so that records can be updated. A had copy of the said **Annexure-B** may invariably be provided by the PDAs to the pensioners concerned for their information. An acknowledgement shall be obtained by the Pension Disbursing Agencies from Office of PCDA (Pension) Allahabad in token of receipt of the requisite Annexure.

Miscellaneous Instructions

17. If a pensioner/family pensioner to whom benefit accrues under the provisions of the order, has already died before receiving the payment of arrears, the LTA will be disbursed in the following manner:

i. If the claimant is already in receipt of Family Pension or happens to be the person in whose favour Family Pension already stands notified and the awardees has not become ineligible for any reason, the LTA under the provisions of this letter should be paid to such a claimant by the PDAs on their own.

ii. If the claimant has already received LTA in the past in respect of the deceased to whom the benefit would have accrued. The LTA under the provisions of this letter should also be paid to such a claimant by the PDAs on their own.

iii. If the claimant is a person other than the one mentioned at (i) and (ii) above, LTA will be paid to the legal heir/heirs as per extant Government Orders.

18. No commutation will be admissible for the revised pension accruing as a result of this revision. The existing amount of pension commuted, if any, would continue to be deducted from the revised pension while making monthly disbursements.

19. Revision of Pension/Family Pension under these orders will not affect the amount of Retirement Gratuity/ Death Gratuity already determined and paid to the pensioners/family pensioners with reference to rules in force at the time of discharge/death.

20. Any overpayment of pension coming to the notice or under process of recovery shall be adjusted in full by the Pension Disbursing Agencies against arrears becoming due on revision of pension on the basis of these orders.

21. The revision of pension/family pension of Defence pensioners arrived in the above manner shall be subject to the findings and recommendation of the committee set up with the approval of the Cabinet to examine the feasibility of increment based formulation recommendation of 7th CPC for revision of pension and decision of the Government thereon if any.

22. These orders issue with the concurrence of Finance Division of this Ministry vide their ID No 10(6A)/2016/FIN/PEN dated 29.10.2016.

Sd/-

(Manoj Sinha)

Under Secretary to the Government of India

31.2

Government of India, Ministry of Defence, Department of Ex-Servicemen Welfare Letter No 17(02)/2016-D (Pen/Pol) dated 4th September 2017

Sub: **Implementation of the Government decision on the recommendations of the Seventh Central pay Commission- Revision of Provisions regulating Pension/Gratuity/Commutation of Pension/ Family Pension including pensionary awards notified in terms of casualty pensionary awards in respect of Commissioned Officers, Junior Commissioned Officers & Other Ranks, Retiring or dying in harness on or after 1.1.2016.**

Sir,

The undersigned is directed to refer to the Government's decisions on the recommendations of the Seventh Central pay Commission notified vide Government of India, Ministry of Defence, Department of Ex-Servicemen Welfare Resolution bearing No 17(1)/2014/D(Pension/Policy) dated 30.9.2016, recommendations of National anomaly committee on methodology for calculation of disability element for Defence Forces and Ministry of Personnel, Public Grievances and Pension, Department of Pension and Pensioners' Welfare Office Memorandum No 38/37/2016-P&PW(A) (I) dated 4.8.2016 as modified vide OM F No 42/14/2016-P&PW (G) dated 24.10.2016. Sanction of the President is hereby accorded for modification in the rules regulating Pension, Family Pension, Retirement/Death/Service Gratuity, Commutation of pension, pensionary awards under casualty pensionary awards including Ex-gratia lump sum compensation in cases of invalidment, etc, to the extent specified in this letter.

2. The provisions of the Pension Regulations, 2008 of Army and various Services Regulations, Instructions and Government Orders issued by this Ministry from time to time, which are not affected by the provisions of this letter, shall remain unchanged.

3. **DATE OF EFFECT**

3.1 The revised provisions of this letter shall apply to the Commissioned Officers including MNS and Territorial Army Officers), junior Commissioned Officers and other ranks of the three services, Non-combatants (Enrolled) in the Air Force, Defence Security Corps and the Territorial Army (hereinafter collectively referred to as Armed Forces Personnel) who retired/discharged/released/invalided out or died in harness on or after 1.1.2016. Separate orders have already been issued in respect of Armed forces Personnel who retired/died before 1.1.2016.

3.2 Where Pension/Family Pension/Death Gratuity/Retirement Gratuity/Commuted Value of Pension or pensionary awards under casualty pensionary awards has already been sanctioned provisionally, or otherwise, in cases of retirement/death occurring on or after 1.1.2016, the same shall be revised in terms of these orders. In cases where pension has been finally sanctioned under the pre-revised orders and if it happens to be more beneficial than the pension becoming due under these orders, the pension already sanctioned shall not be revised to the disadvantage of pensioner.

4. **RECKONABLE EMOLUMENTS**

4.1.1 Commissioned Officers: Pay in the Pay Matrix, Military Service Pay and Non Practicing allowance, if any, last drawn by the officer (Refer-Army Officer Pay Rule 2017, Air Force Officer Pay Rules-2107, Navy Pay Regulations-2017 as may be the case).

4.1.2 Junior Commissioned Officers & Other Ranks; Pay in the Pay Matrix, Military Service Pay, and 'X' Group Pay & Classification Allowance, if any last drawn by the JCOs/OR (Refer – Army Pay Rules-2017, Air Force Pay Rules-2107, Navy Pay Regulations-2017 as may be the case).

4.2 For calculation of all kinds of gratuities, dearness allowance admissible on the date of retirement/discharge/invalided out/death, shall continue to be treated as part of emoluments along with the emoluments as defined in Para 4.1 above.

4.3 SPECIAL PROVISIONS FOR THOSE WHO OPTED TO CONTINUE TO DRAW PAY IN THE PRE-REVISED SCALE OF PAY

4.3.1 Those who have elected to continue to draw pay in the pre-revised scale of pay and have retired/discharged/invalided out of service on or after 1.1.2016, their pension and gratuity, as applicable, shall be calculated under the rules in force immediately before coming into effect of these orders.

4.3.2 The term 'Reckonable Emoluments' for the purpose of pensionary benefits under this Para 4.3.1 shall be the same as defined in Para 3.1 of this Ministry's letter No 17(4)/2008(2)/D (Pen/Pol) dated 12.11.2008 and shall also include Dearness Allowance notified under Sixth CPC Pay structure.

4.3.3 Entitlement of gratuity shall be determined under the order in force immediately before coming into effect of these orders subject to the maximum ceiling as prescribed in Para 8 of this Ministry's letter No 17(4)/2008(2)/D (Pen/Pol) dated 12.11.2008.

4.3.4 Family Pension shall also be allowed in accordance with orders applicable prior to the issue of these orders.

4.4 In the case of Commissioned Officers and JCOs/ORs who have opted for the revised pay structure and have retired/discharged within 10 months from the date of coming over to the revised pay structure, the average emoluments for 10 months period preceding retirement/discharge will be calculated by taking into account pay as follows:

(a) For the period during which pay is drawn in the revised pay structure	Pay drawn in the prescribed Pay Matrix plus Military Service Pay, 'X' Group pay and whole of Classification Allowance (where applicable in case of JCOs/ORs) and Non Practicing Allowance, if any.
(b) For the period during which pay was drawn in the pre-revised pay scales	Pay determined after applying multiplying factor of 2.57 to the sum of existing pay in the Pay Band, Grade pay, Military service Pay, 'X' Group Pay (in case of JCOs/OR) and NPA, if any, drawn during the relevant period plus whole of classification allowance, if any, drawn by JCOs/ORs.

5. **QUALIFYING SERVICE**

5.1 The minimum period of qualifying service prescribed for earning various kind of pension and gratuity by Defence Forces Personnel, shall continue as hithertofore. There shall also be no change in the provisions for determining reckonable qualifying service for calculating pension and gratuity.

6. **PENSION**

6.1 Subject to Para 6.2, there shall be no change in the provisions regulating the amount of pensions including pension determined under casualty pensionary awards. However, the provisions for determining pension based on notional maximum of pre-revised pay scale in respect of JCOs/ORs, shall be discontinued.

6.2 The amount of pension shall be subject to a minimum of Rs 9,000/- and the maximum pension would be 50% of highest pay in the Government (the highest pay in the Government is Rs 2,50,000/- with effect from 1.1.2016). However, the maximum ceiling shall be applicable only in the case of Service/Retiring Pension, Service element of

Disability/Liberalized disability/War Injury Pension and Ordinary Family Pension. The said ceiling is not applicable in the cases of Disability/Liberalized Disability/War Injury element, being authorized under casualty pensionary awards.

6.3 The quantum of additional pension/family pension available to the old pensioners/family pensioners shall be continue to be as follows -

Age of Pensioner/Family Pensioner	Additional quantum of Pension
From 80 years to less than 85 years	20% of revised basic pension/family pension
From 85 years to less than 90 years	30% of revised basic pension/family pension
From 90 years to less than 95 years	40% of revised basic pension/family pension
From 95 years to less than 100 years	50% of revised basic pension/family pension
From 100 years or more	100% of revised basic pension/family pension

The Pension Sanctioning Authorities should ensure that the date of birth and the age of a pensioners/family pensioner, are invariably indicated in the Pension Payment Order to facilitate payment of additional pension by the Pension Disbursing Agencies as soon as it becomes due. Dearness relief shall also be admissible on the additional pension available to old pensioners/family pensioners.

Note: The additional pension payable to old pensioners/family pensioners of 80 years of age and above shall also be applicable to old pensioners/family pensioners of 80 years of age and above in receipt of War Injury Pension/ Disability Pension/Liberalized Family Pension/Special Family Pension.

7. GRATUITY

7.1 The maximum limit of all kinds of Gratuity i.e. Retiring/Retirement/Service/Invalid/Special/Terminal/Death Gratuity shall be Rs 20 lakhs. The ceiling on gratuity shall be increased b 25% whenever the Dearness Allowance rises by 50% of the basic pay.

7.2 DEATH GRATUITY

The rates for payment of death gratuity shall be as under:

Length of qualifying service	Rate of Death Gratuity
Less than One year	2 times of monthly emoluments
One year or more but less than 5 years	6 times of monthly emoluments
5 years or more but less than 11 years	12 times of monthly emoluments
11 years or more but less than 20 years	20 times of monthly emoluments
20 years or more	Half month's emoluments for every six monthly period of qualifying service subject to a maximum of 33 times of emoluments

8. FAMILY PENSION

8.1 Subject to Para 8.2, there shall be no change in the provisions regulating the amount of various kinds of family pensions including family pension determined under casualty pensionary awards and additional family pension applicable to old family pensioners.

8.2 The amount of all kind of family pension shall be subject to a minimum of Rs 9,000/-. The maximum amount of normal rate and enhanced rate of ordinary family pension shall be 30% and 50% respectively of highest pay in the Government which is Rs 2,50,000/- with effect from 1.1.2016. The maximum ceiling is, however, not applicable in the case of Special Family/Liberalized Family Pension, etc, applicable under casualty pensionary awards.

8.3 The dependency criteria for the purpose of family pension shall continue to be the minimum family pension along with Dearness Relief thereon.

9. **EX-GRATIA LUMPSUM COMPENSATION IN CASES OF INVALIDMENT**

9.1 The Ex-gratia lump sum compensation of Defence Service personnel who are boarded out of service on account of disability/war injury attributable to or aggravated by military service, shall be paid @ Rs 20 lakh for 100% disability subject to provisions as stipulated in this Ministry's letter No 2(2)/2011/D (Pen/Pol) dated 26.12.2011. For disability/war injury less than 100% but not less than 20%, the amount of Ex-gratia compensation shall be proportionately reduced. No Ex-gratia lump sum compensation shall be payable for disability/war injury less than 20%. The proportionate compensation would be based on actual percentage of disability as certified by the Invaliding Medical Board, without applying broad banding provisions as contained in Para 7.2 of this Ministry's letter No 1(2)/97/D(Pen-C) dated 31.01.2001.

10. **BROAD-BANDING OF PERCENTAGE OF DISABILITY/WAR INJURY ON DISCHARGE**

10.1 Where an Armed Forces personnel is discharged/retired under the circumstances mentioned in Para 4.1 of this Ministry's letter No 1(2)/97/D(Pen-C) dated 31.1.2001 with disability including cases covered under this Ministry's letter No 15(5)/2008/D(Pen/Policy) dated 29.9.2009 and the disability/war injury has been accepted as 20% and more, the extent of disability or functional incapacity shall be determined in the manner prescribed in Para 7.2 of said letter dated 31.1.2001 for the purpose of computing disability/war injury.

10.2 Rates for calculation of disability where composite assessment is made due to existence of disability, as well as war injury, shall be determined in terms of provision contained in Para 3 (b) of Ministry's letter No 16(02)/2015-D(Pen/Pol) dated 8th August 2016.

11. **EX GRATIA AWARDS TO CADET (DIRECT)**

11.1 In cases of disablement/death, following Ex-gratia award shall be payable subject to the same conditions as hitherto in force in the event of invalidment on medical grounds/death of a Cadet (direct) due to causes attributable to or aggravated by military training-

11.1.1 Monthly Ex-gratia amount of Rs 9,000/- per month.

11.1.2 In cases of disablement, Ex-gratia disability award @ Rs 16,200/- per month shall be payable in addition for 100% of disability during period of disablement subject to prorata reduction in case the degree of disablement is less than 100%. No disability award shall be payable in cases where the degree of disablement is less than 20%.

11.1.3 In cases of death, Ex-gratia amount of Rs 12.5 lakhs.

11.1.4 The Ex-gratia awards to Cadets (direct)/NoK, shall be sanctioned purely on ex-gratia basis and the same shall not be treated as pension for any purpose. However, dearness relief at applicable rates shall be granted on monthly ex-gratia as well as ex-gratia disability award.

12. CONSTANT ATTENDANT ALLOWANCE (CAA)

12.1 Constant Attendant Allowance shall continue to be admissible under the condition as hithertofore at the existing rate from 1.1.2016 to 30.06.2017. However, it shall be admissible at the uniform rate of Rs 6750/- per month, irrespective of the rank with effect from 1.7.2017.

13. COMMUTATION OF PENSION

13.1 There shall be no change in the provisions relating to commutation values, the limit upto that the pension can be commuted or the period after which the commuted pension is to be restored.

13.2 The pensioners who have retired between 1.1.2016 and date of issue of orders for revised pay/pension based on the recommendations of the 7th CPC, shall have an option, in relaxation of provisions of relevant Pension Regulations, not to commute the pension which has become additionally commutable on retrospective revision of pay/pension on implementation of recommendations of the 7th CPC. Option form to be used for this purpose shall be prescribed by the PCDA (Pension) Allahabad along with their implementation instructions.

13.3 The option may be invited only from those who want to commute their pension which has become additionally commutable as per Para 13.2 above and no commutation shall be allowed as a default. In such cases, RO/HOO/PSAs will finalize the cases without waiting for option for commutation of additional pension and such option, if any, received later on 9 within four months from the date of issue of this letter may be processed separately for additional commutation. Option for additional commutation on the basis of revised pension once exercised would be final and in no case it would be entertained at a later stage. Service Hqrs may be deputed as Nodal agencies to carry out such exercise with the respective ROs for the speedy implementation of work and forward such cases to PSAs.

GENERAL INSTRUCTIONS

14. The amount of various pensionary awards admissible tin terms of this order, shall be rounded off to the next higher rupee by the Pension Sanctioning authorities.

15. If the amount of any monthly pension/family pension admissible under the provisions of this letter works out to be less than Rs 9,000/- per month, it shall be stepped up to Rs 9,000/- per month and authorized for payment at this rate.

16. The pension/family pension notified in terms of these orders from 1.1.2016 or thereafter, shall qualify for dearness relief sanctioned by the Government from time to time in accordance with the relevant rules/instructions.

PROCEDURE FOR SANCTION OF REVISED PENSION TO THOSE WHO HAVE ALREADY RETIRED

17. For revision of pensionary wards as per provisions of this letter in respect of Armed Forces personnel who have already retired/discharged/invalided out/died on or after 1.1.2016 and in whose cases, pensionary benefits at pre-revised rates have already been notified, the Records Offices concerned in case of JCOs/OR and PCDA(O) Pune/ Naval Pay Office Mumbai/AFCAO, New Delhi, as the case may be, in respect of commissioned officers, will initiate and forward revised LPC-Cum-Data Sheet as prescribed by PCDA (Pensions), Allahabad, to their respective Pension Sanctioning Authorities (PSAs) for issue of Corrigendum PPOs notifying the revised pensionary awards. Further, implementation instructions to all concerned, shall be issued by PCDA (Pension), Allahabad immediately on receipt of these orders.

18. Pension Regulations of the three Services, shall be amended in due course.

19. This issues with the concurrence of Finance Division of this Ministry vide their ID No 10(03)/2017/Fin/Pen dated 30.08.2017.

Sd/-

(Manoj Sinha)

Under Secretary to the Government of India

31.3

Government of India, Ministry of Defence, Department of Ex-Servicemen Welfare Letter No 17 (01)/2017(2)D (Pen/Policy) dated 17th October 2018

Sub: **Revision of Pension of pre-2016 pensioners/family pensioners in implementation of Government's decision on the recommendations of the 7th Central Pay Commission Concordance tables-regarding.**

The undersigned is directed to convey that instructions were issued for revision of Pension/Family Pension with effect from 1.1.2016 in respect of Armed Forces Pensioners/family pensioners who retired/died prior to 1.1.2016 vide this Ministry's letter No 17(1)/2017/(02)/D(Pension/Policy) dated 5.9.2017. As per the same, revision of pension for pre-2016 Armed Force pensioners/family pensioners under first formulation, was to be done by notionally fixing their pay in the pay matrix recommended by the 7th Central Pay Commission in the level corresponding to the pay in the pay scale/pay band and grade pay at which they retired/died. The notional pay fixation in 7th CPC pay matrix has to be arrived by fixing pay under each intervening Pay Commission based on the formula for revision of pay. The revised rates of Military Service pay, Non Practicing allowance, where applicable, and "X" Group pay & Classification allowance for JCO/ORs, if applicable, notified in terms of 7th CPC orders, shall also be added to the amount of pay notionally arrived at under the 7th CPC pay matrix and shall be termed as notional reckonable emolument as on 1.1.2016 for determining the revised pension/Family Pension in terms of Para 5 of this Ministry's letter dated 5.9.2017.

2. Based on past instructions on fixation of pay in various pay commissions, concordance tables for fixation of notional pay for Armed Force Personnel who retired/died in various ranks during the 4th, 5th and 6th Pay Commission periods (including 3rd Pay Commission for Sailors only) have been prepared and the same are enclosed herewith. In the case of commissioned officers who retired/died in harness before 1.1.1986, these concordance tables may be used based on their notional pay as on 1.1.1986, which was fixed in accordance with this Ministry's letter No 1(3)/98/D (Pen/Policy) dated 27.5.1998. Concordance tables for JCO/ORs who were discharged/died in service prior to 1.1.1986 (prior to 1.1.1973 for Sailors), are under preparation and shall be issued separately.

3. These concordance tables have been prepared to facilitate fixation of notional pay of pre-2016 pensioners/family pensioners by the concerned Record Offices and attached Pay Account Offices in case of JCO/ORs of the three services and PCDA (O), Pune/Naval Pay Office Mumbai/AFCAO New Delhi in case of commissioned officers of Army/Navy/ Air Force respectively. Due care has been taken to prepare these concordance tables based on the fitment tables for fixation of pay from 3rd to 4th (only for Sailors), 4th to 5th to 6" and 6th to 7th Pay Commission. In case of any inconsistency in the concordance tables vis-a-vis the relevant rules/instructions, the notional pay and Pension/Family Pension of pre-2016 pensioners/family pensioners may be fixed in accordance with the rules/instructions applicable for fixation of pay in the intervening Pay Commission periods.

4. The Pension/Family Pension of pre-2016 Armed Forces pensioners/family pensioners may be revised using the appropriate concordance table in accordance with the instructions contained in this Ministry's above quoted letter dated 5.9.2017

5. This issues with the concurrence of Ministry of Defence (Finance Pension) vide their UO No. Part File 1 to 30(01)/2016/fin/Pen dated 27.09.2018.

6. Hindi Version will follow.

Yours faithfully
Sd/-
(Manoj Sinha)
Under Secretary to the Government of India

Chapter-32

Provisions Concerning One Rank One Pension and Other Enhancements

32.1

Government of India, Ministry of Defence Letter No14(3)2004-D (Pen/Sers)/ Vol. III dated 1st February 2006

Sub: Improvement in the pension of Personnel Below Officer Rank (PBOR).

Sir,

I am directed to state that the ex-servicemen have been demanding since long same pension for the same rank and length of service irrespective of date of retirement, popularly known as 'one rank one pension'. A Group of Ministers (GOM) was constituted by the Government in January, 2005 to look into the issue. After detailed deliberations on various aspects, GOM felt that while the demand for 'one rank one pension' cannot be agreed to, there is a justification for improving the pensionary benefits of the PBOR, particularly the three lowest ranks.

2. Finally, GOM unanimously recommended that the pension of pre-1.1.1996 retiree PBOR may be revised with references to the maximum of post 1.1.1996 pay scales. In addition, the weightage of Sepoy, Naik and Havildar ranks for past as well as future retirees be increased to 10, 8 and 6 years respectively subject to the maximum qualifying service of 30 years. The benefit would be given only in respect of service pension.

3. The above recommendations of the GOM have been accepted by the Government. Sanction of the President is hereby accorded to the modification to the extent specified in this letter in the relevant Rules/Regulations/instructions concerning pensionary benefits of the PBOR.

4. After para 5 (b) (I) of this Ministry letter No. 1(6)/98/D (Pension/Services) dated 3.2.1998 relating to weightage for the purpose of calculation of pension, a para (c) is added as follows:

> *(c) With effect from 1.1.2006, the weightage for the purpose of calculations of pension for past well as future retires PBOR of Sepoy, Naik and Havildar ranks will be follows:

Rank (Army)	Rank (Navy)	Rank (Air Force)	Weightage (In years)
PBOR inculding NCs(E)	Equivalents Ranks	Equivalents Ranks	
Sepoy	-do-	-do-	10
Naik	-do-	-do-	8
Havildar	-do-	-do-	6

> * subject to a maximum qualifying service of 30 years. However, in case a person is already getting more than 30 years qualifying service with the existing weightage of 5 years, he would continue getting that and there will be no enhancement of weightage in his case. The pension of past retirees would be recalculated accordingly.

5. The following is added after Para 2.2 (a) of this Ministry's letter No. 1(1)/99/D (Pen/Services) Dated 7.6.1999 relating to revision of pension of post and pre-1.1.1996:

> "with effect from 1.1.2006, pension of pre 1.1.1996 retires in all ranks of PBOR in Army, Navy and Air Force for 33 years of qualifying service shall not be less than 50% of the maximum pay in the revised scales of pay introduced with effect from 1.1.1996 including 50% of Highest classification allowance, if any, of the rank and group held continuously for 10 months preceding retirement subject to a minimum pension of Rs 1913/- per month. Such pension shall be reduced prorata where the pensioner has less than the maximum qualifying service for full pension, that is 33 years"

6. The provision of para 2 of the Ministry's letter No. B/39013/AG/PS-49(a&c)/131/A/D (Pension/services) dated 9.2.2001 read with corrigendum dated 22.2.2001 will stand amended with effect from 1.1.2006 to the above extent.

7. All other terms and conditions of this Ministry's letters mentioned on Para 4,5 and 6 above remain unchanged.

8. The above benefit would be only in respect of service pension including invalid pension, service element of disability pension and war injury pension.

9. These orders are effective from 1.1.2006. No arrears are to be given.

10. Pension Regulations of the three services will be amended in due course.

11. PCDA(P) will circulate to all concerned tables for revision of pension within a period of 4 weeks after getting the same vetted by this Ministry and Defence Finance.

12. This issues with the concurrence of the Finance Division of this Ministry vide their U.O. No. 279(F Pen)/06 Dated 1.2.2006.

Yours faithfully,
Sd/-
(A.K. Upadhyay)
Joint Secretary to the Government of India

32.2

Government of India, Ministry of Defence Letter No 14(3) 2004-D (Pen/Sers)/ Vol.V dated 2nd May 2006

Sub: Improvement in the pension of Personnel Below Officer Rank (PBOR)

Sir,

The undersigned is directed to invite reference to Para 11 of the Ministry's letter No. 14(3)/2004-D (Pen/Sers) Vol-III dated 1.2.2006 issued on the subject mentioned above and to say that the pension tables for revision of pension in terms of the orders issued under this Ministry's letter dated 1.2.2006 as prepared by the office of PCDA(P), Allahabad and vetted by CGDA, New Delhi have been approved by this Ministry in consultation with Defence Finance, enclosed of Appendix-A.

2. Approval of the Government is also hereby accorded to the following:

  i. While preparing the tables, certain anomalies arose, pension of higher ranks PBOR worked out to be less than of the lower rank. In such cases the shortfall in pension has been made up by protecting the pension of such higher rank by stepping up the pension to the level equal to that of the lower rank.

  ii. Where the revised pension as on 1.1.2006 of a pre 1.1.96 pensioner worked out with increased weightage subject to a maximum of 30 years qualifying service and in terms of the provisions of this Ministry's letter No. 1 (2)/97/D (Pen/Sers) dated 24.11.97 and No. 1(2)/98/D (Pen/Sers) dated 14.7.98 happens to be more than the revised pension indicated in the relevant columns of pension tables, the pensioners will get the pension which is more beneficial to him.

  iii. With effect from 1.1.2006, the amount of ad hoc ex-gratia will cease to be paid in respect of pre 1.1.1973 pensioners, since the same has lost its relevance in view of improved pensionary benefits bringing pensionary benefits of pre 1.1.1973 pensioners at par with post 1.1.1996.

  iv. The orders contained in this Ministry's above mentioned letter dated 1.2.2006 will also apply to non combatants (enrolled) (NC's (E)) drawing pension as on 1.1.2006 under the Pension Regulations of the three Services as well as pension rules of erstwhile state forces and various orders issued fromtime to time.

  v. The provisions of these orders, however, do not apply to Commissioned officers and their families and to all the family pensioners of PBOR. These orders also do not apply to UK/HKSRA/KCIOs pensions and Pakistan/ Burma pensioners.

  vi. The orders regarding increase in the weightage contained in this Ministry's above mentioned letter dated 1.2.2006 do not apply to TA pensioners. However, cases for revision of pension of pre-96 pensioners with reference tomaximum of pay scales as on 1.1.1996 will be referred to office of the PCDA(P) Allahabad in the prescribed proforma enclosed at Annexure-A for determining the revised pension taking into account reckonable emoluments, qualifying aggregate embodied service and maximum of the revised pay scales introduced with effect from 1.1.1996.

  vii. No commutation will be admissible on additional amount of pension accruing as a result of revision under these orders. However, the existing amount of pension commuted, if any, would continue to be deducted from the revised pension. In case of service personnel retiring on or after 1.1.2006, the benefit of commutation will however be admissible on the additional amount of pension as a result of these orders up to the existing limit.

viii. As a result of these orders, there will be no change in the amount of retirement gratuity already paid to the pensioners.

ix. An over payment of pension coming to the notice or under process of recovery, shall be adjusted in full by the pension disbursing authorities against arrears becoming due on revision of pension on the basis of these orders.

x. If a pensioner to whom the benefit under these accrues has died/dies before receiving the payment an account of arrears with effect from1.12006, the life time arrears (LTA) will be disposed off as per the extant orders contained in Paras 21.1 to 21.4 of this Ministry's letter no. 1 (2)/98/D (Pen/Sers) dated 14.7.98.

xi. Invalid pension/service element of disability pension in respect of PBOR retirees having less than 15 years qualifying service would also need to be revised in terms of these orders. Specific tables for the purpose have not been prepared for the reason that each of such cases will be unique one as rank, group and qualifying service will differ from case to case and hence on standard tables can be prepared. PDAs will refer such to PSAs concerned as per specimen letter enclosed at Annexure A. Similarly, revision of pension in all War Injury cases irrespective of the qualifying service will also required to be done by the PSAs concerned for the reason that the crucial information relating to last pay drawn and the maximum terms of engagement to the specific rank for which pension would need to be verified with reference to the original records held by the PSAs. Such cases will also be forwarded by the PDAs to the PSAs concerned in the above prescribed proforma enclosed at Annexure A.

xii. A progress report on revision of pension by the Public Sector Banks, ICICI Bank Ltd, HDFC Bank Ltd, UTI Bank Ltd. IDBI Bank Ltd (through their link Branch), State treasuries, Post Offices and Pension Paying Officers in Nepal will be sent by them to office of the PCDA(P), Allahabad on monthly basis till revision is carried out in all the affected cases, in the statement enclosed of Annexure –B and those by DPDOs to PCDA(P) Allahabad as well as their respective CDAs viz, CDA(PD) Meerut and CDA Chennai.

3. The Pension Disbursing Authorities (PDAs) may be authorized by PCDA(P) to carry out revision of pension with effect from 1.1.2006 in affected cases in the lights of these orders without calling for any applications from the pensioners and without any further authorization from concerned Pension Sanctioning Authorities (PSAs) and pay the arrears on account of such revision except in those cases, which are required to be referred to PSAs.

4. The pension revision may be completed by 30.9.2006

5. Detailed instructions for guidance of the PDAs for implementation of the orders will be issued by PCDA(P) Allahabad separately. Similarly, methodology adopted for preparation of tables along with sample calculations for the three lower ranks i.e. Sepoy, Naik and Havildar may be circulated to the PDA by PCDA(P), if considered necessary to facilitate revision of pension by the PDAs expeditiously.

6. The tables for revision of pension attached at Appendix-A will be circulated by PCDA(P) to all concerned including PDAs separately in a time boundmanner. They may get the requisite number of hard copies of the tables printed after following laid down procedure. However, efforts should be made to circulate the tables at the earliest. Case for Govt. sanction, if any required for the purpose may be taken up by CGDA with this Ministry immediately.

7. This issues with concurrence of MOD (Finance) vide their UO No. 772/Fin(P)/2006 dated 20.3.2006.

Yours faithfully,
Sd/-
(Harbans Singh)
Director (Pension)

32.3

Government of India, Ministry of Defence, Department Of Ex-Servicemen Welfare Letter No PC 10(1)/2009-D (Pen/Pol) dated 8th March 2010

Sub: **Implementation of the Government decision of the recommendations of the Cabinet Secretaries' Committee – Revision of pension in respect of Personnel Below Officer Rank (PBOR) discharged prior to 01.01.2006.**

Sir,

The undersigned is directed to state that in order to consider various issues on pension of Armed Forces pensioners, the Government had set up a Committee headed by the Cabinet Secretary. The Committee in its Report have recommended the following for pre-2016 PBOR pensioners –

1.1 Pre-10.10.1997 PBOR pensioners may be brought on par with post – 10.10.1997 PBOR pensioners; and

1.2 To reduce the gap between the pensions of pre & post-1.1.2006 PBOR pensioners, following principle may be followed –

1.2.1 Pension of all pre-1.1.2006 PBOR pensioners may be reckoned with reference to a notional maximum in the post – 1.1.2006 revised pay structure corresponding to the maximum of pre-sixth pay commission pay scales as per fitment table of each rank.

1.2.2 To continue with the enhanced weightages awarded by the Group of Ministers (GOM) of 2006.

2. The above recommendations of the Committee have been accepted by the Government and the President is pleased to decide that ***with effect from 1st July 2009***, service pension/special pension/invalid pension/service element of disability pension/special pension/invalid pension/service element of disability pension and service element of war injury/liberalized disability pension (in release cases only) or all pre-1.1.2006 PBOR pensioners of Army, Navy and Air Force (including DSC and TA) shall be reckoned at 50% of the notional pay in the post- 1.1.2006 revised pay structure corresponding to the maximum of pay scales applicable from 10.10.1997 of the rank and group continuously held for last 10 months preceding invalidment/discharge. The amount so determined shall be the pension for 33 years of reckonable qualifying service including rank weightage except for TA personnel) as provided under this Ministry's letter No 1(6)/98/D (Pension/services) dated 3.2.1998 and enhanced vide this Ministry's letter No 1493)/2008/ D(Pen/Sers)/Vol-III dated 1.2.2006. for lesser period of qualifying service, this amount shall be proportionately reduced. The amount of pension finally arrived at shall be subject to a minimum of Rs 3,500/- per month.

3. Following shall be taken into account of determining notional pay mentioned as at Para 2 above:

3.1 The notional pay in the revised pay structure corresponding to the maximum of pay scale applicable from 10.10.1997 for the rank and group, shall be determined as per the fitment tables attached to SAI 1/S/2008 and corresponding instructions for Navy & Air Force, for each rank and group and shall consist of pay in the pay band plus Grade pay plus "X" Group pay (where applicable) plus Military Service Pay plus 50% of the highest classification allowance (revised rates effective from 1.9.2008), if any, of the rank and group held continuously for 10 months preceding discharge.

3.2 In pre-2006 pay structure, since classification allowance was payable to Army Personnel only, the same shall not be reckoned while determining notional pay in respect of DSC, Navy and Air Force personnel.

3.3 Before arriving at the notional pay in the post-2006 revised pay structure in respect of pre-10.10.1997 retirees, the rank and group equivalent to post-10.10.1997 retirees corresponding to which one has retired shall be determined in terms of SAI 1/S/1998 and corresponding instructions for Navy and Air Force, for considering maximum of pay scales applicable with effect from 10.10.1997.

3.4 Notional pay in the revised pay structure in respect of PBOR granted pay of higher rank under Assured Career Progression (ACP) Scheme shall be determined with reference to the upgraded pay scales granted under ACP upgradation subject to condition that the upgraded pay scale was held continuously for 10 months preceding invalidment/discharge. The classification allowance shall be taken for the rank held and group in which paid.

Note –

In addition to revised service pension determined under these orders, Havildar who are granted Honorary rank of Naib Subedar on retirement, shall be allowed additional pension equal to Rs 226/-.

4. In terms of provisions contained in Para 10 & 12 of this Ministry's letter No 192)/97/D (Pen-C) dated 31.1.2001, service element of War-Injury pension/liberalized disability pension in respect of PBOR invalided out from service on or after 1.1.1996 has been computed with reference to emoluments drawn on the date of invalidment from service but counting service up to the date on which he would have retired in that rank in normal course including rank weightage. The said provision for calculation of service element of war injury pension was extended in respect of pre-1.1.1996 invalided out cases vide this Ministry's letter No 1(2)/98/D(Pen/Sers) dated 14.07.1998 in respect of PBOR invalided out of service prior to 1.1.1996, has been considered as emolument last drawn. In implementation of the recommendations of Cabinet Secretary Committee as at Para 1 above, the President is also pleased to decide that service element of war injury pension/liberalized disability pension in respect of PBOR invalided out of service prior to 1.1.2006 shall be reckoned as under:

4.1 The last pay of all those PBOR who were invalided out of service prior to 10.10.1997 and were in receipt of service element of war injury pension as on 1.7.2009, shall be fixed on a notional basis for the rank held by the PBOR at the time of his invalidment in the following manner:

4.1.1 In the case of PBOR who were invalided out prior to 1.1.1996, the notional pay fixed as on 1.1.1996 in terms of Para 12 of this Ministry's letter No. 1(2)/98/D (Pen/Sers) 14.7.98 shall be the basis for notional fixation of their pay as on 1.1.1996 and its further notional fixation as on 10.10.1997 (without, however, any benefit of notional increment) at the rate given to similar PBOR of the same rank and group after the revision of pay scale with effect from 1.1.1996 and 10.10.1997 under the provisions contained in SAI 1/S/1998 and corresponding instructions for equivalent ranks in Navy and Air Force.

4.1.2 In the case of PBOR who were invalided out during 1.1.1996 and 31.12.1995, the pay last drawn at the time of invalidment shall be adopted for notional fixation of their pay as on 1.1.1996 and its further fixation as on 10.10.1997 (without, however, any benefit of notional increment) at the rate given to similar, PBOR of the same rank and group after the revision of pay scale with effect from1.1.1996 and 10.10.1997 under above mentioned Services Instructions.

4.1.3 In the case of PBOR who were invalided out during 1.1.1996 and 9.10.1997, the pay last drawn at the time of invalidment shall be adopted for notional fixation of their pay as on 10.10.1997 (without, however, any benefit of notional increment) at the rate given to similar PBOR of the same rank and group after the revision of pay scale w.e.f. 10.10.1997 under above mentioned Service Instructions.

4.2 The notional emoluments last drawn in post 1.1.2006 revised pay structure corresponding to the notional pay determined as at 4.1 above in respect of PBOR invalided out of service prior to 10.10.1997 and corresponding to last pay drawn in case of PBOR invalided out of service after 10.10.1997 but before 31.12.2005, shall be determined in terms of the fitment tables attached to SAI 1/S/2008 and corresponding instructions for Navy & Air Force, for rank and group and shall consist of pay in the pay band plus Grade Pay Plus "X" Group pay (where applicable) plus Military Service Pay plus 50% of the highest classification allowance (revised rates effective from 1.9.2008), if any, of the rank and group held at the time of invalidment.

4.3 The service element of war injury pension/liberalized disability pension in respect of all PBOR invalided out of service prior to 1.1.2006 shall be notionally recomputed with effect from 1.7.2009 at 50% of the notional emoluments last drawn (determined as per 4.2 above) in the post 1.1.2006 revised pay structure with reference to the qualifying service already admitted in terms of Government orders issued in implementation of Fifth CPC recommendations. The amount so determined shall be the pension for 33 years of reckonable qualifying service including rank weightage (except for TA personnel) as provided under this Ministry's letter No 1(6)/98/D (Pension/Services) dated 3.2.1998 and enhanced vide this Ministry's letter No 14(3)/2008/D (Pen/Sers)/Vol-III dated 1.2.2006. For lesser period of qualifying service, this amount shall be proportionately reduced. The amount of pension finally arrived at shall be subject to a minimum of Rs 3,500/- permonth. The provisions as at Para 3.2 to 3.4 above along with note thereunder shall equally apply for determining the amount of service element of war injury pension.

NON APPLICABILITY

5.1 Prior to implementation of Government orders issued in implementation of Sixth CPC recommendations, pension of JCOs granted Honorary rank of Lieutenant and Captain was being determined at 50% of fixed pay of Rs 10,500/- and Rs 10,850/- respectively. With effect from 1.1.2006, pension of post 2006 retirees in these ranks is being determined at 50% of their pay in the Pay Band-3 plus Grade pay plus MSP. In case of pre-2006 retirees Honorary Lieutenant and Captain, their revised pension is being paid with reference to minimum of Pay Band-3 Plus Grade pay plus MSP introduced from 1.1.2006 in terms of provisions contained in Para 5 of this Ministry's letter No 17(4)/2008(1)/D(Pen/Policy) dated 11.11.2008. The same may be treated as final and no further revision shall be done in terms of these orders.

5.2 The provisions of this letter, also, do not apply to Commissioned Officers and their families and to all family pensioners of PBOR. These orders also do not apply to UK/HKSRA pensioners, Pakistan & Burma Army pensioners, reservist pensioners, pensioners in receipt of disability element only and pensioners in receipt of Ex-gratia payments.

6. The following elements shall continue to be paid as separate elements in addition to the pension revised under these orders-

6.1 Monetary allowance attached to gallantry awards viz, ParamVir Chakra, Ashok Chakra etc.,

6.2 Constant Attendance Allowance, where admissible.

7. Where the revised pension as on 1.7.2009 worked out in terms of these orders, happens to be less than the existing consolidated pension being paid w.e.f. from 1.1.2006 in terms of 6th CPC Government orders, the pension shall not be revised to the disadvantage of the pensioners.

MISCELLANEOUS INSTRUCTIONS

8. No arrears on account of revision of pension based on notional fixation of pay shall be admissible for the period prior to 1.7.2009.

9. No commutation of pension will be admissible on additional amount of pension accruing as a result of revision of pension under these orders. However, the existing amount of pension, if any, that has been commuted will continue to be deducted from the revised pension.

10. Notional fixation of pay in terms of these orders will not affect the entitlement of retirement gratuity already determined and paid with reference to rules in force at the time of discharge/invalidment.

11. Any overpayment of pension coming to the notice or under process of recovery shall be adjusted in full by the Pension Disbursing Agencies against arrears becoming due on revision of pension on the basis of these orders.

PAYMENT OF LIFE TIME ARREARS (LTA)

12. If a pensioner to whom the benefit accrues under the provisions of this letter has died/dies before receiving the payment of arrears, the Life Time Arrears of pension (LTA) shall be paid in the following manner:

12.1 If the claimant is already in receipt of Family Pension or happens to be the person in whose favour Family Pension already stands notified and the awardee has not become ineligible for any reasons, the LTA under the provisions of this letter should be paid to such a claimant by the PDA on their own.

12.2 If the claimant has already received LTA in the past in respect of the deceased to whom the benefit would have accrued, the LTA under the provisions of this letter should also be paid to such a claimant by the PDA on their own.

12.3 If the claimant is a person other than the one mentioned at 12.1 & 12.2 above, payment of LTA shall be made to the legal heir/heirs as per extant Government orders.

METHODOLOGY FOR IMPLEMENTATION

13.1 All Pension Disbursing Agencies handling disbursement of pension to Defence pensioners are hereby authorized to carry out revision of service pension/special pension/invalid pension/service element of disability pension with effect from 1.7.2009 to the affected pensioners drawing pension with 15 years or more qualifying service as on 1.7.2009 in terms of these orders with applicable rates of dearness relief without calling for any applications from the pensioners and without any further authorization from the concerned Pension Sanctioning Authorities and pay the arrears on account of such revision except in those casesmentioned at Para 14 below which are required to be referred to pension Sanctioning Authorities for issuance of corrigendum PPO indicating revised pension.

13.2 Keeping in view the above decision and to quicken the process of revision of service pension, special pension, invalid pension, service element of disability pension with 15 years or more qualifying service, specific tables (total 135) indicating revised pension payable with effect from 1.7.2009, have been prepared for PBOR of Regular Army, Navy, Air Force and DSC who were discharged/invalided out fromservice prior to 1.1.2006 and drawing pension as on 1.7.2009, and are enclosed as **Appendix** to this letter. The appended tables indicate the existing pension as per Fifth CPC orders, Improved rates of pension (with and without DP), Revised Consolidated pension under Sixth CPC Government orders and revised pension payable with effect from 1.7.2009. Pension Disbursing Agencies will revise the pension with reference to applicable Table for the rank and group in which the PBOR was pensioned with reference to the actual qualifying service as shown in Column-1 thereof as revised rate of pension indicated against each qualifying service is inclusive of rank weightage applicable for various ranks of PBOR. In addition, dearness relief sanction by the Government from time to time is also payable.

13.3 The initial Pension Payment Order (PPO) or its Corrigendum PPO (Corr PPO) indicates rank, group and qualifying service for which the individual has been pensioned. These information are available with Pension Disbursing Agencies as they have revised pension of all such pensioners in the recent past in terms of Government orders issued on improvement in pension and on Sixth CPC recommendations. In case, however, any information regarding qualifying service, rank, group, etc, is not available with Pension Disbursing Agencies, such cases may be referred to Pension Sanctioning Authority concerned on the Performa enclosed as **Annexure-A.** The Pension Sanctioning Authorities concerned will provide the requisite information from the available records within 30 days of the receipt of request from the Pension Disbursing Agencies.

CASES REQUIRING REVISION FROM PSAs

14.1 Pension of PBOR pensioners who are in receipt of Special Pension, Invalid Pension and service element of Disability Pension for less than 15 years of qualifying service would also need to be revised in terms of these orders. Specific Tables for the purpose have not been prepared for the reason that each of such cases will be unique one as rank, group and qualifying service will differ from case to case and, hence, standard tables cannot be prepared. Pension Disbursing Agencies shall refer such cases directly to the Pension Sanctioning Authorities concerned in the format enclosed as **Annexure-A** to this letter.

14.2 Specific tables for revision of pension in respect of pre-1.1.2006 Territorial Army pensioners have also not been prepared as Pension Disbursing Agencies could not revise such case due to non applicability of weightage in qualifying service and provision for reduction in pension in respect of TA pensioners who have completed 15 years or more but less than 20 years of aggregate embodied service. such cases may also be referred by Pension Disbursing Agencies directly to the Pension Sanctioning Authorities concerned in the format enclosed as **Annexure–A** to this letter.

14.3 Similarly, revision of service element of war injury pension/liberalized disability pension in all cases of PBOR irrespective of the qualifying service shall also required to be done by the Pension Sanctioning Authorities concerned for the reason that the crucial information relating to last pay drawn and the maximum terms of engagement to the specific rank for which pension would need to be verified with reference to the original records held by the Pension Sanctioning Authorities. Such cases shall also be forwarded by the Pension Disbursing Agencies to the Pension Sanctioning Authorities concerned through respective Record Office in the prescribed proforma enclosed as **Annexure-B** to this letter.

METHODOLOGY FOR REPORTING

15. An intimation regarding disbursement of revised pension shall be sent by the Pension Disbursing Agencies to the Office of PCDA (P) Allahabad on monthly basis in the format prescribed as **Annexure-C** to these orders. A copy of the said **Annexure-C** may Invariably be provided by the Pension Sanctioning Agencies to the pensioners concerned for their information. Those Public Sector Banks who are disbursing Defence Pension through Central Pension Processing Centers (CPPC), the monthly progress report may be furnished by the CPPC of the bank directly to the office of the PCDA (P) Pension Allahabad.

16. This issues with the concurrence of Finance Division of this Ministry vide their UO No 502/Fin/Pen/2010 dated 08.03.2010.

Yours faithfully,
Sd/-
(Harbans Singh)
Director (Pensions)

32.4

Government of India, Ministry of Defence, Department of Ex-Servicemen Welfare Letter No 1(15)/2012-D (Pen/Policy) dated 17th January 2013

Sub: Implementation of the Government's decision on the recommendations of Committee of Secretaries 2012 on the issues related to Defence Service Personnel and Ex-Servicemen Improvement in pension of JCO/OR retired/discharged/invalided out of service prior to 1.1.2006.

Sir,

The undersigned is directed to refer to the provisions contained in this Ministry's letter No 17(4)/08(2)/D(Pen/ Policy) dated 18.8.2010 which provide that Pension of all ranks of post-1.1.2006 JCO/OR retirees in Army, Navy and Air Force (including DSC and TA) should in no case be less than 50% of notional pay in the revised pay structure corresponding to the maximum of the Fifth CPC pay scales across the three Services. The amount of pension so determined has to be reduced pro-rata if the reckonable qualifying service including ranks weightage (except TA personnel) is less than service required to earn full pension. Further, in terms of provisions contained in Para 13 of this Ministry's letter No 1(6)/98/D (Pension/Services) dated 3.2.1998 read with MOD letter No 17(4)/2008(2)/D(Pen/Policy) dated 12/11/2008, the normal rate of Ordinary family pension of post-1.1.2006 JCO/OR is calculated at a uniform rate of 30% of reckonable emoluments last drawn. However, if an Armed Forces Personnel dies while in service or after retirement with a pension and had rendered a minimum of 7 years of continuous qualifying service, Ordinary family pension at enhanced rate of 50% of the reckonable emoluments last drawn is allowed for a prescribed initial period.

2. A committee of Secretaries headed by Cabinet Secretary was constituted by the Government to consider various issues on pension of Armed Forces Personnel and Ex-Servicemen, who have recommended to increase current weightage in qualifying service of Sepoy, Naik and Havildar by two years and also to establish a linkage in the rate of the family pension with the pension of JCO/OR. The above recommendation of the Committee has been accepted by the Government and the President is pleased to decide that the weightage for the purpose of calculation of Pension in terms of Para 2 of this Ministry's above said letter dated 18.8.2010 for the rank of Sepoy, Naik and Havildar will be taken as 12, 10 and 8 years respectively subject to a maximum qualifying service of 32 years. However, in case an individual's qualifying service works out to be more than 32 years with existing weightage, he would continue to get the benefit of that and there will be no enhancement of weightage in such cases.

2.1 In supersession of the provisions contained in this Ministry's letter No 17(4)/2008(2)/D (Pen/Policy) dated 20.9.2012, the President is also pleased to decide that provisions of this Ministry's letter dated 18.8.2010 shall also be applicable to post-1.1.2006 JCO/OR granted honorary Commission as Lieutenant and Captain. The notional pay in the revised pay structure for these ranks shall be worked out by adding pay in the revised pay band corresponding to the fixed pay of Fifth CPC (in terms of Para 9(a)(i) of SAI 1/S/2008 as amended and equivalent instructions for Navy & Air Force) plus the Grade pay and Military Service Pay introduced under Sixth CPC revised pay structure.

2.2 The other terms and conditions prescribed vide Para 2 & 3 of this Ministry's above said letter dated 18.8.2010 shall remain unchanged.

3. The President is also pleased to decide that the enhanced and normal rate of Ordinary family pension of post-1.1.2006 JCO/OR, determined in terms of Para 13 of this Ministry's above said letters dated 3.2.1998 read with letter dated 12.11.2008, shall in no case be less than 100% and 60% respectively of the pension determined in terms of this Ministry's *ibid* letter dated 18.8.2010 as modified vide this order subject to fulfillment of other prescribed conditions as hithertofore.

4. These orders shall take effect from 24.09.2012 and shall also cover cases of post-1.1.2006 retiree/death in service cases. The financial benefit in past cases shall, however, be granted from 24.09.2012 only.

5. The pension/family pension of all JCO/OR including honorary Commissioned Officers who retired/discharged/invalided out/died while in service on or after 1.1.2006, shall be re-calculated in terms of these orders by the Pension Sanctioning Authorities concerned. However, no commutation on enhanced pension in terms of these orders shall be allowed to the JCO/OR who retired/discharged/invalided out of service prior to date of implementation of this order. Necessary implementation instructions to all concerned shall be issued by Pr.CDA (Pension) Allahabad on receipt of these orders.

6. Pension Regulations of the three Services shall be amended in due course.

7. This issues with the concurrence of Finance Division of this Ministry vide their I.D. No. PC2/20(12)/2012/FIN/PEN dated 10.01.2013.

Yours faithfully
Sd/-
(Malathi Narayanan)
Under Secretary to the Government of India

32.5

Government of India, Ministry of Defence, Department of Ex-Servicemen Welfare Letter No 1(13)/2012/D (Pen/Policy) dated 17th January 2013

Sub: Implementation of the Government's decision on the recommendations of Committee of Secretaries 2012 on the issues related to Defence Service Personnel and Ex-Servicemen Improvement in pension of JCO/OR retired/discharged/invalided out of service prior to 1.1.2006.

Sir,

The undersigned is directed to refer to this Ministry's letter No PC 10(1)/2009-D (Pen/Policy) dated 8.3.2010 according to which with effect from 1st July 2009, pension of all ranks of pre 1.1.2006 JCO/OR retiree in Army, Navy and Air Force (including DSC and TA) has been reckoned at 50% of notional pay in the post 1.1.2006 revised pay structure corresponding to the maximum of the pay scales applicable from, 10.10.1997 of the rank and group continuously held for last 10 months preceding retirement/discharge/invalidment. The amount of pension so determined has to be reduced pro-rata if the reckonable qualifying service including rank weightage (except TA personnel) is less than service required to earn full pension.

2. A committee of Secretaries headed by Cabinet Secretary was constituted by the Government to consider various issues on pension of Armed Forces Personnel and Ex-Servicemen, who have recommended the following to bridge the gap in pension between pre and post-1.1.2006 JCO/OR pensioners.

2.1 The pension of pre-1.1.2006 JCO/OR pensioners may be determined on the basis of notional maximum for the ranks and group across the three services; and

2.2 Current weightage in qualifying service of Sepoy, Naik and Havildar may be increased by two years.

3. The above recommendations of the Committee has been accepted by the Government and the President is pleased to decide that with effect from 24th September 2012, the service pension, invalid pension, special pension, service element of disability pension and service element of war injury/liberalized disability pension (in release cases only) of all pre- 1.1.2006 JCO/OR pensioners of Army, Navy and Air Force (including DSC & TA) shall be recomputed in terms of Para 2 of this Ministry's above said letter dated 8.3.2010 after determining the highest of notional pay in the revised pay structure corresponding to maximum of pay scales of Fifth CPC across the three Services equivalent to the rank and group in which pensioned. Before determining highest of notional pay of equivalent ranks across three Services, 50% of highest classification allowance (rates effective from 1.9.2008) shall also be added in the notional pay of the rank sin Army, wherever applicable.

3.1 The President is also pleased to decide that for computation of pension in terms of this order, the rank weightage in qualifying service for the rank of Sepoy, Naik and Havildar (except for TA personnel) shall be taken as 12, 10 and 8 years subject to a maximum qualifying service of 32 years. However, in case an individual's qualifying service works out to be more than 32 years with existing weightage, he would continue to get the benefit of that and there will be no enhancement of weightage in such cases.

3.2 The notional pay in the revised pay structure for pre- 1.1.2006 JCO/OR granted Honorary Commission as Lieutenant and Captain shall also be worked out by adding pay in the revised pay band corresponding to the fixed pay of Fifth CPC (in terms of Para 9(a)(i) of SAI 1/S/2008 as amended and equivalent instructions for Navy & Air Force) plus the Grade Pay and Military Service Pay introduced under Sixth CPC revised pay structure.

4. The President is also pleased to decide that service element of war injury pension/liberalized disability pension in respect of JCO/OR invalided out of service prior to 1.1.2006 shall be reckoned as under:

4.1 For determining the notional pay last drawn in respect of JCO/OR invalided out of service prior to 10.10.1997, the provisions laid down in Para 4.1 of this Ministry above quoted letter dated 8.3.2010 shall be followed.

4.2 The notional Pay in the pay band of post-1.1.2006 revised pay structure corresponding to the notional pay determined in case of JCO/OR invalided out of service prior to 10.10.1997 vide Para 4.1 above and corresponding to last pay drawn in case of JCO/OR invalided out of service on or after 10.10.1997 but before 31.12.2005, shall be determined at the same number of stage in the fitment table attached to SAI 1/S/2008 or equivalent instructions for Navy & Air Force. For this purpose, the fitment table considered as having highest maximum of pay scales across the three Services for equivalent rank and group in which pensioned, as determined vide Para 3 above, shall be taken into account.

4.3 The notional emoluments last drawn for rank and group shall consist notional pay in the pay band as determined vide Para 4.2 above plus Grade pay, Military Service pay and "X" Group pay, where applicable to the rank and group held at the time of invalidment.

4.4 The service element of war injury pension/liberalized disability pension in respect of all PBOR invalided out of service prior to 1.1.2006 shall be notionally recomputed with effect from 24th September 2012 at 50% of the notional emoluments last drawn (determined as per 4.3 above) in the Post- 1.1.2006 revised pay structure with reference to the qualifying service already admitted. The amount of service element so determined shall be the pension for 33 years of reckonable qualifying service including rank weightage (except for TA personnel). The provisions at Para 3 to 3.3 above, shall equally apply for determining the amount of service element of war injury pension.

NON-APPLICABILITY

5. The provision of these orders do not apply to the family pensioners of PBOR and Commissioned Officer and their family. These orders also do not apply to UK/HKSRA/KCIOs pensioners and Pakistan/Burma pensioners. The following elements shall continue to be paid as seParate elements in addition to the pension revised under these orders –

5.1 Monetary allowance attached to gallantry awards viz, ParamVir Chakra etc.

5.2 Constant Attendance Allowance, where admissible.

6. The provisions of this order shall be effective from 24th September 2012. No arrears on account of revision of pension based on notional fixation of pay shall be admissible for the past period. However, if a pensioner to whom the benefits under these orders accrues has died/dies before receiving the payment on account of arrears, the life time arrears (LTA) will be disposed off as per the extant orders contained in Para 12 of this Ministry above said letter dated 6.3.2010.

METHODOLOGY FOR IMPLEMENTATION

7. All Pension Disbursing Agencies handling disbursement of pension to Defence pensioners are hereby authorized to carry out revision of service pension/special pension/invalid pension/service element of disability pension with effect from 24th September 2012 to the affected pensioners drawing pension with 15 years or more qualifying service in terms of these orders without calling for any applications from the pensioners and without any further authorization from the concerned Pension Sanctioning Authorities and pay the arrears on account of such revision.

8. In order to quicken the proves of revision of service pension, special pension, invalid pension, service element of disability pension with 15 years or more qualifying service, total 25 tables indicating revised pension payable with effect from 24th September 2012, have been prepared for PBOR of Regular Army, Navy, Air Force and DSC who

retired/discharged/invalided out from service prior to 1.1.2006 and drawing pension as on 24th September 2012, and are enclosed as Appendix to this letter. The appended tables indicate the existing pension as on 1.7.2000 and revised pension payable with effect from 24th September 2012. Pension Disbursing Agencies shall revise the pension with reference to applicable Table for the rank and group in which the JCO/OR was pensioned. The revised rate of pension indicated against each qualifying service in the pension tables appended to this letter is inclusive of rank weightage applicable for various ranks. Pension Disbursing Authority shall refer the actual qualifying service as shown in Column-1 for carrying out revision subject to maximum terms of engagement for each rank as applicable from time to time. in addition, dearness relief sanctioned by the Government from time to time and applicable quantum of additional pension for pensioners of 80 years of age and above, is also payable.

9. The initial Pension Payment Order (PPO) or its Corrigendum PPO (Corr PPO) indicates rank, group and qualifying service for which the individual has been pensioned. This information is available with Pension Disbursing Agencies as they have revised pension of all such pensioners in the recent past in terms of various Government orders. In case, however, any information regarding qualifying service, rank group, etc, is not available with Pension Disbursing Agencies, such cases may be referred to pension Sanctioning Authority concerned on the proforma enclosed as **Annexure-A.** The Pension Sanctioning Authorities concerned will provide the requisite information from the available records within 30 days of the receipt of request form the Pension Disbursing Agencies.

CASES REQUIRING REVISION FROM PSAs

10. Pension of PBOR pensioners who are in receipt of Special Pension, Invalid Pension and service element of Disability Pension for less than 15 years of qualifying service would also need to be revised in terms of these orders. Specific Tables for the purpose have not been prepared for the reason that each of such cases will be unique one as rank, group and qualifying service will differ from case to case, and hence, standard Tables cannot be prepared. Pension Disbursing Agencies shall refer such cases directly to the Pension Sanctioning Authorities concerned in the format enclosed as **Appendix-B** to this letter.

11. Specific tables for revision of pension in respect of pre-1.1.2006 Territorial Army pensioners have also not been prepared as Pension Disbursing Agencies could not revise such cases due to non-applicability of weightage in qualifying service and provision for reduction in pension in respect of TA pensioners who have completed 15 years or more but less than 20 years of aggregate embodied service. Such cases may also be referred by Pension Disbursing Agencies directly to the Pension Sanctioning Authorities concerned in the format enclosed as **Annexure-B** to this letter.

12. Similarly, revision of service element of war injury pension/liberalized disability pension in all cases of PBOR irrespective of the qualifying service shall also required to be done by the Pension Sanctioning Authorities concerned for the reason that the crucial information relating to last pay drawn and the maximum terms of engagement to the specific rank for which pension would need to be verified with reference to the original records are held by the Pension Sanctioning Authorities. Such cases shall also be forwarded by the Pension Disbursing Agencies to the Pension Sanctioning Authorities concerned through respective Record Office in the prescribed proforma enclosed as **Annexure-C** to this letter.

METHODOLOGY FOR REPORTING

13. An intimation regarding disbursement of revised pension shall be sent by the Pension Disbursing Agencies to the Office of the PCDA (P) Allahabad on monthly basis in the format prescribed as Annexure-D to these orders a copy of which shall also be provided by the Pension Disbursing Agencies to the pensioners concerned for their information. Those Public Sector Banks who are disbursing Defence pension through Central pension Processing Centers (CPPC), the monthly progress report may be furnished by the CPPC of the bank directly to the office of the PCDA (Pension) Allahabad.

14. This issues with the concurrence of Finance Division of this Ministry vide their I.D No 10(1)/2012/FIN/PEWN dated 10.1.2013.

15. Hindi version will follow.

Yours faithfully
Sd/-
(Malathi Narayanan)
Under Secretary to the Government of India

32.6

Government of India, Ministry of Defence, Department of Ex-Servicemen Welfare Letter No 12(1)/2014/D(Pen/Pol)-Part-II dated 7th November 2015

Sub: One Rank One Pension (OROP) to the Defence Forces Personnel

Sir,

In view of the need of the Defence Forces to maintain physical fitness, efficiency and effectiveness, as per the extant Rules, Defence Service personnel retire at an early age compared to other wings in the Government. Sepoy in Army and equivalent rank in Navy & Air Force retire after 17/19 years of engagement/service and officers retire before attaining the age of 60 years i.e. the normal age of retirement in the Government. Considering these exceptional service conditions and in the interest of ever vigilant Defence Forces, the pensionary benefits of Ex-Servicemen have accordingly, over time, been fixed.

2. It has now been decided to implement “One Rank One Pension” (OROP) for the Ex-Servicemen with effect from 1.07.2014. OROP implies that uniform pension be paid to the Defence Forces Personnel retiring in the same rank with the same length of service, regardless of their date of retirement, which, implies bridging the gap between the rates of pension of current and past pensioners at periodic intervals.

3. Salient features of the OROP are as follows:

i. **To begin with, pension of the past pensioners would be re-fixed on the basis of pension of retirees of calendar year 2013 and the benefit will be effective with effect from 1.7.2014.**

ii. **Pension will be re-fixed for all pensioners on the basis of the average of minimum and maximum pension of personnel retired in 2013 in the same rank and with the same length of service.**

iii. **Pension for those drawing above the average shall be protected.**

iv. **Arrears will be paid in four equal half yearly instalments. However, all the family pensioners including those in receipt of Special/Liberalized family pension and Gallantry award winners shall be paid arrears in one instalment.**

v. **In future, the pension would be re-fixed every 5 years.**

4. Personnel who opt to get discharged hence forth on their own request under Rule 13(3)1(i)(b),13(3)1(iv) or Rule 16B of the Army Rules 1954 or equivalent Navy or Air Force Rules will not be entitled to the benefits of OROP. It will be effective prospectively.

5. The Govt. has decided to appoint a Judicial Committee to look into anomalies, if any, arising out of implementation of OROP. The Judicial Committee will submit its report in six months.

6. Detailed instructions relating to implementation of OROP along with tables indicating revised pension for each rank and each category, shall be issued separately for updation of pension and payment of arrears directly by Pension Disbursing Agencies.

7. This issues with concurrence of Finance Division of this Ministry vide their ID No. MoD (Fin/Pension) ID No. PC to 10(11)/2012/Fin/Pen dated 07 November 2015.

8. Hindi version will follow.

Sd/-

(K. Damayanthi)

Joint Secretary to the Govt. of India

32.7

Government of India, Ministry of Defence, Department of Ex-Servicemen Welfare Letter No 12(1)/2014/D (Pen/Policy)-Part-II dated 3rd February 2016

Sub: One Rank One Pension to the Defence Forces Personnel.

Sir,

The undersigned is directed to refer this Ministry's letter No 1291)/2014/D (Pen/Policy)-Part-II dated 7th November, 2015 notifying One Rank One Pension (OROP) scheme for Defence Forces personnel. Salient features of the scheme have been mentioned at Para 3 & 4 of above said letter with the provision that the benefit of the scheme shall be implemented from 1.7.2014 to all pre-1.7.2014 pensioners, Para 6 of the letter provides that detailed instructions relating to implementation of OROP along with tables indicting revised pension for each rank and each category, shall be issued separately for updation of pension and payment of arrears by Pension Disbursing Agencies concerned.

2. The undersigned is directed to say that in order to quicken the process of revision of pension/family pension, total 101 pension tables indicating rates of pension/family pension under OROP scheme notified vide this Ministry's order dated 7th Nov, 2015, are appended to this order. The appended tables indicate revised rates of Retiring/Service/ Special/ Disability/Invalid/Liberalized disability/War Injury Pension including disability/war injury element and ordinary/ special/liberalized family pension of commissioned Officers, honorary Commissioned Officers, JCOs/ORs and Non-combatants (Enrolled) of Army, Navy, Air Force, Defence Security Corps & Territorial Army retired/ discharged/ invalided out from service/died in service or after retirement. The existing pension of all – 1.7.2014 pensioners/family pensioners shall be enhanced with reference to the actual qualifying service as shown in Column-I of the tables subject to maximum term of engagement for each rank as applicable from time to time. The rate of pension of pensioners/ family pensioners drawing pension more than the rate of revised pension/family pension indicated in annexed tables, shall remain unchanged.

3. The undersigned is also directed to convey that full pension of PSU absorbees who had opted for 100% commutation of pension, shall also be revised under this order with reference to revised pension of the rank determined for regular category of pensioners. However, there shall be no change in restored amount of pension already notified by respective PSAs in their case.

APPLICABILITY

4. The provisions of this letter shall be applicable to all pensioners/family pensioners who had been retired/ discharged/invalided out from service/died in service or after retirement in the rank of Commissioned Officers, honorary commissioned officers, JCOs/OR and Non-combatants (Enrolled) of Army, Navy, Air Force, Defence Security Corps, Territorial Army & Ex-State Forces and are in receipt of pension/family pension as on 1.7.2014.

4.1 The provisions of this order, however, do not apply to UK/HKSRA/KCIO pensioners, Pakistan & Burma Army pensioners, Reservist pensioners and pensioners in receipt of Ex-gratia payments.

METHODOLOGY FOR IMPLEMENTATION

5. All Pension Disbursing Agencies (PDAs) handling disbursement of pension to Defence pensioners are hereby authorized to carry out revision of Retiring/Service/Special/Disability/Invalid/Liberalized disability/War Injury Pension including disability/war injury element and ordinary/special/liberalized family pension of all pre-1.7.2014 pensioners drawing pension as on 1.7.2014 in terms of these orders with applicable rates of dearness relief without calling for any applications from the pensioners and without any further authorization from the Pension Sanctioning Authorities concerned.

6. Where the revised pension as on 1.7.2014 worked out in terms of these orders, happens to be less than the existing pension/family pension as on 1.7.2014, the pension shall not be revised to the disadvantage of the pensioner.

7. Arrears on account of revision of pension from 1.7.2014 till date of its implementation shall be paid by the Pension Disbursing Agencies in four equal half yearly installments. However, all the family pensioners including those in receipt of Special/Liberalized family pension and all Gallantry award winners shall be paid arrears in one installment.

8. The initial Pension Payment Order (PPO) or its corrigendum PPO (Corr. PPO) indicates rank, group and qualifying service for which the individual has been pensioned. This information is available with Pension Disbursing Agencies as they have revised pension of all such pensioners in the recent past in terms of Government orders issued for implementation of recommendations of Sixth CPC, CSC-2009 & CSC-212. In case, however, any information regarding qualifying service, rank, group, etc, is not available with Pension Disbursing Agencies such cases may be referred to pension Sanctioning Authority concerned on the proforma enclosed as Annexure-A. The Pension Sanctioning Authorities concerned will provide the requisite information from the available records within 15 days of the receipt of request from the Pension Disbursing Agencies.

9. In case of any doubt relating to revision of pension in terms of this order, pension disbursing agencies may immediately take up the matter with nodal officers of respective PSAs details of which shall be notified by Pr. CDA (P) Allahabad in their implementation Instructions.

10. The OROP shall be basic pension from 1.7.2014 and therefore, additional pension as applicable to the old age pensioners/family pensioners on attaining the relevant age (80 years and above) shall also be enhanced by the PDAs from 1.7.2014 or the date from which the pensioner attains the age of 80 years or more, whichever is later.

PAYMENT OF LIFE TIME ARRERS (LTA)

11. If a pensioner to whom the benefit accrues under the provisions of this letter has died/dies before receiving the payment of arrears, the Life Time Arrears of pension (LTA) shall be paid in the following manner:

a. If the claimant is already in receipt of Family Pension or happens to be the person in whose favour family Pension already stands notified and the awardees has not become ineligible for any reason, the LTA under the provisions of this letter should be paid to such a claimant by the PDA on their own.

b. If the claimant has already received LTA in the past in respect of the deceased to whom the benefit would have accrued, the LTA under the provisions of this letter should also be paid to such a claimant by the PDA on their own.

c. If the claimant is a person other than the one mentioned at 11 9a0 & 11 (b) above, payment of LTA shall be made to the legal heir/heirs as per extant government orders.

12. The following elements shall continue to be paid as separate elements in addition to the pension revised under these orders:

i. Monetary allowance attached to gallantry awards viz, ParamVir Chakra, Ashok Chakra, etc.

ii. Constant Attendance allowance, where admissible.

iii. Dearness relief as sanctioned by the Government from time to time.

MISCELLANEOUS INSTRUCTIONS

13. No arrears on account of revision of pension/family pension shall be admissible for the period prior to 1.7.2014.

14. No commutation of pension shall be admissible on revised/additional amount of pension accruing as a result of revision of pension under these orders. However, the existing amount of pension, if any, that has been commuted will continue to be deducted from the revised pension.

15. As a result of these orders, there will be no change in the amount of gratuity already determined and paid with reference to the rules in force at the time of discharge/invalidment/death.

16. Any overpayment of pension coming to the notice or under process of recovery shall be adjusted in full by the Pension Disbursing agencies against arrears becoming due on revision of pension on the basis of these orders.

METHODOLOGY FOR REPORTING

17. An intimation regarding disbursement of revised pension shall be furnished by the Pension Disbursing Agencies to the Office of the Pr. CDA (P) Allahabad in the format prescribed as Annexure-B to this letter in the following month in which revision takes place. PDAs shall also ensure that an intimation regarding revision of pension is invariably conveyed to the pensioners concerned for their information irrespective of the fact the same is beneficial to them or not. The Public Sector Banks who are disbursing Defence pension through Central pension Processing Centres (CPPC), the progress report shall be furnished by the CPPC of the bank directly to the office of the PCDA (Pension) Allahabad through electronic scrolls.

18. All other terms and conditions which are not affected by this order shall remain unchanged.

19. This issues with the concurrence of Finance Division of this Ministry vide their ID No 1 to 10(11)/2012/FIN/ PEN dated 2.2.2016.

20. Hindi Version will follow.

Sd/-

(Manoj Sinha)

Under Secretary to the Government of India

32.8

Government of India, Ministry of Defence, Department of Ex-Servicemen Welfare Letter No 1(15)/2012/D (Pen/Pol) dated 6th February 2019

Sub: **Implementation of Government decision on the recommendations of the Sixth Central Pay Commission- Pension of Personnel Below Officer Rank (PBOR) discharged from service on or after 01.01.2016.**

The undersigned is directed to refer to the provisions contained in this Ministry's letters No 17(4)/08(2)/D (Pen/Policy) dated 18.08.2010 as amended vide this Ministry's letter No 17(4)/2008/D (Pen/Policy) dated 20.09.2012 under which a note below Para 3 (v) of the ibid MoD letter dated 18.08.2010 was inserted regarding non-applicability of provisions of letter dated 18.08.2010 to JCOs granted Honorary Commission as Lieutenant and Captain.

2. Further, in supersession of the provision contained in this Ministry's letter No. 17(4)/2008 (2)/D (Pen/Policy) dated 20.09.2012, letter No 1(15)/2012/D (Pen/Policy) dated 17.01.2013 was issued under which it was decided that the provisions of MoD letter dated 18.08.2010 are also applicable to post 01.01.2016 JCOs/OR granted Honorary Commission as Lieutenant and Captain with effect from 24.09.2012.

3. The President is now pleased to decide that provisions of this Ministry's letter dated 18.08.2010 shall also be applicable to post 01.01.2006 JCOs/ORs granted Honorary Commission as Lieutenant and Captain. The notional pay in the revised pay structure for these ranks shall be worked out by adding pay in the revised pay band corresponding to the Fixed pay of Fifth CPC (In terms of Para 9 (a) (i) of SAI 1/S/2008 as amended and equivalent instructions for Navy & Air Force) Plus the Grade pay and Military Service pay introduced under sixth CPC revised pay structure.

4. In view of the above, the note below Para 3 (v) of this Ministry's letter No 17(4)/08 (2)/D (Pen/Policy) dated 18.08.2010 inserted vide this Ministry's letter No 17(4)/08 (2)/D (Pen/Policy) dated 20.09.2012 may be considered as deleted.

5. The financial benefit past cases shall be granted from 01.01.2006 or date of discharge/invalidment, whichever is later. In this regard, concerned PSAs would suo-moto issue Corr PPO based on the data of Post 2006 retired Hony Commissioned Officers held with them.

6. All other terms and conditions shall remain unchanged.

7. This issues with the concurrence of Finance Division of this Ministry of vide their ID No. 10(15)/2015/FIN/PEN dated 02.01.2019.

Yours faithfully

Sd/-

(Manoj Sinha)

Under Secretary to the Government of India

32.9

Government of India, Ministry of Defence, Department of Ex-Servicemen Welfare Letter No 1(1)2019/D(Pen/Pol) dated 4th January 2023

Sub: **Next revision of pension of Defence Forces Personnel/family pensioner under One Rank One Pension (OROP)**

Sir,

The undersigned is directed to refer to the provisions contained in para 3(v) of this Ministry's letter No. 12(1)/2014 /D(PenlPol)-Part-II dated 7.11.2015 regarding re-fixation of pension of Defence Forces Personnel under OROP in future every 5 years

2. The President is pleased to decide that next revision of pension under OROP Scheme would be effective from 1.7.2019. Revision of pension is based on the principles adopted in MoD letter dated 07.11.2015 which are as under:

2.1 Pension of the past pensioners would be re-fixed on the basis of pension of Defence Forces retirees of calendar year 2018 and the benefit will be effective from 01.07.2019.

2.2. Pension will be re-fixed for eligible Defence Forces pensioners/family pensioners on the basis of the average of minimum and maximum pension of Defence Forces Personnel retired in calendar year 2018 in the same rank and with the same length of service.

2.3. Pension for those drawing above the average shall be protected.

2.4. The benefit would also be extended to family pensioners including war widows and disabled pensioners.

2.5. Arrears will be paid in four half yearly instalments. However, all the family pensioners including those in receipt of Special/ Liberalized Family Pension and Gallantry Award Winners shall be paid arrears in one instalment.

2.6. Personnel who opt to get discharged w.e.f. 01. 07. 2014 (on or after 01.07.2014) on their own request under Rule 13(3)I(i)(b), 13(3)II(i)(b), 13(3)III(iv) or Rule 16B of the Army Rules 1954 or equivalent Navy or Air Force Rules will not be entitled to the benefits of OROP

3. Detailed instructions along with tables for revision of pension for each rank and each category under OROP Scheme, shall be issued separately.

4. This issues with the concurrence of Finance Division of this Ministry vide their ID Note No 10(01)/2019/Fin/Pen dated 30.12.2022.

5. Hindi version will follow.

Yours faithfully,
Sd/-
(B L Meena)
Under Secretary to the Govt. of India

32.10

Government of India, Ministry of Defence, Department of Ex-Servicemen Welfare No 1(1)/2019/D(Pen/Pol)/Vol-II dated 20th January 2023

Sub: One Rank One Pension to the Defence Forces Pensioners.

The undersigned is directed to refer to this Ministry's letter No. 1(1)/2019/D(Pen/Pol) dated 04.01.2023 notifying revision of pension under One Rank One Pension Scheme (OROP) with effect from 01.07.2019 to all Pre-01.07.2019 Defence Forces Pensioners/Family Pensioners. Para 3 of the letter provides that detailed instructions relating to implementation of OROP along with tables indicating revised pension for each rank and each category, shall be issued separately.

2. The undersigned is now directed to say that in order to quicken the process of revision of pension/family pension, total 121 tables indicating rates of Pension/Family Pension under OROP scheme are appended to this order. The appended tables indicate revised rates of Retiring/Service /Special/Disability/Invalid/Liberalized Disability/War Injury Pension including Disability/War Injury Element and Ordinary/Special /Liberalized Family Pension of Commissioned Officers, Honorary Commissioned Officers, JCOs/ORs and Non-Combatants (Enrolled) of Army, Navy, Air Force, Defence Security Corps & Territorial Army Retired/Discharged/Invalided Out from Service/died in service or after retirement. The existing pension of all Pre- 01.07.2019 (except pensioners retired on or after 01.07.2014 on pre-mature retirement/own request as provided in para 4 of MoD letter No. 12(I)/2014/D(Pen/Pol)Part.II dated 07.11.2015 as amended vide Ministry of Defence, Department of Ex-Servicemen Welfare letter No. 12(1)/2014/D(Pen/Pol)Part-II dated 06.06.2017) pensioners/ family pensioners shall be enhanced with reference to applicable table for the rank (and group in case of JCOs/ORs) in which pensioned with reference to the actual qualifying service as shown in Column-I of the tables subject to maximum term of engagement from time to time. The rate of pension of pensioners/family pensioners drawing more than the revised rate of pension/family pension indicated in annexed tables, shall remain unchanged.

APPLICABILITY

3. The provisions of this letter shall be applicable to all pensioners/family pensioners who had been retired/ discharged/invalided out from service/died in service or after retirement in the rank of Commissioned Officers, Honorary Commissioned Officers, JCOs/ORs and Non- Combatants (Enrolled) of Army, Navy, Air Force, Defence Security Corps, Territorial Army & Ex-State Forces and are in receipt of pension/family pension as on 01.07.2019 (except pensioners retired after previous OROP revision on pre mature retirement/own request).

3.1 The provisions of this letter, however, do not apply to UK/HKSRA/KCIO pensioners, Pakistan & Burma Army pensioners, Reservist pensioners and pensioners in receipt of Ex-gratia payments and pensioners retired after previous OROP revision on pre mature retirement/own request (as provided in para 4 of MoD letter dated 07.11.2015).

METHODOLOGY FOR IMPLEMENTATION

4. It is provided in para-2.6 of MoD letter dated 04.01.2023 that the pensioners retired on or after 01.07.2014 on premature retirement/own request are not eligible for benefits of OROP. The information regarding premature retirement/own request is not available in the Pension Payment Order (PPO). Hence, table based revision by PDA in such cases is not feasible.

4.1 *Therefore, it is decided that the pension o f all pensioners retired/discharged on or aper 01.07.2014 and before 01.07.2019 will be implemented through corrigendum PPO.* Since, most of the data of pensioners/family pensioners have been migrated in SPARSH application, therefore, revision of pension of migrated pensioners/family pensioners will be done through SPARSH application only. The corrigendum PPO in the case of remaining pensioners retired/discharged on or after 01 .07.2014 and before 01 .07.2019 will be issued by Pension Sanctioning Authorities in affected cases, suo-moto (where rates of pension under these orders are beneficial than the rates of their pension as on 01 .07.2019).

4.2 In all other cases i.e pensioners retired/discharged up to 30.06.2014, invalided out prior to 01.07.2019 and family pensioners, this revision will be implemented based on the pension tables as appended with this order. All Pension Disbursing Agencies (PDAs) handling disbursement of pension to Defence pensioners are hereby authorized to carry out revision of Retiring/Service/ Special/ Disability/ Invalid/ Liberalized Disability/War Injury Pension including Disability/War Injury Element and Ordinary/Special/Liberalized Family Pension of all such pre-01.07.2019 pensioners/family pensioners drawing pension as on 01.07.2019 in terms of this order with applicable rates of dearness relief without calling for any applications from the pensioners and without any further authorization from the Pension Sanctioning Authorities concerned.

4.3 The revised rates of pension under this letter are average of minimum & maximum rate of pension for a rank and a qualifying service of live data of 2018 retirees. Wherever, the rates of higher qualifying service of a rank are lower than rates of lower qualifying service in same rank or data is/are blank for higher qualifying service then the same have been protected by higher rate of lower qualifying service, due to this, many rates in same column appear equal. Similarly, wherever the revised rate of pension under this order are lower in higher rank than rate in lower rank in same qualifying service then the same have been protected with higher rates of pension in lower rank in same qualifying service resulting similar rate in same qualifying service in two adjacent columns.

5. Where the revised pension as on 01.07.2019 worked out in terms of this letter, happens to be less than the existing pension/family pension as on 01.07.2019, the pension shall not be revised to the disadvantage of the pensioner/ family pensioner.

6. Arrears on account of revision of pension from 01.07.2019 till date of its implementation shall be paid by the Pension Disbursing Agencies in four half yearly installments. However, all the family pensioners including those in receipt of Special/Liberalized family pension and all Gallantry award winners shall be paid arrears in one installment.

7. The initial Pension Payment Order (PPO) or its Corrigendum PPO (Corr PPO) indicates rank, group and qualifying service for which the individual has been pensioned. This information is available with Pension Disbursing Agencies as they have revised pension of all such pensioners in the recent past in terms of Government orders issued for implementation of recommendations of 7th CPC. In case, however, any information regarding qualifying service, rank, group etc., is not available with Pension Disbursing Agencies, such cases may be referred to Pension Sanctioning Authority concerned on the proforma enclosed as **Annexure-A** . The Pension Sanctioning Authorities concerned will provide the requisite information from the available records within 15 days of the receipt of request from the Pension Disbursing Agencies.

8. In case of any doubt relating to revision of pension in terms of this letter, Pension Disbursing Agencies may immediately take up the matter with Nodal Officers of respective PSAs, details of which shall be notified by Pr. CDA (P), Prayagraj in their implementation instructions.

9. The revised rates of pension under this letter shall be basic pension from 01.07.2019 and therefore, additional pension as applicable to the old age pensioners/family pensioners on attaining the relevant age (80 years and above) shall also be enhanced by the PDAs from 01.07.2019 or the date from which the pensioner attains the age of 80 years or more, whichever is later.

PAYMENT OF LIFE TIME ARREARS (LTA)

10. If a pensioner to whom the benefit accrues under the provisions of this letter has died/dies before receiving the payment of arrears, the Life Time Arrears of pension (LTA) shall be paid in the following manner:

a. If the claimant is already in receipt of Family Pension or happens to be the person in whose favour Family Pension already stands notified and the awardees has not become ineligible for any reason, the LTA under the provisions of this letter should be paid to such a claimant by the PDA on their own.

b. If the claimant has already received LTA in the past in respect of the deceased to whom the benefit would have accrued, the LTA under the provisions of this letter should also be paid to such a claimant by the PDA on their own.

c. If the claimant is a person other than the one mentioned at 10(a) & 10(b) above, payment of LTA shall be made to the legal heir/heirs as per extant Government orders.

11. The following elements shall continue to be paid as separate elements in addition to the pension revised under this order:

i. Monetary allowance attached to gallantry awards viz. Param Yir Chakra, Ashok Chakra etc.

ii. Constant Attendance Allowance, where admissiole.

iii. Dearness relief as sanctioned by the Government from time to time.

MISCELLANEOUS INSTRUCTIONS

12. No arrears on account of revision of pension/family pension shall be admissible for the period prior to 01.07.2019.

13. No commutation of pension shall be admissible on revised/additional amount of pension accruing as a result of revision of pension under this letter. However, the existing amount of pension, if any, that has been commuted will continue to be deducted from the revised pension.

14. As a result of this letter, there will be no change in the amount of gratuity already determined and paid with reference to the rules in force at the time of retire/discharge/invalidment/death.

15. Any overpayment of pension coming to the notice or under process of recovery shall be adjusted in full by the Pension Disbursing Agencies against arrears becoming due on revision of pension on the basis of this order.

METHODOLOGY FOR REPORTING

16. An intimation regarding disbursement of revised pension shall be furnished by the Pension Disbursing Agencies to the office of the Pr. CDA(P), Prayagraj in the format prescribed as **Annexure-B** to this letter in the following month in which revision takes place. PDAs shall also ensure that an intimation regarding revision of pension is invariably conveyed to the pensioners concerned for their information irrespective of the fact that the same is beneficial to them or not. The Public Sector Banks disbursing defence pension through Central Pension Processing Centers (CPPC), the progress report shall be furnished by the CPPC of the bank directly to the office of Pr. CDA (Pensions) Prayagraj through electronic scrolls.

17. All other terms and conditions which are not affected by this order shall remain unchanged.

18. This issues with concurrence of Finance Division of this Ministry vide their ID No10(01)/2019/Fin/Pen dated 16.01.2023

19. Hindi version will follow.

Sd/-
(B L Meena)
Under Secretary to the Govt.of India

Chapter-33

Important Letters

33.1

Government of India, Ministry of Defence Letter No A/49779/AG/PS4(c)/291/ A/D (Pensions/Services) dated 26th February 1980

CORRIGENDUM

The following amendment is made in this Ministry's letter No A/49779/AG/PS4(c)/1313/A/D(Pensions/Services) dated the 23rd July 1979 regarding assessment of retiring service pension of Armed Forces Commissioned Officers and Personnel Below Officer Rank on the basis of the rank actually held for at least ten months before retirement:

In Para 1

For "continuously for at least 10 months instead of 2 years before retirement, regardless of whether it is held in a substantive or paid acting capacity."

Read "regardless of whether it is held in a substantive or paid acting capacity and, in the case of personnel below officer rank the lowest group for which he is paid, during the last ten months before retirement instead of two years."

2. This issues with the concurrence of Ministry of Finance (Defence) vide their U.O. No. 619-Pen of 1980

Sd/-

(Shiv Rai Jakir)

Under Secretary to the Government of India

33.2

Government of India, Ministry of Personnel, Public Grievances & Pensions, Department of Pension & Pensioners' Welfare Letter No 38/37/08-P&PW(A) dated 11th August 2009

OFFICE MEMORANDUM

Sub: Implementation of the Government's decision on the recommendations of the Sixth Central Pay Commission – Revision of pension of pre-2006 pensioners/family pensioners, etc.

The undersigned is directed to say that in this Department's OM of even number dated 21.5.2009, it was provided that the following documents would be accepted as proof of date of birth/age for payment of additional Pension/Family Pension on completion of 80 years and above.

i. Pan Card

ii. Matriculation certificate (containing the information regarding date of birth)

iii. Passport

iv. CGHS Card

v. Driving license (if it contains date of birth)

2. The matter has been examined further. Considering the difficulty in producing any of the above mentioned documents as proof of age by the old pensioners, particularly those in the rural areas, it has been decided that the Voters ID Card may also be accepted as proof of date of birth/age for payment of additional pension/family pension on completion of 80 years and above subject to the following conditions:

i. The pensioners/family pensioners certifies that he is not a matriculate (The matriculation certificate should be insisted in the case of matriculate pensioners/family pensioners).

ii. The pensioners certifies that he does not have any of the documents mentioned in Para 1 above.

3. The other conditions for acceptance of the documents, as mentioned in the OM dated 21.5.2009, will remain the same.

4. Some doubts have been expressed regarding the date from which the additional pension is to be made effective. In this connection, attention is invited to the clarifications issued vide this Department's O.M. of even number dated 3.10.2008. It is re-iterated that the additional quantum of pension/family pension, would be admissible from the 1st day of the month in which the date of birth falls, only on completion of the age of 80 years, 85 years, etc, (and not in the beginning of the 80th year, 85th year, etc.). All references/representations received in this respect stand disposed off accordingly.

Illustration: If a pensioner/family pensioner's date of birth is 26.1.1930, then he/she will be entitled to the additional quantum of pension on completion of 80 years of age w.e.f. 1.1.2010.

5. It is impressed upon all the Ministries/Departments of the Government of India and the pension disbursing authorities to keep in view the above instructions while disposing of the cases of payment of additional pension/family pension. CGA/CPAO are requested to advise all Pension disbursing/sanctioning authorities to take suitable action in accordance with the above instructions/guidelines and to make suitable entry regarding date of birth in the PPO. Similarly, instructions may be issued by Ministry of Defence and Ministry of Railways to their concerned Accounts Department accordingly.

6. This issues with the concurrence of Ministry of Finance (Department of Expenditure) vide their I.C.U.O No. 261/EV/2009 dated 9.7.2009.

Sd/-

(M.P. Singh)

Director (PP)

33.3

Government of India, Ministry of Defence Letter No 4684/DIR (PEN)/2001 dated 14th August 2001

ORDER

Sanction is hereby accorded in pursuance of MOD ID No. 14(3)/2001/D(O&M) dated 3.8.2001 for delegation of administrative powers with the approval of Raksha Mantri to the Service HQrs in respect of the subjects indicated below:

a.
  i. Division of family pension between eligible family members.

  ii. Initial cases for award of Special Family Pension and ex-gratia for officers.

  iii. Recovery from pensionary benefits first charge being Public Fund dues thereafter Non-Public Fund dues from the residual benefits.

  iv. Payment of dues to NOK of deserters.

  v. Condonation of shortfall in Qualifying Service for grant of pension in respect of PBOR beyond six months and upto 12 months.

  vi. Time bar sanction for filing appeals for Ordinary Family Pension, Special Family Pension, Disability Pension etc. in respect of officers and PBOR beyond 12 months.

  vii. Grant of ex-gratia award to Cadets on death/disability within the Govt. approved terms and conditions.

  viii. Pensionary award to officers dismissed from service otherwise than with disgrace/cashiered.

  ix. Pensionary award to officers who are discharged, called upto to resign or are retired.

  x. Grant of pension to PBOR dismissed from service.

  xi. Grant of Disability Pension to officers.

  xii. First appeal against rejection of Ordinary Family Pension, Special Family Pension, Disability Pension/ Ex-gratia award etc, to officers and PBOR.

  xiii. First claim for pension and gratuity submitted after 12 months from due date where Pension Sanctioning Authority is not satisfied with reasons for delay.

  xiv. Implementation of Judgments delivered by various Courts/CATs including those with financial implications where further appeal is not contemplated.

  xv. Condoning of delays in conducting release medical boards (GOI, MOD Order No. 4684/Dir (Pens)/2001 dated 20 Sep 2001).

b. Approving Authority in the Service HQrs in respect of the above subjects will be AG/COP/AOP/AOA as the case may be, any further re-delegation of these powers will require prior approval of Ministry of Defence.

c. Authorities for authenticating of orders/documents will be the authorities as specified in Ministry of Home Affairs SO No. 2297 dated 3.11.1958. Further, the complaints/written statement in suits in any court of civil jurisdiction or in writ proceedings by/or against the Central Government shall be signed by the authorities, indicated in the Ministry of Law's Notification dated 14.2.1990. Any further devolution of powers in this regard will require approval of MHA and Ministry of Law respectively. Proposal for this purpose, if need be, may be initiated by the Service HQrs, and be referred to these Ministries for issue of necessary corrigendum through D(O&M) Section of this Ministry.

d. Concurrence of Integrated Finance shall continue to be obtained wherever required as hithertofore without involving this Ministry.

2. The relevant Regulation(s) or Pension Regulation for the Army/Navy/Air Force shall stand amended accordingly. Formal amendments to Pension Regulations will, however, be issued in due course of time.

3. In case Pension Regulations and any other Govt Orders/Instructions are required to be amended, necessary proposals in this regard will be initiated by the Service HQrs.

4. Cases for RM's approval will be submitted, wherever required by the Service HQrs, after approval of AG/COP/AOP/AOA. Whenever required such cases should be routed through the Pension Branch of this Ministry.

5. As regards to composition of First Appellate Committee (FAC), the Chairperson of the Committee shall be the AG/COP/AOP in the respective service HQrs, in place of Director/Dy Secretary incharge of Pension Division in the Ministry of Defence. The composition of the second Appellate committee headed by RM/RRM will remain unchanged. However, the cases shall be submitted for recommendations of the Members of the Committee and approval of RM/RRM direct by the Service HQrs.

6. These orders will take effect from the date of issue.

7. This issues with the concurrence of Defence (Finance) vide their U.O. No. 1539/Addl. FA(B) dated 13th August 2001.

Sd/-

33.4

Integrated HQ of Ministry of Defence (Army), Adjutant General's Branch, Additional Directorate General Manpower [MP-8 (I of R)] Letter No A/20105/ MP 8(I of R)(a) dated 15th May 2008

Sub: Change of Name of Wards of Serving/Ex-Servicemen Personnel Below Officers Rank (PBOR)

1. As per Integrated HQ of MoD (Army) letter No A/20105/MP 8 (I of R) (a) dated 28 August 2002, exhaustive instructions on publication of Part-II Orders affecting Kindred Rolls of serving/retired PBOR were issued.

2. This HQ has been receiving number of requests/representations from environment for making changes in the name of wife and children of serving as well as ex-servicemen due to one or the other reason. Since there was no provision for making any changes in kindred roll portion of sheets rolls, no action was taken on these requests/ representations.

3. Now, this proposal has been examined de novo and it has been decided that the following occurrences will be accepted and published in the Part-II Orders for serving/ex-servicemen provided the requests are supported with the requisite documents as mentioned against each:

Ser No	Occurrence	Supporting documents	
		Serving Personnel	**Ex-Servicemen/Widows**
(a)	Addition of surname of PBOR to the name of wife and children of serving and retired PBOR	(i) A declaration certificate by the individual duly authenticated by two witnesses and counter-signed by CO Unit only.	(i) An affidavit sworn in before a first class Magistrate.
(b)	Change in the maiden name of wife	(i) A declaration by the individual duly authenticated by two witnesses and counter-signed by CO Unit only.	(i) An affidavit sworn in before a first class Magistrate.
		(ii) Extract from two national dailies wherein notice regarding the change of name has been published for the general information of the public at large.	(ii) Extract from two national dailies wherein notice regarding the change of name has been published for the general information of the public at large.
		(iii) CTC of School leaving certificate/certificate from Principal of the School.	(iii) CTC of School leaving certificate/certificate from Principal of the School.
		OR	**OR**

		Extract of birth/death register maintained by the village/Panchayat/Municipality. (iv) An affidavit duly sworn in before the first class Magistrate.	Extract of birth/death register maintained by the village/Panchayat/Municipality.
(c)	Change of name of children and own brother/sister	(i) A declaration certificate by the individual duly authenticated by two witnesses and counter-signed by CO Unit only. (ii) Extract of birth/death register maintained by the Village/Panchayat/Municipality. **OR** CTC of School leaving certificate/certificate from Principal of the School. (iii) Extract from two national dailies wherein notice regarding the change of name has been published for the general information of the public at large. (iv) An affidavit duly sworn in before the first class Magistrate.	(i) An affidavit sworn in before a first class Magistrate. (ii) Extract of birth/death register maintained by the Village/Panchayat/Municipality. **OR** CTC of School leaving certificate/certificate from Principal of the School. (iii) Extract from two national dailies wherein notice regarding the change of name has been published for the general information of the public at large.

4. Any certificate or proof produced by serving/retired PBOR, if found to be false at any stage, would render the concerned occurrence null and void and necessary action will be initiated against the defaulters. It is therefore, of paramount importance that the Record Offices satisfy themselves thoroughly on the genuineness of documents produced by the serving/retired PBOR/widows before accepting for publication of occurrences. It may be noted that all requests from ex-servicemen/widows must be routed through concerned Zila Sainik Board and duly countersigned. All old cases pending with units/Record Offices will be cleared by 31 Dec 2008. Necessary amendment in Appendix 'J' documents Procedure JCOs and OR is under issue.

5. This has the approval of the Adjutant General.

6. Suitable ROI may be issued.

Sd/-
(Venugopal MN)
Brigadier
DDG MP 8 (I of R)
For Adjutant General

33.5

Government of India, Ministry of Personnel, Public Grievances & Pensions, Department of Personnel & Training Letter No 18/-3/2015-Estt. (Pay-1) dated 2nd March 2016

OFFICE MEMORANDUM

Sub: Recovery of wrongful/excess payments made to Government servants.

The undersigned is directed to refer to this Department's OM No. 18/26/2011-Estt (Pay-I) dated 6th February 2014 wherein certain instructions have been issued to deal with the issue of recovery of wrongful/excess payments made to Government servants in view of the law declared by Courts, particularly, in the case of Chandi Prasad Uniyal and Ors vs. State of Uttarakhand And Ors, 2012 AIR SCW 4742, (2012) 8 SCC 417, Para 3 (iv) of the OM inter-alia provides that recovery should be made in all cases of overpayment barring few exceptions of extreme hardships.

2. The issue has subsequently come up for consideration before the Hon'ble Supreme Court in the case of **State of Punjab & Ors vs. Rafiq Masih (WhiteWasher), etc, in CA No. 11527 of 2014 (Arising out of SLP (C) No. 11684 of 2012)** wherein Hon'ble Court on 18.12.2014 decided a bunch of cases in which monetary benefits were given to employees in excess of their entitlement due to unintentional mistakes committed by the concerned competent authorities, in determining the emoluments payable to them, and the employees were not guilty of furnishing any incorrect information/misrepresentation/fraud, which had led the concerned competent authorities to commit the mistake of making the higher payment to the employees. The employees were as innocent as their employers in the wrongful determination of their inflated emoluments. The Hon'ble Supreme Court in its judgment dated 18th December, 2014 *ibid* has, inter-alia observed as under:

> *"7. Having examined a number of judgments rendered by this Court, we are of the view, that orders passed by the employer seeking recovery of monetary benefits wrongly extended to employees, can only be interfered with, in cases where such recovery would result in a hardship of a nature, which would far outweigh, the equitable balance of the employer's right to recover. In other words, interference would be called for, only in such cases where, it would be iniquitous to recover the payment made. In order to ascertain the parameters of the above consideration, and the test to be applied, reference needs to be made to situations when this court exempted employees from such recovery, even in exercise of its jurisdiction under Article 142 of the constitution of India. Repeated exercise of such power, "for doing complete justice in any cause" would establish that the recovery being effected was iniquitous, and therefore, arbitrary, And accordingly, the interference at the hands of this Court".*

> *"10. In view of the afore-stated constitutional mandate, equity and good conscience, in the matter of livelihood of the people of this country, has to be the basis of all Governmental actions. An action of the State, ordering a recovery from an employee, would be in order, so long as it is not rendered iniquitous to the extent, that the action of recovery would be more unfair, more wrongful, more improper, and more unwarranted, than the corresponding right of the employer, to recover the amount. Or in other words, till such time as the recovery would have a harsh and arbitrary effect on the employee, it would be permissible in law. Orders passed in given situations repeatedly, even in exercise of the power vested in this Court under Article 142 of the constitution of India, will disclose the parameters of the realm of an action of recovery (of an excess amount paid to an employee) which would breach the obligations of the State, to citizens of this country, and render the action arbitrary, and therefore, violative of the mandate contained in Article 14 of the constitution of India".*

3. The issue that was required to be adjudicated by the Hon'ble Supreme Court was whether all the private respondents, against whom an order of recovery (of the excess amount) has been made, should be exempted in law, from the

reimbursement of the same to the employer. For the applicability of the instant order, and the conclusions recovered by them thereinafter, the ingredients depicted in paras 2 & 3 of the judgment are essentially indispensable.

4. The Hon'ble Supreme court while observing that it is not possible to postulate all situations of hardship which would govern employees on the issue of recovery, where payments have mistakenly been made by the employer, in excess of their entitlement has summarized the following few situations, wherein recoveries by the employers would be impermissible in law:

i. Recovery from employees belonging to Class-III and Class-IV service (or Group 'C' and Group 'D' service).

ii. Recovery from retired employees, or employees who are due to retire within one year, of the order of recovery.

iii. Recovery from employees, when the excess payment has been made for a period in excess of five years, before the order of recovery is issued.

iv. Recovery in cases where an employee has wrongfully been required to discharge duties of a higher post, and has been paid accordingly, even though he should have rightfully been required to work against an inferior post.

v. In any other case, where the court arrives at the conclusion, that recovery if made from the employee, would be iniquitous or harsh or arbitrary to such an extent, as would far outweigh the equitable balance of the employer's right to recover.

5. The matter has, consequently, been examined in consultation with the Department of Expenditure and the Department of Legal Affairs. The Ministries/Departments are advised to deal with the issue of wrongful/excess payments made to Government servants in accordance with above decision of the Hon'ble Supreme Court in **CA No 11527 of 2014 (arising out of SLP (C) No. 11684 of 2012) in State of Punjab and others, etc, vs. Rafiq Masih (WhiteWasher)** etc. However, wherever the waiver of recovery in the above-mentioned situations is considered, the same may be allowed with the express approval of Department of Expenditure in terms of this Department's OM No. 18/26/2011-Estt (Pay-I) dated 6th February, 2014.

6. In so far as persons serving in the Indian Audit and Accounts Department are concerned, these orders are issued with the concurrence of the comptroller and Auditor General of India.

Sd/-

(R.K. Jain)

Deputy Secretary to the Government of India

33.6

Government of India, Ministry of Defence Letter No 1(6)/99/D(Pen-C) dated 15th September 2003

Sub: **Implementation of Government decision on the recommendation of 5th Central Pay Commission regarding ex-gratia awards in the cases of disability of cadets due to causes attributable to or aggravated by military training.**

Sir,

In supersession of this ministry earlier letter No. 1(6) 99/D(Pen-C) dated 11.2.2002, I am directed to convey the sanction of the President to the payment of following ex-gratia awards subject to the same conditions as hitherto in force in the event of invalidment of Cadets (Direct) on medical grounds due to causes attributable to or aggravation by military training-

i. Payment of monthly ex-gratia of Rs 1275/- per month.

ii. Payment of Ex-gratia disability award @ 2100/- per month for the 100% disability during the period of disablement. The amount will be reduced proportionately from the ex-gratia disability award in case the degree of disablement is less than 100%, and

iii. Constant attendance allowance (CAA) of Rs 600/- per month for 100% disability on the recommendation of invaliding medical board.

2. Dearness Relief at applicable rates will be granted on monthly ex-gratia as well as on ex-gratia disability awards at the rates sanctioned from time to time vide Ministry of Personnel Public Grievances & Pension (Deptt. of Pensioner & Pensioners' Welfare) office memorandum No. 42/2/95 P&PW(G), dt. 27.10.97. While calculating dearness relief, monthly ex-gratia and ex-gratia disability award both will be taken together, however, no dearness relief will be granted on CAA.

3. The awards under these orders are sanctioned purely on ex-gratia basis and the same shall not be treated as pension for any purpose.

4. Other rules and procedure regarding assessment/re-assessment of disablement and acceptance of disability as attributable to or aggravated by conditions of military service/training shall be the same as for the regular commissioned officers of the armed forces.

5. The ex-gratia disability awards payment as mentioned Para on above shall be applicable w.e.f. 01.08.1997. The benefit shall be admissible to pre 01.08.1997 cases as well with financial effect w.e.f. 01.08.1997.

6. Rules concerning above mentioned subjects as contained in ministry of defence letter No. 1(5)93-D(Pen-C) dated 16th April, 1996 as amended vide government letter No. 1(5)/93-D(Pen-C) dated 12thMay 1997 read in conjunction with MoD letter of even number dated 5th July, 2001 stand modified to the extent as indicated in the aforesaid paras.

7. This issues with the concurrence of finance division of this ministry vide their U.O. No. 3314/Fin/Pen dated 25th August, 2003.

Yours faithfully,

Sd/-

(P.J. Mathew)

Deputy Secretary of the Government of India

33.7

Government of India, Ministry of Defence Letter No 6(7)/87(Pension/Services) dated 5th April 1991

Sub: **Recognition of marriage after retirement for the purpose of grant of ordinary family pension in respect of Armed Forces pensioners.**

Sir,

1. Under the provisions of Army instruction 51/80 and corresponding Instructions of the Navy and Air Force, marriage after retirement was not recognised for the purpose of grant of ordinary Family Pension. However, on consideration of the early ages of retirement of Armed Forces personnel, marriage after retirement was recognized subject to certain conditions vide Ministry of Defence letter No. 6(7)/87/D (Pens/Sers) dated 02nd Jun 89.

2. Smt. Bhagwati. Widow of Ex-JC-44290 Late Nb/Sub Loknath Sharma of AMC and Smt. Sharda Swamy Widow of a Railway pensioner, who had married after retirement of their husbands, filed writ petition No. 1128 of 1998 and 1204 of 1998 respectively in the Supreme Court claimed that the benefit of the family pension scheme may be extended to them. The Hon'ble Supreme Court in its judgment dated 29 Aug '89 allowed the petitions of Smt. Bhagwati and Smt. Sharda Swamy. This judgment has already been implemented in respect of Smt. Bhagwati by this Ministry.

3. The policy regarding grant of ordinary family pension to post retrial spouses/children of Armed Forces pensioners, in the light of the judgment of the Supreme Court has been considered and the President is pleased to decide that:

a. The benefit of family pension scheme 1964 may also be extended to the post retrial spouses/children born after retirement of the Armed Forces pensioners (officers/personal below officer rank) under the provisions of Army Instruction 51/80 and corresponding Naval and Air Force Instruction;

b. The arrears of family pension may be granted with effect from 22 Sept. 1977 (the date from which contribution of two months emoluments was dispensed with) or from a subsequent date one becomes eligible for family pension, whichever is later. However, where the Armed Forces personnel had contributed two months emoluments in terms of para 11 of A1 51/80 and corresponding Navy and Air Force instructions promulgating 1964 family pension scheme, the arrears of family pension may be granted from the date of death of the pensioner, and

c. Life time arrears, wherever admissible of family pension in respect of spouses of the decreased post-retiral spouses, would also be payable to their family members/heirs where the spouses eligible for family pension were alive on the date of eligibility and who died subsequently for the period from the date of eligibility to the date of death. The application for life time arrears (LTA) should be supported by the following documents:

   i. Death certificate, and

   ii. Proof of relationship of the claimant with the decreased such as in the form of Birth Certificate/Legal heirship certificate/affidavit sworn before a first class magistrate.

4. As the marriages in such cases would have taken place after retirement, there will be no record of such marriages in the service records of the Armed Forces pensioner. As such the living pensioners of this category will be required to apply for endorsement of ordinary family pension entitlements in their PPOs under the provisions of this Ministry's O.M. No.6(4)1369/B/D (Pens/Sers) dated 30th June 88 enclosing therewith registration details of their marriages with the Registrar of Marriages or other component authority under the relevant law. However, in those cases where

such marriage has not been got registered for some valid reason, the cases may be settled on the basis of an affidavit sworn before a First class magistrate.

5. (a) For sanction of ordinary family pension/LTA under the provisions of this letter the eligible members of family would have to apply to the pension sanctioning authority in the attached application forms through the following authority:

	Commissioned Officers	PBOR
Army	All Officers other than of AMC/ ADC/MNS – through AG's Branch/ Org/(b) West Block III RK Puram New Delhi. Commissioned Officers of AMC/ ADC/MNS – Dir Gen Medical Services, MPRS(O), 'L' Block, New Delhi.	Respective Record Offices
Air Force	Air HQ/DPP&P, West Block VI, RK Puram New Delhi.	Air Force Records Office, Subroto Park, New Delhi
Navy	NHQrs/Dte of P&A ,'D' Wing, Nao Sena Bhawan, New Delhi.	NHQrs/Dte of P&A 'D' Wing, Nao Sena Bhawan, New Delhi

(b) The Service HQrs/ROs will complete/get completed Part II/III/IV of the application form (as the case may beand then forward the same to the respective pension sanctioning authority alongwith the requisite papers, documents for further necessary action. In cases where Part III/Part IV of the application form could not be completed by any authority for some reason or the other, the pension sanctioning authority may be approached for sanction of minimum family pension subject to revision at a subsequent stage if an when such particulars become a available.

6. The awards of ordinary family pension which have already been made in terms of this Ministry's letter No. 6(7)/87/D(Pens/Sers) dated 12 Jun. 89 will also have to be revised as per these orders and necessary adjustments made.

7. The relevant provisions of Army instructions AI 62/80 and corresponding instructions of the Navy and Air Force will be modified accordingly, in due course.

8. This Ministry's letter of even number dated 02 Jun 89 on the subject may be treated as withdrawn from the date of issue of this letter.

9. This issues with concurrence of Finance Division of this Ministry vide their I.D. No. 1015-Pen/91 dated 05 April 91.

10. Hindi version will follow.

Sd/-
(Dr. S.K. Sharma)
Director (Pens)

33.8

Government of India, Ministry of Defence Letter No. 12(6)/95/D(Pension/ Services) dated 9th June 1999

Sub: **Amendment to Regulations 16 & 113 of Pension Regulations for the Army, 1961**

Sir,

I am directed to state that under the provision of Regulation 113 (a) of Pension Regulations for the Army (Part - I) 1961, as amended vide CS No. 80/IV/67, a PBOR who is dismissed under the provisions of the Army Act is ineligible for pension and gratuity in respect of all previous service though in exceptional cases, President may at his discretion, grant service pension or gratuity or both at a rate not exceeding that for which he would have otherwise qualified had he been discharged on the same date. Similar provisions in respect of commissioned officers do not exist vide Regulation 16 of PRA (Part -I), 1961.The disparity in the provisions has been engaging attention of the Government for some past time.

2. It has now been decided that all Indian Army personnel including commissioned officers who are cashieving/ dismissed under the provisions of army Act, 1950 or removed under AR 14 i.e. as a measure of penalty, will be ineligible for pension or gratuity in respect of all previous service. In exceptional cases, however, the Competent Authority on submission of an appeal to that effect may at his discretion sanction pension/gratuity or both at a rate not exceeding that which would be otherwise admissible individual so cashiered/dismissed/removed been retired/ discharged on the same date in the normal manner.

3. An individual who is compulsorily retired or removed on grounds other than misconduct or discharged under the provisions of Army Act, 1950 and the rules made thereunder, remains eligible for pension/and/or gratuity as admissible on the date of discharge. This will suo-moto apply to cases of dismissal/removal converted into discharge subsequently.

4. All appeals to the competent Authority in this regard will be preferred within two years of the date of cashiering/ dismissal/removal.

5. Competent Authority for the above provisions will be President in case of Commissioned Officers and GOC-in-C of Command in whose jurisdiction the individual's record office falls in respect of JCOs/ORs. Competent Authority for the purpose of Regn.3 of PRA (Pt. I) as mentioned in Regn. 22 (Table VI) of PRA (Pt. II) will also be the GOC- in-C.

6. Pension Regulations for the Army will be amended in respect of the above provisions in due course.

7. The provisions of this letter shall come into effect w.e.f 1.1.96. However the cases decided between 1.1.96 till date of issue of this letter will not be re-opened.

Yours Faithfully

Sd/-

(Amrit Lal)

Under Secretary to the Govt. of India

33.9

Government of India, Ministry of Defence Letter No 12(6)/95(Pen/Sers) dated 10th August 2000

Sub: Amendment to Regulations 16 and 113 of Pension Regulations for the Army, 1961

The following amendments are made to this Ministry's letter No. 12(6)/95/D(Pen/Sers), dt. 09.06.99 on the above subject:

a. Para 5:

Delete all entries of Para 5 and insert the following:

"Competent authority both for Commissioned Officers and PBORs for Regulations 16 and 113 of Pension Regulations for the Army, 1961, will be the President"

b. Para 7:

Delete all entries of Para 7 and insert the following:

"Provisions of this letter shall come into effect with effect from the date of issue of this Ministry's letter No 12 (6)/95/D(Pen/Sers) dated 09-06-1999. However, past cases will be decided as hithertofore."

2. This issues with the concurrence of Ministry of Defence (Fin/Pen) vide their UO No 2747/Pen/2000 dated 28-07-2000

Sd/-
(Amrit Lal)
Deputy Secretary to Government of India

33.10

Government of India, Ministry of Defence Letter No PC5169/ATP/PC/909/A/04/D(Pen/Sers) dated 6th October 2004

Sub: Continuation of Pension on Change of Nationality by NRI Pensioners

Sir,

I am directed to refer to Regulation 8 of PRA Part-1 1961 and corresponding Regulations for Air Force and Navy, read with Ministry's letter No 12(3)/86/B/2792/D(Pen/Sers) dated 30.05.2003, and to state that when a pensioner becomes a naturalized citizen of a foreign State, PCDA(Pensions), Allahabad has been authorised to decide as to whether the whole or part of the pension or allowance be continued. However, in case of Civil pensioners, change in citizenship by any NRI pensioner does not affect his entitlement to pension. Various representations have been received by the Ministry from affected NRI pensioners and the matter has been reconsidered. The President is pleased to decide that even in the case of Armed Forces Pensioners the entitlement to pension will remain unaffected on change of nationality and pension will continue to be paid by his/her pension disbursing authority. However, the pensioner should intimate the change of nationality, etc, as per the provision contained in Para 13 of this Office letter No 2(l)/89D(Pen/Sers)/Part-I dated 01.10.1991 to the Pension Disbursing Agency as well as to the PCDA (Pensions), Allahabad for updation of their records.

2. Other conditions for payment of pension to NRI pensioners will remain unchanged.

3. Regulation 8 of Pension Regulations for Army Part-I (1961) and corresponding Regulations for Air Force and Navy will be amended accordingly. Para 28(b) of Annexure 'H' of the Scheme for Payment of Pension of Defence Pensioners by Public Sector Banks may also be amended accordingly.

4. This issues with the concurrence of Finance division of this Ministry vide their U.O. no. 4497/FP dated 06.10.2004.

Yours faithfully,
Sd/-
(S R Sharma)
Under Secretary to the Govt. of India

33.11

Government of India, Ministry of Personnel, Public Grievances & Pension, Department of Pension & Pensioners' Welfare Letter No12/5/2020-P&PW(C)-6363 dated 20th February 2020

Sub: **Consolidated instructions on Life Certificate and commencement of family pension if pensioner/ family pensioner is living abroad**

This Department has been receiving grievances of pensioners residing abroad mentioning the difficulties and inconvenience faced by them with respect to submission well as commencement/continuation of family pension. Instructions have already been issued from time to time on the above subject in order to ensure Ease of Living for them. The circulars have been consolidated and are as under:

i. In the case of a pensioner residing abroad, the following methods are available for submission of life certificate –

a. If he/she is drawing pension through any bank included in the Second Schedule to the Reserve Bank of India Act, 1934, the life certificate may be signed by an officer of the Bank.

b. An authorized official of the Embassy of India/High Commission of India/Indian Consulates may issue the life certificate.

c. In case the pensioner is unable to visit the Embassy/Consulate, he/she may submit requisite documents by post to the Embassy/Consulate, including Doctor's Certificate showing the pensioner's inability to present himself/herself in person. Embassy of India/High Commission/Indian Consulate may also assist pensioners/ family pensioners in submission of the Life Certificate.

d. A Pensioner, not resident in India, in respect of whom a duly authorized agent produces a Life Certificate, signed by a magistrate or a notary or an officer of an Indian authorized Bank or Diplomatic Representative of India, is exempted from special appearance.

e. There have been complaints that life certificate submitted over the counter of pension paying branches are misplaced causing delay in payment of monthly pension. In order to alleviate the hardship faced by pensioners, agency banks are instructed to mandatorily issue duly signed acknowledgements. They were also advised to consider entering the receipt of life certificate in CBS and issue a system generated acknowledgements which would serve the twin purpose of acknowledgement as well as real time updation of records. (RBI/2018-1971 DGBA.GBD.No.-1/31.02.007/2018-19, dated 2nd July, 2018)

ii. For commencement of family pension, after demise of a pensioner residing abroad following procedure will be followed –

a. In case the pensioner and spouse are holding a joint account, the requirement of Form 14 has been dispensed with. The spouse may inform the pension disbursing Bank of the death of the pensioner and request the bank for commencement of family pension, through a simple letter. He/she may enclose a copy of death certificate of the pensioner, PPO, proof of his/her own age/date of birth and an undertaking for recovery of excess payment. In other cases, i.e., where the pension is not being credited to the joint bank account of the pensioner, Form 14 will be continued to be obtained by the banks from the family pensioner. However, the condition of attestation of Form 14 has been done away with and witnessing by two persons has been considered as sufficient. (Govt of India, Dept of Pension & Pensioners' Welfare's O.M No.1/27/2011-P&PW(E) dated, 20 September, 2013

b. In case of family pensioners who are unable to visit to India for personal identification, they may be allowed pension/family pension on the basis of a certificate to be issued by an authorized official of the Embassy of India/High Commission of India/Indian Consulate in the country where the pensioner is residing. This certificate is to be issued on verification of Pensioner/Family Pensioner on the basis of the photograph available in the PPO or on the basis of the photograph available on the Passport. (CGA's Authority No.-F. No.1(7)/CPAO Scheme Book/2005/TA/585 dated 22.09.2006)

CPPCs/Branches of all the Pension disbursing banks may be advised to strictly comply with the above instructions.

This issues with the approval of competent authority.

Sd/-
Rajesh Kumar
Under Secretary to the Govt of India

33.12

Government of India, Ministry of Defence Letter No 1034/C/02-D (Pen/Sers) dated 31st October 2003

Sub: **Counting of boy service rendered before attaining the age of 17 years as qualifying service for the purpose of pension/gratuity**

I am directed to refer to the O/o CGDA U.O. No. 5601/AT-P/LXV dated 17.06.2003 and 14.08.2003, and to say that the Govt. letter No. B/39022/AG/PS-4 (A&C)/589/C/D (Pen/Sers) dated 27.03.2002 in respect of Army and Air Force personnel and No. PN/1405/307/CC/C/D (Pen/Sers) dated 13.04.2000 in respect of Naval personnel regarding counting of boy service rendered before attaining the age of 17 years as qualifying service for the purpose of pension/gratuity have been issued.

2. Govt. letters dated 13.04.2000 and 27.03.2002 which have been issued after due consideration and legal advice, do not require any modification/change. You are advised to implement the same and give benefit of counting of 'Boy Service' rendered before attaining the age of 17 years as qualifying service for the purpose of pension/gratuity to all the affected personnel irrespective of their length of service subject to maximum qualifying service.

Yours faithfully

Sd/-

(L.K. Haldar)

33.13

Government of India, Ministry of Defence Letter No B/38076/AG/PS-4(a)/2190/A (Pen/Ser) dated 6th August 1984

Sub: **Calculation of the length of qualifying service for assessment of pension and gratuity in respect of service personnel including Commissioned Officers**

Sir,

I am directed to say that the President is pleased to decide that **in calculating the length of qualifying service for the purpose of pension/gratuity, a fraction of a year equal to three months and above shall be treated as a completed one half year and reckoned as qualifying service** for determining the amount of pension and Service/DCRG.

These orders shall have effect from 28th June 1983.

The existing provisions of the Pension Regulations for the three services may be deemed to have been amended in this respect to the extent of the provisions of these orders. Formal amendment to the aforesaid Regulation will be issued in due course.

This issues with the concurrence of the Finance Division of this Ministry vide UO No 2748/Pen of 1984.

Yours faithfully
Sd/-
Amit Cowshish
Under Secretary to the Govt of India

33.14

Government of India, Ministry of Personnel, Public Grievances & Pension, Department of Pension & Pensioners' Welfare Letter No12/4/2020-P&PW(C)-6300 dated 17th January 2020

CIRCULAR

Sub: Obtaining of Life Certificate by Banks from the doorstep of the pensioners

The undersigned is directed to say that instructions have been issued from time to time for submission of Life Certificate by pensioners, in the month of November every year. Attention is also drawn to the following circulars meant to facilitate submission of life Certificate by Pensioners and ensure Ease of Living for them.

i. CPAO/Tech/Grievances/2010-11/531, dated 30.06.2011, issued by Central Pension Accounting Office, New Delhi, which provides for exemption from personal appearance by pensioners submitting Life Certificate, if the prescribed form in Annexure-XVII of Para 15.2(i) of Scheme Booklet is signed by certain specified authorities.

ii. CPAO/Tech/Life-Certificate/2014-15/31-32, dated 30.01.2015, issued by Central Pension Accounting Office, New Delhi, which highlights the digital Life Certificate mode of submission as part of Prime Minister's "Digital India" scheme.

iii. RBI/2014-15/87, dated 07.05.2015, issued by the Reserve Bank of India, prescribing mandatory issue of acknowledgement to Pensioners on submission of Life Certificate and promoting the use of Digital Life Certificates among Pensioners, which would eliminate the need for their physical presence at branches.

iv. RBI/2017-18/89, dated 09.11.2017, issued by Reserve Bank of India, directing Banks for enabling ease of submitting life Certificate, whereby a pensioner can submit Life Certificate in any branch of the pension paying Bank and the same is uploaded promptly in CBS by the receiving branch itself. It also directs all Banks to ensure Door-Step submission of Life Certificate facility, along with Banking facility to all senior citizens of more than 70 year of age and differently-abled or infirm persons, including pick-up of cash and delivery of cash against withdrawal.

v. OM No. 1/20/2016-P&PW(E), dated 14.11.2017, issued by Department of Pension & Pensioners Welfare, which re-iterates RBI's concern w.r.t. old/infirm pensioners, for which Banks should make concrete efforts to provide the facility of obtaining Life Certificate from their premises/residence and exempt personal appearance.

vi. OM No. 1/20/2018-P&PE (E), dated 18.07.2019, issued by Department of Pension & Pensioners Welfare, which prescribes that pensioners aged 80 years and above may be allowed to give their Life Certificate w.e.f. 1st October every year, which would be valid till 30th November of the subsequent year, in order to provide senior pensioners with an exclusive window at banks, for the activity and avoid the general rush.

2. In spite of detailed instructions, as brought out above, it has been observed that a large number of pensioners (around 8-10 percent) are unable to submit their Life Certificate by the stipulated date i.e. 30th November every year on account of various reasons. The pension disbursing authorities/banks are constrained to discontinue disbursement of their monthly pension, in such cases, due to non-submission of the Life Certificate. Such pensioners face a lot of difficulty in re-commencement of their pension.

3. In order to promote Ease of Living for Pensioners and minimize the cases of non-submission of Life Certificate by the pensioners and ensure uninterrupted disbursement of pension to them, in addition to the instructions contained in Para 1 above, the following instructions are hereby issued for strict compliance:

i. All Pension disbursing banks shall send SMSs/E-mails to the pensioners on 24th October, 1st November, 15th November and 25th November, every year reminding them to submit their Annual Life Certificate by the stipulated date i.e. 30th November.

ii. All Pension disbursing banks shall make an exception list as on 1st December every year, of those pensioners who fail to submit their Life Certificate by 30th November and send SMS/E-mail to the pensioners included in the aforesaid exception list advising them to submit the Life Certificate at the earliest to avoid discontinuation of their pension. The Bank shall also ask such pensioners, through SMS/E-mail, as to whether they are interested in submission of Life Certificate through a doorstep visit by the bank. Wherever a call centre/ App based facility is available, Banks should also encourage taking request for doorstep visits through such modes. The banks shall not charge any Pensioner more than Rs 60/- for such a doorstep visit. In line with the Reserve Bank of India Circular, RBI/2014-15/587, dated 07.05.2015, all banks shall encourage promoting Life Certificate through digital means.

iii. As regards pensioners who have failed to submit their Life Certificate in the year 2019, the banks will prepare an exception list of such pensioners immediately and follow the steps mentioned in sub-para 3 (ii) above.

iv. The CPPCs of Pension Disbursing Banks (in case of more than 1 CPPC in any Bank, then one nominated official on behalf of the bank as a whole) shall report to the Department of Pension & Pensioners Welfare in the months of January. February and March respectively the total number of Central Government Pensioners who have given the Life Certificate, the total number of Pensioners who have not given their Life Certificate along with a break-up of the certificates submitted physically and through digital means, on the following email address: rajesh.kr73@nic.in.

4. CPPCs/Branches of your bank may be advised to strictly comply with the above instructions. The banks are also requested to give wide publicity by putting up these instructions in their websites and also on the notice boards of the branches of the bank, etc.

This is issued with the approval of competent authority.

Sd/-
(Rajesh Kumar)
Under Secretary to the Government of India

33.15

Government of India, Ministry of Personnel, Public Grievances & Pensions, Department of Pensions & Pensioners' Welfare Letter No 21/01/2016-P&PW(F) dated 12th February 2019

Sub: Grant of Invalid Pension under Rule 38 of the Central Civil Services(Pension) Rules, 1972-Clarification regarding

The undersigned is directed to say that Rule 38 and Rule 49 of the Central Civil Services (Pension) Rules, 1972 have been amended vide Notification No. 21/1/2016-P&PW(F) dated 4th January, 2019 (copy enclosed). The proviso to the amended Rule 38 of the CCS (Pension) Rules provides that a Government servant, who retires from service on account of any bodily or mental infirmity which permanently incapacitates him for the service before completing qualifying service of ten years, may also be granted invalid pension in accordance with sub rule (2) of rule 49, subject to the conditions that the Government servant:

a. was examined by the appropriate medical authority either before his appointment or after his appointment to the service or post and was declared fit by that authority for Government service, and

b. fulfils all other conditions mentioned in this rule for grant of invalid pension.

2. In this connection, it is clarified that the condition of qualifying service of ten years for grant of pension under Rule 49(2) of the CCS (Pension) Rules, 1972 shall not be applicable in the case of a Government servant retiring on Invalid Pension on account of any bodily or mental infirmity, under Rule 38. Accordingly, Invalid Pension at the rate of 50% of emoluments or average emoluments, whichever is more beneficial, subject to a minimum of nine thousand rupees per mensem and maximum of one lakh twenty five thousand rupees per mensem, shall be payable to a Government servant who retires under Rule 38 of CCS (Pension) Rules, 1972 even before completing a qualifying service of ten years.

3. All Ministries/Departments are requested that the above clarification may be brought to the notice of Heads of Department. Attached and Subordinate Officers, Controllers of Accounts, Pay & Accounts Offices, etc, under them.

4. Hindi version will follow.

Sd/-

Harjit Singh

Director

33.16

Government of India, Ministry of Defence, Department of Ex-Servicemen Welfare Letter No 12(06)/2019/D(Pen/Pol) dated 16th July 2020

Sub: **Provision of Invalid Pension to Armed Forces Personnel before completion of 10 years of qualifying service - reg.**

Sir,

Government of India, Ministry of Personnel, Public Grievances & Pensions, Department of Pension & Pensioners' Welfare vide their O.M. No. 21/01/2016-P&PW(F) dated 12th February 2019 has provided that a Government servant, who retires from service on account of any bodily or mental infirmity which permanently incapacitates him from the service before completing qualifying service of ten years, may also be granted invalid pension subject to certain conditions. The provisions have been based on Government of India, Gazette Notification No. 21/1/2016-P&PW(F) dated 04.01.2019.

2. The proposal to extend the provisions of Department of Pension & Pensioners' Welfare OM No. 21/01/2016-P&PW(F) dated 12.02.2019 to Armed Forces personnel has been under consideration of this Ministry. The undersigned is directed to state that Invalid Pension would, henceforth also be admissible to Armed Forces Personnel with less than 10 years of qualifying service in cases where personnel are invalided out of service on account of any bodily or mental infirmity which is Neither Attributable to Nor Aggravated by Military Service and which permanently incapacitates them from military service as well as civil reemployment.

3. Pension Regulation of the Services will be amended in due course.

4. The provision of this letter shall apply to those Armed Forces Personnel who were/are in service on or after 04.01.2019. The cases in respect of personnel who were invalided out from service before 04.01.2019 will not be re-opened.

5. All other terms and conditions shall remain unchanged.

6. This issues with the concurrence of Finance Division of this Ministry vide their U.O. No. 10(08)/2016/FIN/PEN dated 29.06.2020.

7. Hindi version will follow.

Yours faithfully,

Sd/-

(Ashok Kumar)

Under Secretary to the Government of India

33.17

Government of India, Ministry of Personnel, Public Grievances & Pension, Department of Pension & Pensioners' Welfare Letter No 1(8)/2021-P&PW(1)-7468 dated 22nd September 2021

Sub: **Submission of Annual Life Certificate for pensioners/family pensioners living abroad.**

Every Central Government pensioner/family pensioner has to submit **Annual Life Certificate** in the month of November for further continuation of pension/family pension. In the case of a pensioner/family pensioner residing abroad, the following methods are available for submission of life certificate —

i. In the case of a pensioner/family pensioner residing abroad and drawing his pension/family pension through any bank included in the Second Schedule to the Reserve Bank of India Act, 1934, the life certificate may be signed by an officer of the Bank. A pensioner/family pensioner gets exemption from personal appearance subject to production of Life Certificate signed by the above mentioned officer of the bank.

ii. A pensioner/family pensioner not residing in India in respect of whom his duly authorized agent produces a life certificate signed by a Magistrate, a Notary, a Banker or a Diplomatic Representative of India is exempted from personal appearance.

iii. Pensioner/family pensioner can also provide Digital Life Certificate online through Aadhaar based biometric authentication system. http://jevanpramaan.gov.in/

[(No. 14.3-CERTIFICATES TO BE FURNISHED BY THE PENSIONERS/FAMILY PENSIONERS-pg 38 SCHEME FOR PAYMENT OF PENSIONS TO CENTRAL GOVERNMENT CIVIL PENSIONERS BY AUTHORISED BANKS (Fifth Edition, July 2021)]

iv. In case of NRI pensioners/family pensioners who are unable to come to India for personal identification, pension/family pension may be allowed on the basis of a certificate to be issued by an authorized official of the Indian Embassy/High Commission of India or Consul of Indian Consulate in the country where the pensioner/family pensioner is residing. This certificate is to be issued on verification of Pensioner/Family Pensioner on the basis of photograph pasted in the PPO or on the basis of photograph pasted on the Passport or any other such document.

v. In case the pensioner/family pensioner is unable to visit the Embassy of India/Consulate, he/she may submit requisite documents by post to the Embassy/Consulate, including Doctor's Certificate showing the pensioner's/family pensioner's inability to present himself/herself in person. Embassy of India/High Commission/Indian Consulate may also assist pensioners/family pensioners in submission of the Life Certificate.

[(No. 16 -Payment of Pension to NRI Pensioners-pg 44 SCHEME FOR PAYMENT OF PENSIONS To CENTRAL GOVERNMENT CIVIL PENSIONERS BY AUTHORISED BANKS (Fifth Edition, July 2021)]

Sd/-
(Rajesh Kumar)
Under Secretary to the Government of India

33.18

Government of India, Ministry of Defence, Department of Ex-Servicemen Welfare ID No 3(3)/2020/D(Pen/Policy) dated 13th October 2021

Sub: Submission of Annual Life Certificate for Pensioners/Family Pensioners living abroad.

Please find enclosed a copy of DoP&PW OM No. 1(8)/2021-P&PW(H) -7468 dated 22.09.2021 on the subject mentioned above wherein for pensioners' awareness, DoP&PW has summarized different modes available to a pensioner/family pensioner living abroad for submission of Annual Life Certificate.

2. It is requested to take necessary action in the matter.

3. This issues with the approval of JS(ESW).

Encl: As Above

Sd/-

(Ashok Kumar)

Under Secretary to the Govt. of India

33.19

Government of India, Ministry of Personnel, Public Grievances & Pension, Department of Pension & Pensioners' Welfare Letter No 38/01(05)/2022-P&PW(A) dated 26th October 2022

Sub: Amount and Conditions for grant of pension under Central Civil services (Pension) Rules, 2021

The Undersigned is directed to say that Department of Pension has notified the Central Civil Services (Pension) Rules, 2021 in supersession of the Central Civil Service (Pension) Rules, 1972. In accordance with sub-rule (1) of Rule 44 of the Central Civil Service (Pension) Rules, 2021, a Government servant, becomes eligible for grant of a pension on retirement under rule 33 (Superannuation Pension), rule 34 (Retiring Pension), rule 35 (Pension on absorption in or under a State Government), rule 36 (Pension on absorption in or under a corporation, company or body), rule 37(Pension on absorption consequent upon conversion of a Government Department into a Public Sector Undertaking), rule 38 (pension on absorption consequent upon conversion of a Government Department into a Central Autonomous Body) or rule 39 (Invalid Pension), after Completing a qualifying service of not less than ten years. The pension in all such cases is calculated at the rate of fifty per cent of emoluments or average emoluments, whichever is more beneficial to him, subject to a minimum of nine thousand rupees per month and maximum of one lakh twenty-five thousand per month.

2. The above rule further provides that a Government servant who retires on Invalid Pension under rule 39 before completing a qualifying service of ten years shall also be eligible for an invalid pension calculated at fifty per cent of emoluments or average emoluments, whichever is more beneficial to him and the Condition of completion of minimum qualifying services of ten years shall not be applicable for grant of pension in his case if he/she fulfills the conditions mentioned in sub-rule (9) of rule 39.

3. In calculating the length of qualifying service, fraction of a year equal to three months and above is treated as a completed six monthly period and reckoned as qualifying service. In the case of a Government servant who has rendered a qualifying service of nine years and nine months or more but less than ten years, his qualifying services for the purpose of this rule shall be ten years and he shall be eligible for pension accordingly.

4. All Ministries/ Departments are requested that the above provisions regarding grant of pension under Central Civil Services (Pension) Rule, 2021 may be brought to the notice of the personnel dealing with the pensionary benefits in the Ministry/Department and attached/subordinated offices thereunder, for strict implementation.

Sd/-

(R.C Sethi)

Deputy Secretary to Government of India

33.20

Government of India, Ministry of Defence, Department of Ex-Servicemen Welfare ID No 1(11)/2020/D(Pen/Legal) dated 28th July 2020

Sub: Processing of Mercy Petitions for grant of service pension under Pension Regulations

As you are aware, Regulations 29 and 41 of the Pension Regulation of Army (PRA, 2008) (Part I) (Regulations 16 and 113 of PRA, 1961) (Part I) provide that an individual who is cashiered/dismissed from service under the provisions of the Army Act or removed under the Rules made thereunder is not eligible for pension or gratuity in respect of all previous service. However, in exceptional cases, the competent authority, on submission of an appeal to that effect by the individual, may at its discretion sanction pension/gratuity or both at a rate not exceeding that which would be otherwise admissible to him on retirement/ discharge. Such appeals are also required to be filed within two years from the date of cashiering/ dismissal/removal from service. Similar provisions exist in the Pension Regulations of both the Air Force and the Navy.

2. The power of the competent authority for deciding the aforesaid appeals was delegated to the AG/ AOP /COP vide Ministry of Defence, Department of Defence, Order No.4684/Dir(PEN)/2001 dated 14.08.2001. Further, vide Ministry of Defence, Department of Ex-Servicemen Welfare Order No.4(24)/2015/D(Pen/Legal) dated 01.09.2016. Secretary, Department of Ex-Servicemen Welfare [Secretary (ESW)] has been designated as the competent authority for deciding aforesaid mercy appeals which are received beyond the period of two years of cashiering/dismissal/ removal from service.

3. It has been seen from the review of such cases forwarded to this Department for disposal at the level of Secretary (ESW), that due to lack of awareness and knowledge about these provisions at the level of lower formations, these appeals are rejected at subordinate levels and reach Service Hqrs or Department of Ex-Servicemen Welfare after many years of filing of such appeals. In many cases, such appeals are filed at the instance of Armed Forces Tribunal (AFT), when the concerned Ex-serviceman files an OA before the AFT for grant of pension or gratuity or both in case of cashiering/dismissal/removal from service. The objective behind the provision for mercy appeal is to provide relief to Ex-servicemen and their family in exceptional situations on compassionate grounds. However, if the process itself gets inordinately delayed, the very objective behind such provision gets defeated.

4. It has also been seen that though the Ex-servicemen, who have been cashiered/dismissed/removed from service are not entitled to pension or gratuity or both as per the provisions of the relevant Pension Regulations, tend to make an application for grant of pension or gratuity or both. It is, therefore, advised that while rejecting such applications as per the provisions of the Pension Regulations, such Ex-servicemen may be informed about the provisions of mercy appeals and may be advised to file mercy appeal, if they so desire, with relevant documents in support of their appeal. Once, such appeals are filed, as stated above, these are to be decided only at the level of Adjutant General/ AOP /COP or Secretary, Department of Ex-Servicemen Welfare, as the case be.

5. These appeals may, therefore, be immediately forwarded by the lower formations through there relevant echelons for disposal at the level of Service Headquarters by the competent authority. Further, in cases where such appeals are filed after a period of two years of cashiering/ dismissal/removal from service, the same may be forwarded to this Department for decision at the level of Secretary (ESW). A Check List indicating the relevant documents to be sent along with such proposal for disposal of such appeals is enclosed. All the field level formations may be sensitised accordingly.

6. This issues with the approval of Secretary (ESW).

Sd/-

(R.K. Chaudhry)

Under Secretary (Pen/Legal)

Explainer: Important Letters

This part contains a brief explanation of certain important and useful letters reproduced in Chapter 33 and also referred to at many other places in this book. The explanations below are in chronological order but not in the order of reproduction in the said Chapter

The letter issued by the MoD on 26-02-1980 (Chapter 33.1) contains the provisions as to how to take the rank into account while calculating pension. Though the 10 months' stipulation now stands abrogated, the letter shows that the pensioner is to get the benefit of his rank held at the time of retirement even if it is held in a paid acting capacity as opposed to substantive capacity.

The letter issued on 06-08-1984 (Chapter 33.13) provides that that in calculating the length of qualifying service for the purpose of pension/gratuity, a fraction of a year equal to three months and above shall be treated as a completed one half year and reckoned as qualifying service for determining the amount of pension and Service/DCRG.

On 05-04-1991 (Chapter 33.7), the MoD had issued instructions on recognition of marriage after retirement for the purposes of pension. It may be recalled that earlier certain disabling conditions had been imposed by the Government on the same but the same were set aside by the Supreme Court.

Vide MoD letter 09-06-1999 (Chapter 33.8) the provisions of Regulations 16 and 113 of the Pension Regulations, dealing with grant of pension to dismissed personnel were amended. The letter itself was amended on 10-08-2000 (Chapter 33.9).

MoD letter dated 14-08-2001 (Chapter 33.3) comprehensively delegates powers to the Services Headquarters on many subjects which were till then within the ambit of the Ministry of Defence only. This was issued with the approval of the then Raksha Mantri.

On 15-09-2003, the MoD had issued a letter (Chapter 33.6) which contained modalities on grant of monthly ex-gratia along with ex-gratia disability allowance to Cadets in various military academies, on sustaining disability.

The letter issued by the MoD on 30-10-2003 (Chapter 33.12) is regarding the counting of Boys' service after a judgment of the Supreme Court. It may be recalled that Boys' Service (or apprenticeship in the Navy) was not counted for the purposes of pension and only the service after the person was transferred to "man's service" was counted.

On 06-10-2004 (Chapter 33.10), the MoD abrogated the prohibitory stipulations on military pensions on change of nationality. This subject has recently been further explained and the procedure simplified vide DoPPW letter dated 20-01-2020 (Chapter 33.11). The Government has also issued instructions on simplification on submission of Annual Life Certificate for pensioners/family pensioners living abroad vide its letter dated 22-09-2021 (Chapter 33.17) as also made applicable to military pensioners vide DESW letter dated 13-10-2021 (Chapter 33.18).

The letter dated 15-05-2008 issued by the Army HQ (Chapter 33.4) contains instructions for changing the names of the next of kin of serving and retired personnel.

The letter dated 11-08-2009 by the DoPPW (Chapter 33.2) contains modalities of the documents that are acceptable for the purposes of granting additional pension on attaining the age of 80 years or more for old pensioners.

The DoPT on 02-03-2016 (Chapter 33.5) had issued detailed instructions giving effect to the observations of the Supreme Court in Rafiq Masih's judgment, wherein recovery from retirees had been prohibited.

On 12-02-2019, the DoPPW issued a letter (Chapter 33.15) clarifying that the minimum service prescribed for disabled personnel for grant of Invalid Pension, that is, 10 years, now stood abrogated. This was followed by a similar letter by the Ministry of Defence (Chapter 33.16), though the same is currently under review due to an anomaly in the same (See Chapter 9.2).

The letter by DoPPW dated 17-01-2020 (Chapter 33.14) provides modalities to simplify the submission of 'life certificate' by pensioners for continuance of pension. It also reiterates the 'doorstep' facility to be offered by banks through digital ways related to obtaining the life certificate, especially for the old and the infirm.

Glossary

Abbreviation	Full Form
AFT	Armed Forces Tribunal
CAA	Constant Attendant Allowance
CGDA	Controller General of Defence Accounts
CPC	Central Pay Commission
CW	Civil Writ
CWP	Civil Writ Petition
DA	Dearness Allowance
DCRG	Death cum Retirement Gratuity
DE	Disability Element
DESW	Department of Ex-Servicemen Welfare
DoPPW	Department of Pension & Pensioners' Welfare
DoPT	Department of Personnel & Training
DR	Dearness Relief
DSC	Defence Security Corps
EOP	Extraordinary Pension
Govt	Government
JCO	Junior Commissioned Officer
LFP	Liberalised Family Pension
LPA	Letter Patents Appeal
MACP	Modified Assured Career Progression
MoD	Ministry of Defence
NC(E)	Non-Combatant (Enrolled)
OA	Original Application
OFP	Ordinary Family Pension
OR	Other Ranks
PCDA(P)	Principal Controller of Defence Accounts (Pensions)
PBOR	Personnel Below Officer Rank
PPO	Pension Payment Order
PRA	Pension Regulations for the Army
SE	Service Element

Continued...

SFP	Special Family Pension
SLP	Special Leave Petition
TA	Territorial Army
TA (case law)	Transfer(red) Application
Vs	Versus
WIE	War Injury Element
WIP	War Injury Pension
WP	Writ Petition
WP (C)	Writ Petition (Civil)
WP (Crl)	Writ Petition (Criminal)